MUSIC, PHILOSOPHY AND GENDER IN NANCY, LACOUE-LABARTHE, BADIOU

Sarah Hickmott

EDINBURGH
University Press

Edinburgh University Press is one of the leading university presses in the UK. We publish academic books and journals in our selected subject areas across the humanities and social sciences, combining cutting-edge scholarship with high editorial and production values to produce academic works of lasting importance. For more information visit our website: edinburghuniversitypress.com

© Sarah Hickmott, 2020, 2022

First published in hardback by Edinburgh University Press 2020

Edinburgh University Press Ltd
The Tun – Holyrood Road, 12(2f) Jackson's Entry, Edinburgh EH8 8PJ

Typeset in 10.5/13 Sabon by
Servis Filmsetting Ltd, Stockport, Cheshire

A CIP record for this book is available from the British Library

ISBN 978 1 4744 5831 3 (hardback)
ISBN 978 1 4744 5832 0 (paperback)
ISBN 978 1 4744 5834 4 (webready PDF)
ISBN 978 1 4744 5833 7 (epub)

The right of Sarah Hickmott to be identified as the author of this work has been asserted in accordance with the Copyright, Designs and Patents Act 1988, and the Copyright and Related Rights Regulations 2003 (SI No. 2498).

Contents

Acknowledgements	iv
Series Editor's Preface	vi
Abbreviations	viii
Prelude	1
1. Music, *Mousike*, Muses (and Sirens)	15
2. Music, Meaning and Materiality: Nancy's *Corps Sonore*	50
3. 'Catacoustic' Subjects and the Injustice of Being Born: Lacoue-Labarthe's Musical Maternal Muse	88
4. Midwives and Madams: Mus(e)ic, Mediation and Badiou's 'Universal' Subject	126
5. From Parnassus to Bayreuth: Staging a Music which is Not One	183
Encore: After Music	222
Bibliography	225
Index	239

Acknowledgements

Many friends and colleagues have informed and shaped this project, some in ways easier to pin down than others: to all, thank you.

Firstly, I owe heartfelt gratitude to my doctoral supervisor, Ian Maclachlan, whose enthusiasm for the original doctoral project upon which this book is based, along with his critical insight and careful attention to the thesis at various stages, were invaluable. Substantial thanks go also to my examiners Marie-Chantal Killeen and Martin Crowley for their critical engagement and thoughtful feedback. I am also grateful for the constructive advice offered by the anonymous readers for EUP, and the series editor Christopher Watkin.

The original doctoral thesis could not have happened without funding (and the book could not have happened without the thesis!): I remain enduringly grateful to the AHRC and also to Merton College for enabling me financially to pursue doctoral work; and to St John's College, Oxford, where I had the great fortune of holding a Junior Research Fellowship, and the University of Durham where the book was completed.

Material in Chapter 2 originally appeared as part of the article '*(En) Corps Sonore*: Jean-Luc Nancy's "Sonotropism"', *French Studies*, 69.4 (2015), 479–93, and material from Chapters 3 and 5 appeared as 'Beyond Lacoue-Labarthe's *Alma Mater*: Mus(e)ic, Myth and Modernity' in *L'Esprit créateur*, 57.4 (2017), 174–88. Permission to reuse this material in its revised form is gratefully acknowledged.

One of the strongest draws of an academic life is the great sense of collegiality and mutual support from fellow travellers; I am especially thankful to those who gave their time to reading and commenting on parts of the earlier manuscript – notably Helena Taylor, Emma Claussen and Jenny Oliver. My extended thanks go to Jo Hicks – his insightful feedback and sarcastic comments helped me to strengthen my argument – and to Anna Bull, who has the impressive ability to know better than I do what my work is really about. Extended thanks are also due to Sarah Mallet, whose generous consideration of my translations doubtlessly improved the end result.

Less immediately tangible – but no less significant – none of this would have come to fruition without the previous help and kind support of various people; in particular, I remain indebted to Barbara Pankhurst, Julie Dashwood, Jeremy Thurlow and Jo Malt for their kindness and intellectual encouragement at important moments in the past.

To Lace, of course, who has accompanied and supported me during every step of this journey, and whose encouragement, kindness and love fill these pages in undefinable but essential ways: thank you, always. And to sweet little Robin and curious funny Iris, whose uterine rhythms accompanied the writing of the book, and whose somewhat more disruptive wordly rhythms have occassionally delayed the final stages – I wouldn't change that for anything, and I can't wait to learn more about you both.

Finally, in memory of my grandparents, Joan and Ron, who I know would have been proud and without whom none of this would have been possible. I am forever grateful to them for teaching me the immeasureable worth of love, kindness and agnosticism, and for sharing with me the music they loved – especially the musicals of Rodgers and Hammerstein, the ragtime of Scott Joplin, Debussy's 'Clair de lune' and Elgar's 'Nimrod'.

Series Editor's Preface

Two or more currents flowing into or through each other create a turbulent crosscurrent, more powerful than its contributory flows and irreducible to them. Time and again, modern European thought creates and exploits crosscurrents in thinking, remaking itself as it flows through, across and against discourses as diverse as mathematics and film, sociology and biology, theology, literature and politics. The work of Gilles Deleuze, Jacques Derrida, Slavoj Žižek, Alain Badiou, Bernard Stiegler and Jean-Luc Nancy, among others, participates in this fundamental remaking. In each case disciplines and discursive formations are engaged, not with the aim of performing a predetermined mode of analysis yielding a 'philosophy of x', but through encounters in which thought itself can be transformed. Furthermore, these fundamental transformations do not merely seek to account for singular events in different sites of discursive or artistic production but rather to engage human existence and society as such, and as a whole. The cross-disciplinarity of this thought is therefore neither a fashion nor a prosthesis; it is simply part of what 'thought' means in this tradition.

Crosscurrents begins from the twin convictions that this re-making is integral to the legacy and potency of European thought, and that the future of thought in this tradition must defend and develop this legacy in the teeth of an academy that separates and controls the currents that flow within and through it. With this in view, the series provides an exceptional site for bold, original and opinion-changing monographs that actively engage European thought in this fundamentally cross-disciplinary manner, riding existing crosscurrents and creating new ones. Each book in the series explores the different ways in which European thought develops through its engagement with disciplines across the arts, humanities, social sciences and sciences, recognising that the community of scholars working with this thought is itself spread across diverse faculties. The object of the series is therefore nothing less than to examine and carry forward the unique legacy of European thought as an inherently and irreducibly cross-disciplinary enterprise.

Christopher Watkin
Cambridge
February 2011

Abbreviations

NANCY

Works in French

Ec	*À l'écoute*
IDV	*Inventions à deux voix: entretiens*
M₁	*Les Muses*
SM	*Sens multiple: la techno, un laboratoire artistique et politique du présent*
SMR	'La Scène mondiale du rock'

Works in English

MSR	'March in Spirit in our Ranks' (in L)

Translations into English

L	*Listening*
M₂	*The Muses*
MM	*Multiple Meaning: Techno, an Artistic and Political Laboratory of the Present*

LACOUE-LABARTHE

Works in French

CM	*Le Chant des Muses*
ES₁	'L'Écho du sujet' (in *Le Sujet de la philosophie: Typographies I*)
IM	*L'Imitation des modernes*
FP	*La Fiction du politique: Heidegger, l'Art et la politique*

LMus	'Une lettre sur la musique' (in *Pour n'en pas finir: écrits sur la musique* pp. 57–72)
MF_1	*Musica Ficta*
PNPF	'Pour n'en pas finir' (in *Pour n'en pas finir: écrits sur la musique* pp. 91–108)

Translations into English

ES_2	'The Echo of the Subject' (in *Typography: Mimesis, Philosophy, Politics*)
HAP	*Heidegger, Art and Politics: the Fiction of the Political*
MF_2	*Musica Ficta*

BADIOU

Works in French

CS_1	*Conditions*
E_1	*L'éthique: essai sur la conscience du mal*
EE	*L'Être et l'événement*
LM	*Logiques des mondes: L'être et l'événement, 2*
PE_1	*La philosophie et l'événement*
PMI	*Petit manuel d'inesthétique*
Sc	'Scolie: Une variante musicale de la métaphysique du sujet' (in LM)
StP_1	*Saint Paul: la fondation de l'universalisme*

Works in English

FLW	*Five Lessons on Wagner*

Translations into English

CS_2	*Conditions*
E_2	*Ethics: An Essay on the Understanding of Evil*
BE	*Being and Event*
LW	*Logic of Worlds*
PE_2	*Philosophy and the Event*
HI	*Handbook of Inaesthetics*
Sch	'Scholium: A Musical Variant of the Metaphysics of the Subject' (in LW)
StP_2	*Saint Paul: The Foundation of Universalism*

Crosscurrents

Exploring the development of European thought through engagements with the arts, humanities, social sciences and sciences

Series Editor
Christopher Watkin, Monash University

Editorial Advisory Board
Andrew Benjamin
Martin Crowley
Simon Critchley
Frederiek Depoortere
Oliver Feltham
Patrick ffrench
Christopher Fynsk
Kevin Hart
Emma Wilson

Titles available in the series

Difficult Atheism: Post-Theological Thinking in Alain Badiou, Jean-Luc Nancy and Quentin Meillassoux
Christopher Watkin

Politics of the Gift: Exchanges in Poststructuralism
Gerald Moore

Unfinished Worlds: Hermeneutics, Aesthetics and Gadamer
Nicholas Davey

The Figure of This World: Agamben and the Question of Political Ontology
Mathew Abbott

The Becoming of the Body: Contemporary Women's Writing in French
Amaleena Damlé

Philosophy, Animality and the Life Sciences
Wahida Khandker

The Event Universe: The Revisionary Metaphysics of Alfred North Whitehead
Leemon B. McHenry

Sublime Art: Towards an Aesthetics of the Future
Stephen Zepke

Mallarmé and the Politics of Literature: Sartre, Kristeva, Badiou, Rancière
Robert Boncardo

Animal Writing: Storytelling, Selfhood and the Limits of Empathy
Danielle Sands

Music, Philosophy and Gender in Nancy, Lacoue-Labarthe, Badiou
Sarah Hickmott

The Desert in Modern Literature and Philosophy: Wasteland Aesthetics
Aidan Tynan

Forthcoming Titles

Visual Art and Projects of the Self
Katrina Mitcheson

Visit the Crosscurrents website at www.edinburghuniversitypress.com/series/CROSS

Prelude

> Without music life would be a mistake.
> Nietzsche[1]

> Il y a d'abord la question de la musique, laquelle,
> étrangement, n'est jamais la question de la seule musique.
> Lacoue-Labarthe[2]

> Selon une très ancienne, très profonde et très solide équivalence – peut-être indestructible –, c'est [la musique] un art féminin, et destiné aux femmes ou à la part féminine des hommes. C'est un art, en tous sens, hystérique. Et c'est pour cette raison, essentiellement, que la musique est l'hystérie. Tout au moins une certaine musique.
> Lacoue-Labarthe[3]

The first aphorism above, from Nietzsche's *Twilight of the Idols, Or, How to Philosophize with a Hammer,* is just one of a vast many that allude to the centrality of music to life, and especially its privileged relation to what makes a life worth living. For Nietzsche, as for many others, this trope locates in music a profound ability to stir not only our emotions but our deepest and most essential selves, and so it links us to something primordial and originary – something other or more than 'worldly'. Music, for Nietzsche, makes life worth living by transcending the drudgery of our daily lives; it removes us from and operates beyond the passing appearances of both language and the mundane. Indeed, that Nietzsche repeatedly invokes aural metaphors in the philosophical

---

[1] Friedrich Nietzsche, *Twilight of the Idols*, p. xxxviii.
[2] MF_1, p. 12. [First, there is the question of music, which, strangely, is never a question of music alone. (MF_2, p. xvi)]
[3] MF_1, p. 198. [According to a very old, very profound, and very solid equivalence – perhaps indestructible – it [music] is a *feminine* art, destined for women or for the feminine part of men. It is a *hysterical* art, in every sense. And for this reason, essentially, music *is* hysteria. At least, a particular music. (MF_2, p. 198)]

task he has set himself, that of *'sound[ing] out idols'*, only makes this constellation of assumptions all the more interesting.[4] He sets out 'to ask questions with *a hammer*', thus framing himself as an iconoclast (*ergo* an 'image-breaker') who will unseat the false, though often *'most believed in'* idols of Western philosophy.[5] And of course idol, like iconoclast, has a strongly ocular bias, and is variously defined as 'an image or similitude of a deity', 'a representation', 'an image, effigy', 'a counterpart, likeness, imitation', 'visible but unsubstantial' or a 'false mental image'.[6] Nietzsche's *'great declaration of war'*,[7] through his sounding out of idols, is therefore premised on the apparent duplicity of the visual domain – the dissimulation of the world as it appears – and the privileged relation of the auditory domain – of sound, hearing and music – to depth, truth and the real. By contrast, then, this book claims that it is in fact the belief that sound – and particularly music – is in some way originary, or at least is more intimately connected to essences or truths, that remains one of the *most believed in* idols of Western philosophy.

Instead, this book takes as its starting point the second citation above, this time from Lacoue-Labarthe (though perhaps not quite in the sense he may have meant it). I read these words as a challenge to the inherited Romanticism that, as this book outlines, continues to pervade much philosophical writing on music. Most importantly, this assertion alerts us to the way in which music, whether considered as an object or artefact, a process, or an idea, is intrinsically enmeshed in 'other' relations, processes, technologies and ideas – to the extent that it is not possible in any way to neatly separate 'it' from the other domains of which it is constituted. Though we may think of a discrete musical work and be able to imagine at least its relative autonomy, once we start to disentangle the complex weave of relations that enabled its emergence, it becomes iincreasingly difficult to distinguish between 'purely' musical questions and those that touch on other aspects of our world-making. And once we start pulling at one thread others begin to work loose too, and quickly we find ourselves faced with the realisation that apparently ontological questions (in the sense of having to do with the identity of

---

[4] Nietzsche, *Twilight of the Idols*, p. xxxiii, italics in original. The title of this work in German is, of course, *Götzen-Dämmerung, oder, Wie man mit dem Hammer philosophirt* – a play on Wagner's *Götterdämmerung* – against which much of this work is a sustained attack. Thus not *all* music makes life worth living – especially not that which Nietzsche sees as heavy, unliberated and ultimately *un*musical music; or, in his words, 'constipated, constipating German music' (i.e. Wagner). See p. 7.
[5] Ibid., p. xxxiii, italics in original.
[6] See 'idol, n.', *OED Online* (Oxford University Press, 2016).
[7] Nietzsche, *Twilight of the Idols*, p. xxxiii, italics in original.

the musical work) were always already sociological and political – even ecological – questions that hinge ineluctably on 'non-musical' factors. Acts of musicking[8] – including supposedly formal innovations – come to be through densely mediated socio-economic, cultural and technological constellations. These include:

- the technological innovations which determine or at least shape sonorous possibilities, which shape even *ideas* about sonorous possibilities (such as instruments; concert halls; paper and pen for notated musics; amplification, recording and playback technologies, etc.);
- the – sometimes also (post-)colonial – plundering of geological, plant and animal life as the material bases for manufacturing instruments, listening venues and music's associated objects (scores, recordings, means of amplification, etc.);
- the pedagogical cultures which train future composers, players, singers and technicians;
- the (often prohibitive) cost of acquiring either instruments, equipment and/or training;
- the availability of leisure time for those who musick at an amateur level (weekends, evenings, paid holiday time, affordable childcare, etc.) and access to informal networks of training, skill sharing, live music cultures and collaboration. Here, of course, it should be noted that *who* has access to leisure time is likely to correlate strongly with demographic factors, such as gender, class, ethnicity and dis/ability;
- histories of court patronage and, latterly, state funding for the arts;
- and institutional (religious, university, and so on) structures of validation that archive, collate and curate various musical artefacts for future use or reference.

To be clear: this list is suggestive, not exhaustive. There is also a whole host of slipperier, more immaterial factors that are even harder to pin down, such as the way in which supposedly neutral aesthetic judgements very often seem to reflect or refract classed politics (and others); the way in which different musical aesthetics assume particular bodily practices (not only for the player but also the listener); the real or imaginary communities that are (often powerfully) intimated through musical experiences;[9] and the culture-specific conventions that govern

---

[8] This is a verb coined by Christopher Small to denote all kinds of musical activity, from composition, performance and listening (whether live or recorded) through to singing in the shower. See Small, *Musicking*.

[9] See Georgina Born, 'For a Relational Musicology', pp. 205–43 for more on this and musical mediation in general.

the organisation of sound phenomena, including changeable distinctions between noise, sound and music. The broader point is that musical actors (composers, performers, technicians, listeners, and so on) are never musicking in a vacuum such that they are simply animating some pre-existing, timeless, musical reserve; rather, a multitude of factors not only mediate musical possibilities but are co-instantiated alongside the musical *qua* musical. In short, *contra* the metaphysical aims of Romanticism, (classical) music is not, and was not, autonomous; and as a result, 'music' is neither a distinct domain or proclivity to which philosophy (or even musicology!) can turn for purely musical insights, nor an *immediate* reservoir of affect which is forever destined to escape the philosophical *logos*.

The recognition that there is no single point of musical origin (in the sense of an independent musical essence) to which we can return should we only be able to siphon off the other (supposedly non-musical) clutter, turns out to be an expedient myth that itself sustains other narratives and beliefs. Throughout this book, then, I reimagine the questions raised by the musical philosophies of Nancy, Lacoue-Labarthe and Badiou from this stance in order to advance – sometimes explicitly, more often implicitly – two major claims:

1. **It is necessary to move beyond what I will here term *musical exceptionalism*.**
   By musical exceptionalism, I mean the philosophical tendency (though the trope is confined neither to philosophy nor philosophers) to position music as something *in excess*; either as something *beyond* what is properly knowable (Badiou might frame this in terms of the sophistical distinction of what can be said and not said; an unsayable beyond that is somehow more deeply or authentically connected to truth, being, etc.) or exceptional in the sense that it is the best exemplar of something (e.g. the sublime, the transcendental absolute, sense, affect, an ostensibly *philosophical* theory/idea). This trope is often sustained by a constitutive forgetting of music's embeddedness in the mediate planes mentioned above (and others) and by investing it instead with a pre-cultural, ahistorical musicality that precedes the emergence of 'actual' music as it appears in the world (and yet somehow remains in touch with it). Much of this stems from an uncritical residual Romanticism, and also correlates closely with what Martin Scherzinger has described as philosophy's 'sonotropism'. Central to this trope is the extent to which these assumptions are in play primarily for high art European musical works: as a result, this book explores this trope largely through

the tension that emerges between the way music is characterised in metaphysical or ontological terms as universal or pre-cultural and ahistorical, and the music that is characterised as aesthetically or ethically valuable – which is very often the canonical works of European high art culture, rather than, for example, non-literate, folk, jazz, popular or non-Western musics. Moreover, when 'other' musics are considered by these philosophers – and they are, sometimes – the social or cultural context is seen to be relevant in ways that are far more rarely the case for the 'absolute' works of the European concert hall. As a result, an exploration of the 'idea' of music in recent French thought opens up onto a thematics of gender, class, race, the body, identity and politics, among others.

2. **For various, interrelated reasons, recent philosophical approaches to music continue to sustain essentialist narratives about femininity.** For reasons that are developed more thoroughly in this book, a philosophical understanding of music seems to have been predetermined to constellate also with questions of gender. As the second citation from Lacoue-Labarthe, above, suggests, there is a longer philosophical history (dating back at least to Plato) that considers music – or at least 'a *particular* music' – to be essentially feminine. While an exploration of ideas about music in recent French thought also brings into frame strongly racialised, classed, ableist (and other) assumptions, as mentioned above, the focus in this book is on the way notions of femininity are both invoked and constructed in explicit ways in this body of work. As a result, it is clear that gender is still deployed as an organisational category in this body of philosophy and, most problematically, in such a way that grants these categories an *a priori* legitimacy. That this happens in philosophy is nothing new – and indeed I am gratefully indebted to the vast body of feminist work that has tirelessly identified, documented and challenged such assumptions. I am, however, suggesting that ideas about music and femininity are intertwined in ways that merit further attention in a body of work that in all other respects claims to upend many of the foundational myths that anchored previous metaphysical thinking. And indeed it is clear that these philosophers are keenly aware of these tropes: Badiou, for example, is deeply committed to philosophical anti-essentialism – he rejects 'difference' as a meaningful category for philosophy and/or politics for this reason (in what follows, though, I am of course going to suggest that he remains attached to a certain kind of femininity that nonetheless depends on an essentialising logic). And in a joint paper from 1983, 'Le "retrait" du politique',

Lacoue-Labarthe and Nancy set out five 'traits' that would allow for a retracing or rethinking of the political, the fourth of which is 'la question de la *mère*' ['the question of the *mother*'] which they '*maint[iennent] avant tout comme l'index d'une question*' ['retain [...] before anything else, as the index of a *question*'].[10] Somewhat surprisingly, then, it is precisely through the figuring of a 'natural' (or at least pre-symbolic) maternality that both Nancy and Lacoue-Labarthe understand music's ontology. In this regard, then, this book remains committed to Badiou's proclaimed anti-essentialism, and begins to answer a question posed, though not explicitly answered, by Nancy and Lacoue-Labarthe themselves.

I

The focus of this book is therefore on the way that recent French philosophical approaches to understanding music both reimagine musical and sonorous philosophies, and yet also inflect and rehabilitate, often unwittingly, long-standing tropes in the philosophy of music. In order to do this, the following chapters explore, expand and critique this line of thinking in its more recent incarnations and especially, as Kara Keeling and Josh Kun describe, at 'a moment [in the humanities] when the study of sound and listening is suddenly more ubiquitous than ever'.[11] Within this remit, however, the role of the specifically musical is somewhat more complicated – it is both the artistic and cultural form that most closely corresponds to the privileged auditory or sonic domain and yet, because of its entanglement with art and culture, it is also 'contaminated' by concerns beyond the 'simply' sonorous. Indeed, as we have seen above in Nietzsche's musico-philosophising, not all music fulfils this auricular ideal. Though philosophy's interest in sound and music has a history extending back much further than Nietzsche, at least to Plato, the twentieth century, and most especially the second half, appears to have witnessed a boom in this area of interest. Martin Jay, for example, has convincingly described this trend in twentieth-century French thought as an 'anti-ocular' turn.[12] In this move towards music and/or sound as a possible 'other' source of knowledge and/or truth, a variety of auditory concepts and acoustic phenomena have been seen to offer a way beyond or against traditional Western metaphysics centred on the primacy of vision as instrumental to knowledge

---

[10] Lacoue-Labarthe and Nancy, 'Le "retrait" du politique', p. 197 [Lacoue-Labarthe and Nancy, 'The "Retreat" of the Political', p. 127].
[11] Kara Keeling and Josh Kun, 'Introduction' in *Sound Clash*, pp. 1–16 (p. 2).
[12] See Martin Jay, *Downcast Eyes*.

(whether through representation/mimesis or visually oriented, empirically minded science). As Keeling and Kun describe, it is an attempt to 'take the culture, consumption, and politics of sound seriously' and stands in contradistinction to 'the nagging dominance of the visual' – or at least a concept of vision that has 'traditionally been linked to reason, knowledge, science, truth and rationality'.[13] Within the French philosophical tradition, however, most of the best-known oto-centric theorisations have specifically concentrated on the concept of rhythm: for example, Henri Lefebvre's *Rythmanalyse*, Henri Meschonnic's *Critique du rythme*, as well as Julia Kristeva's ultimately rhythmic conception of the musico-poetic *chora*, thus leaving the position of music itself in the 'anti-ocular' turn far from clear.[14] Similarly, the theorisations of 'rhythm' often correspond to a description of certain types of literature or writing as 'musical' (in a generic and even metaphorical sense) suggesting a value in the sound pattern of the words and often, perhaps more problematically, merely indicating something imprecise beyond or in excess of the 'literal' meaning of the text. In short, as Peter Dayan has argued, '[m]usic saves language from representation'.[15]

There is also a longer history within French philosophy of thinking about music, Rousseau and Rameau being perhaps the most obvious musical thinkers (and musicians to boot) of the Enlightenment. Without doubt, their work has left a strong impression on subsequent thinkers grappling with musical questions, though the legacy of Rousseau is more often explicitly acknowledged in recent philosophical writing. This book explores the debt to both Rameau and Rousseau in terms of the longer geneaology of thinking about music in Chapter 1, and then in terms of their influence on Nancy's thinking in Chapter 2 and Rousseau's influence on Lacoue-Labarthe in Chapter 3. A conspicuous absence is perhaps the work of Pierre Schaeffer who might be considered – with good reason – the most prominent modern French musical thinker and practitioner, and notably someone who endeavoured to enact a radical break with traditional high art music forms. Though his acousmatic music was certainly innovative in many respects – involving the audition of music/sound detached from its source and thus attempting to attain a 'pure' listening experience – his presence will be felt most keenly in this book via Brian Kane's work. In *Sound Unseen*, Kane proposes an 'alternative history of acousmatic listening as a practice', and in particular one that is 'sutured to a lineage of musical

---

[13] Keeling and Kun, *Sound Clash*, p. 2.
[14] Henri Meschonnic, *Critique du rythme*; Henri Lefebvre, *Eléments de rythmanalyse*; Julia Kristeva, *La Révolution du langage poétique* and *Pouvoirs de l'horreur*.
[15] Peter Dayan, *Music Writing Literature*, p. 131.

phantasmagoria that reaches fruition with the birth of Romanticism, the aesthetics of absolute music, and Wagnerian architectural reforms of the concert hall'.[16] I would strongly urge interested parties to consult this work in more depth, and indeed many of the commitments of this book – particularly as realised in Chapters 4 and 5 – are indebted to this perspective.

Moreover, though Schaeffer's theoretical and practical contributions are no doubt important to the history of French thinking on music and sound, my intention in this book is to make an intervention within a philosophical tradition to which he is only tangentially related. More precisely, the aim of the present volume is to explore the way music is characterised, used or accounted for in a particular body of work: contemporary (post-1968) French thought, by focusing in particular on the work of Alain Badiou, Jean-Luc Nancy and Philippe Lacoue-Labarthe. In spite of the differences in their philosophical-theoretical positions, all of these writers invoke music – both directly and indirectly – to negotiate their relationship to ontological, political, ethical and aesthetic concerns, particularly in terms of how music relates to the (im)possibility of a subject, the condition of truth and the role of philosophical thought itself. In addition to using sound as a tool to steer legitimate philosophical consideration and even methodological concerns beyond an ocular bias, all of the aforementioned philosophers also make reference to examples of actual or 'real-world' music in their work. In particular, then, I will be paying close attention to the extent to which an inherited definition of the 'Idea' of music – one with a strong lineage both in German idealism and its critiques by Schopenhauer and Nietzsche, as well as in Platonic and Aristotelian philosophy – is assumed rather than critically (re)evaluated in otherwise critical thought. Tracing the musical-transcendental baggage of a traditional metaphysical conception of music – as an essentially feminine excess, and one which is too straightforwardly the 'other' of language – brings to the fore an important critical tension that also provides ample ground for a feminist perspective.

II

A guiding aim of this project is, then, to sharpen the critical tools with which we approach the inclusion of music in contemporary theorising, and to embolden a more substantive understanding of the kind of issues that might be at stake when we think about music – especially when

---

[16] Brian Kane, *Sound Unseen*, p. 10.

we lay claim to its supposedly special powers or political meanings. It takes 1968 as a critical moment for two reasons: it is – it hardly needs to be said – of social and political significance following the student and worker protests in Paris and elsewhere. All three of the philosophers considered in depth here were involved – directly or indirectly – with the protests in 1968 and, more importantly, were – and surely remain – committed to many of the principles that guided and motivated this period of unrest. Secondly, 1968 serves as a useful (if approximate) date to mark the transition from the dominance of structuralist to poststructuralist perspectives in French thought.[17] Tzuchien Tho and Giuseppe Bianco highlight that Badiou himself designates the mid-1960s as a turning point for philosophy, citing the 'exceptional set of thinkers who served as professors for the generation who, in 1965, were in their 20s and 30s' as well as noting that it is significant that this is the moment when the nomenclature changes: philosophy – or at least that which is exported largely from France into an anglophone context – becomes 'theory'.[18] This move towards 'theory' (from the Greek θέα 'a view' and ὁράω 'I look, see' gestures towards the partiality of any perspective) perhaps reflects the shift from the proclaimed objectivity and scientism of structuralist approaches to the deconstructive concerns of poststructuralism and the concomitant instability of the texts (literary, philosophical, or otherwise) at hand, and thus the refusal of final or absolute truths. It shouldn't be understated, however, that though poststructuralism both grows from and responds to structuralism, what it sets in motion is a 'fundamental challenge to the defining intellectual ideal of philosophy since Plato: the possibility of attaining knowledge about the ultimate nature and meaning of human existence'.[19] In this respect, the philosophers considered here represent two opposing responses to this definitional moment. Nancy and Lacoue-Labarthe, often writing together and drawing particularly on Nietzsche, Heidegger and Derrida, can be considered as staunch defenders of this position, exploring the consequences (whether personal, political or philosophical) of a world without (absolute) truth and the instability of language, meaning and the subject. In stark contrast, though Badiou is implicated in this pivotal moment – he, too, came of (philosophical) age in the mid-1960s and was no doubt influenced by

---

[17] Barthes's *S/Z* (published in 1970) is often considered the pivotal work in this respect, being structuralist in orientation while simultaneously undermining the structuralist project and paving the way for poststructuralism. See Gary Gutting, *French Philosophy in the Twentieth Century*, particularly p. 249.
[18] Tzuchien Tho and Giuseppe Bianco, *Badiou and the Philosophers*, p. x.
[19] Gutting, *French Philosophy in the Twentieth Century*, p. 251.

it – he has been one of poststructuralism's most relentless and prolific opponents; instead, Badiou makes a strong case for the rehabilitation of philosophy proper (along with its attendant categories of Truth, rationality and knowledge). The slightly shorter chapters on Nancy and Lacoue-Labarthe represent two faces of a shared politico-philosophical commitment and thus the critiques offered – though distinct – are closely related. In contrast, the chapter on Badiou offering the longest sustained interaction with an individual philosopher and his somewhat oppositional approach yields, unsurprisingly, a rather different critique.

The shift towards theoretical perspectives nonetheless imports other complications. Most significantly, despite an alleged anti-ocular turn, it is the continued predominance of the visual (looking, seeing and views being etymologically embedded in the term 'theory') that sits uncomfortably alongside the distinctively auditory considerations at hand. What I am offering here is, necessarily, a partial account and a mere snapshot of a much broader and richer theoretical tradition; there are a number of other thinkers who could have been the focus of sustained attention along these lines and who would have extended the range, scope and value of the considerations. The most conspicuous absences to my mind are the works of Gilles Deleuze and Bernard Stiegler: as Claire Colebrook and David Bennett describe, Deleuze (along with Félix Guattari),

> frequently cite music as their privileged analytic example because it discloses the potential of all art: higher deterritorialisation [. . . It] becomes a privileged example in their work precisely because, as a non-referential regime of signs, it enables us to think how a form of expression (a relation among sounds) enables a form of content (a body and its orientations).[20]

Though it is certainly true that music is a privileged referent and source of inspiration for Deleuze, there is already a substantial and growing body of work that explores this specific intersection of musical and philosophical thought – much of which intertwines and intersects with my own set of concerns, and from a variety of disciplinary perspectives.[21] With this in mind, it seemed cogent not to focus on Deleuze's musical offerings, but rather to point readers in the direction of other work and

---

[20] Claire Colebrook and David Bennett, 'The Sonorous, the Haptic and the Intensive', pp. 68–80 (p. 76).

[21] See, for example, Ronald Bogue, *Deleuze on Music, Painting, and the Arts*; Ian Buchanan, *Deleuze and Music*; Ian Buchanan and Marcel Swiboda (eds), *Deleuze and Music*; Edward Campbell, *Music after Deleuze*; Danielle Cohen-Levinas, 'Deleuze Musicien', pp. 137–47; Brian Clarence Hulse and Nick Nesbitt (eds), *Sounding the Virtual*; Nicolas Marty, 'Deleuze, Cinema and Acousmatic Music', pp. 166–75; Gregg Redner, *Deleuze and Film Music*; Pascale Criton and Jean-Marc Chouvel (eds), *Gilles Deleuze: la pensée musique*; Richard Pinhas, *Les Larmes de Nietzsche*.

hope that they will find their own points of contact. Secondly, though Stiegler has not published a volume dedicated specifically to music, one of his core philosophical concepts, that of *organologie générale* [general organology], is derived from a musicological context – organology was historically the study of instruments – and indeed Stiegler affords music a privileged role in this analytic framework; in addition, Stiegler was also the director of the Institut de Recherche et Coordination Acoustique/Musique (IRCAM) from 2002–6. Though his work is not considered in depth, Stieglerian perspectives are brought to bear in the final chapter, and the role of music in his work certainly deserves more consideration in the future.

III

Music, or at least 'une certaine musique' (as noted by Lacoue-Labarthe above), has a long-standing and powerful association with the feminine and is concomitantly also aligned with the subordinate term in a long list of binary oppositions. At the same time, it is the potential of sound and resonance, as Michelle Duncan describes, to dismantle 'the dualism between subject and object that has governed perception and on which the logic of enlightened reason depends' that has seduced philosophers and theorists to a closer consideration of sound, audition and music.[22] As Jay has explored, the ocularcentrism of Western philosophy – the visual bias which produces the ever proliferating list of binary oppositions – is also indissociably connected to both phallocratic and logocentric regimes: in short, Western philosophy is not merely ocularcentric but also phallogocularcentric.[23] For these reasons, it seems essential to pay especially close attention to the way in which gender constellates with or is constructed alongside theorising purportedly about sound and music; despite its controversial reception with regards to essentialism, Luce Irigaray's foundational work on the way philosophy (and psychoanalysis) locates in the maternal-feminine an illusory ground upon which an originary scene of (patriarchal-masculine) representation can be played has been indispensable.

Though the critical focus is on the way music is (or isn't) related to the feminine, as Kimberlé Crenshaw so necessarily articulated, gendered identity always already intersects with other forms of oppression and discrimination, such as race, class, sexual orientation and (dis)ability – intersecting identities that are considered here though they are not the

---

[22] Michelle Duncan, 'The Operatic Scandal of the Singing Body', pp. 283–306 (p. 299).
[23] See Jay, *Downcast Eyes*, particularly 'Chapter Nine: "Phallogocularcentrism": Derrida and Irigaray', pp. 493–544.

explicit focus.²⁴ Though I aim at no point to validate feminine identity as distinct from overlapping forms of oppression, it will nonetheless be important and interesting to focus more precisely on the way in which race, class and (dis)ability (among other issues) constellate at the nexus of music and contemporary philosophy in future work. While my consideration of the characterisation of music is motivated by a commitment to the perspectives outlined above, I have nonetheless tried as much as possible to be guided by the close reading of the texts at hand (and issues engaged by the broader philosophical projects of their writers) as to the specifically 'musical' considerations that arise as they occur to me; no doubt another reader would identify other angles for consideration.

As a final word of caution, though there is often a substantial blurring between the specifically musical and the 'simply' sonorous – a blurring that is produced partly by the texts themselves as well as by a much broader question of how to define what counts as specifically musical in the first place – I have tried as much as possible to avoid replicating the tendency to see voice and music as near synonyms in philosophical work. Though there is a long and contentious debate about the possibility of music's essentially vocal origins – in part because vocal music is by far the most common and prevalent form of music-making across both geographical and historical planes and in part because they seem to overlap in their capacity for non-semantic but distinctly human expression – both terms too often function as a stand-in for a generic 'beyond' of logocentric meaning. Moreover, there is already a significant body of literature on the voice, especially in its psychoanalytic and phenomenological guises.²⁵ Instead, unless the relationship of music to voice emerges in the writing of the philosophers at hand (such as is the case in the work of Lacoue-Labarthe), I have tried to delimit my attention to the distinctly musical inclusions in their work – by which I mean objects or processes recognised in commonplace discussion as music or having to do with music explicitly (works, performances, composers, recordings, and so on) as well as anything claimed *as* music(al) by these philosophers. In so doing, instead of trying to ask what philosophy can tell us about music, or even what music can tell us about philosophy, the aim here is to explore the way in which a variety of assumptions about what music *is* inhabits these texts.

---

[24] See Kimberlé Crenshaw, 'Demarginalizing the Intersection of Race and Sex', pp. 139–67.
[25] See, for example, Kaja Silverman, *The Acoustic Mirror*; Steven Connor, *Beyond Words*; Michel Chion, *La Voix au cinéma*; Denis Vasse, *L'Ombilic et la voix*; Mladen Dolar, *A Voice and Nothing More*; Adriana Cavarero, *For More Than One Voice*; Don Ihde, *Listening and Voice*; Brandon LaBelle, *Lexicon of the Mouth*; Anja Kanngieser, 'A Sonic Geography of Voice', pp. 336–53.

IV

The main body of the book opens with 'Music, *Mousike*, Muses (and Sirens)' – the first substantive chapter which sketches out some of the key issues in any thinking about music, before exploring in more detail those that are most pertinent to the particular considerations at hand. It also introduces certain crucial tropes and associations – many of which will be more than familiar, some less so – as well as drawing on the musicological literature that has sought to deconstruct in critical and political ways what it is we mean (or often don't mean) when we think or speak about 'music'. I have endeavoured to develop an additive critique of what music 'is' progressively across the three following chapters on individual philosophers and in the final chapter that brings them together; much of this will be very familiar to readers acquainted with Anglo-American musicological discourse from the previous two or three decades – less so to those who are unaware of these developments. It might be noted that there is a distinct lack of musicological perspectives from a francophone context – a fact owing to the relative infancy of socio-politically minded and gender-informed approaches in French musicological discourse.[26]

The second chapter, 'Music, Meaning and Materiality: Nancy's *Corps Sonore*', explores the role of music in Nancy's broader sensuous philosophy along with the genres he draws on for his philosophical meditations: notably rock, techno and *musique savante*. It explores the relationship between music, community and language in his thinking, and locates in Nancy's utilisation of the *corps sonore* a longer genealogy that links Nancy's musical thinking to Enlightenment discourses that simultaneously construct gender in problematic ways. It also addresses tonality as a historical construct and engages with the role of silent, reverent concert hall listening as the assumed space of musical audition, while simultaneously highlighting this construction's participation in and production of particular social, cultural and classed formations. The chapter on Lacoue-Labarthe, '"Catacoustic" Subjects and the Injustice of Being Born: Lacoue-Labarthe's Musical Maternal Muse', develops from the thinking on tonality outlined with Nancy, to develop (notably via Lydia Goehr) a critique of the assumed notion of the musical work: a static, total, bound and autonomous

---

[26] An early and significant exception to this would be Catherine Clément, *L'Opéra, ou, la défaite des femmes*. The infancy of these approaches to the study of music 'encore relativement peu étudiées en France' is attested to in this 2015 call for papers exploring the current state of research, 'Musique et genre', Call for papers, *Calenda*, Published on Friday, 17 July 2015, www.calenda.org/335269

object whose meaning is identifiable only in relation to itself, and one which obscures its means of production and the labour required for its (re)production (regardless of whether it is actually performed). The chapter also considers music's relation to education and pedagogy, as well as probing at Lacoue-Labarthe's construction – via extended notions of (auto)biography – of an essentially musical subject, locating in this gesture his own autobiographical impulse. The fourth chapter, 'Midwives and Madams: Mus(e)ic, Mediation and Badiou's "Universal" Subject' spends some time outlining Badiou's rather different philosophical project, before developing both the critique of concert hall listening and of the work-concept further by addressing the multiple ways in which music is mediated (socially, institutionally, technologically, affectively, educationally, and so on), focusing in particular on the way in which the role of technology has historically been *actively* obscured (or, rather, veiled), in order to produce the illusion of the transcendental and autonomous musical work. Finally, 'From Parnassus to Bayreuth: Staging a Music Which is Not One' brings the three philosophers together – ostensibly via their mutual considerations of Wagner and the ongoing debate as to his music's relation to National Socialism – in order to suggest, through questions of performance and multiply intersecting planes of mediation, a non-reductive approach to both music and gender that refuses to attribute a single essence to either. The concluding analytic thus aims to offer a distinctly musical complement to ongoing debates that seek to move criticism beyond, as Rita Felski describes, 'the Scylla of political functionalism and the Charybdis of art for art's sake'.[27] In short, the final chapter aims to take Nietzsche's hammer one final time to musical 'idols' in order to disrupt yet further any clear opposition between acoustic and visual practices, affective and cognitive modes of musicking, reductive positivism and contextual hermeneutics, instead locating in both music and philosophy a (changeable) repository of tools and techniques that both shape and are shaped by social, cultural, political and performative practices – including articulations of gendered identity.

---

[27] Rita Felski, *Uses of Literature*, p. 9.

1. *Music,* Mousike, *Muses (and Sirens)*

> Elle n'existe pas. C'en est même agaçant; si je me levais, si j'arrachais ce disque du plateau qui le supporte et si je le cassais en deux, je ne l'atteindrais pas, *elle*. Elle est au-delà – toujours au-delà de quelque chose, d'une voix, d'une note de violon. A travers des épaisseurs et des épaisseurs d'existence, elle se dévoile, mince et ferme et, quand on veut la saisir, on ne rencontre que des existants, on bute sur des existants dépourvus de sens. Elle est derrière eux: je ne l'entends même pas, j'entends des sons, des vibrations de l'air qui la dévoilent. Elle n'existe pas, puisqu'elle n'a rien de trop: c'est tout le reste qui est de trop par rapport à elle. Elle *est*. Et moi aussi j'ai voulu *être*. Je n'ai même voulu que cela; voilà le fin mot de l'histoire.
>
> Jean-Paul Sartre, *La Nausée*[1]

In a famous episode towards the end of Sartre's novel, *La Nausée* [*Nausea*], the protagonist, Antoine Roquentin, finds temporary solace in the familiar melody of an old ragtime tune, 'Some of these Days'. The tune he is listening to appears a number of times throughout the philosophical novel and is, he imagines, sung by 'une Négresse' ['a Negress'] – though the song is strongly associated with (and is thus likely the recording by) Sophie Tucker, a Jewish Ukrainian-born American vaudeville and blackface songstress best known as the 'last of the red-hot mamas'.[2] For Sartre, via Roquentin, music not only seems

---

[1] Jean-Paul Sartre, *La Nausée*, pp. 245–6. ['*It* does not exist. It is even irritating in its non-existence; if I were to get up, if I were to snatch that record from the turn-table which is holding it and if I were to break it in two, I wouldn't reach *it*. It is beyond – always beyond something, beyond a voice, beyond a violin note. Through layers and layers of existence, it unveils itself, slim and firm, and when you try to seize it you meet nothing but existents, you run up against existents devoid of meaning. It is behind them: I can't even hear it, I hear sounds, vibrations in the air which unveil it. It does not exist, since it has nothing superfluous: it is all the rest which is superfluous in relation to it. It *is*.' Jean-Paul Sartre, *Nausea*, p. 248.]

[2] See Sophie Tucker, *Some of These Days*, especially 'Blackface' pp. 37–45, 'My Yiddisha Mama' pp. 213–24 and 'The Last of the Red-hot Mamas' pp. 233–41.

to offer respite from the nauseating malaise that guides much of the book – that of Roquentin's 'inability' as Carroll describes, 'to distinguish his conscious self from the objects around him'[3] – but also seems to bypass the ontological duality laid out in Sartre's distinction between the mundane physicality of *être-en-soi* [being-in-itself] and the distinctly human freedom described as *être-pour-soi* [being-for-itself].[4] Though, as sonorous artefact – let us not forget that Roquentin, as always, is listening to the song on the café gramophone – we might be inclined to think of 'it' ontologically as *en-soi*, it is very clear that for Roquentin the 'identity' of the tune is other than the physical or material props that (re)produce the 'vibrations de l'air qui la dévoilent' ['vibrations in the air which unveil it']. Indeed, it *is not* even the vibrations, but rather the vibrations merely reveal or 'unveil' it. Similarly, its 'being' is not dependent on or affected by its surroundings or contingent factors – just as it exists independently of the record that could be broken in two, the passage strongly suggests that it would also be unaffected by such factors as the gramophone breaking or even by an instrumental or vocal failure in live performance: the fundamental essence of the song remains unaffected and unaffectable. It is completely autonomous and free. Or, as Roquentin says elsewhere: 'rien ne peut l'interrompre, rien qui vienne de ce temps où le monde est affalé; elle cessera d'elle-même' ['nothing can interrupt it, nothing which comes from this time in which the world is slumped; it will stop of its own accord'].[5] Towards the very end of the novel, Roquentin asks Madeleine to play the record a final time, during which he muses on 'ce type de là-bas qui a composé cet air' ['that fellow out there who composed this tune'] and (wrongly, again[6]) assuming him to be a 'Juif aux sourcils de charbon' ['Jew with coal-black eyebrows'].[7] In the music he claims to be able to locate a sense of suffering and wonders about the troubles of the fellow who wrote it. More extraordinarily this leads him to suggest that when 'la Négresse' sings this song, two people 'sont sauvés: le Juif et la Négresse. Sauvés. Ils se sont peut-être cru perdus jusqu'au bout, noyés dans l'existence. Et pourtant, personne ne pourrait penser à moi comme je pense à eux, avec cette douceur' ['are saved: the Jew and the Negress. Saved. Perhaps they

---

[3] Mark Carroll, '"It Is": Reflections on the Role of Music in Sartre's "La Nausée"', pp. 398–407 (p. 400).
[4] Sartre characterises music specifically in a similar way in *L'Imaginaire*, see Jean-Paul Sartre and Arlette Elkaïm-Sartre. This is not necessarily consistent with his broader reflections on art, however. See in particular Christina Howells, *Sartre*, pp. 116–44.
[5] Sartre, *La Nausée*, p. 41 [p. 37].
[6] See Carroll. It was actually composed by Shelton Brooks, a Canadian of African descent, and based on a tune published in 1905 by Frank Williams, about whom we have no biographical information; see James J. Fuld, *The Book of World-Famous Music*, p. 511.
[7] Sartre, *La Nausée*, pp. 247, 248 [pp. 250, 251].

were lost right until the very end, drowned in existence. Yet nobody could think about me as I think about them, with this gentle feeling'].[8] There is, nonetheless, a certain circularity to this: music is both a site where suffering is perceptible and also the cathartic balm that soothes this (or at least *his*) very suffering; it reveals a (ontological) lack and yet heals the void it identifies. Ultimately, however, not being a musician, Roquentin resolves instead to write a book which, we realise, may be (despite its self-reflexive framing as a posthumously edited diary of Roquentin from the time of his research for a book on Monsieur de Rollebon) the book we have just read.[9]

La Nausée is, then, at once literary and philosophical, political and (auto-) biographical in the way it fictionalises, via Roquentin, the political and philosophical commitments of Sartre himself. It is yet more intriguing though that music is of such key importance in this endeavour; it is music alone that, as Carroll describes, is 'beyond the physical realm and is free from the vicissitudes of day-to-day existence. The tune is neither *pour-soi* like Roquentin on a good day, nor *en-soi* like the trees that so depressed him.'[10] At the same time, the narrator's existential meditation unwittingly seems to pose more questions than it solves, and brings into frame a number of key difficulties that occur frequently in the philosophy of music: its essence, definition and location, as well as its emotional and psychological impact (its effect and affective capacity more broadly), its similarities and differences to language, and the roles of composers, performers, listeners and, of course, technology, alongside music's relationship to identity, society, culture and politics. Most starkly, perhaps – in the way in which Sartre positions the musical 'object' as resolutely beyond the material props upon which the production of its sounding depends, while also mapping specific identities (the Jew and the Negress) and their attendant sufferings onto nothing more than its sounding – he highlights the way music seems to be both material and immaterial, mediated and autonomous, real and ideal, and deeply and viscerally human yet also beguilingly transcendental.

It comes as little surprise, then, that what music actually 'is', is rather hard to pin down. Indeed, the definitions and conceptions of music are so plentiful and variable that their indisputable entanglement with other (social/cultural) concerns or values seems quite apparent;

---

[8] Ibid., p. 249 [p. 251].
[9] It is interesting, then, that Derrida has spoken explicitly about the 'strong impression' *La Nausée* had on him and the way it creates 'the feeling of existence as excess, "being-superfluous," the very beyond of meaning giving rise to writing' – much like 'Some of these Days' does. See Derek Attridge, *The Singularity of Literature*, p. 36.
[10] Carroll, '"It Is": Reflections on the Role of Music in Sartre's "La Nausée"', pp. 400–1.

there is little geographical consistency, for example: some cultures have no word that can be reliably translated as what, in many European cultures, is called music; or, indeed, have a word that would loosely cover what we tend to mean by music but have no distinction between that and what would be called dance. Equally, what we might broadly assume to come under the umbrella of music would be culturally inaccurate or even offensive in some cases, such as with Quranic recitation. Even within a relatively recent history and within a (broadly speaking) shared culture, the definitions proliferate: for composer Edgard Varèse it is simply 'organised sound'; for music critic and aesthetician Eduard Hanslick it is famously 'form moving in sound';[11] whereas for Luciano Berio it is 'everything that one listens to with the intention of listening to music'[12] (and this, then, of course sets up a different relationship between 'music' and so-called 'noise'). For some, the definition can be broadened beyond the human to include the cacophonous booms and shrieks of industrial machinery and the chirruping of birds and other animals, and even to include the cosmos and the universal harmony of the spheres. While all of this gestures towards the very mutable nature of what (we think) music 'is', suggesting as Jean Molino describes that '[i]l n'y a donc pas *une* musique, mais *des* musiques, pas *la* musique, mais un fait musical. Ce fait musical est un fait social total' ['[t]here is not *one* music, then, but many musics, no music-as-such but a musical fact. That musical fact is a total social fact'],[13] there is of course a long history of thinking about music as a science, and thus defining the essentially musical in terms of properties (overtones, ratios, and so on) that are supposedly eternal and universal and thus not subject to the whims of a particular human culture or society.

This chapter proceeds along three axes: firstly, key moments and configurations in the longer history of musico-philosophical interactions will be sketched out in relation to a number of recurring 'problems' or sites of contention. In so doing, this chapter urges readers towards a critical account of the history of (what we mean by) music – particularly in its instrumental (absolute) guise – and how this relates to changing musical styles and practices. Secondly, music's etymological derivation facilitates a consideration of music's relation to other arts as well as to society and culture more broadly. The final axis introduces some of the ways in which historical and contemporary ideas about

[11] See in particular 'Chapter Three: On the Musically Beautiful' in Eduard Hanslick, *On the Musically Beautiful*, pp. 28–44.
[12] Luciano Berio, Rossana Dalmonte and Bálint András Varga, *Two Interviews*, p. 19.
[13] Jean Molino, 'Fait musical et sémiologie de la musique', pp. 37–62 (p. 38). [Jean Molino and Craig Ayrey, 'Musical Fact and the Semiology of Music', pp. 105–56 (p. 115).]

the interrelationship of music, gender and sexuality have tended to constellate.

MUSIC: TERMINOLOGY, GENEALOGY, HISTORY

I. Allography: The Ontological Problem

Though this book proceeds from the understanding that music has no single, independent, identifiable essence – and therefore the project of trying to define what 'it' is, is rendered somewhat obsolete – the question of music's ontology deserves to be addressed briefly if only to highlight the myriad approaches and difficulties faced. It perhaps helps to be clearer that often one is considering the ontology of different musical things, such as works, performances, recordings or scores, though the relationship between these different musical 'things' is far from clear. In particular, it is useful to flesh out a distinction between autographic (the singular, self-same, written repository of the musical work's identity) and allographic (the double or multiple, performed or sonorous resounding of music beyond or other than its notated version) approaches. Indeed, though sound is often assumed to be central to the concept of what music is, this doesn't necessarily hold for ontological considerations based around the score-copy of a work; as Georges Bloch notes, 'une partition ne s'entend pas, même lorsqu'on la lit. Ce qu'on entend dans sa tête est, d'abord, une abstraction sonore' ['A musical score is not heard, even when it is read. What one hears in one's head is, first of all, a sonorous abstraction'].[14] This is a claim that would lead us also to include mental representations in the possible list of musical things – an idealist perspective that chimes with the way Sartre – or Roquentin – understands the fundamental essence of 'Some of these Days' as precious little to do with the musical text (its notation – not just the sung words), its performance or the instruments/technology used for its sounding. As well as offering a very lucid account of what it means to be a realist, nominalist or idealist when it comes to musical ontology, Lydia Goehr has described musical works as 'ontological mutants': a claim she builds on to make her case for a historicised or genealogical approach to ontology – a position explored further in Chapter 3 of this book.[15]

A primary difficulty is the impossibility of reducing music (presumptively a musical work, which is in itself problematic, as Goehr, noted

---

[14] Georges Bloch, 'Lettre à Philippe Lacoue-Labarthe', pp. 173–202 (p. 175).
[15] Lydia Goehr, *The Imaginary Museum of Musical Works*, p. 2, and 'Part I: The Analytic Approach' for an elucidation of the various positions.

above, goes to great lengths to highlight) to any one of its potential instantiations. Furthermore, when claims are made for locating the essence of music in one type of musical thing, such as in performance, not only are seemingly incommensurate difficulties encountered in relation to its other possible instantiations (does it come into existence when it is first performed rather than when it is 'written', and what if it is never performed?) but also within the category proposed: Which performance? Do recordings of live performances have the same or different ontological statuses? Do (inevitable) wrong notes make it the same or a different piece of music? What if it is played by 'wrong' instruments (by which I mean instruments other than those for which it was scored)? What if it is 'performed' using sampled and synthesised instruments on a computer? And, to push things further still, when large amounts of particular, identifiable works are reworked or recycled, is a new piece created or is it just a new version of the original? Though we might instinctively feel that Jane Birkin's 'Jane B' or Suprême NTM's 'That's My People' are pieces in their own rights, rather than reworkings of a Chopin prelude, this becomes less evident when the piece is explicitly framed as a remixed or re-orchestrated version of the original, such as a trance remix of Barber's *Adagio for Strings* or Schoenberg's orchestration of Brahms's Piano Quartet; and it is less clear still when it is supposedly the piece in question just in a different 'style' – such as a salsa version of Beethoven's Fifth Symphony.[16]

One aspect that is made particularly plain in light of these examples is the presumptive role of the composer-function as central to the work's identity – of the autographical function – both in the sense of the ideologically privileged role of the composer (and possibly their intentions and/or biography) but also the written (rather than performed) location of the musical work – the score-copy – as central to the musical work's ontology. Additionally, this goes beyond – or is at least concerned with something in addition to – the destabilisation of the authorial function as key to interpretation; it is also a historicisation of the 'invention' of the composer-concept. As Georges Bloch states, '[o]n oublie souvent que, avant 1795, il n'y a pas de "compositeur". Il n'y a que des musiciens de statuts sociaux divers (violon du roi, *kapellmeister*, musicien de cour, de rue, de bal, etc.) [. . .] il n'y a ni dichotomie ni même simple distinction entre création et réalisation musicale' ['we often forget that, before 1795, there was no such thing as a "composer". There were merely musicians with varying social

---

[16] See, for example, www.youtube.com/watch?v=cvHrj7p1z34 and www.youtube.com/watch?v=jafWlyfUabw (both accessed 20 October 2016).

statuses (King's violinist, *kapellmeister*, court musician, street musician, *musicien de bal*, etc.) there was neither a dichotomy nor even a distinction between musical creation and its realisation'].[17] This is not to say that prior to this point there were not figures who acted or created in ways that seem fairly indistinguishable from our modern conception of a composer, but that the move to an identified composer-function also entails other significant changes.[18] The two most important points are perhaps drawn from the realisation that prior to this point in the literate high art tradition, 'toute musique est originale, puisque toute occasion ou presque est prétexte à une musique nouvelle' ['all music is original, because almost every situation is a reason for new music']:[19] firstly, the invention of the composer-function is inseparable from the creation of the canon and the (emerging) practice of concert hall listening (itself inseparable from the various revolutions of the eighteenth century and the growing middle classes), which means that works will be heard on multiple occasions and will be played by people who have nothing to do with the person who wrote them. Secondly, and not unrelatedly, this entails a shift in musical consideration towards the written score-copy of the work as the repository of the work's identity.[20] Finally, then, drawing on Lydia Goehr's use of Nelson Goodman's distinction between autographic (irreplicable – there is and can only be one 'Mona Lisa', for example) and allographic arts (which allow for multiple instantiations) is thus useful in attempting to keep in mind some of the difficulties particular to the thinking of musical ontology, specifically when it comes to questions (and assumptions) about music's identity, essence or 'location'.

II. Reluctant Mimesis: Noumena, Phenomena and the Problem of Musical Representation

Another difficulty that has been central to considerations about music's essence is the question of representation and mimesis; as Christopher Hasty describes, music's 'resistance to representation has long been its curse and its promise'.[21] In particular, this forces considerations

---

[17] Bloch, 'Lettre à Philippe Lacoue-Labarthe', p. 177.
[18] Interestingly, however, feminist musicological research focusing on the previously understudied work of Hildegard von Bingen has led to the claim of an astonishingly early example of a self-consciously identified composer-figure. See Susan McClary, 'Why Gender Still (As Always) Matters in Music Studies', pp. 49–60.
[19] Bloch, 'Lettre à Philippe Lacoue-Labarthe', p. 177.
[20] Of course, all of this is entirely commensurate with Goehr's critique of the work-concept mentioned above and explored in more detail in Chapter 3.
[21] Christopher Hasty, 'The Image of Thought and Ideas of Music', pp. 1–22 (p. 1).

of music into a vexed relationship with language (typically seen as mimetic and representational) – a factor that is worth bearing in mind throughout the following considerations. Further still, it refracts in yet more complicated ways with the questions of autography and allography outlined above, depending on where one locates the identity of the musical text: could it be that the performed version is a representation of the essential score-copy, or is the score-copy merely the mnemonic for the 'actual' music in its aural instantiation(s)? In short, is it possible to discern which version is the copy and which is the original – or indeed is it neither and/or both? As mentioned in the 'Prelude', part of the very reason for a renewed interest in music (at least for some recent philosophers) is the way in which, as an auditory phenomenon, it offers a non-visual 'object' of study that evades, avoids or problematises the role of (vision-oriented and linguistic) representation in meaning-making. It is worth setting out in a bit more detail some of what is at stake in these considerations as well as the way in which it has been dealt with in previous attempts to think about music, as it taps into vast questions to do with perception, value, meaning, truth and knowledge.

Since its foundation in Platonic metaphysics, the role of mimesis – usually understood as imitation – has tended to entail a deep anxiety; and indeed it is Plato's foundational redefinition of art as fundamentally mimetic – and thus duplicitous (with regards to truth, rationality and pleasure) – that is at the root of the banishing of the poets from the *callipolis* (the ideal state). As he says to Glaucon in the *Republic*, '[i]f you admit the entertaining Muse of lyric and epic poetry, then instead of law and the shared acceptance of reason as the best guide, the kings of your community will be pleasure and pain' (607a).[22] Underlying all of this of course is a concern with our ability to be able to discern what is or is not true (and consequently good, for Plato). Music's apparent lack of semantic content thus puts it in an especially fraught relationship to representation and so its potential for disclosing or embodying truth; for Plato, this accords music both a privileged and a derogatory status. Though art is definitively mimetic, music nonetheless appears to maintain a more immediate relation to the psyche and a distinct capacity to model *ethos*; as Jeremy Begbie describes,

> Plato weaves Pythagorean and other traditions in a quite stunning synthesis, encompassing the mathematical proportions of the world soul as well as of the human soul and body. Music gives us not only a model of harmonious balance, unity and integrity, it actually implants cosmic harmony into the

---

[22] Plato, *Republic*, p. 361. Just prior to this he has claimed that 'the only poems we can admit into our community are hymns to the gods and eulogies of virtuous men'.

soul of humans [... and in] this way, music and morality become closely linked.[23]

The extent to which we can think of music as non-/representational will be considered in more depth below, but firstly it is helpful to outline how other philosophers have figured music's relation to sensory perception and worldliness more broadly, particularly following the transcendental idealism of Kantian philosophy.

Prior to the Kantian intervention in the *Critique of Pure Reason*, of course there is still a distinction between noumena and phenomena – noumena being objects or things (so, in a Platonic guise, ideas and forms) that are inaccessible to experience (but not to knowledge), and phenomena being what is perceived through the senses. Kant, however, critiques previous metaphysics for conflating the two: for Kant, all things that exist, exist independently of the human mind, but we cannot *know* anything directly about things that exist but are unavailable to our perception. It is therefore crucial to distinguish, as Azade Seyhan describes, 'between the thing as it is synthesized by *a priori* forms of intuition and the thing-in-itself (*das Ding an sich*). The thing-in-itself is not accessible by the faculties and forms a limit to human knowledge.'[24] This 'Copernican revolution' in philosophy placed 'the human mind at the center of all operations of knowledge' and bequeathed to us the prevailing and pervasive notion 'that some primary presence or truth remains inaccessible to consciousness [and it is this that] lies at the heart of the problem of representation'.[25] As several commentators, including Alison Ross, have highlighted, from this point on the entire practice of philosophy stands in an essential relationship to aesthetics (Αισθητική having to do with all that is perceptible through the senses): literary and artistic endeavours foreground the intertwining of (re)presentation and aesthetic (sensory) experience, which philosophy becomes interested in as a 'mode of relation between the forms of material nature and human freedom'.[26] The consequences for the specifically musical for Kant are, however, rather ambivalent: as Marian Hobson describes, 'chez Kant, la musique prend [...] deux valeurs à la fois: elle est l'art à la fois le moins important et le plus élevé, celui qui doit se faire compléter par d'autres arts, et qui pourtant les prime tous' ['with Kant, music takes on two values at the same time: it is both the least important and the

---

[23] Jeremy Begbie, *Resounding Truth*, p. 80.
[24] Azade Seyhan, *Representation and Its Discontents*, p. 5.
[25] Seyhan, pp. 5, 3. It should be noted that there is a sustained and increasingly determined attempt to move beyond the Kantian problematic, for example in the fields of New Materialism, Speculative Realism and Object-oriented Ontology.
[26] Alison Ross, *The Aesthetic Paths of Philosophy*, p. 1 and in general.

most elevated art form, the one which needs to be completed by the other arts and yet also the one which takes precedence over all [other forms of art]'].[27]

This ambivalence is revealed most clearly with regard to instrumental music which, for Kant, may be beautiful but without words its representative function is deficient in its ability not only to convey but also to activate conceptual and rational thinking: it 'occupies the lowest place among the beautiful arts [...] because it merely plays with sensations'.[28] Conversely, however, as we shall see (particularly in Chapter 3) the aesthetic thinking of Kant and his followers has a huge bearing on the development of musical thought in the late eighteenth and early nineteenth centuries, most demonstrably – if ironically – in the way that instrumental rather than texted musical forms come to be privileged as the most highly valued form of music-making. Ultimately it is Hegel who develops many of the concepts initiated by Kant. The theory of art as proposed by Hegel is primarily cognitive and, as with his broader philosophical project, assumes a progressive teleological understanding of art – a narrative that has been central to the musicological understanding of evolving musical styles over time. Though an artwork might indeed be intensely pleasurable, beautiful or emotive, these aspects are insufficient for determining its value. Above all, with regards to music, it is Hegel's idealist emphasis on interiority and immediacy – 'the abstract interiority of pure sound' – that offers a direct voicing of the transcendent and the unity of form and content freed of extra-musical considerations, such as day-to-day life, the contingent and the merely mortal.[29]

Schopenhauer both draws on the Kantian legacy and simultaneously critiques it. One of the most obvious differences is how much of a central role music is accorded in his work; as Jerrold Levinson describes, he 'both accords music a supreme role in the search for personal fulfilment and also views music as a mirror of the underlying nature of things'.[30] As an idealist, like Kant before him (though critical of Kant's understanding of the noumenal), Schopenhauer understands noumenal reality to be only indirectly available to perception: we are offered an incomplete glimpse as it is revealed through its manifestations in objects or phenomena. His name for the thing-in-itself, this deeper or more essential reality, is 'Will' and it is strongly equated with desires and impulses: it is the fundamental principle of both the world and the individual

---

[27] Marian Hobson, 'Kant, Rousseau, et la musique', pp. 290–307 (p. 291).
[28] Kant, *Critique of the Power of Judgment*, p. 206.
[29] Goehr, *The Imaginary Museum of Musical Work*, p. 154. See also p. 157.
[30] Jerrold Levinson, *Musical Concerns*, p. 7.

and articulates a specifically non-rational and non-intellectual urge. For Schopenhauer, music 'stands completely apart'[31] from the other arts: though the arts in general have as their aim the repetition of 'the eternal Ideas grasped through pure contemplation [. . . their] only goal is the communication of this cognition [of the Ideas]', music is explicitly described as 'not an imitation or a repetition of some Idea of the essence of the world'.[32] Though it must be the case that music functions analogously to the other arts and 'in some sense relate[s] to the world as presentation to presented, as copy to original', for Schopenhauer this suggests that music is, instead, a *'copy of the will itself'*.[33] Music is not representative as such, or at least its 'imitative relation to the world must also be very intimate [. . .] because it is instantaneously comprehensible to everyone'.[34] It is this perspective that allows Schopenhauer to explain the seductive powers of music and the profound emotional impact it appears to have. Though (Platonic) Ideas as manifested by the arts are themselves objectivations or presentations of the will (as underlying essence), they 'objectify the will only indirectly' whereas 'music is an *unmediated* objectification and copy of the entire *will*, just as the world itself is [. . .] this is precisely why the effect of music is so much more powerful and urgent than that of the other arts'.[35] Music, rather than depicting 'things' (the world as it appears, in its external aspect) is a copy of the irrepressible and irrational will (which is the world as it is rather than how it appears: its essence or its internal aspect). Music's potential freedom from representation – its explicitly *meta*-physical status – thus endows it with special powers to reveal or at least express fundamental truths about the nature or deeper essence of things than the passing appearance of the world (as representation, language, and so on).

Following on from Schopenhauer, in *The Birth of Tragedy* Nietzsche – perhaps the archetypal musical philosopher – famously discerns two naturally occurring tendencies: he borrows figures from Greek mythology to articulate what he understands as the calm and restrained Apollonian, which is associated with images (or at least the imagistic) and architecture, and the more primitive Dionysian, which is strongly associated with immediacy, excess, intoxication and dancing and is quite evidently influenced by Schopenhauer's idea of the Will. Though clearly Apollo is also associated with music in mythology, it is the

---

[31] Arthur Schopenhauer, *The World as Will and Representation (Vol. 1)*, p. 283.
[32] Ibid., pp. 207–8, 283.
[33] Ibid., pp. 283, 285.
[34] Ibid., p. 283.
[35] Ibid., pp. 284, 285.

Dionysian strain, for Nietzsche, that is the properly aesthetic force; unlike the more rational and cognitive sedimentation of rules and traditions represented by the Apollonian, the Dionysian is considered to be strongly connective, encouraging the forgetting of the self in order to be better and less self-consciously immersed in social gatherings and rites. Music (and its corollary dancing) is to be understood as the most (potentially) Dionysian of the arts, and thus music is characterised as the pinnacle of artistic endeavour. Famously in his early writings, Nietzsche believed that a properly Dionysian and non-imagistic art was being reborn in Wagner's music dramas, though he later changed his mind.

Though post-Kantian philosophy has tended to operate on the assumption that absolute music is non-representational (or at least seriously deficient in its capacity for representation) and, perhaps more problematically still, the assumption that absolute music represents the pinnacle or archetype of the properly musical – the essence of music – musicology, particularly in the last two decades of the twentieth century, has deconstructed both of these assumptions. With regards to the question presently under consideration, the possibility of musical representation is often approached by distinguishing between different types of representation. Thomas Clifton, for example, understands musical representation as presentative rather than denotative,[36] whereas Georgina Born agrees that music lacks denotative meaning but, precisely because of that, figures it as *'hyperconnotative'* in its extraordinary ability to elicit 'imaginary evocation[s] of identity and of cross-cultural and intersubjective empathy'.[37] Indeed, as soon as contemplation is shifted from the largely score-based – specifically musical-syntactic – analysis of European literate music, broader questions about representation emerge. For example, Born and Hesmondhalgh's collection *Western Music and Its Others: Difference, Representation, and Appropriation in Music* asks 'how other cultures are represented in music through the appropriation or imaginative figuration of their own music, and, conversely, how social and cultural identities and differences come to be constructed and articulated in music'.[38] This kind of representation of the Other has a long – often Orientalising – history from the 'Turkish march' or 'Arabesque' trope used by composers such as Mozart and Beethoven through to Bizet's appropriation of the 'Seguidilla' genre (among a multitude of other styles/techniques) to represent the gypsies

---

[36] See Thomas Clifton, *Music as Heard*.
[37] Georgina Born, 'V. Techniques of the Musical Imaginary', pp. 37–58, 32, italics in original.
[38] Georgina Born and David Hesmondhalgh, 'I. Postcolonial Analysis and Music Studies', pp. 1–3 (p. 2).

of southern Spain in *Carmen*, and on to Elton John's evocation of Africa in the 'Circle of Life'. Though all these examples strongly suggest that music does partake in representation, in all of these instances it can of course be argued that representation is taking place at the second degree – all involve the appropriation of a pre-existing musical genre or style being lifted into a different context to represent a different group (accurately or otherwise). But there are also examples where music seems to have some power to represent feelings, moods or atmospheres, without any external reference. For example, as Daniel Albright has described, Schoenberg's period of free atonality places him alongside 'Sigmund Freud (and the painter Edvard Munch and the novelist Joseph Conrad) in a common project to map [i.e. to represent] areas of feeling little explored in previous ages'.[39] The extended chromaticism of works such as *Erwartung* (a texted monodrama, though the claims being made refer expressly to the musical and not the texted aspect) perfectly captures the state of anxiety and inner turmoil of the protagonist, and leads Albright, again, to suggest that 'what onomatopoeia is to outer realism, chromaticism is to inner realism'.[40] Finally, then, though music may struggle to represent if we limit it to the narrower concerns of denotative or semantic meaning, it certainly is implicated in other forms of representation and meaning-making.

III. Music, Logos, Musicology: The Problem of Musical Meaning

As the considerations above suggest, the question of music's representational capacity seems to hinge ineluctably on its relation to language, and to how we understand or construe the similarities and differences between music and language. While we are fairly comfortable with the assumption that language is capable of *saying* something, 'it is problematic how and whether music can "say" anything [though] many composers and musicians have attributed to it a power to reveal something about human life and experience'.[41] And though Kant thinks music needs words if it is to be both beautiful *and* good, as well as to represent concepts and ideas, the Kantian legacy nonetheless also bestows on music a profound ability to reveal truths and be meaningful; at the same time, it is often extremely difficult to say what truth or meaning is revealed though we have little difficulty describing music in more vague terms as 'heroic', 'beautiful' or 'haunting', and so on, even

---

[39] Daniel Albright, *Modernism and Music: An Anthology of Sources*, pp. 4–5.
[40] Albright, *Modernism and Music*, p. 8. Similar claims could be made for other musical works, such as Berg's *Wozzeck*.
[41] Graham, *Philosophy of the Arts*, p. 77.

when the music is purely instrumental. Further still, though music is differentiated from language in its commonplace sense, it is simultaneously considered as a type of language, or language-like; indeed, for Schopenhauer music is explicitly and repeatedly framed as a 'universal language'.[42]

The way the relationship between music and language is construed has not remained entirely consistent over time, but in all instances it seems to be framed in relationship to what we think music 'is' and how music's affective dimension is understood. Voice is often assumed to be central to our understanding of both music and language, and this is perhaps one reason why music has often been considered as a type of language. Daniel Albright has shown how this model of understanding musico-linguistic relations both imagines music to be a language that is intuitively understood by all and simultaneously deficient *vis-à-vis* language.[43] By understanding music as a language, its specific powers are ignored. In contrast, those who have figured music as a non-language often reduce it to arithmetic, ratios or quasi-architectural structure, and 'embrace the idea that music is a species of visual art realized in sound'.[44] This is less in the sense of music's capacity for what we might describe as 'sound-painting' – the sonorous depiction of, say, bells tolling or hens pecking through musical means – but music ideated into quasi-visible structure and form.

As Mark Evan Bonds has shown, the relationship between music's (perceived) essence and its effects – its nature and its power – along with how different historical periods and epochs have conceived of this, is of great interest. Though there are always a multitude of competing theories at any one time, Bonds has argued that in the broadest of strokes the dominant perspectives on this relationship can be divided into three key periods: antiquity through to around 1550; 1550 through to around 1850; and 1850 through to the mid-twentieth century.[45] From antiquity through to the mid-sixteenth century it is not so much that music is capable of 'saying' something, but it has an extraordinary power to mimic or model character, and in its broader conception as *mousike*, as we will see later, is central to a good education and the upholding of social and cultural values. Music's essence was simply conceived of as the 'source of its effect' and this relationship was embodied in the

---

[42] Schopenhauer, *The World as Will and Representation (Vol. 1)*, pp. 283, 289, 290, 291, 292.
[43] See Daniel Albright, *Panaesthetics*, pp. 163–73.
[44] Ibid., p. 175.
[45] See Mark Evan Bonds, *Absolute Music*.

complementary but oppositional figures of Orpheus and Pythagoras.[46] Orpheus is the archetypal musician who used music and its magical powers to charm not only humans but animals too; Pythagoras is the theoretician who is able to show how music's natural basis in number is inseparable from its powerful role in the cosmos. In both cases what music *is* is inseparable from what it *does*; nonetheless, it sets up a series of oppositions between theory/practice, mind/body, abstraction/sensation, and so on.[47] Finally, though it is fair to say and important to acknowledge that most music in antiquity involves some form of oration or chant (along with rhythm and harmony), non-texted music, though uncommon, existed in Plato's time and was in no way exempt from the same set of considerations. Purely instrumental music is not void of ethical content, it is simply much harder to identify 'the *ethos* of absolute music' and thus when in combination with a text it is one of the tasks of someone trained in *mousike* to match this appropriately to 'the *ethos* of the verbal component'.[48]

The second period, from the mid-sixteenth century to the mid-nineteenth century, by contrast, tends to understand music's essence alongside its effect but no longer assesses them as directly causal. By this point the mathematical basis for Pythagoras's ratios was in doubt and so the 'ear, along with the senses in general, began to challenge the mind as a source of knowledge'.[49] Alongside these shifts in the understanding of music's essence, not only did its relationship to language change but, as Andrew Bowie has explored, in the second half of the eighteenth century language too was under interrogation: as a result, it ultimately 'ceases *to be clear what language is*'.[50] The flourishing scientific revolution and its epistemological consequences – along with the difficulty in pursuing a properly scientific analysis of language given that any description of language involves the circularity of also being the medium in which the description (meta-linguistically) takes place – informs the search for a 'purer' language: a search for the origin of language, from which 'impure' natural languages have derived.[51] Though mathematical theories continued to abound – Rameau being a case in point, as we will see, again, later and in Chapter 2 – there is nonetheless a shift towards considerations of music's language-like qualities, particularly through the notion of *melos*. This shift forces the

---

[46] Ibid., p. 10.
[47] Ibid.
[48] Pelosi and Henderson, *Plato on Music, Soul and Body*, p. 60.
[49] Bonds, *Absolute Music*, p. 10.
[50] Andrew Bowie, *Music, Philosophy, and Modernity*, p. 48, Bowie's emphasis.
[51] See ibid., pp. 49–50.

understanding of music and language into closer – almost inseparable and certainly mutually reinforcing – proximity. Music is saved from becoming an art entirely to do with the senses by relating its expressive capacities to similar linguistic capacities;[52] at the same time, as we will see in greater detail in Chapter 2, music becomes a good candidate for a possible origin of language for some thinkers – a move which also helps traverse some of the difficulties in understanding why or how music seems so expressive and to be able to communicate (in the broadest sense) something meaningful without appearing to have anything like a clear semantic content. And so the mutual reinforcing of music's and language's quests for origins continues; music becomes the pre-linguistic origin of language and is also framed *as* a universal language.

In parallel motion to these theoretical developments, both the understanding of music and its attendant practices are also undergoing significant changes, especially as we reach the end of the eighteenth century: it is during this period that the hierarchy of value is inverted, with text-less instrumental or 'absolute' music now occupying the top spot, with texted musical forms deemed less worthy or exemplary of 'good' music. This system of values is quite evident from this period onwards; Schopenhauer, as we have just mentioned, is explicit that music has priority over words, and if music is texted, then the text must be subordinate if it is to be considered 'good' music. The extent to which we have internalised the priority of music in hybrid musical forms, most obviously in opera, is perhaps affirmed in our tendency to speak of the operas of Mozart, Verdi, Bizet or Puccini, and rarely – perhaps never – of those by Da Ponte, Schikaneder, Ghislanzoni, Piave, Meilhac, Adami and Simoni or Illica and Giacosa (the librettists). Similarly, for Nietzsche, the Apollonian is associated with symbolic forms, staid and unnecessary ornamentation and above all, words, which communicate messages at the expense of the Dionysian emotional spirit. In his later work, *Thus Spoke Zarathustra*, which elucidates the concept of the eternal return (which can also be understood as a reformulation of the creative force inherent to the Dionysian), music is again affirmed as superior and more vital than language. With his 'bird-wisdom' he exclaims: 'Sing! Speak no more! – are not all words made for the heavy? Do not all words lie to the light? Sing! Speak no more!'[53] Nonetheless, the Dionysian might be archetypically musical but the Dionysian spirit infuses and informs non-musical art forms: the Dionysian spirit is not to be found in pure music alone but connotes what is *essentially* musical

---

[52] See Bonds, *Absolute Music*, for more on this.
[53] Friedrich Wilhelm Nietzsche, *Thus Spoke Zarathustra*, p. 187.

about music. Crucially, this is primitive and pre-linguistic. All of this simply adds further context to the philosophical perspectives elucidated above; it is, however, necessary to set it out in detail in order to understand what is at stake in the third period.

From the middle of the nineteenth century and owing in major part to both the changing prestige of texted and un-texted musical forms mentioned above along with a set of polemics between Wagner, Hanslick and Liszt, the idea of music's essence and its effects become strictly separated. The notion of absolute music (not the practice: as mentioned, un-texted music dates back to the ancient world) is coined by Wagner, and though the use of the term is inconsistent in his writings, it was first used as a dismissive term to deride purely instrumental music and to bolster his own theories about opera and the *Gesamtkunstwerk*.[54] It is Hanslick's positive appropriation of the term which sets the course of thinking – and especially musicological thinking – on a particular trajectory that has ramifications for at least a century, and it is the legacy of this conception of music that, as this book argues, we are often still in the process of deconstructing. Firstly, as Bonds has described, Hanslick separates essence and effect: it is not that he denies the deeply powerful effects music can produce, but he no longer associates these effects with the question of what music 'is.' Secondly, it is musical form that becomes central to what music 'is' – as can be seen in his well-known definition of music as 'tonend bewegte Form' (translated variously as 'form moved in sounding/tones' or 'tonally moved form', among others), thus settling or at least closing a long debate on music's potential for representation: it simply no longer matters, as all that matters – and is essentially musical – is form. Music no longer *means* anything, as such, and as a result the academic study of music can concern itself entirely with formal analysis and jettison all questions of its emotional, affective, material, performative, social and political dimensions as non-essential to what music fundamentally is. Finally, and especially once the retronym of 'programme music' is coined by Liszt, these two ideas of music (i.e. absolute, autonomous, text-less vs. texted or at least programmatic *ergo* representational, no matter how that happens) are mapped onto specific repertoires. As Bonds describes, 'by aligning the age-old idea of "pure" music with a specific repertory – instrumental, non-programmatic music – these three figures [Hanslick, Wagner, Liszt] together changed the framework of the debate about the relationship between music's essence and effect'

---

[54] See Bonds, *Absolute Music*, p. 1.

and by extension its relation to language and *logos* more broadly.[55] Absolute music is thereafter valued and validated as the superior form of high art music. Concomitantly, music's essence is identified with the rational free-play of formal properties apparently uncontaminated by social context or history, while it is simultaneously framed as a universal language despite being conflated with a particular repertoire – a manoeuvre which completes a thoroughly transcendentalising and universalising gesture.

Surprisingly – or perhaps not – the assumption that music was synonymous with the largely instrumental repertoire of the classical concert hall remained the assumption until the intervention of poststructuralist influenced 'critical musicology' in the last two decades of the twentieth century. This assumption fed into the emergence of musicology – predominantly historical musicology – as a discipline that was by and large palaeographic and philological in its methods: in short, it was generally quasi-scientific, positivist, score oriented and interested in the syntactic relations between notes (primarily in terms of harmony, but also including rhythm and melody) at a local level, and the architectonics of structure in individual pieces or movements as well as across multi-movement works, while also sketching out the autonomous teleological unfolding of changing musical structures/styles across time. Serious consideration about music's relation to bodies, identities, emotions or even performance, as well as non-structural if seemingly 'musical' concerns such as timbre are minimal at best. As Olivia Bloechl and Melanie Lowe clearly recount, musicology was transformed in the 1980s and 1990s by its (belated) encounter with both structuralist and poststructuralist, largely French, left-oriented, 'theory'.[56] It is notable, however, that it has very often been (non-musical) philosophical concepts drawn from this body of theory that were used to analyse musical texts, rather than (post-)structuralist attempts to theorise music itself. Legitimate areas of study rapidly expanded, including a significant body of work on music's relation to, reflection of and reproduction of gender binaries and sexuality, as well as postcolonial perspectives and the growing fields of ethnomusicology and popular music studies (among others). As Susan McClary, one of the early proponents of the so-called 'new musicology' (perhaps more aptly referred to as 'critical musicology', as mentioned above, given its no longer 'new' status) described, this movement was motivated by the need to deconstruct the inherited transcendental baggage of the supposedly autonomous

---

[55] Ibid., p. 12.
[56] See Olivia Bloechl with Melanie Lowe, 'Introduction: Rethinking Difference', pp. 1–52 (p. 21).

and universal value of the music of the high art canon, insisting instead that 'music is always a political activity' and thus also incontrovertibly enmeshed in relations of power.⁵⁷ In so doing, the idea that music might be meaningful beyond its logical, rational, note-relations – that its various social and cultural 'meanings' might be inseparable from what it 'is' – was brought back into consideration, along with increased scholarly consideration of non-literate and non-high art forms of music-making.

Finally, then, before we move to a new set of considerations, I want to suggest another outcome of the genealogy that extends out of the philosophical conceptions of music from the nineteenth century that has perhaps unintended but important consequences for the considerations at hand. It is well documented and understood that Freud had read Schopenhauer and that Schopenhauer's conception of the Will can be seen as a precursor to Freud's theorisation of the unconscious; there has also been much speculation as to the influence of Nietzsche on Freud, especially with regards to the centrality of urges, desires and impulses to the underlying and more primitive Dionysian.⁵⁸ Given that both the Will and the Dionysian are to some extent modelled on music, or music is at least the worldly manifestation of these principles, the Freudian *Trieb* is easily – albeit retrospectively – understood as 'musical'.⁵⁹ The significance of this is made manifest following the structuralist linguistic intervention of Lacan's rereading of Freud: the emphasis is on the visual (cf. 'Le Stade du miroir' ['The Mirror Stage']⁶⁰) and on language, law and representations as constituent (and constituting) parts of the entry into the symbolic order (as well as the structuring of the imaginary). In contrast, the real is understood as 'the ineliminable residue of all articulation, the foreclosed element, which may be approached, but never grasped: the *umbilical cord* of the symbolic'.⁶¹ Though, for Lacan, the symbolic necessarily fails to grasp or have direct access to the real – it falters at every attempt to approach it – the real nonetheless exerts powerful pre- or non-linguistic influences and is an essential part of the psyche as whole. No matter how ungraspable or impossible the real is (from the vantage of the symbolic order), it nonetheless – as is suggested by the citation above – seems to retain some kind of essential link, whether metaphorical or 'actual', to the pre-individuated space of

---

⁵⁷ Susan McClary, *Feminine Endings*, p. 26; see Bloechl, Lowe and Kallberg, *Rethinking Difference in Music Scholarship*, p. 25.
⁵⁸ See, for example, Paul-Laurent Assoun, *Freud et Nietzsche*.
⁵⁹ To be clear, this is not a claim made by Freud, who at any rate was famously amusical.
⁶⁰ See Jacques Lacan, 'Le Stade du miroir comme formateur de la fonction du Je telle qu'elle nous est révélée dans l'expérience psychanalytique', pp. 449–55.
⁶¹ Alan Sheridan, 'Translator's Note', pp. 277–82 (p. 280), my emphasis. This is especially pertinent to the concerns of Chapters 2 and 3.

the womb and the mother-infant dyad more generally. For the subsequent feminist revisionings of Lacan, most evident in the work of Julia Kristeva, this pre-symbolic space assumes a more expressly musical character. She borrows the term *chora* from the *Timaeus* – Plato's dialogue of origins which is fundamentally concerned with the creation of the possibility of truth. As John Sallis describes, the *Timaeus* tells of 'the beginning, the origin, of nature, even a kind of nature before nature, the mother, as Timaeus calls it, of all natural things'.[62] Kristeva uses the *chora* 'pour désigner une articulation toute provisoire, essentiellement mobile, constituée de mouvements et de leurs stases éphémères' ['to denote an essentially mobile and extremely provisional articulation constituted by movements and their ephemeral stases'].[63] She characterises it as a 'space' – albeit one preceding space and time – where, through rupture and rhythm, 'La fonctionnalité kinésique à laquelle nous pensons en parlant du *sémiotique*, est antérieure à la position du signe' ['[t]he kinetic functional stage of the *semiotic* precedes the establishment of the sign'].[64] It is 'in' this primeval womb-space that Kristeva develops her theory of *le sémiotique* [the semiotic], in opposition – though complementary – to the mature symbolic in her theory of signification. The rhythms of the *chora* are articulations of early drives and are coded as essentially musical in their capacity for gestural, pre-symbolic communication. *Le sémiotique* finds its most common articulation in the echolalia of infants and the psychotic babble of the mad, as well as in poetic language; it precedes and is indeed the precondition of the entire symbolic enterprise, though it manifests only in moments of rupture in mature symbolic communication. As Kristeva states, in an extraordinarily Nietzschean vein, '[l]e signe refoule la *chora* et son éternel retour. Seul le *désir* sera désormais le témoin de ce battement "originaire"' ['The sign represses the *chora* and its eternal return. Desire alone will henceforth be witness to that "primal" pulsation'].[65]

We can thus see how at this juncture, both philosophy – strongly influenced by German idealism – and psychoanalysis coordinate in figuring music (or the essentially musical) as pre-linguistic or a proto-language intimately related to desire, bodily impulses and drives; at the same time, by the end of the nineteenth century, dominant musicological perspectives also drew (intentionally or otherwise) on the post-Kantian legacy to validate the free-play of formal syntactical elements as the

---

[62] John Sallis, *Chorology: On Beginning in Plato's Timaeus*, p. 4.
[63] Kristeva, *La Révolution Du Langage Poétique*, p. 23 [Julia Kristeva and Leon S. Roudiez, *Revolution in Poetic Language*, p. 25].
[64] Ibid., p. 26 [p. 27].
[65] Kristeva, *Pouvoirs de l'horreur*, p. 21 [Kristeva, *Powers of Horror*, p. 14].

properly musical, and so conflated the 'idea' of absolute music with a particular repertoire. As a result, one of the guiding aims of this book is to articulate more clearly the often-unacknowledged consequences of this heady alignment of music's purported essence not only with a particular repertoire (this is already well documented, at least within musicology) but also with a theory of the subject and of origins.

IV. Music in the Quadrivium: The Science and Art Problem

Briefly, to conclude this section, it seems pertinent to highlight the way in which discussions about music frequently also involve considerations about whether music should primarily be understood as an art or a science – or indeed both – a consideration that often elicits vehemently polarised responses. From Pythagoras who, as mentioned, considered music's essence to be cosmic mathematical ratios, through to the Boethian *quadrivium* that considered music, along with geometry, arithmetic and astronomy to be one of the four branches of mathematics or science, and onto Leibniz, 'who proposed that the comprehension of music was at base a kind of unconscious calculation or computation',[66] music – or at least its essence – is understood primarily as scientific/mathematical by a number of thinkers. Even when the ratios devised by Pythagoras had been disproven, for the Pythagoreans and those working in his legacy music continued to be understood as intimately related to ratio, mathematics and number. In ancient thought, most clearly as developed by Plato and in the notion of the harmony of the spheres, even when music is considered primarily as an ethical force it is still thought of 'as a *science* that reveals the secrets of nature and exerts a powerful force on the character (*ethos*) of individuals and society as a whole'.[67] The ancient model thus also attests to a different conception of the relationship between science and art in the ancient world; a distinction that is necessary to acknowledge but ultimately beyond the present work to consider in any detail.

Both these ancient conceptions of music, 'as sensuous embodiment of the intelligible universal harmony and [...] as ethical imitation of human passions and characters',[68] coexisted in subsequent European traditions with either conception dominating in different epochs, for different writers, or in different contexts. Though vocal music remained consistently dominant in terms of genre throughout – much literate

---

[66] Levinson, *Musical Concerns*, p. 8.
[67] Thomas J. Mathiesen, 'Antiquity and the Middle Ages', in Gracyk and Kania (eds), *The Routledge Companion to Philosophy and Music*, pp. 257–72, 256, my emphasis.
[68] Karol Berger, 'Concepts and Developments in Music Theory', pp. 304–28 (p. 313).

music from this period is, of course, liturgical – the respective value placed on harmony or melody was more variable. As Karol Berger has clearly laid out, while harmony was the dominant paradigm in the fifteenth and early sixteenth centuries, the end of the sixteenth century witnessed a shift back towards the privileging of music's mimetic ability to model passions and thus an increasing emphasis on melodic or texted aspects, as harmony alone seemed inadequate for conveying ethical education.[69] During the Enlightenment and throughout the *querelles*, music maintained a fairly prominent position, especially as it could be understood as something that bridged both the arts and the sciences and thus served as a useful conceit to consider ideas central to the *siècle des Lumières*, such as the relationship between reason, perception and experience in both artistic and scientific domains. The melodic aspect generally continued to be privileged, though certain key thinkers – especially those influenced by the burgeoning scientific revolution – sought, yet again, a mathematical or scientific basis for music. As suggested above, the sonorous, voice-like character of melody is given greater prominence by Rousseau, whereas Rameau rehabilitates the attempt to think of music in terms of its mathematical relation to proportions and ratios; an endeavour he attempted to prove by drawing on empirical experimentation. His commitment to this scientific understanding could not be clearer than in the opening to the *Traité de l'harmonie* [*Treatise on Harmony*] of 1722 when he states:

> La Musique est la Science des Sons: par consequent le Son est le principal objet de la Musique. On divise ordinairement la Musique en Harmonie & en Melodie, quoi-que celle-cy ne soit qu'une partie de l'autre, & qu'il suffise de connoître l'Harmonie, pour être parfaitement instruit de toutes le proprietez de la Musique, comme il sera prouvé dans la suite.
>
> [Music is the science of sounds; therefore sound is the principal subject of music. Music is generally divided into harmony and melody, but we shall show in the following that the latter is merely a part of the former and that a knowledge of harmony is sufficient for a complete understanding of all the properties of music.][70]

As will be further explored in Chapters 2 and 5, the tension between this double conception of music is not without conflict, however, and ultimately comes down, again, to the privileging of melody over harmony as music's essential musicality (or vice versa). In a more tangible way, the dispute is also enfolded within a larger debate about French

---

[69] Ibid., p. 313.
[70] Jean-Philippe Rameau, *Traité de l'harmonie*, book I, ch. I, p. 1, also cited in Berger, 'Concepts and Developments in Music Theory', p. 313 [Rameau, *Treatise on Harmony*, p. 3].

opera (or *tragédie lyrique*), which is unsurprising given that at this point texted music is still the most exalted form of music – though given the shift that occurs as we approach the nineteenth century, it is perhaps predictable that much of the debate centred around the respective values of the text or the music (whether in terms of the balance between arias and recitatives within an individual opera, or more broadly about whether it is the text or the music that is the driving force behind the opera at large). Ultimately, this becomes a debate about the relative values of Italian and French (style) music, with Rameau (and the Ramistes) attacked initially by the Lullistes for being too 'Italian' (among other things) and then later, in the *querelle des bouffons*, for being too committed to the French tragedic style in the debate with Rousseau, who was a keen proponent of *opera buffa* (and Italian opera more generally). Daniel Chua has written astutely about the specifically musical refractions of the *querelle des Anciens et des Modernes*, showing how until the canonisation of a repertoire (coinciding with the above-mentioned 'invention' of the composer-function) in the nineteenth century, and especially the retrospective 'deification of Bach in the eternal pantheon of absolute music', it was not possible to 'formulate a timeless norm out of its [music's] ephemeral, ever-progressing identity'.[71] Instead, a comparative stylistics is inculcated: music is either 'sacred or secular, old or new, high or low, French or Italian' with the upshot that 'one's judgement depended on which side of the *querelle* one was on: to become ancient was either to be "classic" or out of date; conversely, to be modern was either to be a passing fashion or to be a sign of future perfection'.[72] Finally, then, despite attempts by theorist/practioners such as Rameau to (re)find a scientific, numerical and natural basis for music, the figuring of music in the *querelle* is itself nonetheless distinctly modern, and 'attests to music's epistemological shift from the quadrivium to the trivium [the lower, non-scientific arts of grammar, logic and rhetoric], for quarrelling is a method of positioning style within the relativity [rather than scientific objectivity] of the trivium'.[73]

By the time we reach the nineteenth century, the dominant perspectives in philosophy seem to have shifted towards a conception of music that is not only defiantly non-scientific but, rather, views music as the pinnacle of all art, as is manifest in Walter Pater's famous assertion that 'all art constantly aspires towards the condition of music'. For Schopenhauer, for example, the fact that music does not represent ideas

---

[71] Daniel K. L. Chua, *Absolute Music and the Construction of Meaning*, p. 67.
[72] Ibid.
[73] Ibid., p. 68.

does not mean that music is reducible to the formal (i.e. mathematical) relations between sound phenomena. This is even more the case for Nietzsche, who quips in the *Gay Science* of 1882,

> Suppose one judged the *value* of a piece of music according to how much of it could be counted, calculated, and expressed in formulas – how absurd would such a 'scientific' assessment of music be! What would one have comprehended, understood, recognized? Nothing, really nothing of what is 'music' in it![74]

Ultimately, of course, what becomes quite clear when considering the longer history of the intersections of music, philosophy, art and science is the strong sense in which all of these concerns were never merely musical, but rather tapped into broader ideological debates especially about meaning, reason, education, aesthetics, politics and even the origin and value of society and the state.

MOUSIKE: CULTURE, POLITICS AND EDUCATION

As Sartre suggests, perhaps against himself, music and its different styles, genres and types are often strongly linked to different cultural and socio-economic identities. Though he misreads (or rather 'mis-hears') the musical cues that might allow him to identify a particular musical work as coming from a performer or composer of a particular background or identity, his assumption that one can identify such things from musical cues nonetheless highlights one of the ways in which we often listen to music: music is, in this respect, clearly not separate from society and daily life, but rather is a very complex part of it. As is well known, the word 'music' derives from the Greek word *mousike* (μουσική), which stems from the word 'muse', and simply relates to 'anything pertinent to the muses'.[75] It is often collocated with *techne*; the composite, μουσική τέχνη, refers more specifically to the arts of the muses, and which includes (what we would today call) song, dance and many types of poetry and music. In fact, the ancient conception of *mousike* is so broad that several commentators, including Penelope Murray and Peter Wilson, have suggested that it is 'a contender for the closest term in Greek to our (polymorphous) "culture"'.[76] Consequently, in its original derivation *mousike* is inseparable from other cultural and artistic forms, and especially from poetry, with which the muses were especially associated; indeed,

---

[74] Friedrich Wilhelm Nietzsche, *The Gay Science*, p. 239.
[75] Albright, *Panaesthetics*, p. 1.
[76] Penelope Murray and Peter Wilson, 'Introduction' in *Music and the Muses*, pp. 1–8 (p. 1).

in contemporary parlance they are perhaps associated most strongly with poetry (rather than music), and above all with artistic inspiration. Additionally, though instrumental music certainly existed in the ancient world – albeit as a minor genre – the differentiation between (what we would call) music and poetry, chanting and incantation is far from clear. Prior to the literate revolution and the invention of a written literature that took place between the fourth and fifth centuries BCE, all previous poetry, literature and even philosophy were orally transmitted. This means that the founding works of Western literature – most prominently, of course, the works of Homer and Hesiod – were either sung or narrated, and likely were accompanied by a lyre. Furthermore, as Daniel Albright suggests, even the distinction between different media was less pronounced in the ancient world: 'an artistic medium was not a distinct thing but a kind of proclivity within the general domain of Art'.[77] Thus, though *mousike* might be comprised of many different aspects as described, the practice of *mousike* is a far more wide-ranging and all-encompassing endeavour; 'in the view of Antiquity, they [the muses, and thus *mousike*] belonged not only to poetry but to all higher forms of intellectual life'.[78] Indeed, even the parental lineage of the muses – they are the offspring of Zeus, king of the gods, and Mnemosyne, the personification of memory – guaranteed the authenticity of their arts in an oral tradition, and thus their role as the legitimate repository of cultural memory was their birthright. *Mousike* was fundamentally associated with education (the transmission of cultural messages and information from generation to generation, both implicitly and explicitly) and is thus inseparable from society, culture and politics. Though we often consider music in an abstract or intellectual sense, Danielle Cohen-Lévinas has argued that music is perhaps in an even closer relation to education – especially to a more practical, skills-based learning – because music

> nécessite une connaissance de l'accord, du rythme, du chant choral, de la citare, de la lyre, de la flûte. Elle nécessite par conséquent un apprentissage, ce que nous nommons un métier. Il faut rappeler que la conception musicale selon les Grecs (*Mousiké*) donne naissance aux sept arts libéraux en vigueur au Moyen Âge.
>
> [requires a knowledge of harmony, rhythm, choral singing, and [of how to play] the zither, the lyre, the flute. Consequently, music demands that it should be learnt, what we would call a specialist craft. It is worth remembering that the entire concept of music (mousike), as conceived by the Greeks,

---

[77] Albright, *Panaesthetics*, p. 1.
[78] Curtius, cited in Murray, 'The Muses and their Arts' in *Music and the Muses*, pp. 365–89 (p. 365).

gave birth to the seven liberal arts that came into full force in the Middle Ages.][79]

More precisely, then, as Murray describes, it was through 'the complex interplay of Muses, *mousike* and paideia [education] *that Greek cultural values were articulated*'.[80]

This can be seen perhaps most clearly in Plato, as already suggested above. As Danielle Lévinas-Cohen remarks, '[d]ans la *République*, Platon réserve à la musique une place prépondérante. Elle devient une des disciplines piliers de l'éducation' ['in the *Republic*, Plato gives music a leading position. Music becomes one of the founding disciplines of education']; moreover, owing to the influence of Pythagoras, 'la musique exprime tout à la fois un ordre moral, un ordre arithmétique et un ordre cosmique' ['music is able to express not only a moral order, but also a mathematical and cosmic order'].[81] Though there are many reflections on the technical and practical aspects of music, for Plato music is always also centrally concerned with *ethos* and the possibility of modelling or regulating good moral character for both individual citizens and the city-state at large: it is precisely the ability of *mousike* to mediate – and indeed regulate or attune – between different layers, and to inculcate harmony from the psychological through to the cosmic realm that is of interest. Though the ethical 'content' of music is notoriously difficult to identify, throughout Plato's œuvre there are many attempts to understand and regulate the way in which a correct (i.e. ethical) pleasure can be taken from music as well as its role in the education of citizens through its ability to act as an interface between the soul and the body.

Music is thus thoroughly and inextricably bound up in the daily life of the *callipolis*; it is both a tool for the cementing of social values and a reflection of the society from which it emerges. Babette E. Babich has described how

> the modern tendency to reduce music to the 'organised' art of sound obscures the equiprimordial sense in which *musike* could be regarded, as Nietzsche saw it, as the enabling element of intellectual or spiritual as well as aesthetic and physical education and in which *musike* figures as the determining force of both individual and societal character [*ethos*].[82]

To complicate things yet further, in the *Phaedo*, Socrates aligns *mousike* with the practice of philosophy; in the dialogue he suggests that

---

[79] Danielle Cohen-Lévinas, 'Les Icônes de l'écoute, d'après une lecture de Platon et de Hegel' in *Musique et Philosophie*, pp. 101–21 (p. 102).
[80] Murray, 'The Muses and their Arts' in *Music and the Muses*, p. 389, emphasis in the original.
[81] Cohen-Lévinas, 'Les Icônes de l'écoute' in *Musique et Philosophie*, p. 107.
[82] Babette E. Babich, *Words in Blood, like Flowers*, p. 100.

philosophy is the highest form of *mousike*, and thus troubles easy assumptions that *mousike* is even necessarily to do with art, and concomitantly that music is to do with sound. He says:

> In the course of my life I have often had intimations in dreams 'that I should make music.' The same dream came to me sometimes in one form, and sometimes in another, but always saying the same or nearly the same words: Make and cultivate music, said the dream. And hitherto I had imagined that this was only intended to exhort and encourage me in the study of philosophy, which has always been the pursuit of my life, and is the noblest and best of music.[83]

Similarly, in the *Republic*, Plato explicitly articulates being self-disciplined and virtuous in terms of being a 'true virtuoso' – being musical is thus not necessarily to do with being practically or technically accomplished and trained in specific skills such as singing or playing an instrument, but rather describes the need for a philosopher to attune 'his body in order to make music with his mind' (591d).[84] By describing philosophy as 'the highest form of *mousike*', Plato thus positions musical life as 'an analogue for the life of the mind'.[85] Crucially, as Halliwell describes, it would be wrong to think of this as purely metaphorical; the entire understanding of *mousike* is such that an explicitly 'musico-poetic education and culture' is essential to and inseparable from the 'virtues and balanced passions of "the philosophical nature"' that is induced through this sensuous and aesthetic pedagogical process.[86]

Finally, in returning to the ancient conception of *mousike* I simply wish to highlight music's thoroughgoing relationship to society, education and values. This may, perhaps, seem an obvious point, but it is one that is essential to highlight given the legacy outlined above that, following Kant and Hegel, has understood music and the arts more broadly to be 'separated completely from the world of the ordinary, mundane, and everyday [… and severed] from anything associated with the transient, contingent world of mere mortals'.[87] Moreover, as mentioned, this legacy aligns itself with a particular repertoire which is itself constructed as autonomous, free of function and is thus purportedly in a special relation to absolute freedom and truth, unbound by the passing constraints of daily life. As Hegel describes, it 'cuts itself free from this servitude in order to raise itself, in free independence, to the truth in which it fulfils itself independently and conformably with its

---

[83] Plato, *Phaedo*, pp. 3–4.
[84] Plato, *Republic*, p. 343.
[85] Murray, 'The Muses and their Arts' in *Music and the Muses*, p. 376.
[86] Stephen Halliwell, 'Plato' in Gracyk and Kania (eds), *The Routledge Companion to Philosophy and Music*, pp. 307–16 (p. 315).
[87] Goehr, *The Imaginary Museum of Musical Works*, p. 157.

own ends alone [. . . and] in this its freedom alone is fine art truly art'.[88] Though the final section of this chapter outlines some problematic aspects of the ancient conception of *mousike*, I concur with Babich's assertation that there remains 'an insurmountable conflict between the ancient conception of music and our contemporary understanding of [high art] music [. . . which] refers to a world *apart from* the everyday'.[89] Moreover, by insisting on the lived, material, everyday-ness of music in all its forms, one can launch a productive counter-narrative to the project of European high art culture understood as 'universal, self-justifying, [and] ostensibly place-*less*' – a position that simultaneously derides popular (and other) musical forms for being local, specific, particular, emotional, bodily and trivial.[90] Throughout, I will draw on the body of work described above as 'critical musicology' which sought to challenge the hegemony of this extremely powerful ideological construct; however, though 'critical musicology' was strongly influenced by the (post-)structuralist turn in largely French theory for its own theoretical underpinnings, I wish to suggest that the concept of music is often substantially untheorised – or at least uncritically deployed – in poststructuralist and contemporary theory itself.

MUSES (AND SIRENS): GENDER, AUTHORITY AND ANXIETY

The derivation of 'music' from *mousike*, which inviolably links music to the muses and thus to the feminine in our cultural heritage, will be the subject of the final section of this chapter; this is also indissociably linked to questions of authority, value and legitimacy. Though the genealogy of the muses themselves, the number of them, and their exact skills vary according to author and across time, it is the version articulated by Hesiod in the *Theogony* that has been the major source for subsequent generations. According to Hesiod, the muses were a 'composite of nine sisters (a choir?) who were daughters of Zeus – this gave them Olympian prestige – and their mother "Remembrance" (*Mnemosune*)'.[91] Crucially in this early work – itself an orally transmitted musico-poetic hymn until it was written down in the sixth century BCE – Hesiod makes it clear that the muses have conferred upon him, as poet, two gifts: 'a staff [. . . and] their divine voice, so that I might tell

---

[88] Georg Wilhelm Friedrich Hegel, *Aesthetics*, p. 7.
[89] Babich, *Words in Blood, like Flowers*, p. 100.
[90] Leyshon et al., 'Introduction' in Leyshon, Matless and Revill, *The Place of Music*, pp. 1–30 (p. 5).
[91] Eric A. Havelock, *The Muse Learns to Write*, p. 20.

of things to come and things past'.[92] In figuring the orator of the hymn as a king (represented by the staff or sceptre), the poetic voice is both legitimised and given great power. From this early vision it is clear to see how the muses are both embodiments of all the arts that comprise *mousike* and simultaneously the divine source that inspires and sanctions the (male) poet's voice; the poet is both mediator (between the divine and the audience) and a vessel for a source whose power and authority is external to himself. Moreover, as Penelope Murray has described, in the way that Hesiod establishes a direct link between the muses and the gift of convincing oratory (i.e. rhetoric) we are invited to rethink 'the relationship between poetry and rhetoric, and even between *mousike* and *logos*' – and we might also add music and philosophy.[93]

There is of course a distinction to be made between the *Theogony* as an orally transmitted practice, concerned with the transmission and memorisation of cultural narratives, stories and beliefs, and which formed an essential social function – 'that of preserving the tradition by which the Greeks lived and instructing them in it', and the literate repository we have available to us as a trace of these practices.[94] Though scholars have made many attempts at imagining and reconstructing oral practices (along with specifically musical practices in antiquity) it is of course only from the written texts that remain and that describe oral traditions that we can piece together any idea of these practices, and thus we appear to be stuck with the sense that we are trying to (re)find a lost origin – an origin where there was no distinction between written and oral forms, theoretical and practical accounts and, crucially, between music and literature (and, within that, between poetry and prose). Central to this is of course the fact that, as abundantly mentioned, *mousike*, which becomes interchangeably (and anachronistically) music, song or poetry, among others, did not differentiate in our modern sense between these different artistic media. As we will see, particularly in Chapter 5, the quest for this overdetermined lost origin becomes a major drive of aesthetic aspiration in the late nineteenth century – most iconically, if not actually, with the Wagnerian *Gesamtkunstwerk* which sought an all-embracing synthesis and unification of the individual arts, modelled on a (largely fictive) notion of art at its point of origin in the ancient world.

As Eric A. Havelock has documented, this shift towards a literate culture in the ancient world also changes the way people imagine themselves – even what it is possible to imagine – and also coincides

---

[92] Hesiod, and Norman O. Brown, *Hesiod's Theogony*, p. 54.
[93] Murray, 'The Muses and their Arts' in *Music and the Muses*, p. 371.
[94] Havelock, *The Muse Learns to Write*, p. 8.

with Plato's reconceptualising of art as fundamentally mimetic.[95] At stake in the shift from orality to literacy then is a shifting set of cultural values. Central to this observation is the sense that the emergence of two related, but distinct practices – 'singing, recitation, and memorisation on the one hand (a cultural combination we can conveniently label as orality) and reading and writing on the other (the habit of a documented and literate culture)'[96] – are brought into competition and conflict with each other. Havelock famously asserts that there is a fundamental rupture between the literary and philosophical practices of the (predominantly oral) fifth and sixth centuries and those of the (literate) fourth century; indeed, the ethical life with which Plato is so concerned relies on 'the notion of a moral value system which was autonomous, while at the same time capable of internalization in the individual consciousness, [this] was a literate invention'.[97] Similarly, in the eyes of Havelock, Plato's famous exile of the poets alludes more to a shifting identification of the source of authority; it is less the poet (or indeed the poetry) that Plato attacks, and more the didactic 'instruction it had been their role to provide'.[98] Nonetheless, the Platonic understanding of art (and thus *mousike*) as mimetic, and its indissociable origin as the art of the muses, thus concomitantly describes or sets in motion a set of assumptions and values that also relate to gender. Though in the simplest sense mimesis is often understood as 'imitation', the ramifications of what that means – in terms of authenticity, reality and truth – are far more complicated, both within Plato's own œuvre and for subsequent commentators given that it is used to mean both truthful and bogus imitation. Ronald Bogue – drawing on the work of Mihai Spariosu who has related faithful mimesis and deceptive mimesis to pre-rational and rational mentalities respectively in ancient Greece – has persuasively laid out what this means for the questions at stake here, and deserves citation at length:

> Mimesis in its older meaning seems to be have been allied with ritual, dance, music and play, with performances in which mythic and divine forces are not so much represented as brought into presence through their (re)enactment. Mimesis in this prerational sense is one with 'the non-imitative, ecstatic, or "dionysian" movement of Being.' In Plato, one finds a later, rational conception of mimesis as imperfect representation or imitation of inaccessible Being, as well as a negative characterization of prerational mimesis as hollow simulation and misleading appearance [. . . This dual conception] marks a struggle for domination, an effort to replace the unmediated, amoral power

---

[95] See Eric A. Havelock, *Preface to Plato*.
[96] Havelock, *The Muse Learns to Write*, p. 21.
[97] Ibid., p. 4.
[98] Ibid., p. 8.

of prerational mimesis with the mediated, truth-grounded power of rational mimesis, and to dislodge myth, poetry and rhetoric from their positions of authority and establish in their place the sovereignty of philosophy.[99]

Ultimately, the understanding of both mimesis and *mousike* is deeply ambivalent in Plato. As Spariosu has shown, this is clearly demonstrated in the debate between Socrates and the rhapsode Ion, where rational philosophy is pitted against the magnetic and emotional appeal of pre-rational poetry; at the same time, however, Plato has self-consciously staged this as a dialogue and has Socrates himself reciting Homer and acting in accordance with pre-rational values.[100] Similarly, elsewhere, mimesis is at once necessary and condemned; it is necessary for education (children imitate stories that in turn form or shape them) and yet also condemned for its role in privileging emotion over reason. Of central importance is the way in which, as Potolsky has shown, 'Plato subtly opposes mimesis to the ideals of masculinity. He associates imitation with women, children and the insane, all of whom were expressly excluded from Athenian political life'.[101] Plato's paradigm-shifting conceptualisation which identifies the arts of the muses as fundamentally mimetic also repudiates them for being a 'technology of the past, limited to and by oral culture' and also denigrates them 'as secondary and derivative, distinguished from reason and truth and associated with femininity and childhood [. . . and as a result] poetry comes to seem inappropriate to the needs of current Greek society'.[102]

It is evidently entirely impossible for Plato to dismiss poetry and music completely from the *callipolis*; the muses' long-standing relation to education by no means disappears and the powerful ability of *mousike* to shape the soul remains one of the essential tools for the education of model citizens. As mentioned above there is, however, a vast amount of attention paid to selecting the 'right' forms of artistic practice in order to shape young minds. For now, it is simply necessary to highlight the way in which this conflicting and complicated conception of *mousike* and mimesis sets in chain what is in effect a set of value judgements about what constitutes good or bad, legitimate or illegitimate types of music and poetry, and what the *role* of music in the *callipolis* should be. In short, though Plato at points aligns the highest forms of learning, including philosophy, with *mousike*, and is clearly deeply invested in music's ability to model ethical and harmonious attitudes

---

[99] Ronald Bogue, 'Introduction' in *Mimesis in Contemporary Theory*, pp. 1–12 (p. 2).
[100] See Mihai Spariosu, 'Plato's *Ion*: Mimesis, Poetry, and Power' in Bogue (ed.), *Mimesis in Contemporary Theory*, pp. 13–26.
[101] Matthew Potolsky, *Mimesis*, p. 28.
[102] Ibid., pp. 31, 30.

both individually and in society, he is nonetheless deeply sceptical of mass audiences and popular music (see the *Laws* and the *Republic*) and in general with the idea of music as 'mere' entertainment. The ability of music to elicit strong and pleasurable responses is never in doubt in Plato; in contrast, it is precisely because of this that Plato is so keen 'to deny that pleasure in itself can be the sole criterion of musical value'.[103]

When it comes to the strong – whether pleasurable or painful – reactions that music can elicit, there is another archetypal feminine figure that perhaps brings this heady cultural constellation into view yet more sharply than the muse: that of the siren. Though both the muses and sirens are mythological female figures primarily associated with song, then as much as now, whether they have shared or distinct genealogies is less than clear. The story is infamous: the sirens were dangerous but enticing half-women, half-creatures, whose enchanting song lured mariners to their death on the rocks surrounding their island. Their song is at once irresistible – Odysseus has himself tied to the mast of his ship and plugs his oarsmen's ears with wax in order that he can safely pass the sirens and hear their legendary and magical music – and dangerous: had he not gone to such lengths he and his crew unquestionably would be lured to the shore and to certain death. Though the sirens themselves are charged with a forbidding but compelling eroticism – as not entirely human *femmes fatales* – it is above all 'the siren's *music* that positions her in the flowing spaces between the human, animal, and spirit worlds, between past and present, danger and delight'.[104] Not only have we inherited their legacy – a legacy which posits an insoluble link between sound's capacity to elicit our immediate, spellbinding attention and danger – through our use of the word siren as an alarm or acoustic warning, but the sirenic fantasy also links the act of listening, '[f]rom Homer through Joyce and beyond [...] to subjective displacement, to personal decentering, and to an ecstatic connection to the infinite polyphony of the world that threatens to engulf the self'.[105] As Adorno and Horkheimer famously argued in their critical analysis of the myth, the story of Odysseus is a 'prescient allegory of the dialectic of enlightenment'[106] whereby the rational, bourgeois individual triumphs over the mythical lure of the siren's

---

[103] Halliwell, 'Plato' in Gracyk and Kania (eds), *The Routledge Companion to Philosophy and Music*, p. 312.
[104] Naroditskaya and Austern, 'Introduction: Singing Each to Each' in Austern and Naroditskaya (eds), *Music of the Sirens*, pp. 1–15 (p. 3), my emphasis.
[105] Linda Phyllis Austern, '"Teach Me to Heare Mermaides Singing": Embodiments of (Acoustic) Pleasure and Danger in the Modern West' in Austern and Naroditskaya (eds), *Music of the Sirens*, pp. 52–104 (p. 53).
[106] Max Horkheimer and Theodor W. Adorno, *Dialectic of Enlightenment*, p. 27.

song, but only at the cost of aligning progress and enlightenment with the intellect rather than with (bodily) labour; the oarsmen, after all, are never afforded the painful pleasure of hearing the siren's song, though Odysseus's audition depends on their labour.[107] This potent configuration also orbits around the supposed complementarity of the alluring but monstrous feminine and the power of the voice, audition and music in general to transcend the reason and rationality of the men who find themselves impelled to listen and subsequently obliterated.

In a more explicitly psychoanalytic vein, through the conjoining of the thematics of death, anxiety, femininity and their sonorous realisation, the mythological siren song is figured as the shared sonic essence of both the 'mother's lullaby and the lover's exaltation' and thus as a fantasy that is at once an erotic desire for self-obliteration through sexual climax and also 'a longing for death as a return to the womb'.[108] For other thinkers, the sirens exemplify a nodal point for the coming together of music, sound and queerness; in their visible appearance the sirens clearly transgress the boundaries of the human, but they also represent music's multifarious and even duplicitous nature. As Judith Peraino highlights, they represent the way in which music participates in the 'normalizing and *ab*normalizing of the subject' as well as the way in which 'Western culture has used music to explore, celebrate, manage, and police aspects of gender and sexuality that are irreducible to verbal description and visual representation, as evidenced in the anxiety and ambivalence that frequently condense around music and musicians'.[109] Though a consideration of the sirens and their powerful song is perhaps most obviously a consideration of 'cultural constructs of performance and audition, [and the] diverse links between [the] sounding body and hearing body', it is quite clearly also a particularly neat nexus for the consideration of the cultural constructs that intertwine music, sound,

---

[107] There is, of course, an argument to be made that Adorno, too, in his own musical philosophy also forgets the oarsmen. See Judith Ann Peraino, *Listening to the Sirens*, particularly p. 2.

[108] Austern '"Teach Me to Hear Mermaides Singing"' in Austern and Naroditskaya (eds), *Music of the Sirens*, pp. 58, 56. See the chapter in full for more details of this line of thinking.

[109] Peraino, *Listening to the Sirens*, pp. 7–8. There is an abundance of literature which addresses or alludes to this, either explicitly or implicitly. For example, Fred Everett Maus speaks of the way in which anxieties about the 'unmanliness of musical experience' have fed into the way in which the discipline of music analysis defensively attends to structural, score-based concerns in order to evade (stereo-)typically feminine questions about music's expressive, sensuous nature. See Maus, 'Feminism, Music Theory, Time and Embodiment' in Beate Neumeier (ed.), *Dichotonies*, pp. 61–73 (p. 64). In a different vein, the late Philip Brett argued that not only do homosexuality and music have a long and shared history, but that music has historically acted as a safe refuge for homosexuals, see Philip Brett, 'Musicality, Essentialism, and the Closet' in Brett, Wood and Thomas, *Queering the Pitch*, pp. 9–26.

gender and the subject in both ancient and more recent thought.[110] Indeed, as I hope is evident, much of the above resonates strongly with the essential musicality of Kristeva's pre- and paralinguistic *sémiotique*, as well as with Luce Irigaray's association of liquids and fluidity with the feminine. Ultimately, then, as Linda Phyllis Austern describes, the 'sirenic fantasy relies largely [...] on conceptions of hearing as a passive, feminine sense, and on the links between women, water and the insubstantial, affective flow of music'.[111]

Finally, then, all that remains is to highlight the way in which, despite the centrality of the sonorous dimension to all of these constructs, neither the music of the sirens nor even that of the muses is ever actually heard, as such. Rather, both serve to figure as an ambivalent source of either inspiration or lack that propels the (usually) male poet's artistry; crucially, they themselves are insubstantial – non-existent – except in their subsequent portrayal by the men who depict both them and their songs. In this respect, even Sartre's *La Nausée* is sirenic in structure: though the song 'Some of these Days' does exist and has been sung and recorded by a 'real' singer, Sartre continues to figure the identity of the song beyond that of its realisation. Indeed, as we have seen, Roquentin repeatedly claims that 'elle n'existe pas'. It is precisely this absent presence that serves as the inspiration for his own artistry, with the song figuratively and literally (the lyrics are all about 'miss[ing] your honey') also mirroring and sustaining the lost feminine as manifest in the recent dissolution of his romantic relationship with Anny. Crucially, as Naroditskaya and Austern describe, '[t]he poet, the composer, the painter, the visionary, who (re)presents the song of the siren [or, one might add, the muse] in his own terms usurps her power [... because] her performance is not heard without his mediation'.[112] Indeed, by rejecting entirely the role of Sophie Tucker (and the other performers/instrumentalists/technologies) in the performance of 'Some of these Days', Sartre too goes some way to usurping much of her power. It turns out that the sirens' song, despite its notoriously potent powers, has been man's (re)construct(ion) all along; though they are portrayed as sources of inspiration they are simultaneously and indistinguishably repositories of male fantasy – a fantasy that, when it comes to the sirens, constructs femininity, and especially female sexuality, as inherently

---

[110] Naroditskaya and Austern, 'Introduction' in Austern and Naroditskaya (eds), *Music of the Sirens*, p. 3.

[111] Austern, '"Teach Me to Heare Mermaides Singing"' in Austern and Naroditskaya (eds), *Music of the Sirens*, p. 58.

[112] Naroditskaya and Austern, 'Introduction' in Austern and Naroditskaya (eds), *Music of the Sirens*, p. 10.

dangerous. At the same time, it signals a deep anxiety about all that appears to evade the grasp of the linguistic symbolic, setting in place a familiar chain of binarisms that oppose men/women, culture/nature, language/music, mind/body, and so on. Moreover, though the sirens are a source of inspiration, they are also permanently de-substantialised and *en abyme*; thus to figure man's lack as, essentially, the (sonorous) feminine ultimately serves, *encore*, to send both women and music to the interminable beyond of signification – a gesture that relentlessly aligns women with the subordinate term in the list of oppositions while erasing the lived presence of women in the signifying, symbolic and linguistic domain.[113] As Daniel Albright convincingly shows, this is rarely, if ever, an innocent gesture, because 'fictions of gender and race [amongst others] can be and have been used to inflict harm. Myths tend to have sharp edges.'[114] It is ultimately this metaphoricity – whether of music and/or of gender – to which the rest of this book attends.

---

[113] I am of course referring to Lacan's famous seminar where the feminine is figured, *encore*, in permanent relation to the body (*en corps*) and thus as a constituent lack of the phallogocentric regime of the symbolic. See Jacques Lacan and Jacques-Alain Miller, *Encore*.
[114] Albright, *Panaesthetics*, p. 28.

2. *Music, Meaning and Materiality:* Nancy's Corps Sonore

[L]a jouissance phallique est l'obstacle par quoi l'homme n'arrive pas, dirai-je, à jouir du corps de la femme, précisément parce que ce dont il jouit, c'est la jouissance de l'organe.
Lacan[1]

OUVERTURE

This chapter explores the work of Jean-Luc Nancy, paying close attention to a profusion of musical references across his vast œuvre but homing in on the slim volume, *À l'écoute* (2002), dedicated largely to the question of what (musical) listening affords philosophy.[2] It seems an appropriate point of opening to the questions that are sustained and developed across the book, precisely because it approaches the complex issue of what sound and music do, or could do, for philosophy head on. Or, perhaps more accurately, and less instrumentally, it exposes the way in which philosophy has (had) little purchase on the sonorous precisely because it is beyond signification, if not beyond meaning. All of this is in order to propose the possibility of a philosophy that listens, a philosophy that is attentive to meaning not merely as *logos*, and the passing of sounds always yet to come. For Nancy, it is precisely resonance that is this point of opening.

To begin, then, at the end of the extended essay, *À l'écoute*, we find a short coda based on Nancy's reading of Titian's painting *Venus with an Organist and Cupid* (see Figure 2.1). This musical tableau depicts an

---

[1] Jacques Lacan, *Encore*, p. 15 ['Phallic jouissance is the obstacle owing to which man does not come, I would say, to enjoy woman's body, precisely because what he enjoys is the jouissance of the organ'; Lacan, *On Feminine Sexuality*, p. 7].

[2] I have already made the central argument about Nancy's *À l'écoute* elsewhere, see Sarah Hickmott, '(En) Corps Sonore', pp. 479–93.

Figure 2.1 Titian, *Venus with an Organist and Cupid* (c. 1555), Museo Nacional Del Prado, Madrid. Credit: Museo Nacional Del Prado, Madrid

organist gazing at a nude Venus; she appears to pay him no attention, instead attending to Cupid who is embracing her. Behind these figures we can see out to the fairly modestly landscaped garden of the villa in which the musical scene presumably takes place; the pipes of the organ in the upper left blend almost seamlessly with the lines of trees outside which demarcate the limits of the garden. In an appropriately musical fashion, this 'tail' is more or less inessential to, and independent of, the preceding text, yet ultimately serves to bring it to a more satisfactory close. In effect, Nancy's short oto-iconographical analysis allows for a more lucid recapitulation of the key claims of the short but dense text: firstly, that sound is always already a resounding that folds into itself any distinction between subject/object and inside/outside. Secondly, that sound subsists as a kind of opening or sharing, and in a privileged relation to all the resonances of *sens* (as perception, intelligibility and direction). Finally, in bringing these observations together, Nancy is able to articulate a sonorous theory of the subject – frequently referred to as the *corps sonore* – to complement his broader politico-philosophical project based on a singular plural ontology. In the organist's sensuous gazing at the naked Venus, we learn how 'l'oreille ouvre sur le ventre, ou bien *même elle l'ouvre*' (Ec, p. 84) ['The ear opens onto the belly, or the ear even opens up the belly' (L, p. 45)]. The resonant chamber of Venus's belly is both, Nancy claims, 'le lieu où vient retentir sa musique' ['the very place where his music comes to resound'] and where the inside and outside open up to one another, itself echoed in the externality of the garden scene in the background of an otherwise intimate indoors scene (Ec, p. 84; L, p. 45).

Given both the emphasis Nancy places on the sensuous presentation of the world (on sense *as* meaning(ful) rather than *having* meaning that needs to be located 'elsewhere') and the obviously auditory nature of sensuous lived existence, it seems perfectly logical to offer an acoustemological complement to his other work on the sensuous subject. In addition, it is not only sound that is theorised in *À l'écoute*, but the specifically musical. As Roger Grant notes, it also offers a specifically 'musicological counterpart to his work on the visual and written arts' as a consequence of the inclusion of specific references to music (composers, works, and so on) rather than restricting its focus to abstract, environmental, ecological or non-musical sounds.[3] However, despite a more sustained interest in this short but wide-ranging text in France, the critical reception of *À l'écoute*, both within anglophone French studies and within music and/or sound studies, has been notably lukewarm. In comparison to the rest of his substantial œuvre, even Nancy scholars seem to have been reluctant to engage with this text (a small number of notable exceptions notwithstanding[4]) and thus, despite being a rich text that adds a significant sonorous dimension to his broader philosophical project, it has remained somewhat sidelined.

Though *À l'écoute* is undoubtedly Nancy's major text addressing music and sound and will thus be the major focus, this chapter – along with Chapter 5 – will also confront other musical moments in Nancy's œuvre. Most notably, these come from various references in *Les Muses*; the short chapter 'Musique' in *Le Sens du monde*; two essays from the subsequent English translation of *À l'écoute;* various of the 'inventions' from the set of interviews between Nancy and musicologist-philosopher Danielle Cohen-Lévinas; and, most significantly for this chapter, an interview with Michel Gaillot contributing to a volume on techno music and the published text of a lecture originally given at

---

[3] Roger Mathew Grant, 'Review: Jean-Luc Nancy's "Listening"', pp. 748–52. Of course this is a glib generalisation which ignores all the difficulties outlined in Chapter 1 about how we define 'music' in the first place. Nonetheless, it is Nancy's specific reference to composers and works that I wish to highlight as it demonstrates a clear intention to include what is conventionally – albeit uncritically – understood as music within the text. Indeed, Nancy is explicit about this, when he says: 'J'aimerais [. . .] pousser un peu plus avant, pour aller à nouveau vers la musique, par delà le sonore abstrait' (Ec, p. 58). What is less clear is the positioning of the musical vs. the 'simply' sonorous.

[4] For example, Adrienne Janus, 'Listening', pp. 182–202; Adrienne Janus, 'Soundings', pp. 72–84.

Cité de la Musique in Paris, entitled 'La Scène mondiale du rock' where Nancy suggests that there are 'de bonnes raisons de traiter le rock comme un phénomène philosophique' ['good reasons to consider rock as a philosophical phenomenon'] (SMR, p. 77). As we will see, Nancy, the self-professed 'philosophe non-rocker' (SMR, p. 76) has thus made a rather larger contribution to musico-philosophical thinking than has hitherto been appreciated. Just as Nancy's various musical meditations have received relatively scant attention in anglophone French criticism, scholars in music departments – despite a short-lived initial flurry of excitement – have also been reluctant to engage with the text. As was highlighted in Chapter 1, it may be down to historical disciplinary reasons and musicology's tendency to import concepts seen to have instrumental value as interpretative tools when 'applied' to particular musical works, processes or genres that there has been minimal engagement with À l'écoute and Nancy's œuvre more broadly.[5] Indeed, though the innovations of critical musicology were deeply indebted to poststructuralism and (largely French) theory more generally, attempts to engage with theoretical works that seek to deal with music or sound 'itself' have been notably less prominent.[6] This, however, seems to be changing and 'a new body of work' can be seen to be emerging at the intersection of music studies and philosophy that, as Martin Scherzinger describes, 'instead of bringing philosophy to musicology [...] critically analyzes how music inhabits philosophy itself and then assesses the ethical and political dimensions of these philosophical positions and their relation to lived history'.[7]

This chapter – along with the book as a whole – seeks to contribute to the emerging area of scholarship that Scherzinger identifies above, a field that, to borrow Andrew Bowie's words, is committed to 'rehabilitating the claim that philosophy should be concerned with the idea of what constitutes a meaningful world'.[8] In this respect, though Nancy has received faint praise on occasion – Michael Gallope has suggested that, at least in theory, À l'écoute offers a 'completely different philosophy of music' and one that has the potential to transcend the dualism of approaches focused on either the 'immateriality of sonorous structure [... or the] materiality of practice and context'[9] – given the central importance that Nancy places on the co-valence of sense as

---

[5] In fact, engagement with Nancy's work within anglophone musicology seems to be limited to a handful of reviews of À l'écoute (usually of the English translation) and very little else.
[6] See Chapter 1.
[7] Martin Scherzinger, 'On Sonotropism', pp. 345–51 (p. 345).
[8] Bowie, *Music, Philosophy and Modernity*, p. 46.
[9] Michael Gallope, 'Review: Jean-Luc Nancy. 2007', pp. 157–66 (p. 157).

both sensuousness and meaning, it is all the more surprising that his work has not been taken up more widely in this turn. The text on rock music is, in this regard, particularly 'worldly', and neither disparages rock as merely popular, mass culture entertainment nor idealises it – it is simply a 'porteur d'un sens' ['bearer of sense'[10]] (SMR, p. 77). At the same time, in both the rock and the techno texts, Nancy also considers how the birth of these genres co-emerges alongside other social, political, artistic and intellectual forces, such as mid-twentieth-century philosophy and the 'fin de la métaphysique' ['end of metaphysics'] (SMR, p. 77). In so doing, Nancy lays bare the sensuous criss-crossing of seemingly distinct areas of study, people, geographies and ideologies. Nonetheless, one of the striking features of these texts is simply the hugely different approach to the understanding of rock and techno music when compared to the major musical referent of most of the other musical texts: *musique savante*. Indeed, for all its emphasis on sonority and on what listening offers or affords philosophy, À *l'écoute* still comes across as a 'proper' work of written philosophy, especially in comparison to the less formal style of the rock and techno texts that were originally delivered orally. In the process, À *l'écoute* invokes a metaphysical-ontological notion of what music 'is' in order to remake philosophy's bias towards vision as central to meaning. In contrast, again, the rock and techno texts – which will be engaged with here but approached anew in Chapter 5 – offer considerably less formal meditations on music 'itself', focusing instead on the ethico-aesthetic and political ramifications of particular genres; in so doing, music is characterised in radically different ways across the different texts, leaving an uneasy tension between the different approaches. The major aims of this chapter are thus to critically (re)position Nancy's work on music in relation to two more or less disparate disciplines, and also to pursue a further – explicitly feminist – critique, which locates À *l'écoute* and several other musical moments within a problematic genealogy of thought on sound and/or music. By attending to the specifically musical in Nancy's texts, and then finally returning to his reading of Titian's musical tableau, this chapter aims to locate some of the tensions that arise from what appears to be a fairly uncritical engagement with music, especially in À *l'écoute*, suggesting that there are consequences beyond the explicitly musical moments for Nancy's theory of philosophical listening.

---

[10] *Sens* also connotes 'meaning', and both are at play here and throughout.

THE MULTIPLE ARTS: PRESENTATION AND THE SENSE OF PHILOSOPHY

The central feature of Nancy's philosophy is perhaps his unremitting focus on the senses and their relation to philosophy at large. Though philosophy's 'aesthetic attitude'[11] is, as laid out in Chapter 1, born of a history beginning with Kant, it would seem fair to say that while Nancy is no doubt influenced by this legacy he nonetheless brings something distinctly novel to the table with regards to the sensuous nature of being – or rather 'being *with*'. B. C. Hutchens has described Nancy's broader project as 'a rousing critique of, on the one hand, any transcendental thinking that implies a source of sense "beyond" the world and, on the other, immanential thinking that mimetically conceives of such a source within the world'.[12] Instead, for Nancy, sense is simply the sense of the world *itself*, with no recourse to other grounds, sources, or reserves of meaning. Strongly influenced by Derrida, Nancy's philosophy draws on his work to continue the critique of '*logocentrism* and the determination of being as *presence*',[13] both of which require either a foundational or transcendental signified in order to guarantee epistemological stability and coherence. This does not, however, lead to a world void of meaning – far from it. Though Nancy's philosophy insists on the 'absence de sens' (as given, appropriable, recognisable, etc.) it is precisely 'un sens qui fait sens, dans son absence, on pourrait même dire depuis son absence' ['a meaning that takes on meaning in its absence – one might even say, since its absence'] to which Nancy so intimately and inventively attends (SM, p. 92; MM, p. 94). This absence of meaning points therefore not to a nihilistic embrace of meaninglessness, but simply to the ceaseless deferral of a final, authorising or transcendental meaning; in this respect, Nancy's work is clearly anti- or non-Platonic in that it refuses the identification of meaning with the mimetic copying of fixed and eternal forms or Ideas. In so doing, Nancy's philosophy takes this opportunity – or we might rather say that it is Nancy's philosophy itself that affords this very opening – to play with the various meanings of *sens* as afforded by the contingencies of the French language, and thus to reaffirm the centrality of sensuousness (thus aesthetics in its etymological derivation) to meaning – a meaning that is always presented sensuously or sensorially.[14] Indeed, as Ian Maclachlan

---

[11] Ross, *The Aesthetic Paths of Philosophy*, p. 1.
[12] B. C. Hutchens, *Jean-Luc Nancy and the Future of Philosophy*, p. 33.
[13] Ian James, *The Fragmentary Demand*, p. 12, italics in original.
[14] See Ian Maclachlan, 'Contingencies: Reading between Nancy and Derrida', pp. 139–58 on the role of contingency more broadly.

describes, for Nancy, 'sense [and presumably, therefore, also meaning] always comes in the singularity of a "here and now"'.[15] Unsurprisingly, then, Nancy's critique of traditional philosophical approaches to meaning, that of 'referential ideality'[16] as Alison Ross describes, thus invites an opportunity to rethink the historically difficult relationship between music and meaning. Though we will explore in detail the way in which Nancy characterises music below, in short his philosophy answers the question as to whether meaning is something of which music is capable as soon as it is asked: by virtue of its sensuous presentation in and of the world it simply *is* meaningful. This conviction alone offers a radically refreshing starting point from which to pursue the philosophy of music. Finally, then, embedded within this critique of universal, eternal and fixed meaning as distinct from sense *qua* sensuousness is, as Ian James notes, a triad of thinkers all of whom have been more or less significant to Nancy's work: the Nietzschean critique of Christian-Platonic thought, Heideggerian destruction of the tradition of ontotheology, and the Freudian critique of the subject.[17] While critics such as Simon Critchley have judged Nancy to be, above all, neo-Heideggerian, others such as Ian James have seen his 'initial Nietzschean emphasis against Heidegger [... to be] decisive'.[18] Nonetheless, 'all commentators agree that [...] the task of his philosophy is to enquire into the sense of the world', while also engaging with the 'overcoming of metaphysics' (whether in a transcendental, immanent or substantialist sense) as were many of his contemporaries in the 1960s and 1970s.[19]

With all this in mind, it is easy to see why art – or more precisely, the 'arts' – is a central concern in almost all of Nancy's work. It is tempting to say that, along with the philosophical forebears mentioned above – namely Nietzsche, Heidegger, Freud (perhaps also Lacan) and Derrida – art itself is the other major interlocutor in Nancy's philosophy. *Les Muses* opens with the question '[p]ourquoi y a-t-il plusieurs arts, et non pas un seul?' ['Why are there several arts and not just one?'] (M_1, p. 9; M_2, p. 1). He draws on the figure of the muse both to note its etymological connotations (from *mens*, which has to do with the mind, thinking and spirit), describing how the muse 'anime, soulève, excite, met en branle' ['animates, stirs up, excites, arouses'] before noting that this 'force' has also always been plural: 'Il y a les muses, et non la Muse'

---

[15] Ibid., p. 143.
[16] See Ross, *The Aesthetic Paths of Philosophy*, pp. 136 and 153 in particular.
[17] See Ian James, *The Fragmentary Demand*, p. 12.
[18] Ibid., p. 19. See also Simon Critchley, *The Ethics of Deconstruction*.
[19] Hutchens, *Jean-Luc Nancy and the Future of Philosophy*, p. 5; and see James, *The Fragmentary Demand*, p. 8.

['There are Muses and not the Muse'] (M_1, p. 11; M_2, p. 1). He goes on to assert that this division and diversity is in fact the innate condition of art, and highlights that it is only relatively recently (i.e. since the effects of a largely German Romanticism and the notion of *Kunst*) that art has been referred to in the singular in French, rather than 'les beaux-arts' (M_1, p. 17). Elsewhere, in an interview with Michel Gaillot, he locates this claim more precisely between 1750 and 1850, noting 'que dans ce siècle d'intervalle, l'"art" lui-même est apparu [... et,] en outre, pour corser la chose si je puis dire, l'"artiste" est apparu' ['that in that hundred-year interval "art" itself appeared [... and] over and above that, to thicken the plot, the "artist" also appeared'] (SM, p. 97; MM, p. 99).[20] All of this is simply to highlight the essential multiplicity of art in Nancy's thinking, and to gesture towards some of the crucial ways in which his work diverges substantially from previous (Romantic) thinking on aesthetics. For Nancy, the lack of unity runs parallel to the critical historicising of (singular) 'Art' as born with the Romantics – a moment that coincides also with the birth of philosophical aesthetics. Whereas the post-Romantic baggage leads to a conception of art understood as 'a distinct and autonomous sphere'[21] – a sphere which is concerned with the (re)presentation of meaning *qua* (universal, eternal, transcendent) truth – Nancy attempts to rehabilitate a more ancient, Greek, understanding of the arts. Most importantly, this version draws no clear distinction between 'Art' and its practice: *techne*. As Ian James describes, for Nancy it is the very 'technicity of art and the plurality of artistic techniques that gives rise to the diversity of forms'.[22]

Crucially, then, this observation touches on another central feature of Nancy's thinking on the arts: their essential and constitutive materiality. This is both materiality in the sense of their inseparable craft and practice, as suggested above, and also the bodily materiality of musical participation, Nancy says: 'la musique ne peut être que *jouée*, y compris par qui ne fait que l'écouter. Tout le corps est pris à ce jeu – tensions, écarts, hauteurs, mouvements, schèmes rythmiques, grains et timbres –, faute de quoi il n'y a pas musique' ['music can only be *played*, including by those who only listen. The entire body is involved in this play – tensions, distances, heights, movements, rhythmical schemes, grains, and timbres – without which there is no music'].[23] But it is also in terms

[20] This clearly also coincides with the invention of the composer-function, as was mentioned in Chapter 1, especially pp. 20–1.
[21] Ian James, 'Art – Technics', pp. 83–102 (p. 86).
[22] Ibid., p. 86. See the rest of this article along with James's *The Fragmentary Demand* for more on this idea.
[23] Nancy, 'Musique' in *Le Sens Du Monde*, pp. 133–8 (p. 136) [Nancy, *The Sense of the World*, p. 86].

of Nancy's insistence on the materiality of the medium – even, crucially, when it comes to music, which often seems so tantalisingly immaterial, as was gestured to by Sartre in *La Nausée* and noted in Chapter 1. Nancy describes music and sound specifically as 'matière sonore' ['sonorous matter'], and then clarifies that '[j]'ai écrit "matière" sans doute parce qu'il me venait un désir de rappeler que le son est matériel, physique. Il n'est pas éthéré et presque immatériel comme on peut être porté à le représenter' ['Probably I wrote "matter" because of my desire to remember that sound is material, physical. It is not ethereal and almost immaterial as we can be tempted to represent it'] (IDV, p. 61). The sensuous materiality of the arts is thus the keystone of Nancy's broader philosophical project, as Alison Ross describes:

> Art offers an answer to the problem of presentation posed in Western philosophy [... because] in the arts the emergence of sense from sources of sensible materiality is staged or presented. In this respect art exemplifies the core precepts of Nancy's ontology: specifically, that sense takes place in relations of exteriority and that affect is the hinge that joins materiality and sense as an act rather than a passive state of becoming.[24]

In this respect, not only does Nancy's philosophy afford an 'ontological rehabilitation of pleasure',[25] but it is art itself that offers philosophy an escape from the impasse of representation at large. Indeed, in *Les Muses*, rather than offering a formulation based on mimesis, whereby the material world (and thus art) is always a copy of some 'original', Nancy radicalises Hegel's essentially Platonic formula – that 'art is the sensuous expression of the Idea' – claiming instead that the embodied gesture of painting (or of art in general) is *itself* the Idea. Through art, man sensuously reveals himself *to* himself; 'non pas la sensibilité comme telle, mais la ou les distributions des sens seraient elles-mêmes les produits de l'"art"' ['the distribution or distributions of the senses, rather than sensibility as such, would themselves to be products of "art"'] (M_1, p. 26; M_2, p. 10). For Nancy, painting, for example, is explicitly not the inadequate (re)presentation *of* the Idea (rather it *is* the Idea), and this holds true for song, too, when Nancy states '[c]e fut peut-être, aussi, un chant. Il faut entendre le premier chanteur accompagner le premier peintre' ['It was perhaps, also, a chant. One must hear the first singer accompanying the first painter'] (M_1, p. 121; M_2, p. 69). In *Les Muses*, art is figured as nothing more (and nothing less) than the production *of* sense, but through this gesture (this Idea) sense reveals itself to be produced, 'du sens en tant que ce qui le "produit"

---

[24] Ross, *The Aesthetic Paths of Philosophy*, pp. 151–2.
[25] Ibid., p. 152.

comme tel, c'est d'abord qu'il soit reçu, éprouvé, bref *senti* comme sens' ['insofar as what "produces" it as such is the fact of its being first of all received, felt, in short, *sensed* as sense'] (M_1, p. 53; M_2, p. 28, emphasis in original).

The arts' essential relation to aesthetic perception – again conceived of in its etymological derivation to connote all that is perceptible through the senses – thus affords and sustains its privileged place in Nancy's thought; it is indissociable from Nancy's conviction that we cannot speak of truth in any singular or given sense, and it is for this reason too, no doubt, that '"Art" cannot be evoked in the singular' – a move which 'would reinstall a position of "referential ideality" at the core of his ontology'.[26] As we will see in Chapter 4, this positions Nancy in sharp contradistinction – if not outright opposition – to the evental philosophy of Alain Badiou, for whom philosophy's purpose is the rehabilitation or identification of (Platonic) universal truths as manifest in artistic events (and other domains). Quite conversely, Nancy insists, as Ross describes, that it 'is not truth but meaning or sense on the verge of its emergence that art presents' or, elsewhere, 'the coming of sense over the event of taking place'.[27] Though Alison Ross beautifully presents what is at stake in Nancy's sensuous philosophy, she nonetheless seems to retain a degree of ambivalence as to whether by positioning art as a 'first philosophy' – albeit a pluralistic one – Nancy doesn't in fact reinstate 'art in precisely the position of exception that, in Heidegger's late work, is a matter of considerable ambivalence and debate'.[28] This is a concern worth bearing in mind, and one to which we will return later in this chapter.

It is also worth a brief word about how Nancy's rethinking of art, sense and metaphysics corresponds – indeed is essential to – his thinking on being. Though Ross advances concern at the possibility that Nancy restores art to the position of a first philosophy, it is certainly true that Nancy's broader project is definitively anti- or post-foundational. He writes in *Les Muses* of the illusory nature of foundational thought when he says:

> Le fond ne se produit pas lui-même et il n'est produit en aucune manière. Le fond est l'évidence ou la patence de l'être: l'existence, avec laquelle on ne peut en finir, dès lors, du moins, qu'on ne la manipule pas à quelque fin, l'existence en tant que 'l'infinie multiplicité du monde.' Mais la multiplicité du monde ne reste même pas la multiplicité d'*un* monde: elle qualifie le monde comme hétérogénéité de mondes *en quoi consiste l'unité du monde*. (M_1, p. 51)

[26] Ibid., p. 153.
[27] Ibid., pp. 135, 153.
[28] Ibid., p. 137.

[The ground does not produce itself and is not produced in any manner. The ground is the obviousness or manifestness of Being: existence, with which one cannot have done, at least as long as one does not manipulate it toward some end, existence as the 'infinite multiplicity of the world.' But the multiplicity of the world does not remain even the multiplicity of *a* world: it qualifies the world as heterogeneity of worlds *in which consists the unity of the world.*] (M_2, pp. 26–7)[29]

In this way, Nancy is able to develop his own radical, anti- or post-metaphysical ontology, articulated as *être singulier pluriel* [being-singular-plural], which allows him – as we have seen above in regards to art – to dissociate himself from the shackles of representational thought that identifies Being (and, therefore, the dualisms of subject/object, idea/representation, and so on) through reference to a predetermined ground (substantialism) or to either an external (transcendental) or an internal (immanent) reserve of meaning/spirit/idea 'by which singular beings' identities could be mimetically determined and reflected'.[30] Instead, for Nancy, Being (and meaning *as* sense) *comes into being* (always a being *with*) only in the relational and dynamic space *between* beings (as well as ideas, things, bodies, and so on), which are always exposed to a shared but unknown futurity, but with no preceding (fixed) ground or foundation. Martin Crowley describes how Nancy 'situates the objects of his interest in relation to the broad horizon he calls "sense," namely, the fact of existence [... which is] irreducible to any determinate signification, the opening to and of the world that is re-marked – but not appropriated – by any act of figuration'.[31] Or, as Hutchens states, describing Nancy's ontology, '"we" just is this ability to open ourselves to the spacing of a world, a world that is always "to-come"'.[32] This ontological formulation also permits Nancy to navigate the philosophical terrain between the polar extremes of what the English translator of *Le Sens du monde*, Jeffrey S. Librett, describes as the mythical and the nihilistic; the way in which Western thought has located in symbolic figures or structures, such as religion, totalising and 'full' systems of belief, and thus a guarantee of meaning.[33] Or, in contrast and as mentioned above, its opposite: nihilism as a proposition of (absolute) lack and the consequent relativism of infinite self-difference. As a result of Nancy's careful rearticulation of this dualism, sense – and a concomitant or synonymous 'sense of the

---

[29] Nancy's emphasis. The citation is, despite their differences, from Badiou's CS_1, p. 361.
[30] Hutchens, *Jean-Luc Nancy and the Future of Philosophy*, p. 156.
[31] Martin Crowley, 'Being Beyond Politics', pp. 123–45 (p. 123).
[32] Hutchens, *Jean-Luc Nancy and the Future of Philosophy*, p. 160.
[33] See Jeffrey S. Librett, 'Foreword: Between Nihilism and Myth: Value, Aesthetics, and Politics' in Jean-Luc Nancy, *The Sense of the World*.

world' – is not something that the world either *has* (in reference to some external symbolic guarantee of plenitude) or *does not have* (in reference to an absolute and constitutional lack). Rather, the fact of the world just *is* sense 'on the grounds that there could be nothing else. Sense and the world are coextensive, perfectly commensurate, with no superfluous meanings overhanging this coextensivity.'[34] For Nancy, there is no difference between meaning and the material world in which we find ourselves. He traverses what he sees as a false dichotomy between an illusory plenitude of presence pitted against the equally illusory void of a constitutional lack to articulate the sense of the world 'precisely in the interstitial space *between* these two extremes of myth and nihilism, in the space of their mutual and endless approach'.[35]

FROM 'SONOTROPISM' TO SONOROUS ONTOLOGY

As we have seen in Chapter 1, a philosophical attempt to think about, characterise or describe music – whether in metaphysical, spiritual, aesthetic or ethical terms – has been prevalent in Western thought since Plato. In particular, much philosophical commentary has focused on music's seemingly privileged relationship to both emotions and subjectivity. The genealogy of such a privileged linking of music and the subject runs all the way from Plato's concern about music's profound ability to manipulate behaviour, character and the emotions, through to the lofty metaphysical reflections of German idealism and beyond. In this substantiation of the perceived 'nature' of music – its supposed metaphysical power to reveal some 'essential' facet of human existence – Martin Scherzinger has located what he describes as philosophy's 'sonotropism'. He notes the way in which sonotropism 'proceeds as if music held a metaphysical valence in excess of the usual mediators of language, culture and history'.[36] The trajectory of sonotropism continues, then, to the Schopenhauerian idea of music as 'Will' and arguably further, to poststructuralist attempts to pattern politically engaged philosophical thinking on a kind of musicalised imaginary or virtuality – even a liberating musicalised ontology – such as with Deleuze and Guattari's *ritournelle*.[37] Nevertheless, despite the '*unut-*

---

[34] Hutchens, *Jean-Luc Nancy and the Future of Philosophy*, p. 6.
[35] Librett, 'Foreword: Between Nihilism and Myth: Value, Aesthetics, and Politics' in Jean-Luc Nancy, *The Sense of the World*, p. xv.
[36] Scherzinger, 'On Sonotropism', p. 350.
[37] See, in particular, Gilles Deleuze and Félix Guattari, '1837 – De la ritournelle' in *Mille plateaux*, pp. 381–433.

terable fullness of thought'[38] which music has afforded philosophical thought, the very attempt to *theorise* the audible is centred around the conflict noted in the opening 'Prelude' (the inherent visual bias of theory), leaving the (im)possibility of *theorising* music, or sound, in perpetual debate. Indeed, this is precisely the starting point from which Nancy proceeds, when he states that 'figure et idée, théâtre et théorie, spectacle et spéculation se conviennent mieux, se superposent, voire se substituent avec le plus de convenance que ne le peuvent l'audible et l'intelligible ou le sonore et le logique' ['figure and idea, theater and theory, spectacle and speculation suit each other better, superimpose themselves on each other, even can be substituted for each other with more affinity than the audible and the intelligible, or the sonorous and the logical'] (Ec, p. 14; L, p. 20). Or, more simply, 'on demandera ceci: l'écoute, est-ce une affaire dont la philosophie soit capable?' ['we will ponder this: Is listening something of which philosophy is capable?'] (Ec, p. 13; L, p. 1).

In apparently stark contrast to Western philosophy's historical bias towards vision, Nancy's sonorous counterpoint to his broader ontological project instead finds common ground with a more general trend of critiquing Western metaphysics's ocularcentric discourse, a move which, as already noted in the introductory 'Prelude', has been termed an 'anti-ocular' turn.[39] Adrienne Janus even goes as far as to position *À l'écoute* at 'a culminating moment'[40] of this turn, and, indeed, *À l'écoute* does strive to challenge the predominance of vision as central to knowledge, expounded and expanded genealogically from philosopher-king to philosopher-king. With this in mind, however, Nancy's work at large doesn't eschew the visual in favour of the auditory; indeed, he has written extensively on the cinema, and references to specific music in *À l'écoute* are notably mediated through some kind of visual – the film through which we 'listen' to Mozart's clarinet concerto, or the Titian painting to which Nancy responds with the theatrics of Wagnerian music drama. Elsewhere, the musical resonances or implications of the collected interviews, *Inventions à deux voix*, are explicitly gestured towards in the cover art that shows the score of Bach's two-part invention in E-flat major; similarly, Nancy's presentation on rock music proceeds from an advertisement which reads: '[c]ontre le blues, rien ne vaut le roc' ['against the blues, nothing beats roc'[41]] (SMR, p. 74). Rather,

---

[38] Kant, *Critique of the Power of Judgment*, p. 206, my emphasis.
[39] See Jay, *Downcast Eyes*.
[40] Janus, 'Listening', p. 182.
[41] Nancy uses this advertising slogan, which advocates for the consumption of 'roc' chocolate to combat the blues, as his epigraph and point of departure for the text. The resonances and

then, Nancy is interested in the distribution, or the (re)routing, of the senses, especially in the arts – a move that nonetheless displaces the singular authority of the visual in traditional theorising. Nancy moves against a traditional metaphysical position which had tended to locate in music (and in 'great art' more broadly) a transcendental reserve (of spirit, will, etc.) that neutralised the cultural and historical implications or ramifications – in short, the situatedness – of these aesthetic 'objects', and in this way it is evident that Nancy's anti-ocular turn (or, perhaps more precisely, anti-ocularcentric turn) comes hand in hand with an implicit commitment to a broadly materialist position that acknowledges how seemingly abstract thought necessarily relates to economic, social and cultural conditions.

As a result, then, À l'écoute offers a way of thinking about sound and/or music beyond inherited binaries; commensurate with his singular plural ontology, Nancy resists reinscribing a listening subject and a listened-to object. Instead, the audible appears affirmatively as the perpetual flux of a shared, sonorous world. Nancy's position suggests a potentially radical avenue beyond a dualism that has often seen music considered in either wholly immaterial terms – the closed, positivist approach to score-based analysis or 'purely' formal procedures – or as a mere product of a particular socio-cultural context, with no specificity of its own. Nancy either refuses or exceeds this distinction, and instead positions music as a shared space of resonance; as the auditory distribution of sense (*sens*) in which 'se met à l'écoute simultanée d'un "soi" et d'un "monde" qui sont l'un à l'autre en résonance' ['[is] a simultaneous listening to a "self" and to a "world" that are both in resonance'] (Ec, p. 82; L, p. 43). He also notes how all the senses have both 'passive' and 'active' states (for example, seeing and looking, smelling and sniffing, and so on) and uses this observation to draw a distinction between hearing [*entendre*] and listening [*écouter*], noting how *entendre* is not just 'hearing', but also 'understanding' and even 'intention'.[42] In order to pursue his philosophy of *listening*, rather than *hearing*, he posits that the auditory pairing subsists in a privileged relationship to intellectual or intelligible sense; in short, while *entendre* preserves the dichotomy between a perceiving subject and a perceptible object, Nancy's philosophy of listening demands that 'le sens ne se contente pas de faire sens (ou d'être *logos*), mais en outre résonne' ['sense not be content to make sense (or to be *logos*), but that it wants also to resound'] (Ec, p. 19; L, p. 6). This allows him to challenge the traditional philosophical pursuit

---

play on words are unsurprisingly lost in translation.
[42] See Nancy, À L'écoute, p. 18. Brian Kane explores these distinctions in depth in his article on À l'écoute. See Brian Kane, 'Jean-Luc Nancy and the Listening Subject', pp. 439–47.

of 'truth', or the 'hidden' meaning of sense (as *making* sense or *logos*), and instead to pursue a dynamic, resonant philosophy that subsists in the space of the *renvoi*; in sound that exists only as a *re*sounding. As Nancy states, '[t]out mon propos tournera autour d'une telle résonance fondamentale, voire autour d'une résonance en tant que fond, en tant que profondeur première ou dernière du "sens" lui-même (ou de la vérité)' ['My whole proposal will revolve around such a fundamental resonance, even around a resonance as a foundation, as a first or last profundity of "sense" itself (or of truth)'] (Ec, p. 19; L, p. 6). While it may appear that the *renvoi* reinstates a kind of fundamental ground or essence towards which we can turn, the emphasis on the 're-' negates any claims of foundationalism; any sounding is always already a *re*sounding, with no recourse to an originary or 'pure' sounding.

In particular, the auditory articulation of a sonorous *renvoi* [return] allows Nancy to (re)theorise in ontological terms the specifically ocularcentric aspects of the oppositional pairing of subject-object. Nancy's subject, described as 'un diapason', is one which is 'réglé sur soi' ['tuned to self'] but is nonetheless a 'self' without substance; it is only a 'self' insofar as it exists in the sonorous *renvoi* itself (Ec, p. 37; L, p. 17). Only through this 'return' can the self be said to come into being; through feeling oneself feel [*se sentir sentir*] the self feels itself and is only a self in this feeling. As Nancy himself describes – insisting on the non-metaphorical nature of this sonorous ontology – listening is theorised 'pas comme une figure de l'accès au soi, mais comme la réalité de cet accès, une réalité par conséquent indissociablement "mienne" et "autre", "singulière" et "plurielle"' ['not as a metaphor for access to self, but as the reality of this access, a reality consequently indissociably "mine" and "other," "singular" and "plural"'] (Ec, pp. 30–1; L, p. 12). Nancy also develops his account of subjectivity through his conceptualisation of the *corps sonore* [sonorous body], where both the object and the subject of listening resonate: 'Lequel est toujours à la fois le corps qui résonne et mon corps d'auditeur où ça résonne, ou bien qui en résonne' ['Which is always at once the body that resounds and my body as a listener where that resounds, or that resounds with it'] (Ec, p. 22 n. 2; L, p. 70 n. 11). The remarkable corollary of this, as Adrienne Janus has noted, is that 'all objects, insofar as they resonate' are able, therefore, to be listening *subjects*; this has the consequent (and no doubt intentional) effect of making Nancy's 'human' subject less properly '"subject"-like, less human'.[43] Finally, then, despite the essentially rhythmic constitution – the resonance created by the fundamental

---

[43] Janus, 'Listening', p. 194.

renvoi – of the *corps sonore* that might lead us to think of it in purely temporal terms, Nancy's *corps sonore* also opens onto a spatiality; 'il se propage dans l'espace' ['it spreads in space'] (Ec, p. 22; L, p. 7). This temporal movement even seems to constitute, be a precondition of, or afford the *manifestation* – which Nancy has been keen to insist on as an inherently *visual* domain – of a spatial dimension, and thus to a relation with others. Or, as Wagner's Gurnemanz, cited by Nancy, sings in *Parsifal:* 'Ici, le temps se fait espace' ['Here, time becomes space'] (Ec, p. 33; L, p. 14).

ORIGINS: NATURE AND CULTURE; NOSTALGIA AND COMMUNITY

I. Rameau: The Genealogy of the Corps Sonore

Although unacknowledged in *À l'écoute*, the genealogy of the *corps sonore* returns us directly to the Enlightenment and specifically to Rameau, who coined the phrase to describe the 'natural' and 'scientific' basis for music that he claimed to have found through experimentation. As well as being a significant composer of the Baroque era, Rameau was also a music theorist, and the 'individual who first recognized that all those components [of music] interacted to create a sense of tonality'.[44] Rameau's project was significant in the way it codified, for the first time, what was later seen to be the dominant harmonic practice in literate (high art) European traditions. By 1737, Rameau was able to publish *Génération harmonique* which fully exploited the *corps sonore* as the theoretical basis for his harmonic theory and, via Dortous de Mairan's theories of sound propagation, was closely patterned on Newtonian optics.[45] Furthermore, as Christensen continues, Rameau's prefatory material to the *Génération harmonique* is a calculated emulation of Newton's *Opticks*, which was seen as the paragon of empirical Enlightenment science.[46] The *corps sonore* itself was 'Rameau's term for any vibrating system such as a vibrating string which emitted harmonic partials above its fundamental frequency'.[47] For Rameau, music was a matter for the sciences, and his agenda held at its core a belief not in the creative *invention* of a system to explain harmonic procedures, but in the commitment to the *identification* of the principle from which

---

[44] Joel Lester, 'Rameau and Eighteenth-Century Harmonic Theory', pp. 753–77 (p. 753).
[45] Thomas Christensen, *Rameau and Musical Thought in the Enlightenment*, p. 139.
[46] Ibid., p. 145.
[47] Thomas Christensen, 'Eighteenth-Century Science and the "Corps Sonore"', pp. 23–50 (p. 23).

this apparently 'natural' system can be seen to arise. What interests us here is not so much the linking of music and science; that, of course, has a much longer history as outlined in Chapter 1. Rather, what Rameau's *corps sonore* seeks to provide, via Newton's optical theories, is a purportedly objective account of a harmonic practice divorced from the social and historical context in which it emerged; as asocial, precultural, 'purely' scientific and naturally occurring. Not insignificantly, it would seem, despite his almost obsessive commitment to the *corps sonore* (which by the end of his life was so loaded with metaphysical excess that he saw it to be the generative principle not only of music but also to assume 'cosmic proportions [. . . as] the progenitor of all the arts, sciences, and even religion'[48]), the *corps sonore* was actually no more capable of offering an explanation for subdominant harmony or the minor triad in standard tonal procedures than was any other theory.

II. Rousseau: The (Musical) Origin of the Origin of Culture

In contrast to Rameau's scientific approach, we find points of correspondence also in Rousseau – another Enlightenment progenitor of many contemporary discourses on sound and/or music – who takes an anthropological approach towards the question of sound. In the *Essai sur l'origine des langues*, Rousseau focuses on the voice as that privileged threshold between music and language, or song and speech, and locates in this liminal space between meaning and materiality the originary link that allows language to connect sound and idea – the sensory with the symbolic. For Rousseau, music is seen as an originary 'proto-language' that allows him to posit, as Downing A. Thomas demonstrates, the anthropological missing link that connects semiotics to origins, culture to nature, and man to animal; the origin of the origin of culture.[49] Similarly for Nancy, *diction*, 'la constitution matricielle de la résonance lorsqu'elle est mise dans la condition du phrasé ou du sens musical' ['the matrixlike constitution of resonance when it is placed in the condition of the phrasing or of the musical sense'] precedes both music and language, even though it is common to both (Ec, p. 72; L, pp. 36–7). In Rousseau's originary scene – a scene of communal cultivation in the fields or around the water fountain – he finds that everything, including the origin of art, 'se rapporte dans son principe aux moyens de pourvoir à la subsistance' ['corresponds in its origin to the means of

---

[48] Ibid., p. 23.
[49] Downing A. Thomas, *Music and the Origins of Language*, p. 9. The origin of the origin in the sense that 'music' is prior even to the split from which culture originates.

providing subsistence'].⁵⁰ He differentiates between needs – which he claims lead to 'mediate' communication through gesture or movement – and passions which 'arrachèrent les premières voix' ['stimulated the first words'], finding the idea that the communication of *needs* lies at the root of language, 'insoutenable' ['untenable'].⁵¹ Furthermore, although Rousseau is quick to chastise Rameau's ultimately harmonic conception of the *corps sonore* for effectively universalising an ethnocentric conception of music (because harmony 'ne flate à nul égard les oreilles qui n'y sont pas exercées' ['does not in any way please the completely unpracticed ear'] or 'c'est une langue dont il faut avoir le Dictionnaire' ['It is a tongue for which one needs a dictionary']).⁵² Rousseau's conception remains problematic for different reasons. It is clear that Rousseau insists on a logocentric investment in voice *as* presence; indeed, Derrida famously accorded Rousseau a privileged and singular position in the history of metaphysics as the determination of being as presence, and devoted much of *De la grammatologie* to unpacking the subterranean but ultimately constituent logocentrism of Rousseau's thought.⁵³ As a result of this and, more precisely, because of the way in which he articulates the relationship between music and language in this logocentric formulation, he invests music with a precultural, transhistorical essentialism.

III. Music and Community

Perhaps, though, Rousseau's influence on Nancy's broader philosophical-ontological project is felt much more obviously elsewhere, in their shared conviction that politics originates from the shared space of communal activities. In *La communauté désœuvrée*, Nancy recognises Rousseau – most obviously the Rousseau of the *Discours sur l'origine et les fondements de l'inégalité parmi les hommes*, but the *Essai sur l'origine des langues* is no doubt relevant here too – as the first properly modern thinker of community. Rousseau's nostalgic characterisation, or experience, of community is as 'une rupture (peut-être irréparable) de cette communauté' ['a (perhaps irreparable) rupture in this community'].⁵⁴ Rousseau sets this modern conception of society – founded on a fundamental loss – in contrast to a (fictive) state of nature

---

⁵⁰ Jean-Jacques Rousseau, *Essai sur l'origine des langues*, p. 107 [Rousseau, *Essay on the Origin of Languages*, p. 38].
⁵¹ Ibid., p. 43 [p. 11].
⁵² Ibid., p. 155 [p. 56].
⁵³ See Jacques Derrida, *De La Grammatologie* [Derrida, *Of Grammatology*].
⁵⁴ Nancy, *La Communauté désoeuvrée*, p. 29 [Nancy, *The Inoperative Community*, p. 9].

where natural man in his originary unity has 'amour de soi' ['self-love'] and 'pitié' ['pity'], and no (need of) language proper yet. Nancy, however, as Ian James has shown, inverts Rousseau's supposition.[55] Nancy argues instead that it is not this rupture or loss that impedes our return to an idealised and desired community, but conversely that 'une telle "perte" est constitutive de la "communauté" elle-même' ['such a "loss" is constitutive of "community" itself'].[56] The thought of or desire for a 'return' to community that can be traced from Rousseau, Nancy claims, through to many other philosophers, poets and composers including, of course, Wagner, is perhaps nothing other than 'l'invention tardive qui tenta de répondre à la dure réalité de l'expérience moderne' ['a belated invention that tried to respond to the harsh reality of experience'].[57] Structurally, then, this illusory 'return' – the always already lost community as the condition of the possibility of community – plays an analogous role to the *renvoi* in *À l'écoute*; the dynamism of the sonorous *renvoi* that subsists only ever as a *re*sounding or *re*turn, thus aims to *re*sist at every turn any claim of originary sounding, just as Nancy's inversion of Rousseau denies an originary community. Finally, as Thomas notes, in Rousseau the aesthetic domain emerges as a relation between an individual and a collective; in the end, just as a musical aesthetics *silently* emerges – as an apparently neutral by-product – in Rousseau, the specifically musical appears in Nancy as a folding back on itself of the more essential resonant space of the *renvoi*.

Following on from this, then, it is worth another brief word about the often presumptive relationship of music to community, in part because the idea of community has been so central to Nancy's thought, but also because it is a question that is raised anew in the text on techno music. It has often been through the notion of harmony that the question of community has been attributed a distinctly musical flavour; harmony, with its roots in *harmos* and thus joining or concord, make it almost too easy to map musical harmony (the practice of combining separate tones simultaneously to create a usually pleasurable effect) homologically onto social harmony (the combination of individuals to form a consonant, coherent and unified social whole). As we have seen, this is precisely the positive connotation that Plato affords music; for Plato, music has a unique ability to model harmony on micro- and macro-logical levels. No matter the significant differences in their respective positions, the question of harmonious relations also subtends the musico-philosophical thinking of both Rameau and

---

[55] James, *The Fragmentary Demand*, pp. 175–6.
[56] Nancy, *La Communauté désoruvrée*, p. 35 [Nancy, *The Inoperative Community*, p. 12].
[57] Nancy, *La Communauté désoruvrée*, p. 32 [Nancy, *The Inoperative Community*, p. 10].

Rousseau. Rameau's 'naturalistic *mathesis* which locates the essence of music in harmonic simultaneity'[58] concerns the way in which the overriding harmony of the cosmos might be presented to us in aesthetic experience; in apparent contrast, Rousseau's concern with the alienation of modern man identifies music (or at least its emotional power) with nostalgia, and as a privileged reminder of a lost state of social harmony. For Nancy, the question of community is quite different: it is precisely against any notional recovery of a substantive ideal that Nancy argues, aligning the rehabilitation of an illusory essence, matter or subject (such as the Fatherland) with political terror and fascism. Such an imaginary substance may unify through a figure (such as nationhood, religion, a leader or a supposedly shared identity) but has little to do with *être-en-commun*. Instead of the unification around some kind of delusory identification, it is through our shared exposure to *sens* that Nancy theorises the commonality of being-with, and in particular 'l'être-en-commun comme tel, avant même de l'organiser, de le rapporter à un principe' ['being-in-common as such, even before it is organized or ascribed to a principle'] (SM, p. 84; MM, p. 87).

Nonetheless, in the text on techno, Nancy is reluctant to wholly commit to the idea, proposed by Michel Gaillot, that raves 's'ouvrent en quelque sorte de l'espace et du temps communs, où les individus, par la musique, la danse, par le contexte singulier, inhabituel de ces fêtes, sont comme aspirés dans un "avec", un "ensemble" ou un "partage" autre que celui qui les lie d'ordinaire dans l'espace social' ['some kind of common space and time opens up where it's as if individuals, through the music or the dancing, or because of the singular and unusual context of these fetes, are siphoned into a "with," a "together," or a "share" other than the one that usually binds them to social space'] (Gaillot in SM, p. 74; MM, p. 77). For Gaillot, the spontaneity of emergent raves associated with techno, and its lack of an ideological, political or organisational principle, along with its technological and aesthetic innovation, points towards a capacity for authentic experiences of being-with; it preserves 'un aspect archaïque – archi-originaire si l'on peut dire – dans la mesure où subsistent ou plutôt resurgissent en elle des comportements, qui sont propres au festif en général, tels qu'on pouvait les voir à l'œuvre dans les fêtes des sociétés traditionnelles (dionysies, bacchanales, carnaval . . .)' ['a certain archaic aspect, "archeoriginal," so to speak, to the extent that in it there subsists, or rather resurges, behaviour peculiar to the "festive," in the general

---

[58] Milbank et al., 'Introduction: Suspending the Material: The Turn of Radical Orthodoxy' in Milbank, Pickstock and Ward, *Radical Orthodoxy*, pp. 1–20 (p. 19).

sense (Dionysia, bacchanalia, the carnival, etc.) as we see it at work in traditional societies'] (Gaillot, in SM, p. 71; MM, p. 75). In this way techno, at least for Gaillot, appears to return (us) to the ritualistic and festive (i.e. the Dionysian) aspects of music that have lain dormant or 'anesthesised' in Western musical traditions, or of which the West has only enacted spectacles or simulations. Nancy is cautious about the way in which Gaillot frames this as a return, however, emphasising that there can be no return to the archaic, but that perhaps it is possible to shed light on 'quelque chose qui appartient en effet à un ordre, à une couche, à une strate fondamentale de l'expérience' ['something that in fact belongs to an order, layer, or stratum fundamental to experience'] (SM, p. 72; MM, pp. 75–6). Nancy highlights the (dangerous) nostalgic dimension of the desire to return to something archaic, and stresses his preference for framing it as 'archi-originaire' rather than archaic, and thus something 'qui n'a jamais eu lieu, qui n'aura peut-être jamais lieu et qui est sous toute l'expérience de l'être-ensemble' ['that has never taken place, will perhaps never take place, but which underlies our whole experience of being-together'] (SM, p. 72; MM, p. 76). In this respect, it is perfectly possible to understand techno's aesthetic and technological innovation as key to its archoriginal dimension; it is precisely the 'return' of something entirely novel and thus of something 'qui n'a jamais eu lieu'. Finally, then, without passing final judgement on whether techno corresponds to a nostalgic desire for the archaic, or whether through its innovations it 'returns' us to something sensuously new (or, indeed, both), Nancy asks pertinent questions such as what 'risquerait de n'être que "retour", nostalgie donc, nostalgie de choses tribales, archaïques, de l'idée qu'il y aurait pu y avoir de la fête immédiate' ['might risk, being nothing but "return," and thus, nostalgia [*Nostos* in Greek means 'return' – *Trans*], a nostalgia for things tribal and archaic, for the idea that there may have been soething like an unmediated *fete*'] (SM, p. 72; MM, p. 76).[59] All of this substantially develops Nancy's positioning of the aesthetic, and probes at questions that seem as complex as they are essential. While the aesthetic domain no doubt remains a privileged source of the sensuous immediacy of being-with, musical works or processes and their indisputable entanglement with social forms, practices, institutions, beliefs and politics thus by no means appear to afford music 'itself' any such privileged role.

---

[59] As Nancy points out, archaic festivals are inseparable also from their religious aspects, and so in this respect techno risks 'le retour du sacré simulé' ['the return of a simulated sacred'] (SM, 72; MM, p. 76).

GENS, GENRE, GENEALOGY

Interestingly, Nancy identifies the first instance of this 'return' (here understood as the new return of the underlying dimension that always traverses the shared experience of meaningful worlds) not with the genre of techno, but with that of rock. It is, however, unclear as to whether it is rock/techno that returns us to this experience (especially because they both also involve dancing), or whether it is our conception of these genres (in contrast, perhaps, to our ideating conception of *musique savante*) that returns us to an understanding of music as always already participating in this shared sonorous affectivity. For Nancy, the 'retour' is contemporary with the emergence of rock, which he describes as 'un phénomène énorme. Ce n'est pas par hasard s'il a commencé, et s'est développé en même temps que commençait et se développait une espèce de grande torsion de société, de civilisation qui dans un moment particulier, en 68, a fait craquer tellement de choses' ['an undeniably enormous phenomenon. It is not a coincidence that it began and developed at the same time as another kind of great convulsion, of our society and civilization, began and developed. And at one particular moment, in 1968, it caused a rupture in many areas'] (SM, p. 73; MM, p. 76). In this respect, Nancy explicitly relates rock to the society whence it emerged; a suggestion that is developed more extensively in 'La Scène mondiale du rock', where he expressly describes music as something that 'configure du rapport social. La musique donne une cadence à l'être-ensemble' ['configures the social relationship. Music gives rhythm to the being-together'], and also presents rock itself as 'un phénomène philosophique au sens très large et courant du mot, c'est-à-dire une forme de pensée, de représentation du monde, des valeurs, voire de sens. Ce qu'on appelle aussi une culture' ['a philosophical phenomenon in the largest sense, which is to say a form of thought, of the representation of the world, of values, even of meaning. This, we would also call a culture'] (SMR, pp. 79, 76). Throughout the text, rock is characterised as something which both influences society and is influenced by society (or at least 'external' factors); in this respect rock is considered as both a subject-like form of affective agency and an object-like repository that resounds with contemporary values, meanings, identities and politics. For Nancy, rock played a crucial role in socio-political events such as the fall of the Berlin Wall; indeed, he suggests that there are few 'phénomènes culturels qui puissent revendiquer une pareille vertu de propagation, de contamination, de contagion' ['cultural phenomenons which might be able to claim such capacity for propagation, for contamination, for contagion']; rock is 'un appel [...] à refaire un monde' ['a call to remake the world'] (SMR, pp. 78, 84).

Alongside this conception of rock as a musical force that is able to act on the world, it also appears to reflect prevailing concerns and discourses in its narrative and aesthetic innovations. Nancy explicitly parallels the emergence of rock in the middle of the twentieth century with the concurrent 'fin de la métaphysique' in philosophy. Just as this philosophical trajectory is described as 'le passage d'une époque où la philosophie consistait en une vision du monde ou en un système de vérité, à celle où elle a cessé de se concevoir comme savoir ou construction de systèmes de pensée' ['the passage from an era where philosophy consisted of a vision of the world or a system of truth, to one where philosophy has ceased to consider itself as knowledge or the construction of systems of thought'], rock is understood as a composite genre (rather than a self-authorising musical system) that 'remet entièrement en jeu la question du sens' ['entirely puts back into play the whole question of meaning'] (SMR, pp. 77, 83). As a genre it insists on more than signification in processes of meaning, on 'autre chose que la signification [...] il lui faut l'énergie, la force' ['something other than signification [...] it requires energy, power'] and also sustains a degree of 'autoréflexivité' that would be consonant with this philosophical movement (SMR, pp. 83, 77). With this in mind, the final chapter, 'Narrations', of Pauline Nadrigny's monograph *Musique et philosophie au XXe siècle*, offers a rich supplement to some of Nancy's core observations on rock. By insisting on the interrelation of the sociological and the ontological – as does Nancy in the texts on rock and techno – Nadrigny is able to expose the way in which rock both *figures* itself as a fundamentally modern rupture with the past and simultaneously quests for its origins; it is positioned as 'anhistorique et archétypique' ['ahistoric and archetypal'] and yet 'ne cesse de raconter son histoire, de se raconter' ['never ceases to tell its own history, to tell its own tales'].[60] Finally, then, along with advancing a degree of ambivalence about rock's constitutive relationship to mass-consumer culture and processes of globalisation, Nancy also highlights the way in which rock manifests a fundamental change in the way that different generations relate to each other (he clearly positions himself on the side of the pre-rock generation), suggesting also that it reflects or authorises a changing system of taste and value. Whereas previously a difference was drawn intra-socially between 'les gens cultivés et les autres' ['those that are cultured and those that are not'] because, following rock, music is understood in a

---

[60] Pauline Nadrigny, *Musique et philosophie au XXe siècle*, p. 202.

broader sense *qua* culture itself, the differentiation happens interculturally between those who like a particular genre, say rock, and those who like another, say jazz, or hip hop (see SMR, p. 82).

At the same time, though Nancy brings to the fore the way in which interesting and, one would imagine, important distinctions between different groups of people ultimately sound on the level of the ethico-aesthetic, he nonetheless considers rock as the genealogical starting point for a wealth of sub-genres including 'le pop, la techno, le rap, après être passé par toutes les variantes du rock que vous voudrez, le hard, le *metal*, la *house*, le funk' ['pop, techno, rap, after having passed through all the variants of rock you want: hard, metal, house, funk'] all of which appear to be subsumable under the name 'rock' and between which Nancy draws no fundamental distinction (SMR, p. 77). Though he is aware that genres such as rap and techno do not consider themselves as rock, he nonetheless insists that 'tout le monde sait de quoi on parle quand on dit rock' ['everyone knows what we are talking about when we talk about rock'] (SMR, p. 77). Though much of this likely comes down to his self-professed ignorance when it comes to the actual music, technique or practice of any of these (sub-)genres, it provokes an odd tension with other of his writings.[61] For example, though Nancy at least implicitly continues to understand musical ontology as fundamentally related to society and politics when he considers the relationship between fascism and European art music in 'March in Spirit in our Ranks' – a question to which we will return in depth in Chapter 5 – the ease with which he is able to make intra-genre distinctions when it comes to this repertoire is striking in comparison (see MSR).

NANCY AND THE FEMININE: AESTHETIC GENESIS

> Ève, Hawwah, ce nom fut donné par Adam à la femme parce qu'il signifie 'la vivante'. La Genèse dit : 'parce qu'elle fut mère de tout vivant'. Ève est la vie de la vie, ce qui s'entend du plaisir comme de la mort. Cela s'entend comme cela se divise. La femme est ce qui se divise.
>
> Nancy[62]

---

[61] Nancy is explicit about his ignorance in 'La Scène mondiale du rock'. Similarly, he states 'je suis tout à fait incompétent en technique et en esthétique de la techno' ['I am totally incompetent as far as the technique and esthetics of techno are concerned'] (SM, p. 71; MM, p. 75).

[62] M_1, pp. 113–14 ['Eve, Hawwah: Adam gave this name to woman because it means "the living one." Genesis says: "because she was the mother of all living things." Eve is the life of life, which can be understood to mean pleasure as well as death. It is understoof as it divides. Woman is that which divides itself'] (M_2, pp. 65–6).

With all this in mind, and especially with regards to the musical resonances between Nancy's writing on music and the work of Rameau and Rousseau, Elizabeth Tolbert's assertion that any 'critique of contemporary ideas about music and language must begin with an awareness of their intellectual history, specifically of their roots in Enlightenment discourses about human nature and the origins of human culture' seems compelling.[63] As we have seen, music's 'innate' expressiveness led many Enlightenment philosophers to posit that '[l]anguage, music, and knowledge were all unified in a single divine origin'.[64] This means that language, having subsequently 'split' from a shared origin with music, is still, nevertheless, *directly* connected to the passions and thus allows for an explanation of how language is able to traverse the non-parity of sound and idea. Accordingly, music is then comprehensible – if not properly utterable – as a more immediate and affective proto- or not-yet-language, connecting the natural and non-semantic to the semantic and cultural.[65] Thus music – characterised as 'not (yet) language' – becomes inextricably linked with certain other ideas; a genealogical glance to the philosophy of music demonstrates that it is not only in ancient thought, through the figures of the muses and the sirens, that music has been characterised as essentially 'feminine' – sometimes dangerously so. During the Enlightenment, music is, as Elizabeth Tolbert states, 'elided with the subordinate term in oppositions such as culture/nature, human/animal, mind/body, or reason/emotion. Implicit in music's feminization is its opposition to language, exhibiting qualities such as non-referentiality, syntax without semantics, pure form, the music "itself"'.[66] Western thought's logocentric emphasis on voice (and the materiality of sound) as 'presence', has the corollary of also privileging 'referential meaning [. . . and] metaphorical, as opposed to metonymic thinking'.[67] Consequently, music is castigated as lacking propositional content and is therefore aligned with the 'lesser' term in the corresponding binarisms: as emotional, primitive and certainly feminine. As this dualist thinking demonstrates, debates that seek to position music in a particular way are necessarily involved in (re)articulating all kinds of other (op)positions at the same time.

---

[63] Elizabeth Tolbert, 'Untying the Music/Language Knot' in Linda Phyllis Austern (ed.), *Music, Sensation, and Sensuality*, pp. 77–95 (p. 79).
[64] Thomas, *Music and the Origins of Language*, p. 34.
[65] See Bowie, *Music, Philosophy and Modernity*, p. 54.
[66] Tolbert, 'Untying the Music/Language Knot' in Linda Phyllis Austern (ed.), *Music, Sensation, and Sensuality*, p. 77.
[67] Ibid., p. 81, in the sense that the 'vertical' axis of metaphor presumes a reference *to* something, whereas the 'horizontal' axis of metonymy suggests a potentially infinite deferral of contiguous meaning.

Any contemporary philosophical account of music will necessarily be consistent with, or provide a challenge to, this traditional construction and, given Nancy's determination to destabilise the false dichotomies set up by traditional metaphysical and representational thought, it seems pertinent to explore more thoroughly how these binary oppositions are dealt with, or refuted, in his work. As Gill Howie, following Jean Grimshaw claims, 'it is not incidental that within philosophy the concept of the "feminine" carries specific connotations [... and so] one must analyse the construction of the philosophic canon and consider philosophy a social practice'.[68]

While there remains significant 'disagreement concerning the relevance of social and sexed location to philosophy', feminist philosophers contend that 'the assumption [... of] an irreducible sexual difference has played a key part in the sexual division of labour and power'.[69] Thus, as long as we continue to find it acceptable to *think* in terms of an *essential* difference between the genders and deploy that difference metaphorically as a signifier of a natural and biologically fixed, rather than socio-culturally constructed meaning, we will continue to reproduce that 'difference' in the material world. For similar epistemological reasons (that are themselves part of the critique of Western thought's ocularcentrism) post-Enlightenment ways of knowing, or validating what counts *as* knowledge, have tended towards a privileging of rationality that has also been critiqued from a feminist perspective. The epistemological consequences of being a woman, or a feminist, thus raise methodological questions about both the reading and writing of philosophical texts; not only does the metaphorical articulation of masculine and feminine terms as fixed bearers of meaning make philosophy uncritically complicit – perhaps even involved – in perpetuating an apparently 'natural' difference between the sexes in the 'real' world, but it concurrently aligns the hegemonic masculine position – and consequently philosophy itself – with non-identity, neutrality, rationality and objectivity.[70] A materialist feminist approach demands that *all* philosophy be seen as a situated social practice, and that the standpoint of a self-same, invariably white, male, all-knowing philosopher-king is also a historically-specific subject position. The commitment to a philosophy which concerns itself with the sensuous presentation of the 'real' world (as in, the material world in which we find ourselves presently

---

[68] Gill Howie, 'Feminist Philosophy' in Oliver Leaman (ed.), *The Future of Philosophy*, pp. 105–19 (p. 105).
[69] Ibid., pp. 105, 106.
[70] This is a key tenet of Luce Irigaray's work. See *Ce Sexe qui n'en est pas un* and *Speculum de l'autre femme*. This line of thinking will be developed more extensively in Chapter 5.

and as the only one available to us) should necessarily remain attentive to the position of women in this 'real' world, while also considering the philosophical positioning of women to have a bearing on this, and vice versa. With this in mind, the final and critical rereading of Nancy's *À l'écoute* proceeds not simply from an anti-ocular orientation but from a specifically anti-phallogocular perspective.

In *Les Muses*, Nancy visits the caves of Lascaux – also, by extension, Plato's cave – in order to (re)theorise the Platonic metaphysics of creation, and the role of the aesthetic in this creative act. Through this gesture Nancy indubitably also enlists a classical figure of femininity: the muse; Nancy's œuvre is, however, remarkably silent when it comes to articulating any specific position in relation to gender and sexuality. Kalliopi Nikolopoulou has demonstrated how in *Les Muses*, 'a thematic link is established through recurring images of femininity'.[71] She continues to ask, '[w]hy does discourse on art – after art's declared end – need femininity as a necessary topos in order to exist at all?'[72] Through his invocation of a mythological feminine imaginary (in particular, the muse figure who '*compels* the poet to do her bidding'[73]) and the metaphorics of 'gesture and its etymological link to gestation',[74] Nancy positively rehabilitates the unequivocal materiality of the aesthetic domain that, in some approaches to the philosophy of aesthetics, has been maligned as proof of the art works' status as mere 'copy'. 'By linking processes of carnal and aesthetic creation', as Nikolopoulou demonstrates, Nancy articulates a 'dissipated ancient Greek sense of materiality, for the meaning of *aisthesis* was precisely sense *qua* sensuousness'.[75] Of course this works well for Nancy's larger project, focused as it is on the always already sensuous presentation of the world and on (re)articulating all the senses of sense (*sens*), comprised as intelligibility, as perception and as direction. Nonetheless, Nancy does this by resorting to metaphorical figures of femininity, which runs the risk of eclipsing – or at least conflating – the lived experience of a historically-specific feminine subject position with a fixed mythological imaginary feminine. Or, as Nancy says himself, 'la jeune fille [la muse] qui est à la fois l'extrémité infiniment fragile de l'art et le passage infiniment ténu de la belle forme dans la transformation de la forme en vérité, cette jeune fille n'a d'autre existence que celle des fruits qu'elle présente' ['the girl [the muse] who is at once the infinitely fragile

---

[71] Kalliopi Nikolopoulou, '"L'Art et Les Gens"', pp. 174–93 (p. 176).
[72] Ibid., p. 176.
[73] Nancy, M_2, p. 9, cited in Nikolopoulou, '"L'Art et Les Gens"', p. 187.
[74] Nikolopoulou, '"L'Art et Les Gens"', p. 187. As Nikolopoulou explains, both gesture and gestation etymologically derive from the same Latin root, *gerere*, which means 'to bear or to carry'.
[75] Ibid.

extremity of art and the infinitely tenuous passage of beautiful form in the transformation of form into truth – this girl has no other existence than that of the fruits she presents'] (M_1, p. 96; M_2, p. 54).

Finally, as Robin James has demonstrated, just as the invocation of the metaphorical feminine has consequences, so too does the invocation of music as a metaphor – and in ways that often overlap with this feminine metaphoricity. In 'Affective Resonances: On the Uses and Abuses of Music In and For Philosophy', a formidable article which makes several claims about Nancy's *À l'écoute* that complement the argument advanced in this chapter, James draws our attention to the way in which affect is often presented as an alternative to theories centred on representation or vision and, crucially, that music is often used 'as a metaphor for affect'.[76] Though James in no way challenges the notion that music is affective, she simply urges philosophers to augment their theorising about an abstract and affective quasi-magical and extra-logical 'music' with a fuller understanding of musical practices, musicology and music theory, especially in order to help us better understand 'how actual *music* (practices, theories, works) can help us understand the political dimensions of affect'.[77] James also outlines the way in which the philosophical recuperation of metaphorical musical affect too often simply recasts the set of binaries described above. Vision, representation and meaning (*logos*) are associated with masculinity, activity, whiteness and rationality, while the object of the gaze, sound, 'music' and sensuous (a-logical) meaning are associated with feminine passivity, the body and Otherness; rather than disrupting the fundamental binary, the male philosopher is able to appropriate 'feminized experiences of being affected or acted upon while avoiding the denigration and marginalization that go with these experiences *when they are attributed to women*'.[78] It is thus James's contention that a long history which associates femininity with aesthetic receptivity is indeed rehabilitated to philosophical ends, but 'in terms that reinforce an underlying patriarchal, Orientalist value structure'.[79]

RENVOI À JEAN-LUC NANCY (BETWEEN SILENCE AND SOUND)

In the second section of *À l'écoute* the *corps sonore* is theorised more precisely. Here we find Nancy's articulation of an acoustic plural

---

[76] Robin James, 'Affective Resonances', pp. 59–95 (p. 59).
[77] Ibid., p. 60.
[78] Ibid., p. 68, James's emphasis.
[79] Ibid., p. 68.

ontology replete with maternal metaphorisations: it is the '[c]onstitution matricielle de la résonance' ['matrix-like constitution of resonance'] or, as Nancy asks, 'qu'est-ce que le ventre d'une femme enceinte, sinon l'espace ou l'antre où vient à résonner un nouvel instrument, un nouvel *organon* [...] L'oreille ouvre sur la caverne sonore que nous devenons alors' ['What is the belly of a pregnant woman, if not the space or the antrum where a new instrument comes to resound, a new *organon* [...] The ear opens onto the sonorous cave that we then become'] (Ec, pp. 72–3; L, p. 37). Or: 'le bruit de son partage (d'avec soi, d'avec les autres): peut-être encore une résonance plus ancienne dans le ventre et du ventre d'une mère' ['the noise of its sharing (with itself, with others) resounds: perhaps the cry in which the child is born, perhaps an even older resonance in the belly and from the belly of a mother'] (Ec, p. 79; L, p. 41). Adrienne Janus has considered *À l'écoute*, and particularly Nancy's conceptualisation of the *corps sonore*, to be compatible with the kind of 'otocentric' feminist genealogy that she finds in the antiphallogocularcentric philosophy of Luce Irigaray. She draws a parallel between the 'dynamic multiple resonances propagated by the embodied female self' and Nancy's *corps sonore* as an 'organ of acoustic parturition from which is born the multiple resonances that give birth to sense'.[80] However, it provokes an uneasy tension with Irigaray's playful but critical reappropriation of the link between the womb and the *matriciel* (via *la matrice*) and ultimately to what she sees as Plato's foundational gesture of metaphysical matricide.[81] Too often, and in spite of the careful destabilisation of a straightforward subject-object dichotomy and Nancy's insistent rejection of any original sounding, this mapping onto the maternal-feminine womb/belly risks figuring the *corps sonore* as a receptacle – or at least a space, a 'somewhere else' [*ailleurs*] than the resonance itself, a risk that is fully exposed later when Nancy asks 'ce ventre qu'il regarde n'est-il pas *le lieu où vient retentir sa musique*' ['But isn't this belly that he is gazing at *the very place where his music comes to resound*']? (Ec, p. 84; L, p. 45, my emphasis). Certainly, it is a considerable limitation that Nancy's sonorous ontology, in spite of itself, requires the resonant chamber of a mother-womb-matrix for its articulation, and resonates with Irigaray's critique of the dominant specular economy which reduces feminine and maternal sexuality to an ultimately unproductive womb, and the illusory ground

---

[80] Janus, 'Listening', p. 187.
[81] See Irigaray, *Speculum de l'autre Femme*, particularly 'L'ὑστέρα de Platon', pp. 301–457. It is worth noting that there are also strong resonances with Derrida's deployment of the 'stéréographique' tympanum in his consideration of philosophy's limits. See Derrida, 'Tympan', in *Marges de la philosophie*, pp. i–xxv.

upon which the male philosophical fantasy is staged. The recurrent slippage between the morphological and the metaphorical maternal reinstates a kind of (specifically gendered) foundationalism that seems to be so at odds with Nancy's larger, anti-foundationalist thinking. Furthermore, he equates the *possibility* of sense with sound; resonance and sonority become the *pre*-condition of significance, while somehow also being *beyond* meaning (*l'outre-sens*). Similarly, in 'March in the Spirit in our Ranks', to which we will return in Chapter 5, music's essentially 'ineffable' quality is aligned not with oversignification which Nancy sees as a fascist perversion, but explicitly, again, with 'a beyond-significance [*outre-signifiance*]' (MSR, p. 58). In one of the most problematic passages of *À l'écoute*, where Nancy specifically suggests that we turn 'à nouveau vers la musique, par-delà le sonore abstrait' ['again toward music, beyond abstract sonority'] (Ec, p. 58; L, p. 30), he asks us to heed three demands. Firstly, that we treat '"pure résonance" non seulement comme la condition mais aussi comme l'envoi même et l'ouverture du sens' ['"pure resonance" not only as the condition but as the very beginning and opening up of sense'] (Ec, p. 59; L, p. 31). Secondly, we should 'traiter le corps, avant toute distinction de lieux et de fonctions de résonance [. . .] comme] caisse ou tube de résonance de l'outre-sens' ['treat the body, before any distinction of places and functions of resonance [. . . as] a resonance chamber or column of beyond-meaning'] (Ec, pp. 59–60; L, p. 31); he also compares this to the soundboard of a violin and the 'little hole' in the clarinet. And, thirdly, from this point, to consider the 'subject' *as* (the echo of) the 'l'outre-sens' ['beyond-meaning'] (Ec, p. 60; L, p. 31). Given that this has been theorised around the 'resonant chamber' of the maternal belly-womb, we might want to question how it is that 'before any distinction of places' (or functions) – the Artaudian-Deleuzian Body without Organs, to which Nancy intentionally refers – the sonorous body is *already* feminine? We are left to assume that the belly-womb-matrix does not *count* as a function or a specific distinction. It is instead, like the resonance Nancy theorises, both anterior and posterior, elsewhere or beyond, and timeless.

Nancy also invokes the auditory dimension of the not-yet-subject through the birth-cry of the vagitus – or even the infant still *in utero* – to insist on the materiality of sound as meaning. In many respects, it closely resembles Julia Kristeva's theorisations of *le sémiotique* – the gestural and communicative 'space' of the pre-symbolic (ergo pre-linguistic) – through the (somewhat more conscious, if still problematic) appropriation of Plato's maternal-feminine *chora*. Just as with Nancy's *corps sonore*, the *chora* is both spatial and temporal, and as '[n]i modèle, ni copie, elle est antérieure et sous-jacente à la figuration donc à la spécularisation' ['Neither model nor copy, the *chora* precedes and underlies figuration and thus specularization'].[82] We might wonder, then, whether Judith Butler's well-known critique of Kristeva – that she 'defends a maternal instinct as a pre-discursive biological necessity, thereby naturalizing a specific cultural configuration of maternity' rather than seeing the maternal body itself as 'a production of a given historical discourse, an effect of culture rather than its secret and primary cause' – would apply to Nancy too.[83] It certainly seems that Nancy's *corps sonore*, while introducing bodily materiality as indissociable from meaning in a certain sense, also goes a fair way to obscuring – even de-materialising – the maternal-feminine body as a 'lived' body, instead identifying it, as Butler claims of Kristeva, as 'bearing a set of meanings that are prior to culture itself'.[84]

Along with the tendency to describe or articulate music in reference to an uncritically 'fixed' conception of the (maternal) feminine, Nancy also maintains other aspects of the inherited discourses on music and sound (though, no doubt, they are also articulated in relation to the feminine as well). Just as, for Nancy, '[l]a femme est ce qui se divise' (and thus 'woman' ceases to articulate a clear distinction between inside/outside, internal/external, subject/object, and so on) this is more or less homologically mapped onto music's (or sound's) liminality; its ability to traverse the supposed borders or boundaries of a 'subject'. Nancy often characterises music as an uncontrollable invasion; 'la présence sonore *arrive:* elle comporte une *attaque*' ['sonorous presence *arrives* – it entails an *attack*'] (Ec, p. 34; L, p. 14). While this co-mingling of sound is figured, also, positively – as the inherently 'shared' nature of sound, or the essential sonority of the being-with – it is also recast in alarmingly familiar terms. He asserts that 'le visuel serait tendanciellement mimétique, et le sonore tendanciellement méthexique (c'est-à-dire dans l'ordre de la participation, du partage ou de la contagion)' ['the visual is tendentially mimetic, and the sonorous tendentially methexic (that is, having to do with participation, sharing or contagion)'] (Ec, p. 27; L, p. 10), thus preserving a line of thought directly from Plato that sees music as having a privileged and direct access to the soul, and to be intimately related to interiority; a lineage that doubtlessly assists – *persists* – in also keeping other inheritances in play. As outlined above, there is a long history of figuring aesthetic

---

[82] Kristeva, *La Révolution Du Langage Poétique*, p. 24 [Kristeva, *Revolution in Poetic Language*, p. 26].
[83] Judith Butler, 'The Body Politics of Julia Kristeva', pp. 104–18 (pp. 104, 106).
[84] Ibid., p. 105.

experience in terms of a feminised passivity or receptivity, and indeed it seems clear that Nancy too participates in this assumption; Robin James has shown convincingly the extent to which this assumption is omnipresent in *À l'écoute*, where vision is associated with masculinity, while being '"resonant" is to experience "acoustic penetration"'.[85] This provokes not only an uneasy tension with feminist ontologies 'for which bodily integrity is an almost unquestioned good', but leads to the question, as Diane Perpich outlines, of 'whether Nancy's conception of bodies as subject to a law of inevitable, multiple intrusion is not in some ways a very white, masculine move, attached to a horizon and history of privilege that should give feminists and others pause'.[86] Simultaneously, though Nancy's work, in a certain sense, may be doing crucial work in terms of rehabilitating a sonorous and affective dimension to philosophy, by retreading the path of a feminised aesthetic passivity, femininity itself is only valued 'when it appears in males, only when it dons the trappings of whiteness, and thus continues to marginalize women and non-whites *as listeners*'.[87] Indeed, as we will see shortly, the Titian painting which Nancy enlists as a visual support for his sonorous ontology displays the naked Venus apparently unaware of the organist's music. In Jonathan Sterne's compelling introduction to *The Audible Past* – an interdisciplinary and thought-provoking history of sound that avoids many of the pitfalls of musicology or theory working independently – he cautions against invoking such assumptions, which he sees as stemming from a kind of otic essentialism. As he points out, the difference between sight and sound has often been preconceived as emerging from naturally occurring 'biological, psychological, and physical facts', and it is from this implied assumption that even supposedly 'cultural' analyses of sound (and music) emerge.[88] Sterne constructs a compelling 'audio-visual litany' which demonstrates the inherent dualities in our sound-thinking. It includes, among others, observations such as: 'hearing immerses its subject, vision offers a perspective' or 'hearing is about affect, vision is about intellect' or 'hearing tends toward subjectivity, vision tends toward objectivity'.[89] All of this, he goes on to say, 'idealizes hearing [. . . and thus voice as speech and as presence] as manifesting a kind of pure interiority'.[90]

---

[85] James, 'Affective Resonances', p. 67, citing Nancy, *Listening* (L, p. 3).
[86] Diane Perpich, 'Corpus Meum', pp. 75–91 (pp. 85–6).
[87] James, 'Affective Resonances', p. 68.
[88] Jonathan Sterne, *The Audible Past*, p. 15.
[89] Ibid.
[90] Ibid.

With this in mind, it becomes somewhat easier to explain how quiet – perhaps even 'silent' – the *corps sonore* is. While certain sounds have 'theoretically' been allowed in – certainly the vagitus departing from the womb and the borborygmous of the digesting belly – the remainder comes primarily from the canon of high art music. We have a reference to Mozart's clarinet concerto (although, rather interestingly, heard only through the spectacle of a film, *Le Concert de Mozart*) and, above all, several references to Wagner (Ec, p. 63). In spite of the invasive nature of sound that Nancy theorises, Janus observes how the *corps sonore* 'never takes on the substantiality and volume of the noises that both attack and envelop us in a world where we increasingly use the noise of one technology [. . .] to block out the other'.[91] As Janus continues to ask,

> [h]ow much does the relative suppression of noise in his space of listening resemble a nineteenth-century concert hall? Why does he not make use of concepts associated with recent developments in music that would potentially be productive [. . . For example,] the concept of 'renvoi' as reverberation, offering and return, as the subject sensing itself sensing, is never linked to the notion of a feedback loop.[92]

We might wonder whether there really is any sound in the *corps sonore* at all. While examples of sounds are invoked, they are instrumentalised in articulating not a philosophy of sound but the (maternal) *space* of its endless return, the *renvoi*; resonance as a first principle, and as precondition or possibility. It is not the 'beat' itself, but that rhythm, as he states elsewhere, 'n'"apparaît" pas, il est le battement de l'apparaître en tant que celui-ci qui consiste simultanément et indissociablement dans le mouvement de venir et de partir des formes ou des présences en général, et dans l'hétérogénéité qui espace la pluralité sensitive ou sensuelle' ['rhythm does not *appear*; it is the beat of appearing insofar as appearing consists simultaneously and indissociably in the movement of coming and going of forms or presence in general, and in the heterogeneity that spaces out sensitive or sensuous plurality'] (M_1, p. 46; M_2, p. 24). Perhaps the title of the middle section, 'Interlude: musique mutique', is rather more revealing than at first it might appear. Finally, through his etymological meditation on the word *mot* (from *mutum*, then, variously, *mu*, *motus*, *muô*, *mouth*, and so on) we find the same pull towards a story of origins as in Rousseau, replete with an evocation of an originary scene of harvest and cultivation (see Ec, p. 48).

---

[91] Janus, 'Listening', p. 198.
[92] Ibid., p. 200.

Nancy's collaborator and colleague, Philippe Lacoue-Labarthe, whose own musical offerings we will consider in depth in the following chapter, suggests that philosophy has often aspired to 'un *dire pur* (d'une parole, d'un discours purement transparent à ce qu'ils devraient immédiatement signifier: la vérité, l'être, l'absolu, etc.)' ['a *pure saying* (a speech, a discourse which is purely transparent to what its signs ought to signify unmediatedly, i.e. truth, being, the absolute, etc.)'].[93] We might wonder here whether Nancy is guilty of entertaining the dream of a 'pure listening', upon which an anti-ocular philosophy could be built? De-historicising listening in order to think of it as a 'natural' phenomenon to which we can legitimately turn simply buys into a problematic essentialism, rather than understanding the inheritance of our ears as always already cultural. As Sterne asserts, '[t]here is no "mere" or innocent description of interior auditory experience. The attempt to describe sound or the act of hearing in itself – as if the sonic dimension of human life inhabited a space prior to or outside history – strives for a false transcendence' and reinstates the kind of philosophy against which Nancy is trying to turn by asserting a sonic but nonetheless 'universal human subject'.[94]

CODA

Finally, this chapter (re)turns to Titian's painting. Nancy concludes his meditation on listening by reading this painting as a manifestation of the specifically musical *corps sonore* in action. He asks: 'ce ventre qu'il regarde n'est-il pas le lieu où vient retentir sa musique, et n'est-ce pas aussi bien de la résonance de son instrument qu'il est à l'écoute?' ['But isn't this belly that he is gazing at the very place where his music comes to resound, and isn't it also the resonance of his instrument he is listening to?'] (Ec, p. 84; L, p. 45). He argues that this properly theatrical scene by way of the perspective of the trees and the supposedly 'outside' space against which this more intimate scene of music-making is played intermingles so that 'le dedans et le dehors ouvrent l'un sur l'autre' ['the inside and the outside open up to each other'] (Ec, p. 84; L, p. 45); the trees outside expand the pipes of the organ, and thus the 'resonance' of the scene as a whole. Nevertheless, why does Nancy require the naked body of a woman – and Venus, as the archetypal image of feminine sexuality, no less – to propound his musical theorisations? Janus suggests, in her reading of the same

---

[93] Lacoue-Labarthe, 'La Fable', in *Le Sujet de la philosophie*, p. 9 [Lacoue-Labarthe, 'The Fable', pp. 43–60 (p. 43)].
[94] Sterne, *The Audible Past*, p. 19.

moment in *À l'écoute*, both that Nancy offers 'the embodied mass of Titian's fleshy Venus as a buffer' and also that the scene presents a 'visual image of a mode of listening that is different to that of Schopenhauer, Wagner, and the early Nietzsche, indeed different to the whole Western (Helleno-Christian) tradition of musico-theological listening since Plato'.[95] As Janus acknowledges, in this sacrificial tradition of musical listening, auditors are required to sublimate their bodily responses to the music and instead attend to primarily structural or harmonic features in order to ideate the sonorous in visual or spatial terms. However, while Venus's fleshy body is instrumental in suggesting, even demanding, that listening be conceived in corporeal and not just intellectual terms, the role of Venus's body in facilitating the organist's bodily response – his (and our) experience of a 'sensual excess' – is, nonetheless, contestable. In so doing, the female body is simply (re)aligned with the apparently sensuous, methexical, 'watery' – to follow Janus – nature of sound, and all in music – the properly *musical* – that is irreducible to *logos* or sense (as meaning).

Moreover, although Nancy is happy to acknowledge that the organist is certainly gazing sensually at the naked Venus, he contends that the gaze is directed towards her belly (presumably in order to make his argument that the musician's gaze merely directs us to the belly-womb-matrix on, in, or with which the *corps sonore* is able to make itself resound, and thus folds the visual aspect into a more essential relationship to sonority), but it seems evident that the organist's gaze is actually directed towards Venus's crotch. Do we not find, rather more revealingly, a psycho-sexual scene of acoustic self-identification, whereby the male organist (read, also, philosopher) – effectively blinded by the threat of castration – has to continue to play his 'organ' in order to initiate an otic disavowal of what he has (not) seen. Furthermore, for all Nancy's emphasis on sound as sharing and opening, there is no reciprocity between Venus and the organist; he cannot solicit her (or Cupid's) attention, locked as they are in their pre-cultural dyad. While she is required for *his* hearing and/or listening, the painting suggests that she cannot hear anything at all. She is absent, elsewhere, not whole; permanently beyond the phallic circulation of law, language and meaning or, as Lacan famously put it in *Encore: le séminaire, livre XX*, 'il n'y a pas *la* femme, la femme n'est *pas toute*' ['*woman* does not exist, woman is *not whole*'].[96]

Finally, and perhaps most curiously of all, Nancy is keen to insist

---

[95] Janus, 'Soundings', pp. 79, 80.
[96] Lacan and Miller, *Encore*, p. 14 [Lacan, *On Feminine Sexuality*, p. 7].

that 'on fera répondre à ce tableau la musique de Wagner, au moment où Tristan, à la voix d'Isolde, s'écrie: "*Quoi, j'entends la lumière?*"' ['one can reply to this painting with music by Wagner, the instant that Tristan, to Isolde's voice, cries out: "*What, am I hearing light?*"'] (Ec, pp. 84–5; L, p. 46). Although the musical response undoubtedly enables Nancy to fold the implicit sonority of the painting into a more explicit relation with sound and/or music, why Nancy views this music in particular as an obvious response to Titian's painting is far from clear. Nonetheless, it is certainly revealing in terms of the musical framing it alludes to. What Nancy offers us as 'proof' of his theoretical position is as before, the libretto, and rather strangely the score of the vocal line from Isolde's last utterance ('[unbe]wußt höchste Lust'/'unconscious supreme bliss') at the end of the opera, with *no mention* of the music accompanying them. Neither the quiet *tremolo* strings accompanying Tristan's final words nor the echo of the 'last consolation' motif in the woodwind, nor the timbre and texture of the voices and instruments, nor even the luscious minor plagal cadence – itself a *re*-sounding of the long-awaited resolution of the Tristan chord, only heard for the first time a few bars previously and coinciding with Isolde's death/transfiguration – appear to be of any interest.[97] Beyond the perhaps easy observation that Nancy, despite appearances, is not actually talking about music at all, he nonetheless offers us an interesting musical chronology of the *corps sonore*. Nancy's theorisation of a philosophical listening takes us directly from Rameau's attempt at systematising and codifying a nascent tonality, through to Wagner – and not just any Wagner, but Wagner's *opus metaphysicum*, *Tristan und Isolde*, where tonality begins its journey towards modernist disintegration and fragmentation. The 'Tristan chord', in failing to resolve, by 'resolving' onto a dissonance – a dissonance only resolved 'properly' and thus (temporarily) restoring tonality nearly four hours later, at the very moment Nancy cites – brackets our 'mute' musical scene of philosophical listening as synonymous with the reverently 'silent' reception of canonic, predominantly tonal, works in the classical concert hall. The time-space of Nancy's *corps sonore* is an entirely tonal space, which serves, at the same time – as was Rameau's agenda in the original articulation of the *corps sonore* – to de-historicise and naturalise tonality. Indeed, if we return yet again to the supposed 'representation' of the *corps sonore* in Titian's painting, we find a third instance of the internal/external dichotomy with the trees also circumscribing what is private and public; a distinction that has been crucial to the history of music,

---

[97] For more on the motives in *Tristan and Isolde*, see Roger Scruton, *Death-Devoted Heart*.

and the precise example – the mansion garden – that Richard Leppert gives as a 'prototype of the modern concert hall, which delineates a physical space for a certain kind of music, whose sonorities are the acoustic signs of a certain privileged group of people'.[98] Concomitantly, then, if silence and the delimited space of the concert hall are one and the same – remembering that Nancy's philosophical space of *renvoi* does not refer to the articulation of a 'beat' but the gap *between* the beats that allows the temporal-spatial matrix to unfold – the heyday of the Western high art tradition and its canonic works are also rendered neutral, transhistoric and asocial. In sharp contrast, the musical reflections on the ethico-aesthetic ramifications of techno and rock are *always* made through an understanding that they relate, constitutively, to the society and culture whence they came. Similarly, though jazz and rock (and its multitude of sub-genres) are credited with rehabilitating an essential 'force' – especially because they are 'à la fois une musique et une danse' ['both a music and a dance'] (SMR, p. 79) – that subsequently effects changing morals or traditions on the socio-cultural level, they are never afforded such a privileged role *vis-à-vis* interiority and Nancy's resonant ontology. Whether one is convinced, or not, by Nancy's assertions about rock and techno, the attempt to grapple with the worldliness of specific musical genres leads to far harder, though considerably more interesting, questions about music's affective relation to politics and society.

Ultimately, then, Nancy's insistence in *À l'écoute* that we should 'remonter du sujet phénoménologique [...] à un sujet résonant' ['[go] back from the phenomenological subject [...] to a resonant subject'] (Ec, p. 44; L, p. 21) thus appears to be founded on a fairly well-worn metaphysical sonotropism. Although he claims that the move 'de l'ordre phénoménologique jusqu'au retrait et au recel ontologique, n'est pas par accident un pas qui passe du regard à l'écoute' ['from phenomenological order to ontological retreat and recoil, is not accidentally a step that goes from the gaze to listening'] (Ec, p. 45; L, p. 21) this move necessarily resorts to an essentialising of sound and listening as somehow subsisting outside of time or culture and, more tellingly, perhaps, still relies on the very traditional realm of the (erotic) male gaze directed towards the naked female body for its final exposition. While it may be the case that what Nancy is trying to offer us in *À l'écoute* is a methodology for philosophy, one where, as Janus claims, we are asked to 'attend to resonances of perception and meaning yet to

---

[98] Richard D. Leppert, *The Sight of Sound*, p. 32.

emerge and always passing away',[99] it nevertheless remains problematic to figure this in terms of an essentially 'natural' maternal-feminine, and to frame it against the apparently neutral backdrop of tonality figured *as* synonymous with music (in general).

---

[99] Janus, 'Listening', p. 189.

3. 'Catacoustic' Subjects and the Injustice of Being Born: Lacoue-Labarthe's Musical Maternal Muse

> Pas de femme, donc, si j'ai bien lu. Fors la mère bien entendu. Mais cela fait partie du système, la mère est la figure sans figure d'une figurante. Elle donne lieu à toutes les figures en se perdant au fond de la scène comme un personnage anonyme. Tout lui revient, et d'abord la vie, tout s'adresse à elle et s'y destine. Elle survit à la condition de rester au fond.
> Derrida[1]

This chapter approaches two texts by Lacoue-Labarthe, both of which focus – more or less explicitly – on the relationship between music and philosophy. The first, 'L'Écho du sujet', is from the well-known collection *Le Sujet de la philosophie: Typographies I* (1979) and is, Derrida claims, the 'déploiement le plus impressionnant' ['most impressive unfolding'] of a theme that runs across Lacoue-Labarthe's work: that of 'l'*autos* et de son rapport-à-soi comme rythme' ['the *autos* and its self-relation as rhythm'].[2] The second text, which is far less well-known – in fact, I would venture to say, almost entirely unknown – is a succinct but lucid transcript[3] of a talk given through the 'Petites conférences' series at the Nouveau Théâtre de Montreuil: *Le Chant des Muses: petite conférence sur la musique* (2005). Aimed, as it is, at a young and non-specialist audience, the style and register are apposite to the context and are thus the absolute opposite of the rigorously academic and exceed-

---

[1] Jacques Derrida, Claude Lévesque and Christie McDonald, *L'Oreille de l'autre*, p. 56 ['No woman or trace of woman, if I have read correctly – save the mother, that's understood. But this is part of the system. The mother is the faceless figure of a *figurant*, an extra. She gives rise to all the figures by losing herself in the background of the scene like an anonymous persona. Everything comes back to her, beginning with life; everything addresses and destines itself to her. She survives on the condition of remaining at the bottom' Derrida, *The Ear of the Other*, p. 38].

[2] Jacques Derrida, *Psyché*, p. 627 [Derrida, 'Introduction: Desistance', p. 31].

[3] Or rather, a retrospectively rehabilitated transcript as '[e]n raison d'un dysfonctionnement technique' ['because of a technical malfunction'] only the last third and the following questions were saved. See the 'Avertissement de l'auteur' in CM, p. 9.

ingly technically and philosophically dense 'L'Écho du sujet'; and yet very little, *theoretically*, is found in one that isn't in the other. Indeed, both focus on several clear themes: the (essential) relationship between music and philosophy; the subject's relationship to sound/sonority and, ultimately, the specifically musical; the fundamental link between music and language, as well as teasing apart the supposedly 'musical' aspects of language itself (prosody, diction and lexis). And, most obviously, both apparently reach the same conclusion: that the specifically *musical* aspects of the 'catacoustic' subject – the subject that is given to 'itself' pre-specularly through echo, rather than through reflection – is profoundly and inescapably linked to the maternal.[4] In the following analysis of these texts and their treatment of such themes, I will also make occasional reference to what could be considered Lacoue-Labarthe's major work on music – *Musica Ficta: Figures de Wagner* – where relevant, as well as to some of the essays collected in the recently published volume dedicated specifically to Lacoue-Labarthe's writings on music;[5] *Musica Ficta* in particular, however, will be the focus of a more sustained critique in the concluding chapter. Ultimately, then, the aim is to offer both a critical (largely in this chapter) though ultimately sympathetic (as we will see in Chapter 5) reading of Lacoue-Labarthe's still 'stubbornly under-appreciated' œuvre: an absence that is all the more remarkable, as Martin Crowley describes, given that he was 'so closely involved in the development of such a key part of recent French thought'.[6]

LEGACIES AND LEGENDS: UNPICKING THE PHILOSOPHICAL INHERITANCE

It seems germane to begin by tracing the broader strands of Lacoue-Labarthe's patient but dense thinking, before relating them to the specifically musical concerns at hand. His work is seen to be influenced primarily by Derrida, Nietzsche and Heidegger, although a debt to Benjamin is often overlooked, certainly in anglophone criticism,[7] and often focuses on – or takes as its springboard – the topics of German Romanticism, tragedy, the Heideggerian legacy and its deeply problematic relation to Nazism. Much of his work, from its early underpinnings in the revolutionary verve of the late 1960s, has been in the form of

---

[4] Elsewhere I have already made several key parts of the argument made here and in Chapter 5; see Sarah Hickmott, 'Beyond Lacoue-Labarthe's *Alma Mater*', pp. 174–88.
[5] See Philippe Lacoue-Labarthe, *Pour n'en pas finir*.
[6] Martin Crowley, 'Review: *Philippe Lacoue-Labarthe*', p. 130.
[7] See John McKeane, *Philippe Lacoue-Labarthe*.

collaborations with his friend and colleague, Jean-Luc Nancy, who, as explored in the previous chapter, has also been strongly influenced by Heidegger and Derrida, and with whom he shares a profound concern about, and interest in, concepts such as community, aesthetics and politics. As with many of his contemporaries thinking and writing in the exhilarating momentum of what has been labelled (sometimes with objection) as poststructuralism, disillusionment with structuralism alongside contemporary political instability (and the failed revolution of May 1968) led to a renewed engagement with important historical figures such as Marx and Freud (via Lacan) – including from a feminist perspective – as well as with anarchism and phenomenology. A major influence on Lacoue-Labarthe, as with Nancy, is of course Derridean *déconstruction*: a reading strategy or approach to texts that challenges and exposes a reliance on, or assumption of, hierarchical binaries that fix meaning as monolithic, oppositional and singular, and instead explores the multiplicity of signifiers and the perpetual interplay of differences that constitute, but are never reducible to, their meaning, leading to what is perhaps Derrida's most famous concept: *différance*. Furthermore, the destabilisation of meaning parallels a decentering not only of the author but of the subject at large (again, famously, through Derrida's critique of the logocentric metaphysics of presence) and thus, implicitly and sometimes explicitly, critiques the fiction of the objective, universal, self-same, straight, white male. At root, then, Lacoue-Labarthe emerges from a group of figures whose core concerns are ultimately at the level of language though who, more importantly, 'insist upon the power of writing to transform rather than simply represent our experiences'.[8]

We can now turn to a consideration of how these concerns are dealt with in a specifically Lacoue-Labarthian vein; his own theoretical framing of subjectivity as – again drawing on the 'de-' prefix – *désistance*, and its underpinnings in what are likely his major philosophical contributions: his rethinking of mimesis and his formulation of (onto)typology. When it comes to the formulation of properly philosophical 'concepts' (rather than readings of, for example, Hölderlin, Celan or Wagner) there are clearly two major interlocutors: Derrida and Heidegger, with an important third role played by Nietzsche. As John McKeane hints, following the Derridean project and its insuperable role in Lacoue-Labarthe's thought, it might be more appropriate to consider him not so much as a philosopher but as a practitioner of deconstructive reading, which instead 'looks at philosophical texts, stripping them of any

---

[8] Ibid., p. 1.

privileged status [. . .] without affording privileged status to their concepts as opposed to the repetitions and rhythms through and by which they are written'.[9] He thus explicitly rejects the notion that philosophy, through its reification of seemingly abstract or conceptual thinking, 'is able simply to sideline the difficulties posed by language'.[10] Further still, he identifies in this aspiration one of philosophy's constitutively metaphysical moments; its hope of 'un *dire pur* (d'une parole, d'un discours purement transparent à ce qu'ils devraient immédiatement signifier: la vérité, l'être, l'absolu, etc.)' ['a *pure saying* (a speech, a discourse which is purely transparent to what its signs ought to signify unmediatedly, i.e. truth, being, the absolute, etc.')].[11] His contention, then, as Ian James summarises, is 'that philosophical discourse, in its metaphysical moment, is itself responsible for the distinction between philosophy and literature' and is a foundational move that allows philosophy to preserve its (false) illusion of objective purity.[12] In this respect it should be clear that Lacoue-Labarthe's philosophy – unsurprisingly, given the extent of their collaborations – is interwoven with major strands of Nancy's philosophical agenda. Finally, this deconstruction of philosophy's own metaphysical constitution places him firmly in the neo-Heideggerian tradition of the overcoming of metaphysics; the legacy of which he both perpetuates and, significantly, critiques in deconstructive readings that reveal the *un*thought of Heidegger's project. Most provocatively, this critique has led to the claim that Heidegger's well-known affiliation with the Nazis can be traced back not only to his political actions – he not only joined the Nazi party in 1933, for which he ultimately failed to apologise, clarify or retract his apparent support for National Socialism – but to his philosophical thought too (see FP [HAP], in particular).

These (re)positions and inheritances unsurprisingly have numerous resonances and consequences for his formulations of the (*désistant*) subject and (originary) mimesis, which are closely related to each other: given music's complex historical relationship to mimesis, as set out in Chapter 1, it will be interesting to see how Lacoue-Labarthe deals with the relationship between music and mimesis. Mimesis is generally taken to mean 'representation' or 'imitation', both of which presuppose a pre-existing and preceding 'presentation' (being, object, form, and so on) upon which the representation or imitation is modelled; of which it is a merely secondary and (often) impoverished imitation of the 'real thing'. For Plato (as for his student, Aristotle), mimesis is the representation

---

[9] Ibid., p. 6.
[10] Ibid., p. 61.
[11] Lacoue-Labarthe, 'La Fable', p. 9 [Lacoue-Labarthe, 'The Fable', pp. 43–60 (p. 43)].
[12] James, *The Fragmentary Demand*, p. 21.

of nature and ideal forms/worlds; in and of itself it is neither straightforwardly good or bad, but through its entanglements with truth and deception it can have respectively positive or negative consequences for the individual and the polis. It is also, in Plato's theorisation, intractably connected to education and knowledge as demonstrated by the allegory of the cave; as noted in Chapter 1, Plato also redefines art as essentially mimetic – though as we have seen, music has a particularly complicated configuration in this regard. As Potolsky notes, this 'conceptual revolution' has some considerable knock-on effects, most obviously that once art (and particularly poetry) is 'figured as secondary and derivative, distinguished from reason and truth and associated with femininity and childhood, poetry comes to seem inappropriate to the needs of current Greek society' and thus the poet is expelled from the ideal city-state.[13] Furthermore, this provokes considerable difficulty when it comes to 'ideal' education. Children need to be told stories, the 'acceptable ones' which will instil in them virtuous characteristics; narratives that, through imitation and emulation of exemplary figures, will in turn form them as model citizens – an irreducibly mimetic process (377c).[14] Historical narratives told, rather than demonstrated, in a *diegetic* rather than *mimetic* fashion are preferable in this regard; Plato is deeply suspicious of theatrical mimesis (such as in tragedy) which produces sympathetic feelings in the audience based on emotion, not reason, the effects of which can be felt, he claims, far beyond the theatre.[15]

Just as with Nancy, Lacoue-Labarthe's post-Heideggerian project is concerned with the overcoming of metaphysics, and thus refuses to ground or locate Being through reference to a predetermined fixed and unchanging point of reference; thus identities are no longer mimetically determined as a mere reflection of some extra-worldly absolute and immaterial signified that guarantees subjectival and epistemological stability. Furthermore, this is interwoven with the thinking of a neo-Heideggerian and 'deeper' history of Being, or *Seinsgeschichte*; indeed, as McKeane has pointed out, it is Lacoue-Labarthe's (along with Heidegger's) contention that 'Western philosophy can and should be referred to as a unitary tradition, and what's more, as one requiring deconstruction i.e. requiring that we unpack the various stages of its construction and bring to light the various Others that have been excluded during this process'.[16] However, it is Lacoue-Labarthe's supposition – both with and against Heidegger – that the (problem-

---

[13] Potolsky, *Mimesis*, p. 30.
[14] Plato, *Republic*, p. 71.
[15] See Potolsky, *Mimesis*, p. 27.
[16] McKeane, *Philippe Lacoue-Labarthe*, pp. 5–6.

atic) thinking of mimesis is primary, and more deeply rooted than the (failed) thinking of Being.[17] This mode of thinking occasions a fundamental rupture with the Socratic tradition inherited from Plato onwards: mimesis is no longer to be thought as the (re)creation of a more fundamental (and unmediated) nature but instead describes identity (in the broadest sense) and acts of (re)creation (i.e. *poiesis*, whether as *physis* or *techne*) as a dialogue with or a response to what has preceded (which was itself a response to what preceded that, and so on, *ad infinitum*). It is therefore a theory of originary mimesis – a theory of (re)creation without recourse to a fixed origin from which it emerges; mimesis *as* origin – or, as McKeane confirms, of 'mimesis without model'.[18] This has two immediate and obvious consequences: mimesis is no longer the process by which something is reproduced; it simply *is*, itself, *poiesis*, and, secondly, Being is fundamentally and constitutively abyssal. It turns towards an essential relationality and asserts, as Alison Ross describes, that 'meaning is not beyond presentation, [but] that all occurs in history, God and all, as experience'.[19]

As indicated above, this has particular consequences for the Lacoue-Labarthian subject. As John Martis demonstrates, Lacoue-Labarthe draws on and expands the common French usage of *désistement* (as in 'withdrawal or standing down of a person from a political position, a law suit, and so on'[20]) to explicate his formulation of the subject that comes into being always already and only through an exposure to something beyond or outside of itself. Of course, *désister*, as Derrida has noted, shares a familial relationship with a whole host of Latinate words, such as consist, persist, insist, assist, and so on, all marked by their shared root: *sistere*, meaning 'to (cause to) stand'. What Lacoue-Labarthe's formulation thus highlights is the essential paradox of originary mimesis: the subject is only a subject through its withdrawal – its standing down (and this, as we shall see, is of central concern to the rhythmic and catacoustic subject articulated in 'L'Écho du sujet'). Or, as Martis describes, '[w]hat is depicted *en abyme* is the infinite deferral of the identity of what is withdrawn. The subject is, in its very subjectivity, "revealed" as a withdrawn subject, and so on.'[21] Mimetic deconstruction, figured elsewhere in Lacoue-Labarthe's work as an *hyperbologique* [hyperbologic], concomitantly directs his project towards both aesthetics and politics; if identity (as well as origins or

---

[17] See 'Œdipe comme figure' in IM.
[18] McKeane, *Philippe Lacoue-Labarthe*, p. 155.
[19] Ross, *The Aesthetic Paths of Philosophy*, p. 132.
[20] John Martis, *Philippe Lacoue-Labarthe*, p. 41.
[21] Ibid., p. 59.

essences) are now secondary effects of a more fundamental or primary technique (mimesis without model/origin) his concern is now with how these 'secondary terms [are] worked into form by a figure'.[22]

'WOULDN'T YOU JUST DIE WITHOUT MAHLER?'

> Il faut bien avouer que le moi n'est qu'un écho
> [It must be confessed that the self is nothing but an echo]
> Valéry

> Tout est rythme [Rhythmus],
> le destin tout entier de l'homme est un seul rythme céleste,
> de même que l'œuvre d'art est un unique rythme
> [All is rhythm; the entire destiny of man is one celestial rhythm,
> just as the work of art is a unique rhythm]
> Hölderlin

> ... parce que toute âme est un noeud rythmique
> [... because every soul is a rhythmic knot]
> Mallarmé[23]

And so now we can turn to the consideration of the specifically musical in Lacoue-Labarthe's œuvre. 'L'Écho du sujet' proceeds from what Lacoue-Labarthe intuits to be true, based on a trilogy of citations, above, from Valéry, Mallarmé and Hölderlin, all of which suggesting that the self is either an echo (presumably, following Lacoue-Labarthe's thinking of originary mimesis, without origin) or a rhythm. This 'hunch' is put into play with the observation that in the history of modern philosophy, on at least two highly prominent occasions, a certain confessional mode of philosophising – as well as a sort of pathological delirium, or even madness proper – has played out alongside the would-be musician status of those philosophers: Rousseau and Nietzsche. Furthermore, Lacoue-Labarthe notes, a parallel trajectory exists in the literary domain, citing the examples of Proust, Diderot and Laporte, as well as Mann and Hesse. This allows him to make sense of and add context to what is evidently the guiding question of the text:

> quel rapport y a-t-il entre *autobiographie* et *musique*? Ou, plus précisément, et pour expliciter quand même un peu les choses: qu'est-ce qui lie entre elles l'autobiographie, c'est-à-dire en fait la contrainte ou la compulsion (*Zwang*) autobiographique (le besoin de raconter, de s'avouer, de s'écrire), et la musique – la hantise ou l'obsession de la musique?

---

[22] Ross, *The Aesthetic Paths of Philosophy*, p. 114.
[23] All given as cited by Lacoue-Labarthe. ES_1, pp. 219, 220; ES_2, pp. 139, 140.

[What connection is there between *autobiography* and *music*? More precisely, and to make things a bit more explicit: What is it that ties together autobiography, that is to say, the autobiographical compulsion [*Zwang*] (the need to tell, to confess, to write oneself), and music – the haunting by muisc or the musical obsession?] (ES$_1$, p. 221; ES$_2$, p. 140)

And, finally, how does this relate to 'la problématique plus générale du *sujet*'? ['the more general problematic of the *subject*'] (ES$_1$, p. 221; ES$_2$, p. 141, Lacoue-Labarthe's emphasis). Just as we have seen with Nancy, Lacoue-Labarthe appeals to the intraphilosophical distinction between the visual and the audible in order to explore whether it is possible to go '*en deçà* du "seuil théorique" lui-même [...] au lieu où la *théorie du sujet* (mais peut-être, aussi bien, le *sujet de la théorie*) devrait, si j'ose dire, se voir' ['to the *hither side* of the "theoretical threshold" itself [...] to the place where the *theory of the subject* (but perhaps also *the subject of theory*) would see itself'] (ES$_1$, p. 227; ES$_2$, p. 145, Lacoue-Labarthe's emphasis) and thus to disarm philosophy/theory of what is, from Plato through to Lacan, its privileged specular weaponry, asking instead 'ce qui arrive lorsque l'on remonte de Narcisse à Echo [...?] Qu'est-ce qu'un phénomène "catacoustique"?' ['what happens when one goes back from Narcissus to Echo [...?] What is a "catacoustic" phenomenon?'] (ES$_1$, p. 227; ES$_2$, p. 146).

'Catacoustics' is the branch of acoustics that studies echoes and derives, as Amittai F. Aviram notes, from the Greek verb '*katakouein*, which means both "to listen to" and "to obey"'.[24] Thus, the word both neatly encapsulates what is to become Lacoue-Labarthe's figuring of a pre-specular, inner-echo and the inescapable demand of the musical obsession. He takes as the central 'object' of his enquiry the widely known text by the psychoanalyst, Theodor Reik, *The Haunting Melody*, that documents a twenty-five-year-long attempt at understanding his own experience of an 'hantise musicale'; the involuntary return of a melody following the death of his friend, mentor and fellow psychoanalyst, Karl Abraham. It is far beyond the scope of this chapter to offer a thorough summary of what is an exceedingly well-worked and strikingly dense text; nonetheless, a brief excursus to explain the key moments of both Reik's text, and Lacoue-Labarthe's reading of it, is necessary.

I. Autobiography

The starting point of the narrative for our purposes is when Reik, upon hearing of the death of Abraham, decides to take a walk in the (snowy

---

[24] Amittai F. Aviram, *Telling Rhythm*, p. 215.

and *unheimlich*) forest and realises that he is being 'haunted' by the chorale from the final movement of Mahler's Second Symphony – a haunting that provoked the auto-analysis-cum-autobiography and that continued until he gave the memorial speech at Abraham's funeral. Reik initially struggles to understand the association of Mahler with Abraham, observing that Abraham did not even like Mahler's music, until he notes that Mahler found the inspiration for the chorale at the funeral of his mentor, von Bulow. This realisation thus produces, as Lacoue-Labarthe comments, a complementary set of artistic/analytic filial pairings: through Mahler's identification with his mentor, von Bulow, and Reik's identification with his mentor, Abraham, we are left with Bulow/Mahler (with Beethoven in the background) and Abraham/Reik (with Freud in the background). A number of key moments follow, which allow Reik to proceed with the analysis. Firstly, following the memorial speech given by Reik, Federn makes a 'Freudian slip' when he offers his thanks for the speech just heard by Abraham – an error that leads Reik to wonder whether Federn wished him dead also, or whether he saw him as an equal or successor to Abraham – a feeling he dismisses as impossible but that, nonetheless, through self-analysis, reveals to him a sense of rivalry. Secondly, he witnesses a funeral procession where a young boy asks his mother why there is music as the dead cannot hear it. This incites the feeling – and his recognition – of an underlying guilt; the realisation that we do not share quickly enough our feelings of love and affection with the (still) living. Finally, he is proud of a moment in the memorial speech – the repetition of an i-vowel – that he considers to be particularly stylish, and the sense of style is linked, for Reik, to Abraham's 'proper' north German character and accent (especially in comparison to his own 'improper' Austrian accent) and consequently to the mother tongue. Thus, through Reik's auto-analysis, this heady trilogy of guilt, rivalry and style become essentially linked to the autobiographical impulse. 'Style' – often called, in an Aristotelian vein, *lexis* by Lacoue-Labarthe – appears to be essentially musical, or at least what lends music, drawing on Benveniste, its 'signifiance' and thus its participation in a shared (and inherently social) material and worldly universe of signs. As Lacoue-Labarthe demonstrates, what interests Reik here 'n'est pas de l'ordre, à strictement parler, du langage mais, intéressant la langue, intéresse dans la langue, dans l'usage de la langue [. . .] sa part *musicale*, prosodique ou mélodique' ['is not, strictly speaking, of the order of language. Rather, it affects a language, and affects in the use of a language [. . .] its *musical* part, prosodic or melodic']; in short, 'la voix: l'intonation, le débit, le ton, les inflexions, le mélisme, le rythme, voire le timbre (ou ce que Barthes appelle le "grain")' ['the *voice*: intonation, elocution, tone, inflections, melsima, rhythm, even timber (or what Barthes calls "grain")'] and thus 'une stylistique' ['a stylistics'] (ES$_1$, pp. 243–4; ES$_2$, p. 159). He continues to explain how these aspects – which are not properly linguistic, according to Lacoue-Labarthe – undercut and escape 'la partition métaphysique (théorique) qui les sous-tend toujours: sensible/intelligible, matière/forme, corps/esprit, chose/idée, etc.') ['the metaphysical (theoretical) distinctions that always underlie them (sensible/intelligible, matter/form, body/spirit, thing/idea, and so on)'] and are, as well as being untheorisable, also 'social, historique, culturel, esthétique, – bref, *éthique*, au sens rigoureux du mot *êthos*' ['social, historical, cultural, aesthetic – in short, *ethical*, in the strict sense of the word *ethos*'] (ES$_1$, p. 244; ES$_2$, p. 160). Lacoue-Labarthe thus invites the suspicion that certain essential characteristics – supposedly untheorisable as they may be – are nonetheless equally applicable to aspects of both language and music, thus neatly deconstructing a clear music/language binary in the process.

II. Allo-/Heterothanatography

Of course, this doesn't fully explain either the observed connection between the musical obsession and autobiography, or the subject's reaction to – or affinity for – a particular piece of music. Needless to say, it is not insignificant that the symphony haunting Reik is Mahler's Second, also known as the 'Resurrection', after the poem (Klopstock's 'Die Auferstehung') that forms the text of the final movement (the haunting melody). The first movement begins with the death of the hero (the *Totenfeier* or Funeral Rites), the second through fourth movements remember happy times with the deceased and then subsequently meditate on the meaninglessness of life, and finally the fifth movement (re)presents the redemption and resurrection of the hero/protagonist. Thus we are presented with a narrative symphonic form – much as Mahler later withdrew the programme from circulation – which, through the resurrection of the hero, enacts the narcissistic wish for posterity, and the impossibility – well observed by Freud – of conceptualising one's own death, except as (still living) witness to it. However, while there is ample material for analysis in the text and programme of the chorale, Reik pushes the question further – and certainly beyond anything foreclosed by Freud's well-known amusicality – to try and understand the connection between the psyche and music 'itself'; the *characteristic* parallelism that Reik observes between himself and Mahler with regards to their respective filial pairs (compounded, further, by Bulow's admiration for Mahler as a conductor, but not as a composer, and

Abraham's respect for Reik as a *theorist*, but not as a practitioner) pushes him to locate the significance of the haunting melody in an unremittingly elusive and unconscious, but nonetheless perceptible, stylistics. Music's *signifiance* is thus, as Lacoue-Labarthe surmises in a Nietzschean or Heideggerian vein, associated with the 'représentation d'une *Stimmung* inconsciente' ['representation of an unconscious *Stimmung*'] (ES$_1$, p. 273; ES$_2$, p. 186). Style is, therefore, double: 'c'est tout d'abord un phénomène de diction ou d'énonciation [. . .] mais c'est aussi le "caractère": l'incisé et le grave, le prescrit (ou le pré-inscrit), le "programmé" d'un sujet – soit, dit-il, l'inconscient' ['it is first of all a phenomenon of diction or enunciation [. . .] But it is also "character": the incised and the engraven, the prescribed (or pre-inscribed), the "programmed" in a subject – in other words, he says, the unconscious'] (ES$_1$, p. 251; ES$_2$, p. 166). This returns us, then, to the intraphilosophical distinctions already commented upon by Lacoue-Labarthe (such as the visual and the audible), the musical subject's relation to these divisions and the omnipresence of the specular threshold: all that is inadmissible *theoretically* seems to be provoked by music and yet is intelligible only through speculation. Nonetheless, the *désistant* and split subject – the subject apprehended through its mirror image, and who is therefore split from 'itself', from the (always already) dead other from whose non-separation the not-yet-subject constituted its non-identity, thus necessitating the subject's own imaginary death – appears to find a residue of its pre-specular echo in the affective dimension of music. The (tragic) catharsis is the 'première reproduction ou répétition, ce premier mimème *immédiat* de l'Un originaire [. . .] la musique guérit en somme' ['first reproduction or repetition, the first *immediate* mimeme of the originary One [. . .] in short, music heals'] (ES$_1$, p. 275; ES$_2$, p. 187), says Lacoue-Labarthe. Consequently, autobiography is reconceived as always allothanatography (or more properly, heterothanatography – allo- implying a doubling of the *same* subject, rather than radical exteriority of an absolute other), and the duplicity of style (as both enunciation and *ethos*; the subject as writer and as written) appears to ensure music's link to at least one crucial facet of heterothanatography; music's 'essential' nature based on repetition homologically mimes – or actually *is*, it is not clear – the unconscious repetition of the subject in its 'détermination fondamentale [. . .] comme "ethos" ou comme caractère' ['fundamental determination [. . .] as "ethos" or as character'] (ES$_1$, p. 272; ES$_2$, p. 185). For both Reik and Lacoue-Labarthe, then, music is consequently characterised as saving the subject from itself – or rather, from its own death: music 'resurrects'.

MUSIC AND LANGUAGE

Music thus reveals itself as just another mode of the subject writing 'itself'. And indeed, for Lacoue-Labarthe, the link between music and language is absolutely fundamental. In *Le Chant des Muses*, Lacoue-Labarthe is guided by such apparently simple questions as *what* is music and *why* do we have it? More specifically, he reminds us that we need the verb 'faire', which implies a 'qui' – we need a human (or possibly an animal) agent, as music doesn't just 'naturally' occur. Although unacknowledged in the text – presumably owing to genre constraints – one would imagine that this is underpinned by a neo-Heideggerian deconstruction of a straightforward binary opposition between natural (*physis*) or artificial (*techne*) modes of production. He draws our attention to the etymology of music, deriving as we well know from *mousike*, which simply refers to 'l'art des muses' in general, and not just what we now think of music in the narrow sense (CM, p. 19). The muses, as he points out, are the daughters of Zeus and Mnemosyne – a now forgotten goddess of memory, from which we derive both memory and 'mental' – and are generally thought of as the goddesses of 'les beaux-arts' (i.e. painting, sculpture, architecture, poetry, music, theatre and dance) which means art as *techne* (from which we derive technology), and thus art retains a strong link to artifice (see CM, pp. 20–1). However, he recants, this ignores an earlier conception of the muses that attaches them particularly (exclusively, even) to poetry and music, noting that all poetry was previously 'sung' or at least 'chanted'; the muses in their original incarnation, then, are 'porteuses de la musique, [et] sont les déesses de la poésie' ['bearers of music, [and] goddesses of poetry'] (CM, p. 21). He continues by explaining that *poiesis* simply means production, making or creation (as Daniel Albright has stated, 'we might speak of the poetics of a sonnet, and we might speak of the poetics of a sofa'[25]) and that *within* this [*poiesis*] there is, as previously mentioned, *techne*, and also *physis*, which accounts for 'natural' production; it is simply synonymous with the whole concept of 'nature' and the physical world around us (see CM, p. 21). And yet, poetry is considered 'l'art par excellence [. . .] le plus "poïétique" [. . .] la plus pure' ['the art *par excellence* [. . .] the most "poetic" [. . .] the most pure'] for the reason, claims Lacoue-Labarthe, that it is the art of *language* (CM, p. 22). Whereas Daniel Albright draws from the etymology of *poiesis* the conclusion that *poetics* 'does not exalt the literary

---

[25] Albright, *Panaesthetics*, p. 2.

as much as it seems',[26] for Lacoue-Labarthe, it is rather that language – as a distinctly human accomplishment – is seen to straddle thought, memory and meaning, and in its designation as the first 'technique' renders us, also, 'un être "technique"' ['a "technical" being'] (CM, p. 22). These formulations allow Lacoue-Labarthe to make his two principal claims about music: firstly, that music is fundamentally linked to language and, secondly, that it is an art – or more precisely 'une poïèsis technique' ['a technical *poiesis*'] (CM, p. 23).

The links with language do not stop there, however. The fundamental link that Lacoue-Labarthe observes between music and language (that of their being *techne)* ensures that music is seen not as a natural phenomenon – not just as environmental 'bruits' – albeit with the confusing caveat he accords the possibility that *certain* animal sounds, particularly those of birds and other 'mugissements ou beuglements, hurlements, etc' ['bellowing or mooing, howling, etc.'], remind us that the first musical instruments we know of are those made from hollowed bone and that may have been used to imitate the sounds of our prey (CM, p. 24). Imitation is thus key. He continues, rather surprisingly – given a declaration made earlier about his intention to treat the matter purely philosophically – by taking 'un petit tour du côté de la science' ['a little detour into the realm of science'] to show that various studies have demonstrated at least two things: firstly, that perhaps the only proper sense the child has in the womb – before its birth – is that of hearing, and that, secondly, although it can't hear sounds from the exterior very well, it can hear almost directly 'la voix de sa mère: il entend sa mère parler' ['the voice of its mother: [in the womb] the baby hears its mother speak'] (CM, pp. 24–5). This means the infant must be aware of the alternations between 'bruit/silence' and 'grave/aigu', leading Lacoue-Labarthe to claim, consequently, that the infant *in utero* is first and foremost exposed to what is *already* musical in language. This aspect of language is of course *prosody*, from the Greek, *odos*, which is 'song'. Thus it seems our first experiences (and the essential facet?) of both music and language are of the natural melody, the 'song' of the mother tongue *in utero*; its cadence, melody, rhythm, intonation and phrase.

Lacoue-Labarthe concedes, even emphasises, that these are insufficient grounds to account for music, which as '*une poïèsis "technique"* [. . .] a besoin d'instruments; et ces instruments sont chargés de produire un certain effet, que rien de "naturel" ne peut produire' ['a "technical" *poesis* [. . .] demands instruments; and these instruments are required to

---

[26] Ibid., p. 2.

produce a particular effect that cannot be produced by anything "natural"'] (CM, pp. 28–9, Lacoue-Labarthe's emphasis). Nevertheless, this does not seem to impede the return to the mother tongue and the inevitably Rousseauian turn of events: through music's ability or attempt to 'retrouver sa mélodie' ['refind its [language's] melody'] he reveals that each type of music thus corresponds to its language 'type' (CM, p. 30). He supports this claim with the example of European orchestral music, stating that after listening to only a little bit, even if one doesn't recognise the particular work or composer – 'cela dépend de votre culture' ['that depends on your culture'] – with just the slightest familiarity one will recognise whether the work is, for example, Russian or Italian (CM, p. 30). And not because the music is texted, he says (he's speaking particularly of the symphony, it seems), but because of 'la mélodie et la prosodie, le rythme' ['melody, prosody, and rhythm'] which are based on, or imitate (*calqué sur*) the language from which they come (*sur la forme de la langue de départ*) (CM, p. 31). Not only does this seem naively simplistic, but one is immediately struck by a plethora of examples that seem to refute this claim: what, precisely, in a Bach fugue corresponds to his Germanic mother tongue? Or in Purcell's *Fantasias* for viols, to his English mother tongue? Or in Berio's fiendishly virtuostic *Sequenzas*, to his Italian mother tongue? Or in John Cage's aleatoric music, to his American English mother tongue? And what about when Bizet writes music that is meant to sound like southern Spain – where are we meant to locate his French mother tongue then? And it seems fairly evident– curiously and complexly mediated via images, the other arts, recording technologies and historical, social and political factors (among many others) – that Vaughan Williams's identifiable pastoral 'voice' bears a (stylised) link to the British countryside rather than to English prosody, just as Mosolov's 'Iron Foundry' relates to post-Revolutionary Russia and the hyper-industrialisation of the Soviet Union. In fact, the only (tenuous) example which springs to mind would be something like the grandiose theme of the final movement of Sibelius's Second Symphony, which relentlessly places the stress on the first beat (though that in itself is entirely standard – it is the fact our attention is drawn to this that is notable) that it is tempting to draw a parallel with Finnish phonology and the invariably stressed first syllable. And this example is, perhaps, telling, coming as it does from a composer whose output was profoundly associated with the formation of Finnish national identity. Indeed, the repertoire to which Lacoue-Labarthe refers – the symphonic works of the classical and Romantic concert hall – unsurprisingly coincide with nascent and emergent European nationalities and nationalisms. His central claim here – that music is recognisable as, and is traced from, the *melos* of the mother tongue – is either untrue, or positions music that doesn't 'work' according to this framing as non-music or, at least, unmusical music.

The Heideggerian-inflected Rousseauianism doesn't stop there, however. He claims perhaps an even more striking example would be that of jazz (even when the music in question is instrumental, it comes, as does all music according to Lacoue-Labarthe, from a vocal origin) which develops from gospel music or the blues – which themselves derive from work songs, he states. He asks his reader/listener: 'qu'entend-on dans cette musique?' ['What do we hear in this music?'], replying, '[l]a langue des Noirs américains [. . .] l'anglais parlé – mal, si l'on veut, avec un accent, une élocution "étranges" – par des Africains déportés d'Afrique de l'Ouest aux Etats-Unis comme esclaves et qui ont gardé, forcément, l'accentuation, le rythme, la prosodie de leur langue d'origine' ['the vernacular of black Americans [. . .] English spoken – badly, if you want, with an accent, a "strange" elocution – by Africans deported from West Africa to the United States as slaves and who inevitably kept the accentuation, the rhythm, and the prosody of their mother tongue'] (CM, p. 31). Evidently, this characterisation conveniently skates over – or wilfully ignores – the complexity of the emergence of jazz and blues music.[27] It seems particularly problematic that he completely ignores histories that have demonstrated a genealogy shared with minstrelsy; the fetishisation of 'primitive' orality; and the construction of 'authenticity' through the cataloguing gaze of white men and their recording technologies that sought the most rural, 'rough' and reprobate examples, marketing the resulting recordings as 'race records' until the 1940s. Of course, this history seeks to highlight how in turn it also constructs notions of 'blackness' – inherently linked to criminality, drinking, violence and sexual excess – for the largely white audiences that bought these records.[28] Indubitably, this is just one (prominent) version of the history of the blues; there is of course no singular or authoritative version – and indeed other scholars and musicians have contested at least aspects of such accounts.[29] However, its complete omission in the service of a transparently mimetic, essentialising and naturalised account is troubling both politically and in terms of Lacoue-Labarthe's own critique of mimeticism. Comparably, Lacoue-

---

[27] Though he does offer a different description of jazz in the brief 'Remarque sur Adorno et le jazz, d'un désart obscur' in Lacoue-Labarthe, *Pour n'en pas finir*.

[28] Of course this is also a woefully inadequate explanation of the emergence of blues cultures, but it serves merely to highlight some of the aspects that have been overlooked in Lacoue-Labarthe's construction.

[29] For a variety of positions see, for example, work by Paul Gilroy, Henry Louis Gates, Jr, Angela Y. Davis, Houston A. Baker, Elijah Wald and Richard Middleton.

Labarthe finds a similar phenomenon with rap and hip hop, which he claims to be another vocal music that derives directly from the vernacular of young blacks, this time living in the suburbs of Los Angeles, which when transposed to France becomes the vernacular of the Maghreb or other Africans living in the *banlieue*. Here, Lacoue-Labarthe's argument starts to collapse, even in its own terms: does rap thus correspond to ('badly') spoken English or French? Or are black American and black or Maghrebi French all so generically 'other' that it ceases to matter to distinguish between them? And does rap *music* have nothing to do with it after all? His justification seems to be, indirectly, that (white?) people find it much harder to rap successfully – 'ceux dont la langue natale est le français ont beaucoup plus de mal à s'y faire' ['for those whose mother tongue is French it is a much harder task'] (CM, p. 33) – and therefore it must have something to do with the way non-white people *speak*; their (lexical) *style*. No doubt, stylistics has something to with the overall aesthetic but, firstly, many French rappers *do* in fact speak French as their native language (white or not); secondly, this characterisation erodes the complex socio-economic and cultural conditions with which this music is linked as well as its (often) engaged politicism; and, thirdly, it completely ignores not only the musical/instrumental (where present) but also the richly literary and complexly crafted reliance on word play, extended metaphor, alliteration, double entendre and lyricism in exchange for a simplistic homological mapping onto the prosodic aspects of the vernacular. While it is easy to demonstrate the problematic underpinnings of this type of argument when Lacoue-Labarthe speaks of popular music forms through his omission of their complex and well-studied relationship to social, political and cultural concerns – these musics are so often studied sociologically (rather than in terms of aesthetics) in relation to the sub-cultures from which they emerge or are a part of – it perhaps rouses less immediate suspicion in the passages dealing with literate high art music; the possible reasons for which I will now address.

CULTURE, HISTORY AND ABSOLUTE MUSIC

In *The Imaginary Museum of Musical Works: An Essay in the Philosophy of Music*, Lydia Goehr launches a compelling critique of the way analytic philosophy has attempted to apprehend or conceptualise the musical work. Her argument is centred around the fact that analytic philosophy tends to treat its subject matter scientifically or naturalistically, and thus 'tallies with the belief that concepts are historically and ideologically neutral, unaffected by contingent changes, and undetermined in all essential respects by those "myths" or "prejudices" inherent in our different cultural, social, political and aesthetic milieux'.[30] Goehr is struck by the limited repertoire that philosophers consider when trying to make generalising claims about the 'nature' of music, asking why it is that

> theorists have chosen to focus on classical, concert music? For what reasons have ancient, Asian, folk, jazz and popular forms of music mostly been left out of the inquiry? These are complicated questions, and they are made all the more so when we realise that even 'classical music' is a troublesome concept which, having entered musical language at the turn of the nineteenth century, has already taken on two distinct meanings: to denote music written in 'classical style' in the second half of the eighteenth century and to denote European 'concert' music in its entirety.[31]

Goehr explores a variety of theories from different branches of analytic philosophy and demonstrates that as soon as one tries to apply their definition or description of what music *is* to a non-Western, popular, folk or non-literate musical tradition it starts to fall short – or outright fail. She thus proposes a genealogical or historical approach to musical ontology; an approach that exposes the context of a particular concept and is thus able to 'contribute to knowledge and, when desirable, social change'.[32] Although this critique could be seen to have little purchase on Lacoue-Labarthe's work – he is, after all, a decidedly continental philosopher, and he does consider more than just 'classical' music, at least in *Le Chant des Muses* and on the odd occasion in some of the essays collected in *Pour n'en pas finir* – I think its aptness is rather striking; unsurprisingly, it has been in relation to his claims about popular music or 'classical' (in the sense of genre, rather than epoch) music that either pre- or post-dates the formation of the classical/Romantic canon that the problematic aspects of his conceptualisation of music are most clear.

In both 'L'Écho du sujet' and in *Le Chant des Muses*, there is a notable lack of consideration as to what actually constitutes the musical 'work'. While Lacoue-Labarthe's arguments about the essential link to the 'musical' aspects of spoken language might lead us to think that he is considering music primarily as performance, the recourse to Mahler (and particularly the programmatic elements of the 'Resurrection' Symphony which both Reik and Lacoue-Labarthe rely on) in 'L'Écho du sujet' is contingent on aspects also present in the score-copy of the work and certain 'syntactical' procedures (of which more later).

---

[30] Goehr, *The Imaginary Museum of Musical Works*, p. 78.
[31] Ibid., p. 80.
[32] Ibid., p. 4.

Music's allographic nature is thus completely unaccounted for; music is at once both instantiated through performance, and yet no performance is identical to the work 'itself' (nor is it identical to the score). This problem has been dealt with in a number of ways, as Goehr has explored, but what attempts at reconciling this difficulty have in common is the failure to recognise this as a product of a certain historical conceptualisation of the musical 'work' that is specific to a particular time period and geographical area. Indeed, *literate* musical traditions are themselves a minority form, with the concept of the absolute musical 'work' (i.e. un-texted, bound, autonomous, sublime and accessible through the almost *unworldly* composer-genius) specific to just a few hundred years of European musical history. Given this, musicologist Gary Tomlinson has even suggested we would do well to substitute 'carmenology' or 'cantology' for 'musicology', given that by far the dominant form of 'music' – globally and historically – is song forms; a move that 'might unsettle rather than confirm our easiest assumptions' as well as 'serv[ing] to remind us that music signifies not an ideologically neutral, cross-cultural array of sounding phenomena but rather a constructed cultural category – one indeed that is, as we delimit it, and viewed against the long historical *durée*, recent and local'.[33] Furthermore, the ideology of this supposedly autonomous musical aesthetic emerges alongside Romantic idealism in general, and can be described as 'an interplay between two claims': 'The first claim concerns the *transcendent* move from the worldly and particular to the spiritual and universal; the second concerns the *formalist* move which brought meaning from music's outside into its inside.'[34] Whereas when Lacoue-Labarthe asks, early on in Le Chant des Muses, 'pourquoi fait-on de la musique?' or 'pourquoi y a-t-il la musique?' ['Why do we make music? Why is there music?'] (CM, p. 16) and argues that it must be something to do with our very first emotions, Goehr would remind us that until about 1800 the response to 'why' or 'what' is music would have been answered with regard to its '*extra-musical* function and significance [. . .] shaped by the functions music served in powerful institutions like the church and the court'.[35] Music, in its Romantic conception, has henceforth been 'separated' from the mundane and quotidian, the transient and mortal, and instead allows for the unmediated *immediacy* of expression. Accordingly, the classical music forms – the concerto, symphony and 'sonata form' in particular as the archetypes – are not contingent on any 'extra-musical' occasion but

---

[33] Gary Tomlinson, 'Vico's Songs', pp. 344–77 (p. 344).
[34] Goehr, *The Imaginary Museum of Musical Works*, p. 153.
[35] Ibid., p. 122.

are 'independently designed and independently coherent'.[36] Thus, with Schopenhauer and Nietzsche clearly on the horizon, we see how easy it is for music – under this conception – to be understood as expressing (pure) will and primary essences.

Classical music forms, and 'sonata form' in particular, invite us to consider another aspect that is remarkably overlooked – perhaps symptomatically – by Lacoue-Labarthe: harmony. Central to the construction of these musical forms is the role of functional harmony and the supposedly autonomous dialectic of tones. In sonata form, which is the quintessential form of the first movement of any symphony, a dialectic is set up between the first 'subject' (or thesis) in the tonic key and a contrasting second 'subject' (antithesis) in a related key, followed by a development section where these ideas are explored and expanded, leading finally to a recapitulation where both subjects return, but this time with the second subject co-opted into the same key as the first subject (synthesis).[37] The extent to which we can straightforwardly read socialities or cultural forms – for example, the first (often heroic) subject has been frequently characterised as 'masculine', with the second (often lyrical) subject marked as 'feminine' – onto musical forms has been hotly contested.[38] Nonetheless, the teleological drive of functional harmony is at least one of the ways in which tension and release, passion and desire – and thus subjectivity – are constructed or represented in this repertoire. Susan McClary has demonstrated that the emergence of tonality – and its standardisation in thinkers/composers such as Rameau, as seen in the previous chapter – is a musical convention that is constructed/constructs analogously 'to such [eighteenth-century] emergent ideals as rationality, individualism, progress, and centred subjectivity'.[39] In this respect, the autonomous tonal works of the concert hall parallel the emergence of bourgeois subjectivity, particularly in the way in which they both project teleologically through time a nonetheless coherent and organic whole; an entity with an identifiable essence. Further still, in a recent Bourdieusian ethnography of classical music practices, Anna Bull has argued convincingly that bourgeois ideals are built into the aesthetic and its contingent practices. Discipline and restraint – long-documented cornerstones of bourgeois identity – are cultivated through classical music practices

---

[36] Ibid., p. 164.
[37] The Hegelian overtones of this standard musicological explication of sonata form are far from coincidental.
[38] See, for a variety of positions, work by Susan McClary, Richard Taruskin, Lawrence Kramer and Georgina Born.
[39] Susan McClary, *Conventional Wisdom*, p. 61.

and, significantly, are 'inscribed onto the body in rehearsals'.[40] It is all too easy to forget that this supposedly autonomous music isn't just played spontaneously, but that the idealised version we get either in the concert hall or in recorded forms is the product of innumerable hours of work – an extraordinary amount of labour (in fact, we would do well here to remember Lacoue-Labarthe's own assertion that we must allow ourselves to hear the *ergon* beneath the *organon* (see FP, p. 108; HAP, p. 68)). Aside from the hours dedicated to private practice, the orchestral player submits to hours spent stop-and-start – an essential rehearsal procedure if one is to coordinate 60-odd players into a seemingly organic whole – under the control of the conductor who, in turn, sculpts or forms the ideal aesthetic. In so doing, Bull argues that it is not that enjoyable and pleasurable aspects of music are eradicated; quite inversely, strong and embodied emotions are cultivated but controlled – pleasure is instead channelled, or 'inheres in the *control over* the totality of the group and the musical whole'.[41] In this way, the ideology of this aesthetic – as abstract, rational, disembodied, and so on – is justified, demanding simultaneously bodily transcendence (individual desires, responses or pleasures must be subjugated to the demands of the whole) and the disciplining of these very bodies (that are nonetheless required to play this 'transcendent' music). This is just one way in which musical subjectivities might be formed or figured in line with the ideology of a particular aesthetic, no matter how abstract it might claim to be. We can thus see how music might be profoundly associated with, or experienced as, deeply emotional; that is to say above, beyond or aside from any pre-symbolic associations with the maternal voice.

Even though the bounds of the tonal dialectic are notably expanded in the musical language of Mahler's late Romanticism, which purposefully plays with the limits of these forms – and the central role of 'free-play' to the Romantic notion of autonomous music should be duly noted here, he never 'breaks' or escapes them; tonality even in its most expanded form remains central to the pulsional movement through time that allows for a sense of 'narrative' (which Lacoue-Labarthe is so keen to remark upon). And yet, Lacoue-Labarthe is absolutely silent about this when it comes to any question of what is 'essentially' musical; just as for Rousseau – who we have seen already to be so influential on Lacoue-Labarthe's thinking about music – harmony seems to be an inconvenient, corruptive or at least a *post hoc* embellishment of what

---

[40] Anna Bull, 'The Musical Body', p. 159.
[41] Ibid., p. 160.

is *essentially* musical (i.e. melody and rhythm). We therefore have a deeply contradictory understanding of music whereby Lacoue-Labarthe appears to want to claim it as a universal language (albeit against himself, we might imagine) by importing the musico-transcendental baggage of a Romantic conception of music, while also neglecting to take account of the role of functional harmony – the 'free' play of tones – which is clearly a, if not *the*, distinctive feature of this repertoire. While there is certainly a case to be made for a neo-Heideggerian project which seeks to relate music and/or rhythm to a deeper or more fundamental history of Being, and thus excludes the local or epochal aspects from its purview – in this case, perhaps, functional harmony – Lacoue-Labarthe nonetheless retains an unmistakable and epochally distinct conception of what music *is*, i.e. a bound and self-sufficient musical work with an identifiable and organic essence, stemming from a post-Romantic transcendentalising of aesthetics. Furthermore, such inherent conflicts (which are, necessarily, built into the very concept of such a thoroughly man-made 'offering' that nonetheless also claims cosmic transcendence) are found not only in recent philosophy but also in the work of the progenitors of this discourse, as Goehr argues is revealed by Kant's aesthetic claims and ideals: 'purposiveness without purpose' and 'disinterested attention'.[42] Having suppressed the 'spatial axis of harmony', music's drive through time is understood only as a rhythmic repetition compulsion which forcefully impels its writing/written subject regardless; it is, as Catherine Pickstock argues, just a 'version of music as a universal language, which perpetuates the Wagnerian error' – despite Lacoue-Labarthe's damning critique of Wagner elsewhere[43] – 'of imagining that music has a "pure" essence, free from the mediation of verbal and symbolic convention'.[44]

CATACOUSTICS I

With all this in mind, it seems potentially fruitful to bring such perspectives to bear on Lacoue-Labarthe's most sustained development of the musical or catacoustic subject as figured in 'L'Écho du sujet', largely via his analysis of Reik's auto-analysis. Lacoue-Labarthe seems always to be interested in moments of failure; moments that reveal, foreclose or short-circuit some 'deeper' logic at work, and, for this reason, offer themselves as hermeneutic windows worthy of decon-

---

[42] See Goehr, *The Imaginary Museum of Musical Works*, p. 158.
[43] This is most evident, of course, in *Musica Ficta*, as well as in a number of the essays in *Pour n'en pas finir* and is a question to which we will return in Chapter 5.
[44] Catherine Pickstock, 'Music: Soul, City and Cosmos after Augustine', pp. 243–77 (p. 255).

structive philosophical reflection or praxis. Indeed, in 'L'Écho du sujet', it is Reik's failure to realise what is at work, unwittingly binding the musical obsession (catharsis), the autobiographical impulse and lexis (as style) together. Moreover, in this instance, according to Lacoue-Labarthe, Reik's failure is, paradoxically, his success; what Reik's text reveals – perhaps more profoundly than Reik realised – is the failure of the theoretical *tout court*. Lacoue-Labarthe – having articulated his conception of the abyssal and 'desistant' subject that is neither the writing nor written subject but rather permanently lost 'between' the two in order to explain, *contra* Plato, that first-person narrative, or *haple diegesis*, is strictly speaking impossible – returns to a key moment in The Haunting Melody in order to expose what Reik has implicitly identified as the autobiographical impulse (as opposed to the autothanatography that is actually written). The excerpt is, appropriately, *en abyme:* an extended citation from the programmatic description of Mahler's Second Symphony. It describes how, on the way back from the funeral of someone important, one finds oneself reminded of happy memories such that the overwhelming grief provoked by this person's death is temporarily lifted or forgotten. As one (re)awakens from this, not only is one filled with guilt, but

> il se peut que [. . .] l'incompréhensible remue-ménage de cette vie devienne agitation fantomatique de silhouettes dans une salle de danse; de la nuit profonde, vous regardez, mais c'est si loin que vous ne pouvez entendre la musique. Il vous manque le rythme, clef de ces mouvements; les tournoiements, les virevoltes de ces couples vous paraissent insensés.
>
> [it may be that the [. . .] never understandable bustle of life becomes ghastly as the moving of dancing figures in an illuminated dance hall into which you look from the dark night, from so far away that you cannot hear the music. The turning and moving of the couples appears then to be senseless.] (Reik, cited in ES$_1$, p. 282; ES$_2$, p. 193)

In short, as Lacoue-Labarthe notes, he is describing the 'étrangement du familier' ['estrangement of the familiar'] (ES$_1$, p. 283; ES$_2$, p. 194), a thoroughly *unheimlich* scene. Crucially, then, what this reveals for Lacoue-Labarthe is that rhythm 's'entend. Il ne se voit pas [. . .] Sans rythme [. . .] la danse (c'est une valse) se désorganise et se défigure. Autrement dit, le rythme, qui est ici d'essence spécifiquement musicale (acoustique), est antérieur à la figure ou au schème visible dont il conditionne l'apparition comme telle' ['is heard. It is not seen [. . .] without rhythm [. . .] the dance (it is a waltz) becomes disorganized and disfigured. In other words, rhythm, of a specifically musical (acoustic) essence here, is prior to the figure or the visible schema whose appearance, as such [. . .] it conditions'] (ES$_1$, p. 283;

ES$_2$, p. 194), In other words, the rhythmic impulse is both pre-specular and the precondition of the specular, 'la *répétition* ou la contrainte temporelle (et non topologique ou spatiale) comme facteur de diversification à partir de quoi peut se reconnaître, s'installer et se disposer du réel' ['the *repetition* or temporal (not topological or spatial) constraint that acts as a means of diversification by which the real might be recognized, established, and disposed'] (ES$_1$, p. 283; ES$_2$, p. 194), both impelling and undoing, eliciting and interrupting the whole theoretical framework from within. Likewise, rhythm is also 'la condition de possibilité du sujet' ['the condition of possibility for the subject'] (ES$_1$, p. 285; ES$_2$, p. 195), and yet it 'excède, commence à excéder ou à entamer l'économique. À le ruiner de l'intérieur' ['begins to exceed and broach the subject's economy, and ruin it from within'] (ES$_1$, p. 277; ES$_2$, p. 189). As Amittai Aviram has observed, this would place Lacoue-Labarthe, alongside Nancy, firmly in the Nietzschean tradition that Kristeva assumes in her characterisation of the *chora*, for whom 'the musical or rhythmic is a state of being outside of and prior to the social, verbal, thinking subject, while the latter is a kind of construct that simultaneously represents (in images and in symbols) and represses its musical other, which is also its origin'.[45]

Fortunately, however, Lacoue-Labarthe does not leave it there. Having set out with the intention of finding the link between the autobiographical impulse and the musical obsession – now identified as, essentially, (pre-specular) 'rythme' – he suddenly retracts and suggests that actually 'il faudrait probablement désolidariser, autant qu'il est possible de le faire, la question du rythme [. . .] de toute problématique *musicale*' ['it would probably be necessary to dissociate as much as possible the question of rhythm from any *musical* problematic'] (ES$_1$, p. 289; ES$_2$, p. 199). To explain this claim he complicates what appeared to be a more or less straightforward conception of rhythm; rhythm now bifurcates into what seems to be a modern, Platonic idea (i.e. what he has articulated so far) and a more ancient notion (pre-Socratic, following Leuccipus, Democritus and Heraclitus). Via Benveniste, again, he explains how '*rhuthmos* ou *rhusmos* [. . .] signifie primitivement schema: la forme ou la figure' ['*rhuthmos* or *rhusmos* [. . .] means originally [. . .] form or figure'] ES$_1$, p. 289; ES$_2$, pp. 199–200), and is, rather, 'rhythm' (or whatever we now want to call it) as broached by time; it is 'la forme dans l'instant qu'elle est assumée par ce qui est mouvant, mobile, fluide, la forme qui n'a pas de consistance organique [. . .] improvisée, momentanée,

---

[45] Aviram, *Telling Rhythm*, p. 197.

modifiable' ['the form at the moment it is taken by what is in movement, mobile, fluid, the form that has no organic consistency [...] improvised, momentaneous, modifiable'] (Benveniste, cited in ES_1, pp. 290–1; ES_2, p. 201). In the coming together of these two aspects, then, is where we find what has previously been identified as *ethos*: type, imprint, style (*lexis*), etc. Concomitantly, then, there is also an uninterrupted filial link in the movement 'du type à la disposition (*Stimmung*), à l'humeur et à ce qu'on n'appelle quand même pas en vain le *caractère*' ['from the type to disposition (*Stimmung*), to humor and what is not inappropriately called the *character*'] (ES_1, p. 290; ES_2, p. 200), a relation that is best understood, unsurprisingly, as an 'echo'. Finally, then, Lacoue-Labarthe returns briefly to the properly *musical* problematic, to remind us that even in the *Republic*, music is subject to the same distinctions as linguistic discourse: *logos* and *lexis*. Musical discourse is dealt with (as Lacoue-Labarthe has also done so far) as the strict equivalent of *lexis*, enunciation; however, unlike *lexis* itself (in discourse) specifically *musical lexis* is, Lacoue-Labarthe argues, itself mimetic. Music 'doit s'accommoder (*akolouthein*) au *logos*' ['must accommodate itself (*akolouthein*) to the *logos*'] (ES_1, p. 291; ES_2, p. 201). Music (or rather, musical lexis) is subsequently understood as fundamentally imitative (but, crucially, as with his figuring of originary mimesis, without origin). And, indeed, this is achieved 'selon des critères au reste fixes, traditionnels, soit (et cela concerne principalement l'harmonie) des traits "éthiques" (mollesse, supplication, violence, courage); soit, quant il s'agit du rythme, des *caractères*' ['according to fixed, traditional criteria, whether these relate (principally as regards harmony) to "ethical" traits (lack of vigor, suppliance, violence, courage), or, in the case of rhythm, to characters'] (ES_1, p. 292; ES_2, p. 201). In this way, pre-specular rhythm (the measure, metre and prosody of the mother's voice *in utero*) is 'calculé sur la *diction* en tant qu'elle imite ou représente un *caractère*' ['judged in relation to *diction* inasmuch as this imitates or represents a *character*'] (ES_1, p. 292; ES_2, p. 202), and *this* rhythm (as broached by time) – just as with the *unheimlich* dance movements witnessed, soundless, at a distance – is social, conventional and historical. Perhaps here it would be wise to recall the muses' profound link with both politics and (correct, virtuous) education (*paideia*) and, thus, in a modern formulation, *Bildung*, which at root literally means form(ation). As Azade Seyhan has claimed in a different – but not altogether unrelated – context, the literary (or musical) work 'becomes the embodiment or sensory representation of knowledge'.⁴⁶ Rhythm allows the manifestation of the always ungraspable *ethos*, therefore, at the perceptible but inassimilable interstices of consonance and dissonance, *eurythmy* and *arrhythmia* (see ES_1, p. 292; ES_2, p. 202). And this is the case just as much with music as with language, and is why, Lacoue-Labarthe claims, via Reik, that 'le retour du choral de Mahler était simplement dû à l'analogie des circonstances [... et par conséquent] n'excède en rien les limites officielles de la psychanalyse' ['the return of Mahler's chorale wa due simply to an analogy of circumstances [... and consequently] does not exceed in any way the official limits of psychoanalysis'] (ES_1, p. 293; ES_2, p. 203).

CATACOUSTICS II: EDUCATION, FORMATION, PAIDEIA

> As my father I have already died, as my mother I am still living and growing old.
> Nietzsche⁴⁷

There is, therefore, an implicit if undeveloped way of thinking a political and ecological philosophy of music – in the sense that music is a spatio-temporal, technical and aesthetic way in which humans (inter) relate to, create or constitute, their social, cultural and historical environments – in Lacoue-Labarthe's formulation of what he describes as a 'catacoustic' musical subject. Perhaps none of this is so surprising, given the essential link between music, *mousike*, the muses, and education (*paideia*) and cultural values in ancient Greek thought – as laid out in the first chapter – and Lacoue-Labarthe's reformulation of mimesis – itself central to education. I would like to suggest that what is essential and most fruitful in Lacoue-Labarthe's thinking of music – itself a category I hope to have shown is, in itself, in need of deconstruction – is both the emphasis he places on the constitutive technicity of music (the need of instruments, organs, training, practical and compositional techniques) and his rather insistent (re)linking of its relation to *mousike* (*techne*) which, as we have seen, comprises all the skills of the muses and, as we have noted in Chapter 1, is broadly synonymous with our modern concept of culture. By this measure, music is unthinkable except in relation to the social (and therefore the cultural, political, and so on) and is imbued with – and imbues – social, cultural, educational and moral values. Lacoue-Labarthe's careful and

---

[46] Seyhan, *Representation and Its Discontents*, p. 18.
[47] Friedrich Nietzsche, *Ecce Homo*, p. 7.

patient tracing of the deeper history of rhythm as intimately linked to '*la forme ou la figure*', and thus to sculpture, offers a powerful image of, or way of thinking about, music's role in sculpting or forming citizens in line with the cultural and social values of the time. It also allows us to think about how music participates in the very model of education that Lacoue-Labarthe himself has so rigorously critiqued: that of exemplarity (a model that has been summarised elsewhere, quite succinctly, by Jaeger: 'Education is the process by which a community preserves and transmits its physical character. For the individual passes away, but the type remains'[48]). From this vantage point, even the most abstract aesthetic partakes in the sculpting of bodies, minds, desires and values; as an intellectual and a physical education, *mousike* figures or forms both individual and social characters: in short, *ethos*.[49] In this respect, Lacoue-Labarthe's choice of *katakouein* (meaning 'to listen' and 'to obey') seems particularly apt, inviting as it does a consideration of how music is imbricated in the socio-politic and also relates to power, control and ideology. It gestures towards the compelling 'nature' of music (that both Reik and Lacoue-Labarthe feel so keenly on an emotional level) while also suggesting that this arises – at least substantially – from the co-individuation of social and personal norms, values and aesthetic preferences, rather than from an extra-worldly reservoir of truth, spirit or pure, unbridled emotion that only music has direct access to. Furthermore, it also allows – as Lacoue-Labarthe has made abundantly clear – for an account of how the (musical) writing subject also always writes another: style, whether musical, literary or philosophical (here Lacoue-Labarthe's careful deconstruction of a straightforward distinction between music and language is particularly useful), betrays the duplicity of the subject, and the ever-present other that can be traced in any (auto-/allo- or bio-/thanato-) graphical gesture. Catacoustics thus offers a compelling way of thinking about music's role – and a role moreover that does not differ substantially from literature, the visual or plastic arts, philosophy, science or psychoanalysis – in processes of meaning-making, mimesis, the creation and upholding of values, and the formation of minds, bodies and desires in irreducibly cultural, aesthetic and political ways.

In fact, another well-known text draws together so many of these same themes: autobiography, style, education, ethics, the ear and hearing (and its *unheimlich* nature), and the mother tongue: Derrida's *Otobiographies*. Moreover, within it, Derrida highlights a

---

[48] Werner Jaeger, *Paideia: The Ideals of Greek Culture*, p. xiii, cited in Iain D. Thomson, *Heidegger on Ontotheology*, p. 155 n. 13.
[49] See Babich, *Words in Blood, like Flowers*, p. 100.

distinction between educational institutions (which he characterises as 'acoustique' and 'acroamatique' – arcane, exclusive, cerebral and predominantly oral, as in Aristotle's teachings for his inner circle), and texts/venues which are meant for public consumption and are thus accessible: the very duality we have between the two texts at hand here – Lacoue-Labarthe's *Le Chant des muses* and 'L'Écho du sujet'. For all Lacoue-Labarthe's tentative distancing, and his reluctance to be named as a 'philosophe', he is no doubt partaking in the very discourses he is critiquing – there could be no other way, of course – and it is striking that the text destined for a wider public consumption, *Le Chant des Muses*, makes claims, quite emphatically, that the far more sophisticated and nuanced 'L'Écho du sujet' appears to make but only with reluctance, caveat or in a non-committal manner. There is no reading of *Le Chant des muses* that allows for such a complex articulation of how we might think about music and its relation to the social, preferring instead the thoroughly naturalised account of music's fundamental link to the mother tongue and thus to emotions. While on one level this might be explained as a consequence of the genre – after all, the teenagers to whom the text was originally addressed have not had the years of philosophical training required to grapple with something as dense as 'L'Écho du sujet' – it nonetheless seems irresponsible to fill impressionable young minds with claims that one would not sign one's name (or 'name') to, at least wholeheartedly, in a properly academic context.

So, to return to Derrida's *Otobiographies* which reads, among other things, Nietzsche's *On the Future of Our Educational Institutions*, and highlights both a critique of the cultural machinery of the state – particularly of the (university) education system functioning under the illusion of academic freedom – while also suggesting the possibility of a subterranean fascism at work, depending on the interpretation of Nietzsche's text. The educational institution is figured as an *omphalos* – an indistinguishable ear/mouth/umbilical cord that connects the student to the institution and thus to the state. The state educational institution, acting in place of the mother, in fact forges a link with the (dead) father/state; it is in this power – this co-optation of the living mother in service of the dead father – that Derrida locates the uncanny and the text's potential fascism, while also commenting on the specifics of the ear/hearing (as we have seen elsewhere) and the fact that the ear is the most 'open' organ, the organ famously without eyelids and thus the possibility of closure. As the students take notes, the (uncritical, for all the emphasis on academic freedom) passive ears accept and transmit through their pens – a profusion of umbilical cords – the teachings of the state. From a singular mouthpiece, the academic apparatus is multiplied into many ears and hands, the 'établissement pour la culture (*Bildungsanstalt*)' ['cultural establishment'].[50] Again, we are returned to familiar themes such as posterity, (auto)biography and the writing subject; through the writing and signing of a name – the father's (or the state's) name – we are returned to immortality; we continue to live after our death by signing a (dead) patronymic with the still living pen (umbilical cord) of the (m)other. The supposedly living feminine (with the name 'woman' standing at the origin of the (re)production of 'truth') is thus instrumentalised in the service of signing the dead father's name.[51]

MUSES, MEMORY, MATERNALITY

> Selon une très ancienne, très profonde et très solide équivalence – peut-être indestructible –, c'est [la musique] un art féminin, et destiné aux femmes ou à la part féminine des hommes. C'est un art, en tous sens, hystérique. Et c'est pour cette raison, essentiellement, que la musique est l'hystérie. Tout au moins une certaine musique.
> Lacoue-Labarthe[52]

So, then, the question beneath all of this – just as in Lacoue-Labarthe's 'L'Écho du sujet' – continues to be how and with what name do we sign, and how is this essentially – constitutively – a signing of (an) other? Unfortunately, (this time), Lacoue-Labarthe does not stop at the catacoustic and socialised account of music offered already. He returns to the question of music, and specifically the question of why it seems to have such a profound emotional effect on us. In turning to a different text in Reik's œuvre, *The Ritual*, he explains that Reik had once thought that rhythm was not, essentially, musical. In this text, Reik explores myths about the origin of music, discovering that primitive and archaic instruments in the Jewish (biblical) tradition cannot, properly, be considered as instruments, but as mere 'machine[s] à faire du bruit' ['noise-making machine[s]'] (ES_1, p. 294; ES_2, p. 204). This impels Reik to a deeper meditation on the shofar, which as a primitive

---

[50] Derrida, Lévesque and McDonald, *L'Oreille de l'autre*, p. 52 [Derrida, *The Ear of the Other*, p. 35].
[51] See Gayatri Chakrovroty Spivak, 'Feminism and Deconstruction, Again: Negotiating with Unacknowledged Masculinism' in Teresa Brennan (ed.), *Between Feminism and Psychoanalysis*, pp. 206–24 (p. 216).
[52] MF_1, p. 198 [According to a very old, very profound, and very solid equivalence – perhaps indestructible – it [music] is a *feminine* art, destined for women or for the feminine part of men. It is a *hysterical* art, in every sense. And for this reason, essentially, music *is* hysteria. At least, a particular music (MF_2, p. 105)].

'instrument' with which he is familiar, leads him to recognise the profound and unusual emotional effect, despite the fact that '[l]es trois groupes de notes [...] ne se différencient que *par un changement de rythme*' ['The three sets of sounds [...] *are only distinguishable by change of rhythm*'] (Reik cited in ES_1, p. 295; ES_2, p. 204, Lacoue-Labarthe's emphasis). As a result of this, he decides that the shofar is 'plus proche d'un instrument de percussion, de la crécelle primitive ou du *bullroarer* décrit par les ethnologues, que de la trompe ou du clarion' ['closer to a percussion instrument, to the primitive rattle or the *bullroarer* described by ethnologists, than to the horn or bugle'] (ES_1, p. 294; ES_2, p. 204); its profound emotional effect comes from the way it somehow reconnects us with something archaic and unknown. Ultimately, then, Lacoue-Labarthe considers it as an 'appel à la résurrection' ['call to resurrection'] (ES_1, p. 295; ES_2, p. 204) (not forgetting to remind us once more of the subject of Mahler's Second Symphony; again, claims Lacoue-Labarthe, music saves us from our own death), and in this 'point énigmatique' he locates this deep emotion's resistance to analysis.

The result of this is twofold, elucidates Lacoue-Labarthe: firstly, Reik suspects that something non- or ante-musical is understandable in terms of rhythm; secondly, that 'l'émotion que provoque en nous telle "musique" archaïque n'est pas une émotion proprement musicale' ['the emotion elicited in us by such an archaic "music" is not a properly musical emotion'] (ES_1, p. 295; ES_2, p. 204). Thus it appears that music is not in itself the cause of the emotion – at least in the sense of eliciting or producing an emotion due to purely musical procedures – but that music, or 'musical' rhythm, remains, somehow, linked to the sense of something that precedes, but nonetheless determines us; it is the point of access that allows us, anamnesically, to recognise something fundamentally (pre-) originary. Though never mentioned explicitly, much of this would seem to tally with Lacoue-Labarthe's conviction that mimesis – and what seems to be its complex but essential relation to the musical, rhythmic or catacoustic constitution of the subject – is of an older and deeper nature than the properly Heideggerian problematic of the history of Being. The rough and raw power of the proto-musical shofar is thus understood, Lacoue-Labarthe states, as the repetition of the inaugural murder of the *Urvater* – the well-known origin of art as proposed by Freud in *Totem and Taboo* – but this time recast with 'music' rather than tragedy as its first resounding.[53] This is not

---

[53] Though there is perhaps no fundamental distinction to be made here (i.e. between music and tragedy) – especially given the way in which Lacoue-Labarthe understands our modern conception of music (*savante*) to be inextricably bound up in its quest to reinvigorate

surprising though, Lacoue-Labarthe says, given that precisely what we have established is that the analytic, or theoretical, schema necessarily involves a specular reduction, and thus we are always returned to the (theatrical) Oedipal scene (see ES_1, p. 296; ES_2, pp. 204–5); the hated or feared father who inspires, encouraged by 'la préférence maternelle qui [. . .] suscite le premier héros-poète' ['the maternal preference that inspires the first hero-poet'] (ES_1, p. 296; ES_2, p. 205), to the collective, foundational, but phantasmatic, murder. Again, we are trapped at the specular threshold, where music can incite in us some recollection of something pre-originary, and yet is also only attainable from the vantage of an ineluctably scopic/theoretical (and thus theatrical) schema.

But there is more. Although Lacoue-Labarthe cautions that, strictly speaking, going beyond the specular model is quite impossible, he nonetheless suggests – noting the 'voix maternelles' ['maternal voices'] that overwhelmed the musician-philosopher, Nietzsche – that the musical 'echo' corresponds to the mother: 'De quoi d'autre que la mère pourrait-il y avoir au juste réminiscence?' ['Of what else, other than the mother, could there in fact be reminiscence?'] (ES_1, p. 297; ES_2, p. 205). And this is where 'L'Écho du sujet' rejoins with *Le Chant des Muses*: in both instances the conclusion is linked to an essential maternality. Lacoue-Labarthe reminds us in *Le Chant des Muses* that the infant *in utero* cannot distinguish between its body and that of its mother – space or distance (between the mother and child) does not yet exist; rather, anything (any sound) provokes an immediate reaction, a movement, the child is '*ému*' [moved, stirred, etc.]; music is thus first and foremost an art of emotion. Furthermore, and perhaps more clearly than in 'L'Écho du sujet' – although I think it is implicit there too – this echoing of an originary maternal emotion is linked to instrumentation and amplification. This allows him to reaffirm his earlier claim that although, as we have seen, *prosody* (song) is linked to the mother tongue, music is necessarily also a *techne*, and thus dependent on instruments. Given that the transmission of sound isn't immediate like sight (although how this stands in relation to his much earlier claim that sound is 'pire que les images, qu'on peut à tout moment ne pas regarder, il y a la musique à laquelle on ne peut pas échapper' ['worse than images, which at any moment one can choose not to look at, there is music from which there is no escape'] (CM, p. 18)) we thus need assistance in order to '*clarifier* – de lui donner une puissance qu'elle n'a pas' ['*clarify* – to give it a power that it does not have']; the task of music is to '*clarifier* l'étouffement

itself in the spirit of Greek tragedy – the elaboration of this line of thinking is the subject of Chapter 5. This all obviously rings heavy with Nietzschean overtones: see, of course, Nietzsche, *The Birth of Tragedy*.

(maternel) du son' ['clarify the (maternal) suffocation of sound'] (CM, p. 37).[54] This helps explain an earlier claim that no matter the style or genre of a song, in order to sing 'de manière vraiment artistique, il faut un apprentissage encore plus difficile' ['in a truly artistic way, it is necessary to undergo a gruelling training'] (CM, p. 29). This makes of it a properly *technical* art, distinct from the utterly naturalistic 'music' of the mother's *melos* though we can 'retrouve[r] un peu de la musique *d'avant* (la naissance) ou de la musique "antérieure" dont j'ai parlé' ['refind a little of the music from *before* (birth) or the "anterior" music of which I spoke'] (CM, p. 30). Further still, it allows him to explain the concern over amplification in general – Bach's desire for an ever-bigger organ or the permanently expanding Romantic orchestra (see CM, p. 41) – as the search, the attempt to *retrouver* that very first *émoi* [emotion] (*é-moi* [and me]). Finally, then, in 'L'Écho du sujet', Lacoue-Labarthe reintegrates the *unheimlich* to complete the picture:

> Quoi d'autre pourrait en nous résonner, faire écho, nous paraître familier? Rappelez-vous: 'l'antique patrie des enfants des hommes', 'l'endroit où chacun a dû séjourner en son temps d'abord' – le 'je connais cela, j'ai déjà été ici.' Je l'ai déjà entendu, donc. Platon pensait que ce sont les mères qui imposent ou impriment à chacun son type. Par quoi d'autre en effet serions-nous 'rythmés'?
>
> [What else could echo, resonate in us, seem familiar to us? Let us recall the 'place where each of us once dwelled,' the 'I know this, I've already been here' – and thus, 'I've already heard it.' Plato thought that mothers are the ones who impose or imprint upon each of us our type. How else, in fact, would we be 'rythmed'?] (ES$_1$, p. 297; ES$_2$, p. 206)

In both instances, in order to work this theoretical (re)positioning the same manoeuvre is performed: he invokes the help of science – or at least a scientist of sorts! Despite claiming early on in *Le Chant des Muses* that although science might have interesting things to say about music, he is nonetheless going to treat it from a purely philosophical perspective, at the final hurdle (as already mentioned) he makes 'un petit tour du côté de la science' (CM, p. 24). It is clear that without this foundation he has no way of claiming that the only sense available to the infant *in utero* is that of the mother's voice – indeed this is not a position that philosophy alone could prove (nor, for that matter, is there scientific clarity on the matter) – and thus his essentialising claims about the natural (maternal and emotional) basis of music fall short. Perhaps

---

[54] Though 'clarify' reads slightly oddly in English, I have decided to retain the English cognate because of Lacoue-Labarthe's insistence on his choice of 'clarification', which comes from the Latin *clarus* and was used originally as an adjective to describe the voice, and not for colours and/or light.

more spectacularly – although he is careful not to claim it, *explicitly*, as proof of his theoretical position – in 'L'Écho du sujet', he turns to a short 1927 text, 'Musique et inconscient', by Georg Groddeck, a physician, psychoanalyst and founder of psychosomatic medicine. He claims that he is 'l'un des rares [psychanalystes] au demeurant à s'être affronté au problème de la musique' ['one of the few [psychoanalysts], finally, to have confronted the problem of music'] (ES_1, p. 297; ES_2, p. 206); the excerpt he offers us is extraordinary in its own right, articulating (with the authority of an early twentieth-century psychoanalyst who certainly considers his work 'science') this very point that Lacoue-Labarthe has been so keen to make: the role of the uterine sensory environment in forming the essential musicality – and thus music's essence – of the not-yet-subject. Groddeck states:

> Les données physiologiques de la période qui précède la naissance, où l'enfant n'a rien d'autre à découvrir par ses impressions que le rythme régulier du cœur maternel et du sien propre, mettent en lumière les moyens dont se sert la nature pour inculquer aussi profondément à l'homme le sentiment musical [. . .] le musical trouve son origine avant la naissance.
>
> [The psychological data from the period preceding birth, in which the infant discovers nothing from his own impressions but the regular rhythm of the mother's heart and his own, illuminate the means used by nature to inculcate in man a musical feeling [. . .] the musical has its origins before birth.][55]

This alone is evidently uncritical and problematic in the context of the discussions in both this chapter and the preceding one on Nancy. However, if we turn to the rest of the Groddeck text (un-cited in Lacoue-Labarthe's text except for the excerpt from which the above citation comes), which Lacoue-Labarthe without doubt must have read, the results are quite illuminating. While the excerpt seems at best naively idealistic and at worst misguidedly uncritical, the remainder of the text is manifestly problematic. Right from the beginning there is an 'unworlding' of music, or at least its withdrawal into unconscious desires and drives, when he states: 'la musique ne vient pas de la partie consciente de l'âme et ne s'adresse pas au conscient, mais sa force afflue de l'inconscient et agit sur l'inconscient' ['music does not come from the conscious part of the soul nor does it speak to consciousness, rather its power both flows from and acts upon the unconscious'].[56] More significantly, after a long etymological meditation on the word 'clef' he is able to make what seems to be his major point: that music

---

[55] Georg Groddeck, 'Musique et Inconscient', pp. 3–6 (p. 6), also cited in ES_1, p. 297; ES_2, p. 206.
[56] Groddeck, 'Musique et Inconscient', p. 3.

is both fundamentally linked to maternality – specifically the pregnant maternal body – and also to the mechanics of the reproductive act itself. He states that:

> l'étymologie a toujours de semblables affirmations quand elle touche à la reproduction et à la grossesse. De toute manière la clôture concerne un espace vide, elle est réalisée grâce à la clef [. . .] Prenons alors les cinq lignes et les quatre intervalles où sont les notes, on obtient le nombre neuf. Et neuf est le nombre de l'achèvement, de la grossesse. L'espace des notes serait par là le symbole de la mère nourricière, et la clef le symbole du masculin, qui féconde et ferme l'intérieur féminin.[57]

> [etymology always has such claims when it touches on reproduction and pregnancy. Anyhow, the closure concerns an empty space which is achieved by means of a key [. . .] If we take the five lines and four spaces upon which notes are placed, we get the number nine. And nine is the number of achievement of a full-term pregnancy. The space for the notes would in that way be the symbol of the nurturing mother and the key the masculine symbol which fertilises and closes the feminine interior.]

This passage is no doubt worthy of extensive commentary, but for now let us focus on two of the most striking aspects: firstly, the recurring theme that assumes that music (as an idea or concept in its ontological or metaphysical determination) is unambiguously equivalent to literate high art music produced in Europe over a few hundred years: 'classical' music. A move which, as already noted, voids the music of the social and cultural context of its production (and reception) figuring it instead as timeless, placeless, ahistoric, and a thoroughly neutral category. Secondly, although this occurs in explicitly gendered terms – and unsurprisingly also in terms of passivity and activity – it is the choice of *mère nourricière* (rather than simply *mère*) that strikes me as most interesting and instructive: it suggests not only a nurturing mother, but also a foster mother – or even a wet nurse – both of which are provisional roles, or rather feature as supplements or stand-ins for a 'real' mother, just as we have seen that the educational institution is figured in Derrida's reading of Nietzsche. This suggests that just as Lacoue-Labarthe is keen to stress the essential splitting or doubling of the father (as both symbolic and real) in the Lacanian psychoanalytic frame work on which he draws in 'L'Écho du sujet', the mother (or the 'mother') is necessarily also (at least) double. The (symbolic) nurturing provided by the *mère nourricière* (whether as foster mother/wet nurse – or indeed caregiver, in the hope of challenging the assumption of a (biologically) sexed basis for such a role – or even as the stand-in educational institution) is clearly distinct from, or at least supplementary

[57] Ibid., p. 4.

to, the 'real' space of gestation, and yet this is never clearly delineated (as it is with the father).

Finally, we are brought to another observation of an uncanny similarity between (Derrida's commentary on) Nietzsche's *Ecce Homo* in *Otobiographies* and Lacoue-Labarthe's two texts – again in relation to the question of the mother. Derrida comments on the striking hesitancy in Nietzsche's delivery; he states:

> La chance de mon existence *(Das Glück meines Daseins)*, son unicité *peut-être* [...] tient à sa fatalité: pour l'exprimer en forme d'énigme *(Rätselform)*, je suis, en tant que mon père, déjà mort *(als mein Vater bereits gestorben)*, en tant que ma mère, je vis encore et je vieillis *(als meine Mutter lebe ich noch und werde alt)*.
>
> [The good fortune of my existence *[Das Glück meines Daseins]*, its unique perhaps [...] lies in its fatality: I am, to express it in the form of a riddle [*Rätselform*], already dead as my father [*als mein Vater bereits gestorben*], while as my mother, I am still living and becoming old [*als meine Mutter lebe ich noch und werde alt*.]⁵⁸

Similarly, as we have seen, Lacoue-Labarthe repeatedly uses a comparably tentative structure through the use of the conditional ('Quoi d'autre pourrait en nous résonner?' [What else could resonate in us?] or 'Par quoi d'autre en effet serions-nous "rythmés"?' [How else, in fact, would we be 'rythmed'?]) or *perhaps* more explicitly in *Le Chant des Muses*, '*peut-être* qu'elle retrouve un peu de la musique *d'avant*' ['*Perhaps* [the voice, through the act of singing] will be able to refind a little of the music *of before*'] (my emphasis). As Derrida notes, through this seemingly careful and non-committal 'peut-être' Nietzsche – and thus Lacoue-Labarthe – in fact retain the possibility that this 'situation chanceuse' ['chancy situation'] may nonetheless have a 'caractère exemplaire ou paradigmatique' ['exemplary or paradigmatic character'].⁵⁹

LACOUE-LABARTHE'S ALMA MATER

> Que tout philosophe soit inscrit dans son discours, qu'il s'y marque, à son corps défendant ou non, qu'il soit par conséquent toujours possible de pratiquer une lecture autobiographique de n'importe quel texte philosophique, la chose n'est pas nouvelle, elle est même probablement constitutive, depuis Parménide, de l'énonciation philosophique comme telle.
> Lacoue-Labarthe⁶⁰

---

⁵⁸ Nietzsche, *Ecce Homo*, p. 7; also cited in Derrida, Lévesque and McDonald, *L'Oreille de L'autre*, p. 28 [*The Ear of the Other*, p. 15], my emphasis.
⁵⁹ Derrida, Lévesque and McDonald, *L'Oreille de l'autre*, p. 28 [*The Ear of the Other*, p. 15].
⁶⁰ ES₁, pp. 222–3 [That every philosopher should be inscribed in his (or her) own discourse, that he should leave his mark there, by or against his will, that it should always be possible

And so finally the analysis demands our return to Lacoue-Labarthe's texts, to the stories they tell aside from themselves, and to the (m)others inscribed therein. The first point relates to Lacoue-Labarthe's reluctance to deconstruct the category of 'music' itself. While he patiently and determinedly demonstrates that certain overlapping features of both music and language (lexis, style, rhythm, *melos*, and so on) prove fruitful in showing a less than clear distinction between what we can safely affirm is either 'just' music, or 'just' language (rather than music being an originary or proto-language, as we saw in the Rousseauianism of Nancy's theorisation) his thinking is nonetheless inflected with a residual transcendentalist metaphysics; indeed, John McKeane has also noted this to be the case in his archival work that explores Lacoue-Labarthe's almost completely unknown and at the time unpublished writings on opera – some of which are now available in *Pour n'en pas finir*.[61] While he *does* consider music other than that belonging to the canonical repertoire of Western literate music – his mention of jazz, rap and blues in *Le Chant des Muses* and elsewhere accounts for a sizeable proportion of the music referred to – the way he goes about it, rather than getting him off the hook, actually compounds the problem; instead of moving from his deconstruction of a clear music/language binary to a nuanced account of how we might then think about this ambiguous relation and their interactions with society, culture, and politics, he instead retains a notion of an organic musical work – one with a fixed essence. All the more disturbingly for a scholar so critical of mimetology and, moreover, profoundly troubled by Heidegger's quest for fundamental philosophical languages, he then articulates the fixed essence of musical works in relation to distinct languages – as if these were also neatly geographically bound, timeless and fixed, and not riddled with their own set of imperialist, classist and nationalist politics. This seems all the more disappointing given the potentially fruitful line of (musical) enquiry implied in much of his thinking of 'catacoustics'.

Secondly, in both texts, his invocation of hegemonic, masculinist and 'objective' scientific discourse (or pseudo-scientific discourse – though of course if we are to believe Lacoue-Labarthe's own position *vis-à-vis* the fictioning nature of all discourses, then surely *all* science is pseudo-science?) in order to career his own discourse towards the maternal closures he seeks seems deeply suspicious – not least because without the concession to (pseudo-)science in each instance, the weight of his

therefore to practice an autobiographical reading of any philosophical text, is hardly new. Indeed, since Parmenides, this fact has probably been constitutive of philosophical enunciation as such] (ES$_2$, p. 142).

[61] See McKeane, *Philippe Lacoue-Labarthe*, p. 112.

argument is remarkably reduced. Again, not only does it rehabilitate a long-standing trope in the history of Western thought on music – that of its essential relation to the feminine, to its concomitant passivity and to emotions – but, in invoking 'science' to make his point, he grounds a contestable philosophical fiction as 'fact' (although for Lacoue-Labarthe this too would still be a fiction). Indeed, this trope is one that Lacoue-Labarthe is all too aware of but is reluctant to intervene in or to attempt to imagine ways beyond its impasse, apparently settling instead for its inevitability. In *Musica Ficta*, he explicates both Nietzsche and Heidegger's critiques of the fundamental passivity of the Wagnerian aesthetic state,

> comme le comble de la plasticité, de la malléabilité, de l'impressionnabilité. Comme pure 'matérialité', si l'on préfère, selon – là encore – une très ancienne équivalence (*materia/mater*) qui, au-delà de telle ou telle ressource étymologique de telle ou telle langue naturelle, s'ancre aussi bien dans la détermination aristotélicienne – si même elle n'est pas bien antérieure – de la fémininité ou de l'essence du féminin. (MF$_1$, pp. 199–200)

> [as the height of plasticity, malleability, impressionability. As pure 'materiality,' if we prefer, according to – again – a very old equivalence (*materia/mater*), which, beyond any particular etymological resource of any particular natural language, is also anchored in the Aristotelian – if not more ancient – determination of femininity or the essence of the feminine.] (MF$_2$, p. 106)

The conclusions that emerge once we place Lacoue-Labarthe's texts on musical ontology – 'L'Écho du sujet' and *Le Chant des muses* – alongside his major work on the aesthetics or ethics of a particular music – *Musica Ficta*[62] – are unsettling, to say the least. In both, the function of anamnesis is integral to a central argument: in 'L'Écho du sujet' and *Le Chant des Muses* it is the anamnesic *recognition* of the mother that provokes music's profound and cathartic emotional effects. The affective dimension of music is inseparable, for Lacoue-Labarthe, from a recollection of its maternal-feminine origins – and indeed he uses an extraordinarily explicit account of this in Groddeck to support this claim. And yet, the anamnesic quality of Wagner's music – especially as described by Baudelaire – is one of the aspects that informs some of his most stinging critique, as will be considered further in

---

[62] Though it would be unfair not to acknowledge that Lacoue-Labarthe is himself deeply hesitant and cautious about whether this text is actually *about* music (or even Wagner's music) rather than, as the title suggests, 'figures de Wagner', I would nonetheless suggest that supposing that the two could ever be neatly separated simply sets one up for another set of charges of essentialism and commitment to the ideology of an autonomous musical object that is distinct from the social, cultural and political contexts in which it is produced, performed and received.

Chapter 5. Indeed, as Lacoue-Labarthe carefully points out, anamnesis is not only a recognition or recollection 'd'une tradition (d'une origine)' ['of a tradition (an origin)'] (MF$_1$, p. 117; MF$_2$, p. 56) but, far more importantly, it is also a forgetting (of history). As Martis has argued, 'Lacoue-Labarthe's concern with Wagner's music [. . . is] as historically emblematic of the possibility that music can offer the subject self-appropriation, either as *feeling* or as *figure*'.[63] It allows the subject, on a very affective level, to experience something as a pure and untainted origin – as essence and thus destiny. In this framing, Lacoue-Labarthe's critique of Wagnerianism is absolutely on a par with Nietzsche's; the endless melody renders it too feminine, too passive and, ultimately, lacking in (virile) style – indeed, as both Lacoue-Labarthe and Derrida have commented abundantly, style 'n'est pas sans connotation sexuelle' ['is not without sexual connotation'] (MF$_1$, p. 200; MF$_2$, p. 106). We are thus left to suppose that although music – or what is essentially musical – is fundamentally feminine, in order for it to be aesthetically or ethically valid it needs to be made *less* feminine; without the potent thrust of style to contain, give shape to, form and figure the unbound feminine mat(t)er, it remains dangerous (implicitly fascist, even). And is this not precisely the image in the Groddeck text cited above: 'la clôture concerne un espace vide, elle [la clôture] est réalisée grâce à la clef' or 'le symbole du masculin, qui féconde et ferme l'intérieur féminin'? It is an empty, meaningless, nothingness that threatens to engulf the subject unless plugged by the male member. Of course, Pandora's 'box' must remain firmly shut.

And yet, Lacoue-Labarthe's account of subjectivity is figured along similar lines: the abyssal and desistant subject is constituted as a subject only through this exposure to a radical exteriority (without any implication that there ever was – or ever could be – a point or a subject 'prior' to this exposure). However, as so much feminist scholarship has bountifully noted, 'theories that de-center the (masculine) subject paradoxically privilege the feminine by turning her into a seductive figure of absence. To put it simply, they celebrate woman by effectively making her disappear.'[64] Lacoue-Labarthe's desire to 'remonte[r] de Narcisse à Echo' now seems particularly apt; for what else is the myth of Narcissus and Echo than the celebration of Narcissus's tragic death (a death that nonetheless allows him to flourish – to flower – symbolically, and thus poetically) and simultaneously, to follow Lynne Huffer again, elsewhere, 'the story of a woman disappearing?'[65] Echo's voice remains,

---

[63] Martis, *Philippe Lacoue-Labarthe*, p. 241 n. 48, Martis's emphasis.
[64] Lynne Huffer, 'Blanchot's Mother', pp. 175–95 (pp. 177–8).
[65] Lynne Huffer, *Maternal Pasts, Feminist Futures*, p. 75.

but idealised, unattainable and, significantly, disembodied. The question of whether Lacoue-Labarthe's figuring of the 'desistant' (and catacoustic) subject is possible without recourse to a feminised (m)other for its coherence is, certainly, beyond the scope of this book – I will nonetheless return to what is most productive in Lacoue-Labarthe's thinking for music in the concluding chapter. We might, however, turn one final time to the name Lacoue-Labarthe, to his mus(e)ical fantasy of maternal origins, and to his own musical obsession and autobiographical compulsion.

In an unpublished interview cited by McKeane, Lacoue-Labarthe states, 'je n'ai jamais pu ne pas penser à l'injustice qui nous fait naître' ['I have never been able not to think of the injustice that causes us to be born'].[66] In this light, Lacoue-Labarthe's often obsessive, occasionally tortured and, above all, patiently persistent writing recounts as much his own nostalgic projection of irrecoverable origins as it does a theory of the subject – though we would do well to remember, of course, that these are axiomatically indistinguishable for Lacoue-Labarthe: the subject of theory and the theory of the subject are necessarily conterminously produced. In this way, and without apologising for the ill-considered maternal fiction upon which he makes a dubious claim to fact – a fiction that for all its emphasis on mat(t)er, dematerialises the female body leaving only the acousmatic imago of the 'living' feminine as necessary supplement to the (dead) male subject – Lacoue-Labarthe's account is, nonetheless, deceptively coherent. Indeed, perhaps *his* failure is also his paradoxical success, revealing precisely one way in which the 'subject' is worked into a form by a figure. Music, as he states, primes: 'elle déclenche le geste autobiographique. C'est-à-dire, aussi bien, le geste théorique' ['it sets off the autobiographical gesture. Which is to say, as well, the theoretical gesture'] (ES_1, p. 233; ES_2, p. 151). 'L'Écho du sujet', in particular, is beguilingly honest: it is all about his (m)other.[67]

---

[66] McKeane, *Philippe Lacoue-Labarthe*, p. 1 (McKeane's translation).
[67] I am, of course, making further reference to Lynne Huffer's article, 'Blanchot's Mother', already mentioned, which makes a similar claim about Blanchot.

4. Midwives and Madams: Mus(e)ic, Mediation and Badiou's 'Universal' Subject

> [L]e cinéma c'est d'abord l'invention d'une technique
> Badiou[1]

> [W]e are used to associating 'technology' largely with twentieth-century music: Theremins and synthesizers, and the tools of electronic music. But oboes and violins are also technologies. Acknowledging this simple fact might make us question the values and ideas that we have come to attach to certain technologies. Even more importantly, though, the history of the orchestra shows the indivisibility between technology and aesthetics.
> Emily Dolan[2]

> The question of technology, of modernity, of techne is in my opinion not a very important question. There are always technical questions, but there is no capital newness in the question of technology. There is no direct ethical question of the relation between ethics and technology. Ethical questions, for me, are questions in the field of truth.
> Badiou[3]

Following the neo-Heideggerian infused poetics of many leftist French philosophers (Nancy and Lacoue-Labarthe included), a distinctly different (counter-)movement can be traced in the work of Alain Badiou. Whereas Nancy and Lacoue-Labarthe remain committed to the essentially Nietzschean-Heideggerian (and latterly Derridean) overthrow of Platonic metaphysics, Badiou, though arguably a post- (rather than anti-) Heideggerian, purposefully and clearly provocatively identifies himself not only as a neo-Platonist, but as the twenty-first-century's heir to Plato. Indeed, amidst his extensive and ceaselessly proliferating

---

[1] PE$_1$, p. 97 [cinema is, first of all, the invention of a technology (PE$_2$, p. 81)].
[2] Emily I. Dolan, *The Orchestral Revolution*, p. 22.
[3] Badiou, 'On the Truth-Process', open lecture at the European Graduate School, para. 9, www.lacan.com/badeurope.htm (accessed 11 June 2019).

œuvre we find his acclaimed 'hyper-translation' of *La République de Platon*, a text that seems to confirm, as François Laruelle argues, the suspicion that Badiou sees himself (or asks us to read him) in relation to Plato the way that Lacan saw himself in relation to Freud: as a rereading or making available of its fundamental truth. As a result, though Badiou is quite evidently a *soixante-huitard* through and through – and indubitably the trace of his enduring fidelity to those events is written into his philosophy in a much more explicit way than with Nancy or Lacoue-Labarthe – we find a commitment in Badiou to philosophical principles that seem to run against the grain of much continental thought in the late twentieth and early twenty-first centuries: to truth, universality, science (largely as mathematics), 'great' art, and to a rigorous, rational and organised philosophical system. Concomitantly, this comes also with a rejection of conventional ethics, aesthetics, sophistry and rhetoric, any discourse centred on the 'other' (including human rights), multiculturalism and diversity, environmentalism, and political correctness (including feminism, though Louise Burchill suggests his position on this has shifted slightly over the last few years[4]). The upshot of this is, perhaps not unsurprisingly, a philosopher who seems extremely difficult to place: while identifying and philosophising as a Maoist-sympathising communist militant, his aesthetic predilections (for all his rejection of aesthetics as philosophy) are explicitly and unapologetically for high art Western culture; his pronouncements on love seemingly in line with the validation of traditional, monogamous marriage; and his assertion of its fundamentally heterosexual basis (even though not necessarily biological in basis, sexuation is necessarily binary) at odds with contemporary understandings in queer theory.[5]

This chapter will explore Badiou's relatively infrequent pronouncements on music in the rather different context of this anti-deconstructionist neo-Platonic philosophy. Chapters 4 and 5 of his major work on music, *Five Lessons on Wagner* – particularly the analysis of *Parsifal* therein – will provide the backbone of much of what is discussed, alongside musical 'moments' scattered rather more diffusely elsewhere in his œuvre, notably in *Petit Manuel d'inesthétique*, *L'éthique: Essai sur la conscience du mal*, and the little commented upon, marginal 'chapter' from *Logiques des mondes*, 'Scolie: Une variante musicale de la

---

[4] See Louise Burchill, 'Feminism' in Steven Corcoran (ed.), *The Badiou Dictionary*, pp. 126–32, particularly p. 132.
[5] That said, this is not a claim that Badiou, in the French context, is unique in his lack of engagement with queer perspectives – far from it. See, for example, *Queer Theory's Return to France – Paragraph*, 35.2 (2012), 462–4, special edition edited by Oliver Davis and Hector Kollias – for more on queer theory's late arrival in France.

métaphysique du sujet', among others. In so doing, I hope to show that despite Badiou's self-positioning as a Platonist, and his characterisation of his work as the necessary antidote to the tired poetics of Heideggerian influenced modern sophistry, there are nonetheless interesting points of contact between his work and that of Nancy and Lacoue-Labarthe when it comes to the specific themes that constellate around the consideration of music. One of the most salient (and welcome) features of Badiou's writing on music is that he doesn't appear to imbue it with any particular essence (unlike, as we have seen, the fundamentally pre-linguistic maternal-feminine origins of music as articulated by Nancy and Lacoue-Labarthe).[6] Nevertheless – and rather differently to the previous two chapters which probed at the philosophical projects of Nancy and Lacoue-Labarthe, homing in on their characterisation of music to reveal a problematic and essentialising blind spot that stands in sharp contrast to their broader post-metaphysical thinking – this chapter exploits Badiou's writing on music as one critical angle (undoubtedly of many) through which a feminist objection to his concept of universal truth might still be launched. Ultimately, despite Badiou's indubitable innovations which have provoked a new and invigorating set of challenges for a leftist philosophy appropriate to the trials of the twenty-first century, the critique of Badiou is finally more severe than those of Nancy and Lacoue-Labarthe; while there is undoubtedly much of great political import in Badiou's philosophy (particularly his articulation of the self-serving hypocrisy of much human rights discourse and the warmongering economic neo-imperialism it serves to obscure), his *opinions* on music – and moreover, the way they are instrumentalised – are nonetheless extremely problematic. Through their careful consideration this chapter aims to show how his thinking on music highlights how certain core axes of his thought are fundamentally intertwined with the deep-seated misogyny present in much of his work.

As alluded to above, Badiou's philosophy is a stringent and well-wrought maieutic system, one which sees philosophers, extending Plato's analogy to midwives, as 'maquerelles des Idées, nous [philosophes] présentons les vérités aux clients potentiels' ['madams of Ideas, we [philosophers] present truths to our potential clients'].[7] The role accorded

---

[6] Even Badiou is not immune, on occasion, to these kinds of metaphors, however. In PMI, he states: 'ce pouvoir de la langue est précisément ce que le poème ne peut nommer. Il effectue, en puisant dans *le chant latent de la langue*' ['this power of language is precisely what the poem cannot name. It effectuates this power by drawing on the latent song of language'] (PMI, p. 43; HI, p. 25, my emphasis). This, however, is not typical of the way in which Badiou understands music on the whole.

[7] Private correspondence between Badiou and Mehdi Belhaj Kacem, attested to in Mehdi Belhaj Kacem, Alexandre Costanzo and Alain Badiou, *Esthétique et philosphie*, p. 73.

to philosophy here brings into sharp relief the difference between the core beliefs or values of the Nancy-Lacoue-Labarthian project and the Badiousian one. In order to discuss in any detail the characterisation of music for Badiou's thinking – especially as music appears to be accorded no specific essence or unique role – it is first necessary to briefly delineate the key structures, claims and orientations of Badiou's thought. After outlining the key terms essential to the understanding of Badiousian philosophy – notably, truth (as universal), ontology (as mathematical set theory), the 'event', the (immortal) subject, and the 'conditions' of philosophy (art, love, science, and politics) – this chapter then puts this into dialogue with feminist thought, particularly through a critique of the idea of the universal, and then continues with a critical discussion and analysis of Badiou's musico-philosophical playlist, which stretches from Haydn through to contemporary classical music. In so doing, I will continue to draw on the musicological perspectives offered in the previous chapters on Nancy and Lacoue-Labarthe and will also bring into the frame more recent work by Emily Dolan, Brian Kane and Mark Evan Bonds (among others) in order to probe in more detail at the complicated interrelation of music, mediation and technology. In more concrete terms, then, this chapter will argue that Badiou's preference for Hans-Jürgen Syberberg's film version of Wagner's seminal and final opera *Parsifal* is revealing, bringing to the fore the ways in which music is multiply mediated – especially by technology and its in/visible relation to particular aesthetic, socio-cultural and ideological formations. Alongside this, inconsistencies and incoherencies in the way Badiou identifies pure and impure art forms (i.e. music vs. cinema), technologically and non-technologically mediated arts (and non-arts or 'entertainment'), and artistic responses to aesthetic 'events' will be highlighted in order to demonstrate the way in which Badiou's system is responsive (perhaps purposefully) only to the inherited conceit of an autonomous, transcendent work (though he would no doubt reject this historicising) – something that is confirmed by his own musical timeline. For Badiou, the history of music (or truths in the specifically musical domain of art, which is itself (Art) understood as a 'condition' of philosophy – we will return to this) runs from the 'Haydn-event' (i.e. the invention/formalisation of classical forms) through to contemporary classical music, which is largely understood as faithful responses to the 'Schoenberg-event' (i.e. the invention of serialism) and possibly some jazz, with all other musics disparaged and relegated to the status of entertainment or non-art (and thus of no concern to philosophy). Indeed, it also the case that whatever musicking is happening in the Titian painting analysed by Nancy (see Figure 2.1) is of no interest to Badiou because, dating from *c.* 1555, it pre-dates any identification of musical truth in

Badiou's work. While much of my critique can be explained as the product of a fundamentally different philosophical orientation (I am, quite evidently, a historicising sophist, by Badiou's account!) this chapter nonetheless hopes to demonstrate several inconsistencies and problems internal to Badiou's own thought along the way. Finally, by demonstrating that form is itself technologically and socio-culturally mediated (i.e. musical forms and processes are themselves inherently contingent, multiply mediated and irreducibly enmeshed in their relations to particular social, cultural and political configurations, the effects of which can be discerned in Badiou's own musical periodisation), and in ascertaining that Badiousian truths only pertain to the purely formal innovations or procedures of music, the inherited and geo-historically particular synecdochic relation between form and music (or art more broadly) profoundly troubles his claims to universality. Consequently, the very idea that music (or any 'art') could be absolute – divorced from the society that produces it – or at least its 'truth-procedure' could be – is itself the product of a very particular (and relatively recent) ideological configuration. Furthermore, this ideological configuration has been complicit with and instrumentalised by capitalist ideologies such as our supposed (neoliberally conceived) freedom, autonomy and individualism (including the very human rights discourses Badiou explicitly rejects); in short, the very structures incommensurable with Badiou's universal truths. Ultimately, then, the crux of this chapter leads to two claims. Firstly, and despite a Badiousian turn of late,[8] that recent musicology has much to bring to the table of (post-)postmodern theory and philosophy, and that the import of such critical interventions should not be underrated in avoiding a Thermidorian – to use a Badiousian term – musical(ogical) turn. Secondly, that Badiou's invisible role as the mediator or adjudicator of the distinction between truth and opinion reveals a distinctly Pythagorean (rather than Platonic) philosophical gesture, while also revealing an (in)aesthetic system that rehabilitates sets of hierarchical binaries that seem especially problematic in light of the self-evident misogyny found on numerous occasions in Badiou's texts.

PHILOSOPHICAL SYSTEMS, ANTIPHILOSOPHY AND SOPHISTICAL RHETORIC

Perhaps the most striking contrast between the Nancy-Lacoue-Labarthian project and that of Badiou's is their fundamentally opposi-

---

[8] See, among several recent examples, James Currie, 'Music After All', pp. 145–203, and several texts by J. P. E. Harper-Scott.

tional understandings and characterisations of philosophy itself. While Nancy and Lacoue-Labarthe seek to redress the (im)balance between the statuses of literature (or the literary-poetic) and philosophy by identifying philosophy's supposedly neutral and objective voice as its very own founding metaphysical moment – thus philosophy is strictly indistinguishable from literature – Badiou seeks to rehabilitate philosophy in its classical sense. For Badiou, 'La philosophie est théorie générale de l'être et de l'événement, tels que noués par la vérité. Car une vérité est le travail *auprès* de l'être d'un événement évanoui dont il ne reste que le nom' ['Philosophy is the general theory of being and the event as tied together by truth. A truth is the work that takes place *near* the being of a vanished event of which the name alone remains'] (PMI, pp. 45–6; HI, p. 26, Badiou's emphasis). In this way, his philosophical project at large makes a concerted plea, as Oliver Feltham describes, 'for a return to philosophy, for an end to the end of philosophy and its endless deconstruction'[9] and, moreover, as Fabien Tarby articulates, he remains committed to 'une histoire de la vérité, dont la succession renvoie à des problèmes et des thèses éternelles' ['a history of truth, which is progressively elaborated in reference to problems and theses that are themselves eternal'] (PE_1, p. 154; PE_2, p. 132). Badiou's understanding or formulation of 'truth', 'being' and 'event' will be delineated more clearly below, but for now it is his identification of philosophy as a 'general theory' – and one moreover that is systematic and identifies truth as universal – that gives us pause for thought; subtending all of this is, quite clearly, an entirely different conception of language than that which we have found in Nancy and Lacoue-Labarthe. For Badiou, then, while a philosopher might leave traces of his particular writing style, philosophy is fundamentally, as the translator of the English version of *Philosophie et l'événement* describes, 'a protocol of transmission pertaining to something not constituted by the writing process itself [. . . It] is always *didactic* writing: its rationale consists in conveying the Idea.'[10] The philosopher's words – whether written or spoken – provide the means, or the material support, but are ultimately detachable from the information that they convey. Thus, in absolute contrast to Nancy and Lacoue-Labarthe, there is an essential and fundamental difference between literary writing (which is to do with the bounds of language itself) and properly philosophical writing for which language and its accrued specific technical terminology is simply the quasi-material sup-

---

[9] Oliver Feltham, 'Philosophy', in Bartlett, Clemens and Badiou (eds), *Alain Badiou: Key Concepts*, pp. 13–24 (p. 13).
[10] 'Translator's Preface', in Alain Badiou and Fabien Tarby, *Philosophy and the Event*, p. vii, emphasis in original.

port that allows the philosopher to convey his message: rationally, logically and unbound by any limitation of language *qua* language.[11]

And, indeed, nowhere is this more evident than in Badiou's proposition of 'antiphilosophy' and his diatribes against sophistry. While the task of philosophy, for Badiou, is to orientate the thinking of thought to truth, what antiphilosophers and sophists have in common is a rejection of or relativising of 'Truth'. Whereas antiphilosophy remains, in some sense at least, philosophy – and indeed in some substantial way it functions to counter philosophy 'proper' in that through the antiphilosophy/philosophy confrontation a task is announced, 'philosophy is always heir to antiphilosophy'[12] – sophistry is, by contrast, its negative double. The primary objection to sophistry is its delimitation of 'philosophy' to the play of language (games) and the signifier, and their replacement of (universal) Truth with a multitude of contingent opinions. As Badiou states, sophists are '[c]eux pour qui l'opposition fondamentale n'est pas entre la vérité et l'erreur ou l'errance, mais entre la parole et le silence, entre ce qui peut être dit et ce qui est impossible à dire' ['those for whom the fundamental opposition is not between truth and error, or errancy, but between speech and silence, that is, between that which can be said and that which it is impossible to say'] (CS_1, p. 60; CS_2, p. 6), or in his well-known maxim that serves as a corrective to the sophistical error that '*[i]l n'y a que des corps et des langages*' ['*There are only bodies and languages*'] (LM, p. 9; LW, p. 1, Badiou's emphasis), to which Badiou retorts '*sinon qu'il y a des vérités*' ['*except that there are truths*'] (LM, p. 12; LW, p. 4, Badiou's emphasis). It is worth highlighting that, as we have seen, this kind of sophistical practice has consequences for the way music (which as we have seen in Nancy is also, fundamentally, silent) tends to be categorised – or even instrumentalised – where it is enlisted to supplant or at least plug the void beyond the limits of what language cannot say; a move that, given the Lacanian identification of the symbolic (linguistic) realm with phallic/paternal law has, as its consequence, the (re)alignment of the maternal-feminine with the properly (non-linguistic) musical. Evidently this fundamentally different perspective has profound ramifications for Badiou's understanding of music. Finally, however, the sophists *do* in fact serve a 'purpose' for philosophy, in that they 'nous rappelle que la catégorie de Vérité est vide' ['[remind] us of the emptiness of the

---

[11] Interestingly, it is over this issue that Badiou disagrees with his long-time colleague and collaborator Barbara Cassin. See, for example, Barbara Cassin, *L'effet sophistique*. It is also worth noting, I think, that although he asserts philosophy's ability to communicate quite straightforwardly, his writing is extraordinarily dense and difficult to understand!

[12] Alain Badiou, 'Who Is Nietzsche?', pp. 1–11 (p. 10).

category of Truth'] (CS$_1$, p. 75; CS$_2$, p. 19); while philosophy affirms the category of Truth, the negative figure of the sophist 'prevents philosophy from becoming self-enclosed and mistaking itself for a meta-discourse that consequently substantializes the empty category of truth as a privileged access to the real'.[13] In short, philosophy *is not* truth itself, but should rather affirm the (com)possibility of heterogeneous truths as found in its four conditions: love, science, art and politics.

BEING (MATTER AND ONTOLOGY) AND EVENT (DIALECTIC AND IMMORTALITY)

In terms of its philosophical foundations, Badiou's philosophy, as Fabien Tarby describes and as announced by Badiou's magnum opus, *L'Être et l'événement*, is primarily committed to two things: matter (which is 'mathématisable [et] logique'), and 'l'exception humaine' (which functions dialectically as a category of negation in the guise of an event) (see PE$_1$, p. 155). Less frequently acknowledged, though important, it would seem, is that though Badiou rejects the poetics that ensue from philosophy's Heideggerian deconstruction, through the title he nonetheless conscripts himself into a lineage that runs from Heidegger's *Being and Time* through to, less controversially, Sartre's *L'Être et le néant*. As Oliver Marchart asserts, 'there are many more similarities between Badiou and his alleged adversaries, the modern "sophists" [... i.e. poststructuralists ...] than there are incompatibilities'.[14] At stake in rehearsing the common ground he occupies with other poststructuralists is acknowledging their shared commitment to the possibility of a post-foundational thinking; the commitment to a *re*thinking of materialism and the rescinding of the idealist transcendental – whether in terms of God, essence, soul or spirit, or any totalising absolute including the illusory quest for lost origins. Tarby articulates this in terms of the horizontal nature of our material, (hum)animal, real(ity) and the verticality of idealism, while highlighting that 'nul matérialisme n'a jamais pu soutenir une horizontale pureté. Il y a toujours eu une sorte de supplément ou d'incise' ['There has never, in fact, been a materialism capable of maintaining a horizontal purity. There has always been some sort of supplement or parenthetical clause'] (Tarby in PE$_1$, p. 162; PE$_2$, p. 141) – a difficulty that is frequently traversed through the invocation of the Lacanian and distinctly human symbolic, which in turn changes our relationship to the (no longer immediate) real (Tarby in PE$_1$, p. 162;

---

[13] Samo Tomsic, 'Sophistry' in Steven Corcoran (ed.), *The Badiou Dictionary*, pp. 317–20 (p. 320).
[14] Oliver Marchart, *Post-Foundational Political Thought*, p. 111.

PE$_2$, p. 141). The innovation we are presented with in Badiou, through the event, is the possibility of accounting for our more-than-animality without simultaneously invoking a (fixed or eternal) transcendental.

The first of the two major terms for Badiou, then, is that of 'being'. His mathematical ontology is a sustained attempt to dissolve the residual Romanticism in Heidegger's thinking of the unrecognised ontological difference subtending the entire history of Western thought. Badiou's position *vis-à-vis* ontology is developed, through Cantorian set theory, perhaps most rigorously in the opening movements of *L'Être et l'événement*, and it explores how what *is* (as such) is *multiple*; there is no fundamental consistency or *unity* – one-ness – to what *is*, but rather a radically infinite multiplicity. Crucially, the multiple is not substantialised, but is itself 'le régime de la présentation' ['the regime of presentation'], insisting that 'l'un est [. . .] un résultat opératoire [. . . mais] le domaine de l'opération n'est pas un (car l'un *n'est pas*), et que donc il est multiple, de ce que, *dans la présentation*, ce qui n'est pas un est nécessairement multiple' ['the one [. . .] is an operational result [. . . but] the domain of the operation is not one (for the one *is not*), and that therefore this domain is multiple; since, *within presentation*, what is not one is necessarily multiple'] (EE, p. 32; BE, p. 26, Badiou's emphasis). Presentation, or rather 'présentation structurée' ['structured presentation'] [EE, p. 33; BE, p. 27) thus effects a particular situation – 'Il n'y a que des situations' ['There is nothing apart from situations'] (EE, p. 33; BE, p. 28) – and yet remains ungrounded by a transcendental One as *l'un* is just an operational effect or result. Thus, critically, 'Le multiple, dont l'ontologie fait situation, ne se compose que de multiplicités. Il n'y a pas d'un. Ou: *tout multiple est un multiple de multiples*' ['The multiple from which ontology makes up its situation is composed solely of multiplicities. There is no one. In other words, *every multiple is a multiple of multiples*'] (EE, p. 37; BE, p. 31, my emphasis). Or, as he states perhaps more lucidly elsewhere: 'l'ontologie, si elle existe, doit être la théorie des multiplicités inconsistantes en tant que telles. Ce qui veut aussi dire: ce qui vient à la pensée de l'ontologie est le multiple, sans autre prédicat que sa multiplicité. Sans autre concept que lui-même, et sans rien qui garantisse sa consistance' ['ontology, if it exists, has to be the theory of inconsistent multiplicities as such. This means that what lends itself to the thought of ontology is a manifold without a predicate other than its own multiplicity. It has no concept other than itself, and nothing ensures its consistency'].[15] In short, ontology cannot be identified in reference *to* anything else – it has no substance – nor

---

[15] Badiou, *Court traité d'ontologie transitoire*, p. 29 [Badiou, *Briefings on Existence*, p. 36].

is it transcendental; it does not *mean* anything. So, for example, to be a man or a woman or a musician means nothing, as such – or is at least of no ontological interest; these are simply passing identifications/presentations borne of particular situations that are merely superfluous gloss to the properly ontological. These fundamental points of Badiou's ontology are important for several reasons (and likely many more than it is possible to enumerate here). Firstly, these theorisations are at the very core of Badiou's determination not to slip into the fallacy of what is ultimately a theological ontology (i.e. the logic of the transcendental One). Secondly, Badiousian multiplicity must be differentiated from the Deleuzian (and Guattarian) multiplicity which is related to the 'virtual'– and thus remains in some effective or essential link with the 'actual'– rather than the 'infinite' or the 'eternal'. Thirdly, the mathematical determination of being both acknowledges and troubles the Heideggerian distinction between the ontic and the ontological, and thus between *étant* and *être*. Certainly, the infinite multiplicity describes the ontological field, and not *merely* the ontic, but precisely what it also highlights, as Tarby acknowledges, is Heidegger's residual idealism in his desire to 'reach the ontological, *beyond* the ontic'.[16] Finally, then, in this resistance to figure the ontological field as in/accessible to philosophy, and which also discards 'being' as an *object* of philosophy (i.e. something about which philosophy can, as self-imagined master discourse, either have direct access to or reveal truths about – a theme that will recur in many other fields as we will soon see), 'ne fait que *délimiter* l'espace propre possible de la philosophie' ['all it does is *delimit* the proper space of philosophy'] (EE, p. 22; BE, p. 15, Badiou's emphasis). In this way, then, the radical thesis proposed – that 'les mathématiques sont l'ontologie' ['mathematics is ontology'] (EE, p. 21; BE, p. 15) – means that philosophy, in that it necessarily *speaks*, speaks only 'metaontologically' about being, whereas mathematics makes intelligible the infinite and eternal multiplicity (of being). It is in this way, precisely, that mathematics simply *is* ontology.[17]

The second crucial term for Badiou's philosophy is *l'événement*. An event can happen in any of four domains – art, love, science and politics – which are also the conditions of philosophy (of which, more below). As mentioned above, Badiou draws on Cantorian set theory (of the specifically Zermelo-Fraenkel variety) for his ontological project, and the development of Cantorian set theory is itself one of these events or, more precisely, simply the *name* of the event (to which Badiou is

---

[16] Fabien Tarby, 'Being' in Steven Corcoran (ed.), *The Badiou Dictionary*, p. 26.
[17] See Alex Ling, 'Ontology' in Bartlett, Clemens and Badiou (eds), *Alain Badiou: Key Concepts*, pp. 48–60 (pp. 48–9).

faithful). In its most fundamental sense, an *événement* is decidedly unpredictable, and has the potential (even if not realised) to effect monumental change in the domain in which it occurs through its disruptive and reconfiguring effects that demand 'une *nouvelle* manière d'être' ['a *new* way of being'] (E_1, p. 61; E_2, p. 41, Badiou's emphasis). As Badiou states, '[l]'événement crée une possibilité, mais il faut ensuite un travail, collectif dans le cadre de la politique, individuel dans le cas de la création artistique, pour que cette possibilité devienne réelle' ['The event creates a possibility but there, then, has to be an effort – a group effort in the political context, an individual one in the case of artistic creation – for this possibility to become real; that is, for it to be inscribed, step by step, in the world'] (PE_1, p. 19; PE_2, p. 10). In and of itself, the event guarantees nothing, as it requires faithful subjects to carry out the work (the truth-procedure) it induces or demands. In this way, Badiou draws an emphatic distinction between 'truth' and knowledge: though knowledge is generated by truth (procedures), it is always specific and incomplete, and certainly not *éternel* as is truth. Whereas knowledge is partial, truth (even if it evades us) is absolute (see LW). Crucially, then, the event is not located in particular situations, but is rather a '*supplément*' ['*supplement*'] (E_1, p. 61; E_2, p. 41, Badiou's emphasis), or, in Lacan's sense, 'une "trouée"' ['hole'] (E_1, p. 63; E_2, p. 43). It is this way of thinking which allows Badiou to sidestep any reference to a meaningful, transcendental beyond; the truth-procedure that unfolds 'from' the event is strictly *not* drawn from a pre-given (set of) truth(s) – 'Il n'y a pas de Ciel des vérités' ['there is no heaven of truths'] (E_1, p. 63; E_2, p. 43) – but rather *induces* new ways of being. The event and its attendant truth-procedure are both contingent and 'une *rupture immanente*' ['*immanent break*'] (E_1, p. 63; E_2, p. 42, Badiou's emphasis); a rupture in that the event was nowhere present *in* the given situation (hence, then, its unpredictability), and yet also immanent in that the ensuing truth-procedure unfolds in a particular situation. Above all, then, the event is (or at least *describes* as 'it' has no substance as such) a disruption to or a reconfiguration of the present situation; in its wake a (new) subject is induced. The order, here, is crucial, and Badiou is absolutely clear on this point: though the trace of the event is only sustained by its faithful subject, '[l]e sujet ne pré-existe nullement au processus. Il est absolument inexistant dans la situation "avant" l'événement. On dira que le processus de vérité *induit* un sujet' ['the subject, therefore, in no way pre-exists the process. He is absolutely nonexistent in the situation "before" the event. We might say that the process of truth *induces* a subject'] (E_1, p. 63; E_2, p. 43, Badiou's emphasis). Because 'Truth' is strictly speaking supplementary to '*ce qu'il y a*' ['*what there is*'] the (faithful) subject induced through fidelity to the event 'outre-passe l'animal' ['goes beyond the animal'] even if 'l'animal en est le seul support' ['the animal remains its sole foundation'] (E_1, p. 61; E_2, p. 41, Badiou's emphasis). Or, properly speaking, the subjectivation induced by the event makes the subject *immortel*. Because truth, for Badiou, is *éternel*, so the subject that is produced as a faithful response to its trace is *immortel*; and as Badiou describes, we all have this opportunity: 'À tout animal humain est accordée, plusieurs fois dans sa brève existence, la chance de s'incorporer au présent subjectif d'une vérité' ['Several times in its brief existence, every human animal is granted the chance to incorporate itself into the subjective present of a truth'] (LM, p. 536; LW, p. 514).

In this way, the eponymous '68 slogan to which Badiou often refers and to which he remains faithful, 'soyez réalistes, demandez l'impossible' ['be realistic, demand the impossible'], helps to clarify what is at stake and knots together several key elements: the impossible (or the void) of a particular situation (the situation here being capitalism) is what makes that situation, as such, possible, or at least identifiable/thinkable in its totality. But it is only im/possible 'dans l'ordre établi' ['within the established order'] (PE_1, p. 21; PE_2, p. 11) or in the current (state of the) situation. The event is thus the supplement to the 'what there is' (i.e. again, capitalism) but is nowhere present *in* the situation; as a result, if faithfully maintained, it induces a change of situation. To be explicit: a non-capitalist form of socio-economic organisation is nowhere present *in* the capitalist situation, but its non-existence (in the situation) is what enables us to think capitalism as the organising structure that there is. In this context, a political event (such as 1968) would be the supplemental rupture (whose trace is sustained by faithful subjects) that declares or proposes a (universal) truth that is both immanent to the situation and yet is nowhere contained within it. Furthermore, for Badiou, the slogan takes on extra resonances when we realise that it can also be understood in its Lacanian overtones – after all, the Lacanian real is the quintessential what there is (not) that is both constitutive *and* beyond any symbolic manifestation (Lacan famously said 'l'impossible, c'est le réel, tout simplement' ['the impossible is the real, quite simply']¹⁸). Further still, this brings us back into dialogue with Badiou's difficult-to-think mathematical ontology: Lacan also described the real as 'c'est la mathématique' ['it is mathematics'],¹⁹ and thus helps one to imagine the way in which it is incorrect to think of the

---

[18] This was a claim made in a 1967 seminar ('La logique du fantasme') cited in Didier Castanet, 'Éditorial. "L'impossible, c'est le réel, tout simplement"', pp. 5–7 (p. 5).

[19] See Castenet, 'Éditorial. "L'impossible, c'est le réel, tout simplement"'.

ontic and ontological as oppositional – they are *both* only identifiable in terms of infinite multiplicities and there is no 'pure' ontological field to which we can return – and the way in which the event is properly exterior ('inhumain' as Badiou describes, see PE_1, p. 23) to the 'what there is' of the situation, without being pre-determined, predictable, inevitable or, indeed, transcendental as such. All we can do is wait for an 'event' – a truth – to change the configuration of the situation and of knowledge.

MUSICAL MARGINS: 'UNE VARIANTE MUSICALE DE LA MÉTAPHYSIQUE DU SUJET'

> I have made a discovery thanks to which the supremacy of German music is ensured for the next hundred years.
> Arnold Schoenberg[20]

Having laid out in book one of *Logiques des mondes* his formal theory of the subject (or *meta*-physics) Badiou turns to a properly musical subject to elucidate over the course of a mere ten pages 'une version compacte quelque peu décalée' ['a distilled, if slightly altered, version'] (Sc, p. 89; Sch, p. 79). This slight chapter is described as a 'Scolie', an explanatory comment, interpretation or exegesis usually given in the margin,[21] and thus formally gestures towards music's illustrative but by no means central role in Badiou's thinking and, at the same time, suggests a hesitancy in grappling with music in any depth that is even more profoundly marked in *Five Lessons on Wagner*.[22] For our purposes, this modest chapter is of particular interest because it is the only place in Badiou's œuvre where his theory of the subject (or anything approaching the formal rigour of his major philosophical texts) is laid out in terms of music; even the book devoted to Wagner is unusually scant when it comes to the dense technical terms that proliferate almost everywhere else. In order to do this, he elucidates his metaphysical theory of the subject in thirteen points – remembering that the subject is by no means reserved for solely human subjects, but also artistic,

---

[20] Schoenberg, cited in Willi Reich, *Schoenberg: A Critical Biography*, p. 130. Noted also by Badiou, see LM, p. 80; LW, p. 90.
[21] 'scholium, n.' *OED Online* (Oxford University Press, March 2016; web, 26 April 2016).
[22] Michael Gallope has also described *Five Lessons on Wagner* as being 'framed by a measure of hesitancy'. See Michael Gallope, 'The Universal Form of Badiou's Wagner', pp. 342–8 (p. 342). It should be noted that music is not alone in this marginal treatment: *Logiques des mondes* contains two other *scolia*, 'Scolie aussi impressionant que subtil: Le Foncteur transcendental', and of more direct structural equivalence to the musical *scolie*, 'Scolie: Une Variante politique de la physique du sujet-de-vérité', which offers a similarly tentative defence of Mao's political restraints in inducing a new political body/organ-isation.

scientific, amorous, political subjects – elucidating further each of the thirteen points in relation to music. For example, his first point: 'Un sujet est une relation indirecte et créatrice entre un événement et un monde' ['A subject is an indirect and creative relation between an event and a world'] is subsequently expounded by invoking 'comme monde la musique allemande à la fin du XIXe siècle et au début du XXe' ['as a "world" German music at the end of the nineteenth century and the beginning of the twentieth'] (Sc, p. 89; Sch, p. 79) and the post-Wagnerian disintegration of tonality as found in the music of not only Wagner, but also Mahler, Bruckner, Richard Strauss and the early Schoenberg and Korngold; a world which is fundamentally changed by 'l'événement-Schoenberg' ['the Schoenberg-event'], an event whose trace creates a new musical world and which 'casse en deux l'histoire de la musique, en affirmant qu'un monde sonore est possible qui ne soit pas réglé par le système tonal' ['breaks the history of music in two by affirming the possibility of a sonic world no longer ruled by the tonal system'] (Sc, p. 90; Sch, p. 80). Crucially, the trace is not the dodecaphonic or serialist technique itself, but rather the body of musical works (which include serial/dodecaphonic compositions) that are responses to 'l'impératif que détient la trace' ['the imperative harboured by the trace'] (Sc, p. 90; Sch, p. 80).

Badiou then continues to sketch out the different subjectivities induced by the eventual trace, and the different configurations or negotiations of the new subject in the form of openings or closures (what Badiou terms 'points'). For Badiou, the subject 'est une séquence qui comporte des continuités *et* des discontinuités [with the old world], des ouvertures *et* des points. Le "et" s'incarne en sujet. Ou encore (en-corps): Un sujet est la forme conjonctive d'un corps' ['is a sequence involving continuities and discontinuities, openings and points. The "and" incarnates itself as a subject. Or again, it is em-bodied: A subject is the conjunctive form of a body'] (Sc, p. 93; Sch, p. 83, Badiou's emphasis). Moreover, it is, in the current example, according to Badiou, with the differing musical responses under the names Berg (oriented to openings with the old world) and Webern (oriented towards points of closure with the old world) as incorporated into the subject 'musique sérielle' ['serial music'] that the truth of the Schoenberg-event is proven or revealed (see Sc, p. 94; Sch, p. 83). Similarly, it is under the names Mozart and Beethoven as incorporated into the subject 'style classique' ['classical style'] (i.e. the invention of the architectonics of large-scale forms) that we find proof of the Haydn-event (see Sc, p. 94; Sch, p. 84). Ultimately, then, it is in this *post hoc* identification of subjective constructions, bodies and works that truth is announced, or 'dépliée point par point, elle ne tient dans aucune formule unique' ['unfolded point by point, and is not contained in any single formula'], thus on a more fundamental level 'l'événement-Schoenberg prononce la vérité du monde musical post-wagnérien de la fin du XIXe siècle et du début du XXe' ['the Schoenberg-event pronounces the truth of the post-Wagnerian musical world of the end of the nineteenth and beginning of the twentieth century'] (Sc, p. 95; Sch, p. 85). In short, the truth of the Schoenberg-event functions to reveal something about a previous situation. Badiou sees the music of the late Romantic period to be 'une distorsion extensive du style classique' which in turn leads to 'une totalisation structurale [. . . et] une saturation émotive, une angoissante recherche, finalement en vaine, de l'effet' ['structural totalization [. . . and] an emotional saturation, an anxious and ultimately hopeless search for the effect'] (Sc, p. 95; Sch, p. 85). It is in this way, for Badiou, that serial music reveals the truth of the classical style which has reached its saturation. Given, then, that the truth induced by an event relates to the truth of the previous situation, this leads to an entirely teleological narrative that passes in a strictly filial fashion, and Badiou is absolutely clear about this:

> il n'y a aucune intelligence contemporaine du style classique et de son devenir-romantique, aucune vérité éternelle, et donc actuelle, du sujet musical initié par l'événement-Haydn, qui ne transite par une incorporation à la séquence sérielle, et donc au sujet familièrement nommé 'musique contemporaine'. (Sc, p. 96)

> [there is no contemporary understanding of the classical style and its becoming-romantic, no eternal and therefore current truth of the musical subject initiated by the Haydn-event which does not pass through an incorporation into the serial sequence, and therefore into the subject commonly named 'contemporary music'.] (Sch, p. 85)

We might only note for now the way this reconstructs or realigns the history of universal truths with an entirely conventional narrative of European music history (though this is unacknowledged, it is simply 'l'histoire de la musique'); and, moreover, one that is unable to account for (or is at least unable to attribute any value or interest to) non-filial relations such as the ways in which Webern influenced Schoenberg: if the compositions of Webern and Berg constitute the body of the serial subject as induced by the Schoenberg-event, there is no way of articulating in these terms the interconnecting and mutually reinforcing influences that the various members of the Second Viennese School had on one another (or indeed on anyone else). Nor does it offer us any way of understanding works within a composer's œuvre that break the teleological narrative (such as Schoenberg's late return to elements of tonality and even neo-classicism); or at least it denigrates them as having nothing to do with universal truths. It also reconstructs a conventional narrative which ignores the contribution of women composers who, if we were interested in the 'serial subject', could also include, for example, Ruth Crawford Seeger and Elisabeth Lutyens (though, again, it is unable to account for this in terms of filiation as it is not entirely clear that either were particularly inspired by Schoenberg; nonetheless, they wrote works that are, *encore*, incorporable into the serial body), and finally refuses the possibility that influences from other domains (especially when it comes to technology and what Badiou would term 'entertainment' music) or non-formal procedures can be related to or understood in terms of the history of truths. In addition, the process of influence is substantially dematerialised, suggesting that truths are communicated 'telepathically' rather than through 'specific events [here in the conventional sense] and materialities'; as Piekut describes,

> influence [figured only in terms of formal innovations discerned retrospectively – usually in the score – by the attentive scholar] becomes a technique for erasing all the mediators that actually perform the act of influence. Any relation of influence surely relies upon many things to work – how else does composer A touch composer B, separate by fifty years, than by virtue of her scores, performances, recordings, or writings?[23]

In short, just as Badiou's philosophy describes the *post hoc* identification of events (of which all remains is the trace), his philosophical system seems apt only to describe – again, *post hoc* – what we already know to have been significant and canonical musical events (in a generic rather than Badiousian sense), thus obliterating alternative, minoritarian or counter-histories and rendering the work done to uncover some of these histories as having nothing to do with 'truth'.

In closer detail, Badiou concludes this brief excursus into a musical world by giving examples of composers or musical works in relation to the four affects that 'signalent l'incorporation d'un animal humain au processus subjectif d'une vérité' ['signal the incorporation of a human animal into subjective truth-process'] (Sc, p. 96; Sch, p. 86). The first, *terreur*, is described as 'une discontinuité décisive, qui installerait d'un seul coup le nouveau monde' ['a decisive discontinuity that will institute the new world in a single blow'] (Sc, p. 96; Sch, p. 86); the second is *angoisse*, and is figured as a 'recul devant l'obscurité de tout ce qui est discontinu [...et] cet affect signe le désir d'une continuité, d'un abri monotone' ['retreat before the obscurity of the discontinuous [... and] this affect signals the desire for a continuity, for a monotonous shelter'] (Sc, p. 96; Sch, p. 86); the third, *courage*, 'affirme l'acceptation

---

[23] Benjamin Piekut, 'Actor-Networks in Music History', pp. 191–215 (p. 202).

de la pluralité des points, de ce que les discontinuités sont à la fois impérieuses et multiformes' ['affirms the acceptance of the plurality of points, of the fact that discontinuities are at once inexorable and multiform'] (Sc, p. 96; Sch, p. 86); and, finally, *justice*, which 'affirme l'équivalence, au regard de la prééminence du devenir-sujet, de ce qui est continu et négocié, et de ce qui est discontinu et violent' ['With respect to the pre-eminence of becoming-subject [...] affirms the equivalence of what is continuous and negotiated [...] and of what is discontinuous and violent'] (Sc, pp. 96–7; Sch, p. 86). This final affect, *justice*, about which Badiou speaks at much greater length than any of the others, also affirms that these various 'modalités subjectives' ['subjective modalities'] (i.e. negotiation or violence) cannot be hierarchised in terms of value, and thus that '[l]a guerre peut valoir autant que la paix, la négociation autant que la lutte, la violence autant que la douceur' ['War can have as much value as peace, negotiation as much as struggle, violence as much as gentleness'] (Sc, p. 97; Sch, p. 86). Once these basic affective modalities have been established, Badiou continues by mapping them homologically onto various composers' responses to the Schoenberg-event. So, for example, he aligns the fundamental rupture or break of a terroristic affect with the music of Boulez who, as he claims, 'était sans égards pour la "musique française" de l'entre-deux-guerres' ['cared little for the "French music" of the inter-war period'] and thus 'dans son inflexible volonté d'incorporer la musique, en France, à un sujet qui en Autriche et en Allemagne avait un demi-siècle d'âge, Boulez n'hésitait pas à introduire [...] une certaine dose de terreur' ['in his inflexible will to incorporate music in France into a subject that in Austria and Germany was already half a century old, Boulez didn't hesitate to introduce [...] a certain dose of terror'] (Sc, p. 97; Sch, p. 86). Interestingly, this is later characterised as little more than a geo-culturally induced imperative when Badiou claims that Boulez 'ne pouvait ni ne devait éviter une certaine dose de terreur pour désembourber la prétendue "musique française"' ['[neither] could nor should have avoided a certain dose of terror in pulling so-called "French music" from the mud'] (Sc, p. 98; Sch, p. 87). This quite explicit value judgement is all the more striking coming just a few lines after he proscribes making value judgements about the relative value of the four affects – all of which are necessary – concluding that to fall prey to such opining 'n'est qu'un effet d'opinion' ['is to succumb to mere opinion'] (Sc, p. 98; Sch, p. 87). Apparently the same proscription doesn't hold true for music itself (which would appear to have an absolute rather than a relative value – an idea to which we will return later). He then continues to align *angoisse* with the music not only of Stravinsky, but also of Berg and Dutilleux, and which he understands to maintain a fundamental relation to at least 'reste[r] [normé] par l'ouverture plutôt que par l'abrupt des points' ['still [be] governed by the opening rather than by the abruptness of points'] (Sc, p. 97; Sch, p. 87). Striking, yet again, is the way he characterises those placed under the affective modality of *angoisse* who, he claims, took for granted 'l'existence d'un seul monde-musique' ['the existence of a single music-world'] (Sc, p. 97; Sch, p. 87); in denying the new musical world, named serialism, Badiou signals what he takes to be their false belief in tonality as constituting the only musical world. Again, this is a point to which we will return in light of Badiou's own pronouncements on music which suggest a singularly European (if not only tonal) musical world. Under the affect of *courage* he places Webern, who '[cherche] les points dont le nouveau monde-musique doit faire la preuve qu'il peut en décider' ['in seeking out those points whose outcome the new music-world must prove itself capable of deciding'] (Sc, p. 97; Sch, p. 87); and, finally, he claims that Boulez, ultimately, learned *justice* in his later years: 'entre 1950 et 1980 [. . .] il a acquis le pouvoir de détendre quand il le faut l'abrupt de la construction, de développer ses propres ouvertures' ['between 1950 and 1980 [. . .] he acquired the power to slacken the abruptness of the construction when needed and to develop his own openings'] (Sc, pp. 97–8; Sch, p. 87).

PHILOSOPHY AND ITS CONDITIONS: SCIENCE, LOVE, POLITICS AND ART

As already noted, any of Badiou's truth-procedures take place in the domain of one of philosophy's four conditions, or generic procedures: science, love, politics and art. At their most basic and essential level, the conditions of philosophy as announced by Badiou are one of the features that refuse the temptation of philosophy to consider itself a master discourse; philosophy itself is incapable of truth (given that it is not independent) but can refer to the conditions *outside* of it wherein truth may be located. It is this exteriority of the conditions, the '"outside" [. . .] required for its [philosophy's] own taking-place',[24] as Justin Clemens describes, and their irreducibility to philosophy (or to each other), that is key. The crucial and singular role of philosophy, then, is not to provide (the content of) truth(s) itself – as if that were possible – but rather the identification *of* 'truth' is the central and

---

[24] Justin Clemens, 'Conditions' in Steven Corcoran (ed.), *The Badiou Dictionary*, pp. 68–73 (p. 68).

irreplaceable role of philosophy in Badiou's thought. 'La philosophie est', as Badiou claims, 'l'entremetteuse des rencontres avec les vérités, elle est la maquerelle du vrai. Et de même que la beauté doit être dans la femme rencontrée, mais n'est nullement requise de la maquerelle, de même les vérités sont artistiques, scientifiques, amoureuses ou politiques, et non pas philosophiques' ['Philosophy is the go-between in our encounters with truths, the procuress of truth. And just as beauty is to be found in the woman encountered, but is in no way required of the procuress, so it is that truths are artistic, scientific, amorous, or political, and not philosophical'] (PMI, p. 21; HI, p. 10). Philosophy identifies the singular, but ultimately empty, category of Truth and, in so doing, philosophy is both 'un diagnostique de l'époque [... et] une construction [...] d'un concept de vérité' ['a diagnosis of the epoch [... and] a construction [...] of a concept of truth'] (PE_1, p. 150; PE_2, p. 130). It is essential to remember that each of the conditions is distinct and irreducible to any of the others – and this would be one reason that we might have, for example, specific language and terminology in order to discuss condition-specific considerations on their own terms. They are truths precisely *because* they are autonomous and, as Clemens, again, describes, 'self-authorising, self-problematising, self-limiting, and self-sustaining processes'.[25] At every level, then, Badiou's project is also part of the ongoing attempt to resolve philosophy's residual Romanticism: the fields of love, science, art and politics are neither inaccessible to theory (i.e. because they are somehow beyond language) nor transcendentally grounded nor identifiable with meaning as such, but rather they produce truths across four domains (and four only) that are at once universal (not predicated on anything else) and singular (linked to a particular situation). As Simon Critchley has described, it is precisely a 'situated universality' that Badiou's project attempts to articulate.[26]

Badiou's conception of history, then, is also closely related to – or even mutually dependent on – the way he understands truth; indeed the only history there is for Badiou, in any fundamental and certainly philosophical sense is, as Corcoran describes, 'the history of truth, or rather of truth*s*'.[27] His work challenges or refutes the idealism of two classical positions: that of traditional metaphysics and also that of 'democratic materialism' (what he claims to be the dominant ideology of the (postmodern) present day), both of which, in different ways, oppose truth

[25] Ibid., p. 69.
[26] See Simon Critchley, *Infinitely Demanding*.
[27] Steven Corcoran, 'History/Historicity' in *The Badiou Dictionary*, pp. 147–52 (p. 147), emphasis in original.

to history (and vice versa). Traditional metaphysics defends truth, contending that it exists outside of the historical context in which it may appear – truth is eternal and transcendental – while democratic materialism claims, conversely, that there can be no eternal truth; all truths are relative, discursive and ultimately reducible to particular social and historical configurations. The upshot of all this, for Badiou, is that truth and history are thoroughly (even necessarily) commensurate with each other; the event is both immanent to the particular (historical) situation (in any one of the four conditions) *and* is only an event (i.e. produces a truth) if it addresses all (i.e. is universal). Crucially, then, a truth-process '*ne se communique pas* [...] Pour tout ce qui concerne les vérités, il est requis qu'il y en ait *rencontre*. L'Immortel dont je suis capable [...] doit être *directement* saisi par la fidelité' ['cannot be communicated [...] In all that concerns truths, there must be an *encounter*. The Immortal that I am capable of being [...] must be *directly* seized by fidelity'] (E_1, pp. 73–4; E_2, p. 51, Badiou's emphasis). Consequently, the event (of which all that we can speak is its name: 1848, 1968, Mallarmé, Schoenberg, Cantor, an amorous encounter, and so on) is only discernible *post hoc* as a trace, and in relation to the subjective formations/responses it induces (for example: fidelity, denial, occultation, resurrection), all of which entail not only new subjective forms (the event is properly *incorporé*) but also a new situation (in whatever domain the event took place). A body is thus 'la dimension mondaine du sujet. Et "trace" ce qui, à partir de l'événement, détermine l'orientation active du corps. Un sujet est donc une synthèse formelle entre la statique du corps et sa dynamique, entre sa composition et son effectuation' ['the wordly dimension of the subject and "traces" that which, on the basis of the event, determines the active orientation of the body. A subject is therefore a formal synthesis between the statics of the body and its dynamics, between its composition and its effectuation'] (Sc, p. 89; Sch, p. 79).

THE PROBLEM OF PARTICULARISM AND THE UNIVERSALITY OF TRUTH

In Badiou's extraordinary excursus into an explicitly musical subject in *Logiques des mondes*, the crucial roles of history, worlds, truth and event are prominently foregrounded as we have seen – all of which are inextricably bound up with his understanding of universality. In his major work theorising and describing his conception of the universal, *Saint Paul: La Fondation de l'universalisme*, Badiou describes how 'l'énergie d'une vérité, ce qui la fait exister dans le monde, est identique à son universalité' ['the impetus of a truth, what makes it exist in the world, is identical to its universality']. Moreover, the subjective form of this universal truth 'sous le nom paulinien d'amour' ['under the Pauline name for love'] consists only in the way it is addressed 'à tous les autres, Grecs et Juifs, hommes et femmes, hommes libres et esclaves' ['to all the others, Greeks and Jews, men and women, free men and slaves'] (StP$_1$, p. 97; StP$_2$, p. 92). While, I would contend, his (re)figuring of eternal truths challenges classical metaphysical (including Platonic) conceptions in interesting and both productive and potentially contentious ways, it is the universal address and its knock-on impact on notions such as difference, or 'particularism', that really rub against the grain of so much recent thought. The centrality of this to Badiou's philosophy cannot be overemphasised; not only are truth-procedures only truth-procedures in that they are absolutely indifferent to differences (see E$_1$, p. 46; E$_2$, pp. 26–7) but, he claims, 'toute la prédication éthique sur l'autre et sa "reconnaissance" doit être purement et simplement abandonnée' ['the whole ethical predication based upon recognition of the other should be purely and simply abandoned'] (E$_1$, pp. 42–3; E$_2$, p. 25). His entire philosophy is a rallying call to 'faire valoir une singularité universelle à la fois contre les abstractions établies (juridiques alors, [in St Paul's time] économiques aujourd'hui), et contre la revendication communautaire ou particulariste' ['mobilizing a universal singularity both against the prevailing abstractions (legal then, economic now), and against communitarian or particularist protest'] (StP$_1$, pp. 14–15; StP$_2$, p. 14). Moreover, he frames the entire project of identarian liberation movements as fundamentally complicit with the throes of neoliberal capitalism (this is evidently quite difficult to reconcile with the incontestably positive outcomes of feminism and the civil rights and gay liberation movements for the *lives* – and not just the neoliberal economy – of many, though far from all, women, non-white and LGBTQ+ individuals – none of which, it might be added, Badiou is . . .).

To return to Badiou's own words: 'Les deux composantes de l'ensemble articulé (homogénéité abstraite du capital et revendications identitaires) sont dans une relation de miroir et d'entretien réciproque' ['The two components of the articulated whole (abstract homogeneity of capital and identarian protest) are in a relation of reciprocal maintenance and mirroring'] (StP$_1$, p. 14; StP$_2$, p. 13). His charge is, in effect, a more philosophically dense charge of the classic (white, cis male, able-bodied, and so on) activist: 'You're dividing the movement! There's no war but class war!' (though Badiou would no doubt problematise the term 'class'). Or, as he states elsewhere, what we have now is 'la sociologie culturelle, pour les besoins de la prédication, à feu la lutte des classes' ['a cultural sociology preached, in line with the new-style sermons, in lieu of the late class struggle'] (E_1, p. 41; E_2, p. 23). He then goes on to ask, rhetorically, and more than a little sarcastically, 'Qui peut prétendre que va de soi la supériorité du cultivé-compétent-gestionnaire-sexuellement-épanoui? Mais qui défendra le religieux-corrompu-terroriste-polygame? Ou se fera le chantre du marginal-culturel-homéopathe-médiatique-transsexuel?' ['Who will maintain the self-evident superiority of the competent-cultivated-sexually liberated manager? But who will defend the corrupt-religious-polygamist terrorist? Or eulogize the cultural-marginal-homeopathic-media-friendly transsexual?'] (StP_1, p. 14; StP_2, p. 13). Much of this, it seems, is provocative polemics aimed at inciting a reaction but also, ultimately, at unseating cherished and uncritical notions, many of which are, quite evidently, co-optable to free market profiteering. More succinctly it is the self-evident universality of capitalism (in our present situation) that requires, for Badiou, 'a struggle of universalism against universalism, not of particularism against universalism'.[28] It is not that Badiou denies difference (or even that differences manifest in particular ways in particular worlds) but conversely that difference is, ultimately, *all that there is*; the generic multiplicity of being is not, however, localisable in any one identity configuration. This leads Badiou to be able to say, for example, that '[i]l y a autant de différence entre, disons, un paysan chinois et un jeune cadre norvégien qu'entre moi-même et n'importe qui – y compris moi-même. Autant, mais donc aussi *ni plus ni moins*' ['There are as many differences, say, between a Chinese peasant and a young Norwegian professional as between myself and anybody at all, including myself. As many, but also, then, *neither more nor less*'] (E_1, p. 44; E_2, p. 26, Badiou's emphasis). While there is without doubt some serious cause for reflection (about difference and identity and their relationships to capitalism) based on some of Badiou's claims, his position also has the consequence of flattening all differences (no doubt intentional given his singular interest in infinite multiplicities) such that the structural and systemic oppressions of our present situation (and thence their relationships to capitalism) cease to matter. It is quite evidently true that the hypocrisy of the supposed (Western) commitment to 'democratic materialism' (i.e. the ethics of 'recognising the other', in favour of diversity, multiculturalism, plurality of opinions and cultures premised on a fundamental and universal equality, i.e. 'human rights') is easily shown, in practice, to mean 'freedom' for those, and only those,

---

[28] Alain Badiou, 'Appendix: Politics and Philosophy' in *Ethics: An Essay on the Understanding of Evil*, p. 114.

who believe in democracy (which in turn ultimately is shown to be the free market). This internal inconsistency and hypocrisy is, indubitably, grave and, it would seem, not only indisputable but a rallying wake-up call to the present realities of economic neo-imperialism. At the same time, however, Badiou's incendiary invective against 'identity politics' smoothes over a playing field – albeit one constructed by a particular world situation – that is fundamentally not smooth, and moreover for reasons that are indispensable to the very functioning of capital that Badiou aims to critique. His reproach is also cruel, patronising and self-serving, demanding that there be no significant difference between managers, terrorists or transsexuals, or that the politics of sexual liberation and polygamy do not also inflect a long, important and ongoing history of sexism, trans/misogyny and racism, particularly once the dynamics of power, control and consent are brought into frame. Not only is the levelling gratuitous, but so too is the flattening; individuals are reduced to the composite of their supposed identities and voided of any reflective capacity (unlike Badiou, apparently) to recognise the ways in which their battles are instrumentalised against them by market forces – not to mention the pragmatic reasons why an individual might opt 'in' to the system, even against themselves (or their politics). The ways in which Badiou – and philosophy at large – can be seen as co-opted into the neoliberal economic system (as if books were not commercial as well as informative or as if holding a professorship at the prestigious ENS doesn't offer institutionally sanctioned legitimacy along with the opportunity to preach and practice radical politics) are simply ignored. It is hard to see how this is anything other than a stereotyped caricature of identity politics and a woeful under-description of the complexities of (historically) identity-based movements that, in the twenty-first century tend to constellate around intersectionality, performativity, association and ally-ship. It also runs to the thoroughly absurd logical conclusion, as suggested above, that the only group not guilty of the vanity and fallacy of 'identity politics' is the (ever neutral) straight, white, bourgeois, cisgender, able-bodied man (such as Badiou) – as if his (non-)identity was not also an identity that is substantially responsible for privileging voices (such as his own) and for its easy identification of/as the universal.[29] In what follows, I hope to make it plain that this commitment to

---

[29] Similarly, Sara Ahmed identifies the way in which, for thinkers such as Badiou and Žižek, 'identity politics' are derided and disparaged for creating a new set of marketable products (not only books, magazines, etc., but also lecture circuits) asking us to note 'the irony that Žižek and Badiou might not need to create a so-called "segment of identity politics" to guarantee their own lecture tours (indeed the critique of identity politics is probably more profitable and more inductive to the logic of capital)'; see Sara Ahmed, 'Melancolic Universalism'.

a flawed universality poses problems not only in the way that Badiou consequently rejects feminism (while, nonetheless, maintaining a concept of 'femininity') but also for his thinking on aesthetics.

ART AGAIN, OR *INESTHÉTIQUE*

The question of art – and especially how art *vis-à-vis* a universal Badiousian truth-procedure plays out – ultimately, then, will be the final focus of this chapter, most specifically of course in terms of 'musical' art. (Though Badiou offers no theory as such of 'art' or the specifically 'musical', he nonetheless pronounces on, or, rather, identifies the truth-procedures of various 'musical' events as his philosophy sets itself up to do.) From the off, however, Badiou's delimiting of this category (art) is itself contentious, as is his theory of *inesthétique*. While Elie During claims that 'Badiou's writings make constant use of artistic examples and paradigms, taken from both "high" and "low" culture',[30] it is extremely hard to see much evidence for this except, perhaps, for his meditations on the horses painted in the Lascaux caves (though being prehistoric it seems evident that they refuse this distinction), his otherwise relentless bemoaning of the 'democratisation of taste', cultural diversity and plurality, and his utterly disparaging remarks on all non-'high' art (to which he would hardly even accord the title of 'art'). To wit (and to mention just a couple of instances):

> En réalité, il n'y a pas d'art populaire. C'est une expression dépourvue de sens. En quoi l'adjectif 'populaire' vient-il spécifier ou déterminer le mot 'art'? C'est une catégorie qu'il faut abandonner. Il y a la musique, c'est tout. *La musique sera jugée à partir de sa capacité à traiter des inventions formelles.* On verra alors que le degré de complexité, d'inventivité de la musique dite savante est sans commune mesure avec celle dite populaire. Il a fallu d'ailleurs dire 'savante' uniquement parce qu'une musique se disait 'populaire'. Cette dernière doit être appelée musique de divertissement, ce qui n'a rien d'infamant. (PE_1, p. 95, my emphasis)

> [In reality, there is no such thing as popular art. The expression is meaningless. In what way does the adjective 'popular' specify or determine the word 'art'? This category has to be jettisoned. There is music, full stop. *Music will be judged on the basis of its capacity to deal with formal inventions.* It will, then, become clear that the degree of complexity, of inventiveness, of so-called serious music is without any common measure with that said to be popular. It was necessary, moreover, to say 'serious' solely because there was music said to be popular. The latter should be called music of entertainment, which is in no way defamatory.] (PE_2, p. 80, my emphasis)

---

[30] Elie During, 'Art', in Bartlett, Clemens and Badiou (eds), *Alain Badiou: Key Concepts*, pp. 82–93 (p. 82).

And again (and yet more egregiously):

> la 'musique contemporaine' [i.e. musique savante contemporaine], c'est-à-dire de cela seul qui, au XXe siècle, a mérité le nom de 'musique' – si du moins la musique est un art, et non ce qu'un ministre a cru devoir subordonner à une éprouvante fête. (Sc, pp. 91–2)
>
> ['contemporary music', that is, of the only thing that in the twentieth century merited the name of 'music' – if we grant that music is an art and not that wich some minister subjects to the demands of gruelling festivals.] (Sch, p. 81)

Thus, the disdain with which he considers (all) non-'high' art forms is abundantly clear; though he mentions 'popular' or 'entertainment' arts most often in his invectives, he quite clearly also includes folk, non-literate and quite possibly non-Western forms of music-making. There is a singular and revealing – though non-committal – exception for jazz, which though not explicitly described in terms of truth, must nonetheless 'être incorporée à l'histoire de la musique savante' ['be incorporated within the history of serious music'], though this is because jazz 'a progressivement rejoint [...] les problèmes les plus sophistiqués de la musique savante' ['was [...] to progressively intersect with the most sophisticated problems of serious music'].[31] This is a position advanced across several texts, and appears to be motivated or justified by his commitment to defending 'l'idée d'unité de l'art, son unité de toujours' ['the idea of art's unity, the unity it has always had'] (PE$_1$, p. 97; PE$_2$, p. 81). While these (contentious) assertions are presupposed as a non-historicisable fact, in *Inesthétique*, he plays close attention to the historical formulas that have connected art and philosophy – particularly in relation to truth – in distinctly different ways. It is his contention that there have been three previous conceptions of the relationship between art and philosophy, all of which are also related to education (as with Lacoue-Labarthe). Firstly, there is the didactic or Platonic view of art that identifies its essence in mimesis, and therefore in the production of the *effect* of truth (which is in fact extrinsic to it) resulting in art's banishment – or at least its strict control. Secondly, the Romantic or German/hermeneutic schema whose thesis is 'que l'art *seul* est capable de vérité. Et qu'en ce sens il accomplit ce que la philosophie ne peut qu'indiquer' ['that art *alone* is capable of truth. What's more, it is in this sense that art accomplishes what philosophy can itself only point toward'] (PMI, p. 12; HI, p. 3, Badiou's emphasis), all of which leads to

---

[31] Does this not simply imply a discourse of assimilation, whereby 'other' traditions must simply assimilate to the apparently universal (though distinctly Western, Eurocentric, bourgeois) tradition in order to be considered 'real' art?

a hysterical glorification of art. Thirdly, the classical or Aristotelian *dispositif* which, like the didactic schema, claims that art, with its essence in mimesis, is incapable of producing truth but, in contrast, 'Ce n'est pas grave, parce que la *destination* de l'art n'est nullement la vérité. Certes, l'art n'est pas vérité, mais aussi bien il ne prétend pas l'être, et donc il est innocent' ['This incapacity does not pose a serious problem [. . .] This is because the *purpose* [*destination*] of art is not in the least truth. Of course, art is not truth, but it also does not claim to be truth and is therefore innocent'] (PMI, p. 13; HI, p. 4, Badiou's emphasis). It is this conviction, as Badiou goes on to describe, which leads to the Aristotelian articulation of art's relation or role with regard to the passions and to catharsis, and thus figures art as fundamentally therapeutic rather than cognitive or revelatory (see PMI, p. 13; HI, p. 4). Ultimately, then, these different approaches cast the specific relationship between art and truth in three distinct ways: in the didactic view truth is singular but not immanent; in the Romantic view it is immanent but not singular; and in the classical view truth is neither immanent nor singular, though it may appear to be – art is effectively an 'opération publique' ['public operation'] (PMI, p. 14; HI, p. 5). Badiou's radical proposition in *Inesthétique* then, is to offer a fourth schema or method for the understanding of the relationship between art and truth: as both singular *and* immanent (i.e. universal and singular – in the way it is linked to a specific situation).

The role of philosophy, *vis-à-vis* art, then, is 'distinguer [la vérité] de l'opinion' ['to distinguish truths from opinion'] (PMI, p. 29; HI p. 15). However, this is strictly not aesthetics in the conventional sense, where art is an 'object' for philosophical speculation and where art is also beholden to philosophy's interpretation and the (illusory) 'truths' *about* it that philosophy itself (and alone) is able to provide; instead, 'l'art *lui-même* est une procédure de vérité' ['Art *itself* is a truth procedure'] (PMI, p. 21; HI, p. 9, Badiou's emphasis). Or, as Badiou describes in the epigraph:

> Par 'inesthétique', j'entends un rapport de la philosophie à l'art qui, posant que l'art est par lui-même producteur de vérités, ne prétend d'aucune façon en faire, pour la philosophie, un objet. Contre la spéculation esthétique, l'inesthétique décrit les effets strictement intraphilosophiques produits par l'existence indépendante de quelques œuvres d'art. (PMI, epigraph, unnumbered).

> [By 'inaesthetics' I understand a relation of philosophy to art that, maintaining that art is itself a producer of truths, makes no claim to turn art into an object for philosophy. Against aesthetic speculation, inaesthetics describes the strictly intraphilosophical effects produced by the independent existence of some works of art.]

We might note, however, that while Badiou is adamant that philosophy is only philosophy in 'se gardant de *juger* le poème [or the artwork in general] et, singulièrement, de vouloir [. . .] lui administrer des leçons politiques' ['abstain[ing] from *judging* the poem, and, most of all, from the wish [. . .] of imparting any political lessons based upon it'] (PMI, p. 46; HI, p. 27, Badiou's emphasis), he has nonetheless quite clearly circumscribed and rhetorically defined – albeit within a fantastically well-wrought philosophical system – what we will admit into the arena of art (and thus truths) by *a priori* elimination of popular (and other) arts: by *judging* them, ultimately, as *not art*. It is absolutely unclear in what way this is anything other than the kind of 'opinion' that philosophy should be distinguishing from truths – except that the whole system has been built around Badiou's pre-philosophical exclusion of certain types of (non-) art and thus appears at first glance, to be internally consistent.

HANS JÜRGEN SYBERBERG'S (AND WAGNER'S) *PARSIFAL*

Now we will turn to Badiou's other major text on music, *Five Lessons on Wagner*, which is admittedly hesitant at committing itself to being a book *about* music. After an unusually personal preface in which Badiou gushes emphatically about his lifelong affection for the music of Wagner – a love inherited from his mother and cemented by life opportunities[32] – he indicates more than a little resistance to the idea of writing a book on Wagner (see the 'Preface'). He also describes how he was able to draw on this long-standing Wagnerian love affair in the *Concours* – the competitive national exam that awards places to the top-ranked students to the *Grandes Écoles* – where he devoted the concluding paragraph of an essay on 'What is a genius' to *Parsifal*. The text itself has an unusual history, given that it comprises the amalgamated and edited version of a series of lectures (and the notes thereof) worked into a text originally in English – though the lecture notes were in French – by Susan Spitzer. Strangely, then, the French version of this text is actually a translation of the original English text, *Five Lessons on Wagner*, and not written directly by Badiou's own hand (though the content evidently derives entirely from the aforementioned lectures), the result of which is an uncharacteristically lucid and easy-reading text.

---

[32] For example, in his role as the 'Oberbürgmeister of Toulouse', Badiou's father was personally invited to the 'New Bayreuth' under the direction of Wieland Wagner; he also gave Badiou and his school friends seats in the mayor's box when he brought *Tristan und Isolde* to Toulouse (see FLW, p. ix).

Interestingly – and I think aptly – Badiou characterises the Wagner question as a specific genre for philosophy, one which, he claims, 'created a new situation with respect to the relationship between music and philosophy' (FLW, p. 56) but also suggests that Wagner has thus become a necessary 'subject' for any philosopher to approach. The first three lessons lay out, almost as a literature review, the historical and extant positions on the 'Wagner case' as he sees them and summarise the core objections levelled at him from Nietzsche through to Adorno and on to Lacoue-Labarthe alongside a few moments of personal reflection, analysis and commentary. Lessons four and five, 'Reopening "The Case of Wagner"' and 'The Enigma of *Parsifal*', offer much more in terms of Badiou's own analysis of the questions at hand, bringing it into a closer – though by no means as explicit as in his writing in general – dialogue with Badiou's philosophy (and politics) at large. The fourth chapter, 'Reopening "The Case of Wagner"' sets out to right what Badiou sees to be some of the false accusations levelled at Wagner in previous philosophical tracts, notably to do with the imposition of the 'endless melody' (FLW, pp. 76–7); the way in which 'the Other's suffering is dissolved in a rhetoric of compassion' (FLW, p. 77); the charge that Wagner's music is ultimately dialectical in a resolving or reconciliatory sense (see FLW, p. 78); that the music is ultimately subjected to the narrative (see FLW, pp. 78–9); and that Wagner is unable to create a new sense of time, especially in terms of 'waiting' (see FLW, pp. 79–80). These fundamental questions about Wagner's musical practice and aesthetics – which ultimately hinge on the ever-present question of whether his music has some essential link to anti-Semitism and fascism – will be dealt with in a comparative analytic with Nancy's and Lacoue-Labarthe's perspectives in the following and final chapter of this book. For now, it is to Badiou's characterisation, analysis and understanding of *Parsifal* as mentioned on occasion in lesson four and as the subject proper of lesson five that we will turn our attention.

In 'Reopening "The Case of Wagner"' one of the central concerns is to pull a little at the inherited idea that Wagner, though he makes you wait – seemingly endlessly – for a resolution, is finally in the service of the ultimate (dialectical) resolution and, moreover, one that therefore dissolves all difference, in a formidable and totalising gesture of closure. Thus, to give only the best-known example (and one that has already come up in Chapter 2), in *Tristan und Isolde*, though we may wait around four hours for the desired resolution of the dissonance set up in the 'prelude', we nonetheless get the resolution we have patiently waited for – and we might add in an almost excruciatingly sublime way that obliterates the suffering and, finally, the death of the protagonists alongside which this musical gesture of closure is carefully coordinated. Badiou, however, approaches this question of difference and closure from a rather different angle, arguing that the radically different 'colour scheme' (FLW, p. 99) of each opera instead indicates that 'there is no one single, unifying pole towards which the music is somehow oriented as such, but rather an exploration of diverse possibilities' (FLW, p. 99). In short, each opera is oriented towards exploring the possibility of a particular '*hypothesis*' (FLW, p. 99). Rather than seeing Wagner's infamously lengthy operas as the way in which he manipulatively builds such extraordinary tension so as to require a final gesture of ultimate and totalising resolution of all differences, he senses in Wagner's 'difficulty in concluding' a distinctive hesitancy, and one, moreover, that 'had a tendency to leave several interpretations of hypotheses open' (FLW, p. 100). Badiou's own proposition – that Wagner's (overly) long operas in fact present us with a question to which Wagner is reluctant to conclude definitively – is then explored in relation to the various hypotheses that Badiou claims three of the operas present. While *Götterdämmerung* and *Die Meistersinger* deal with, respectively, the question of what comes after the gods – proposing (in Badiou's analysis): 'humanity, regarded in a revolutionary sense, an utterly generic, not specific sense' (FLW, p. 101) and 'the essence of Germany' to which (in Badiou's analysis, again) is proposed, 'high art' (FLW, p. 103) – *Parsifal* asks (as does Nietzsche): 'Is there something beyond Christianity?' (FLW, p. 103). The Christian symbolism employed in *Parsifal* is certainly without doubt, though Badiou, as usual, approaches it from a rather different angle: he suggests that the answer offered by Wagner to the question is that 'what is beyond Christianity is actually the full affirmation of Christianity itself' (FLW, p. 103). Of course this chimes rather nicely with Badiou's own proposal of an essentially Christian materialism developed from his understanding of the fundamental message of the Pauline universal; but it also offers a very different take on one of the classic critiques of *Parsifal* – that 'Redemption to the Redeemer' is a deeply anti-Semitic 'solution' to the problem of Jesus being born a Jew, and thus that he, too, needs redeeming. In stark contrast (and with no acknowledgement of how this either subverts or runs alongside – or even challenges – the problem of anti-Semitism in *Parsifal* in this regard) he claims that:

> 'Redemption to the Redeemer' means: Christianity has ceased being a doctrine of salvation, and it is only through the figural or aesthetic reaffirmation of the Christian totality, which in a certain way de-Christianizes and de-idealizes it, that something beyond Christianity can be found [. . .] *Parsifal* is the eternal return applied to Christianity. Christianity returns, but it does so

in an aesthetically affirmed mode, that of the 'Redemption to the Redeemer', as though it had to return as something different from, yet based on, itself. (FLW, p. 103)

All of this is initially presented fairly didactically without much (if any) recourse to either the music or libretto of *Parsifal*, but it is then followed by a section dealing with the '*musical structure of the three [Götterdämmerung, Die Meistersinger and Parsifal] endings*' where his claims are fleshed out with more reference to the works at hand. Though the specifics of the analyses offered of *Götterdämmerung* and *Die Meistersinger* are beyond our concerns here (only because neither receive the same level of sustained engagement as does *Parsifal*), it is notable that for *Götterdämmerung* – as we will see is also the case for *Parsifal*, which hinges on Hans Jürgen Syberberg's centennial film production – the elucidating examples given often pivot around a particular performance or staging (in *Götterdämmerung* it is the Chéreau-Boulez collaboration). In contrast, this is not the case for *Die Meistersinger*, though the subject matter of this work is itself concerned with the question of aesthetics, art, performance and, thus, representation.

The discussion of *Parsifal* begins from where the analysis of *Die Meistersinger* left off: with the issue of renunciation as exemplified most clearly in the finale. Having outlined already the hypothesis Badiou claims is presented in *Parsifal* – that of the redemption of Christianity in a de-Christianised form, and thus the renunciation of the 'old' Christianity – he explores how this plays out, and interestingly it intersects on multiple occasions with the question of gender. He describes the 'old Christianity' as represented by Titurel and his son Amfortas on multiple occasions as 'moribund' (FLW, p. 110), explaining this as a result of Christianity's fixation on a survivalist mode, a parochial outlook and its 'defensive dimension' (FLW, p. 110). Badiou then claims that when all that is being aimed for is survival, 'you are defenceless against the insistence of the sexual drive' (FLW, p. 110), and thus we are seamlessly led into a consideration of Amfortas's infamous wound – not forgetting that Amfortas is a representative of the old Christianity. As Badiou describes, he 'has a disgusting, oozing fatal wound, owing to the fact he could not resist temptation' (FLW, p. 110); this 'utterly obscene wound' is then, as Badiou argues just a few lines below, 'aptly filmed by Syberberg with terrifying obscenity as a vagina displayed on a cushion' (FLW, p. 110, see Figure 4.1). Not only does Badiou consequently identify vaginas as disgusting, obscene, a force of devastating *jouissance*, and the danger of not resisting temptation, his gesture is all the more disturbing given that the 'vagina displayed on a cushion' is

Figure 4.1 Act I, Scene 4. Credit: Zoetrope

just one incarnation of Amfortas's wound in Syberberg's production (nor is there any suggestion that it actually *is* a vagina or, rather, a vulva); though it is also displayed in a vulva-like manner in the 'prelude' (see Figure 4.2) it is rather, as David Schwarz describes,

> a unique 'performing object' in Syberberg's film. It changes in every scene it appears. As a performing object with no internal consistency from moment to moment, it is the purest form of Icon – one in which meaning is projected at every moment, changing the object each time it is seen.[33]

It is interesting, then, that the only meaningful identification Badiou projects onto Amfortas's 'disgusting, oozing fatal wound' is that of a 'vagina', and a vagina that is somehow associated with a moribund Christianity in need of both renunciation and redemption.

Ultimately – misogynistic language temporarily placed to one side – Badiou makes a strong case for the central role of compassion (*Mitleid*) in *Parsifal* as being aligned with self-denial – because 'survival is actually a form of *self*-concern, which explains why it does not protect us from the obscenity of *jouissance*' (FLW, p. 111). We are thus faced with

---

[33] David Schwarz, *Listening Awry*, p. 153.

Figure 4.2   Overture. Credit: Zoetrope

the pairs 'compassion/self-denial' and 'Christianity/survival' which are musically (re)presented, Badiou claims, 'through the theme of Amfortas and his wound, and, on the other, through the theme of Parsifal, which is practically understated, barely phrased in the brass' (FLW, p. 111). Amfortas's theme is characterised as 'lyrical' and 'fearsome' ('lyrical' has a long history of being perceived as stereotypically 'feminine' in music, and we have just noted Badiou's own fear regarding female genitalia) while Parsifal's, as mentioned, is 'understated', though there is no discussion of how that comes about musically save the reference to the brass (FLW, p. 111). All of this is simply to highlight that we are left to go on Badiou's word alone that this is the case, as there is no illustrative reference to techniques of musical representation, orchestration, tonal/chromatic/diatonic relations, phrasing, timbre – let alone strictly *formal* relations. Again, he says:

> [i]n terms of the music, I would say that this whole finale, concerned as it is with replacing moribund, narcissistic, deathly Christianity with a new, reaffirmed Christianity around the idea of a central, innocent self-denial, will attempt to represent what I would call the evaporation of sovereignty into gentleness, or the transmutation of sovereignty into gentleness. That is what I think is really at stake in the music of the finale. *Whether it succeeds or not is partly a question of analysis and taste.* (FLW, p. 112, my emphasis)

This is not to suggest, of course, that a musical justification for these claims could not be found; rather, it is to emphasise that, again, when

Badiou speaks 'of the music' in Wagner he rarely lives up to his word (and not only in terms of the restricted and formalistic terms he has set for himself elsewhere). Likewise, his invocation of the roles of 'analysis' and 'taste' are instructive parameters he permits into the musico-philosophical discussion of Wagner that elsewhere he has repeatedly maligned (at least in terms of their interest for philosophy whose role is to birth, as 'midwife', the truth-procedures of any of the four conditions and avoid opinion).

So to return briefly to the analysis of *Parsifal*, we have quite evidently been presented already with a strong and problematic intersection with considerations of gender and sexuation, but this is not the only place this question comes up explicitly in his analysis. Because Badiou's only referent for *Parsifal* is explicitly Syberberg's film version, the question of gendered identity and sexuation becomes more or less unavoidable. Syberberg took the absolutely original move of having Parsifal played by two different actors (actually three actors, if you include the child Parsifal we witness in the animated 'prelude', in addition to the singer, Rainer Goldberg, who provides the vocal part throughout): a young man and a young woman. Parsifal has appeared, up until this pivotal moment, in more or less conventional fashion as a young man played by Michael Kutter (save that 'he' does not provide the vocal part but instead a singer's voice is over-dubbed to his lip-syncing and he is also considerably younger than most operatic singers tackling the part on stage). However, at the well-known point of transformation – a deeply Oedipal scene where Parsifal is seduced, as Badiou states, 'by a kind of weird mother [Kundry] who is both dead and alive, a sexual vampire of sorts' (FLW, p. 113) – Parsifal either splits or is doubled – initially through a process of substitution and finally combination (see FLW, p. 113) – and the adolescent boy is first replaced by, then appears alongside, an adolescent girl. Though Parsifal initially yields to the kiss, he abruptly breaks away, thus representing two stages of transformation (one in relation to his own psychical and sexual maturation and the other in relation to compassion – the wound it provokes him to 'feel'). This brings Badiou to suggest that a Christian renewal will also be to do with 'the heralding of a new sexuation' (FLW, p. 113) – a not altogether unwelcome proposal. This strikingly queer gesture – insofar as we continue to hear the voice of tenor Rainer Goldberg being emitted, now 'from' the body/mouth of Karin Krick – which Badiou understands to show that, as already suggested, it is 'as if only either by combining the two sexes or showing that there is no difference between them or that they are hard to tell apart could represent the redemption of the deathly sensuality and obscene *jouissance* in which the Christianity of the past has exhausted itself' (FLW, pp. 112–13). Later on, he also refers to Parsifal as 'the universal signifier' (FLW, p. 142) – a claim which one can see to be substantially buoyed by Syberberg's symbolic presentation of masculine and feminine poles within a single 'character' (or 'signifier', as Badiou also claims, see FLW, p. 140). Though we will return to this striking visual, technological and symbolic splitting between masculine and feminine poles, between actor and singer, voice and body, for now it is necessary to bring this into closer dialogue with Badiou's understanding and characterisation not only of the feminine, but also feminism, as found elsewhere.

BADIOU AND FEMINISM, AND THE FEMININE (GENERIC) ♀

> Les différences nous donnent, comme font les timbres instrumentaux, l'univocité reconnaissable de la mélodie du Vrai.
> Badiou[34]

As suggested previously Badiou aligns feminism, fairly uncritically, with all the other (and ever proliferating) identity-based movements. He cites it specifically in relation to his critique of 'ethical ideology' as manifested in human rights discourse and the prescription that we should respect the 'other', or those different from us, but only with the caveat, as he points out 'que le différent soit démocrate-parlementaire, partisan de l'économie de marché, support de la liberté d'opinion, féministe, écologiste ...' ['that the different be parliamentary-democratic, pro free-market economics, in favour of freedom of opinion, feminism, the environment ...'] (E_1, p. 41; E_2, p. 24). More concretely, he explicitly frames his project as a battle against 'le culte des identités nationales, raciales, sexuelles, religieuses, culturelles tentant de défaire les droits de l'universel' ['the cult of national, racial, sexual, religious and cultural identities seeking to undo the rights of the universal'].[35] For Badiou, then, the primacy of the universal trumps all other claims, and the prescription of the demand to respect the other (and our infinite particularisms) as the sole 'universal' to which we can legitimately refer is merely the misguided and illusory outcome of a sophistical logic. For Badiou, feminists are caught in the (false) logic of an ethics of difference,

---

[34] StP_1, p. 113 [Differences, like instrumental tones, provide us with the recognizable univocity that makes up the melody of the True] (StP_2, p. 106).
[35] Badiou, *Second manifeste pour la philosophie*, p. 10 [Badiou, *Second Manifesto for Philosophy*, p. 4].

one that was clearly exposed when it came to the debate over the headscarf in France. According to Badiou, the logic goes something like this: feminism is rooted in an ethics of difference which demands respect for difference (for example, here, based in sex/gender), but is ultimately hypocritical because it rejects differences that conflict with its own (sense of difference/identity) as was borne out with (some) feminists' support for the burka ban (which they saw to index male domination and patriarchal control over women's bodies). Secondly, as with any position which refutes the neutrality of the universal, it does so from the false basis of starting from a particularist difference as given (or constructed) in a specific (historical) situation: in this way Badiou is (rather welcomely) deeply anti-essentialist. The foundations of this kind of argument are discussed in detail in his major text on the (neutral) universal, *St Paul*, notably including a lengthy discussion that aims to rehabilitate St Paul from the claims, 'souvent soutenu, que Paul soit le fondateur d'une misogynie chrétienne' ['frequently maintained, that Paul is the founder of a Christian misogyny'] (StP_1, pp. 110–11; StP_2, p. 103). His major claim is that Paul's significant contribution is that 'On ne peut transcender les différences que si la bénévolence à l'égard des coutumes et des opinions se présente comme *une différence tolérante aux différences*' ['Difference can be transcended only if benevolence with regard to customs and opinions presents itself as *an indifference that tolerates differences*'] (StP_1, p. 106; StP_2, p. 99, Badiou's emphasis), and which is summed up in the prescription: 'ne soyez pas un discutant des opinions' ['do not argue about opinions'] (Rom. 14.1, cited in StP_1, p. 107; StP_2, p. 100).

Absolutely unacknowledged, then, in Badiou's œuvre, and perhaps symptomatically so, is the fact that feminism itself has a long and arduous history (both in terms of theory and praxis) in (re)theorising, understanding, negotiating and challenging the concept of the 'universal'.[36] Furthermore, and perhaps closer to Badiou's thinking, for some feminists this *also* comes hand in hand with a long-standing critique of relativism, including specifically feminist objections to the entire project of human rights (reaching, in many ways, a similar conclusion to Badiou: that the whole project of human rights functions as an 'opt-in' to the status quo, in this instance capitalist patriarchy, and thus

---

[36] For a variety of positions on this debate see, for example, Leila Ahmed, *Women and Gender in Islam*; Hazel V. Carby, 'White woman listen!'; Kimberlé Crenshaw, 'Demarginalizing the Intersection of Race and Sex', pp. 139–67; Jodi Dean, *Solidarity of Strangers*; Jean Grimshaw, 'Philosophy, feminism and universalism', pp. 19–28; bell hooks, *Feminist Theory*; Chandra Talpade Mohanty, 'Under Western Eyes', pp. 333–58; and Jill Steans, 'Debating women's human rights as a universal feminist project', pp. 11–27.

in some fundamental sense it does not significantly challenge or alter the systemic oppressions of capitalist heteropatriarchy). In this respect, Badiou's generally reactionary and remarkably un-nuanced perception of feminism bears little relation to feminism as it is actually practised or theorised, and instead throws out a whole body of work that has itself spent so much time and energy devoted to the extraordinarily difficult question of the relation between the local and the global or the particular and the universal. Indeed, feminism is given such short shrift in all of Badiou's work that his characterisation and understanding of it simply does not chime with the realities of either feminist activists or academics. As Mari Ruti compellingly describes:

> many of them [supposed 'identity' movements, in Badiou's terms] are actually not identarian at all but often work quite diligently to forge cross-identarian or postidentarian alliances. For instance, contemporary feminism, at least in its more theoretical valences, is rarely a movement for the liberation of 'women,' understood in some essentialist sense, but one that questions the very meaning and construction of gender and sexuality. Moreover, such feminism usually strives to combine an analysis of heteropatriarchy with an analysis of other related forms of social inequality, such as racism and class disparities.[37]

Though Badiou is typically dismissive of feminism, he nonetheless accords the feminine 'position' an important role in his philosophy. As noted, he objects to what he sees as a (philosophical) position that proceeds from a particularism – that of 'woman' – rather than that of a universal. In this respect, it is Irigaray, for Badiou, who is the quintessential 'anti-philosophe' in the way that she espouses 'a violent determination of philosophy on the basis of the category of "woman"'.[38] It is for Badiou an illusory basis from which to proceed – not because he denies difference – but because (multiple/infinite) difference is simply what there is in the world. As he describes,

> [t]out est différent de tout, tout est autre que tout. Étant donné que je suis dans une ontologie qui est radicalement une ontologie du multiple, la différence, l'altérité, c'est ce dont je pars; c'est le régime d'être [. . .] Je n'introduis la relation qu'au niveau de l'apparaître; c'est une catégorie du monde, non de l'être. (PE_1, p. 70)

> [Everything is different from everything else, everything is other than everything else. Given that I am in an ontology that is radically an ontology of the multiple, difference or alterity is what I set our from: it's the regime of being [. . .] I only introduce relations at the level of appearing; it's a category pertaining to world and not to being.] (PE_2, p. 57)

---

[37] Mari Ruti, *Between Levinas and Lacan*, p. 88.
[38] Private communication between Burchill and Badiou, 2011, cited in Louise Burchill, 'Feminism' in Steven Corcoran (ed.), *The Badiou Dictionary*, p. 131.

This, however, is where things start to become more complicated. Though Badiou reduces the *category* 'woman' to an appearance that has nothing to do with either truth or Being (which simply consists of infinite multiplicities) he nonetheless insists on oppositional poles or positions, which he continues to name 'man' and 'woman' or 'masculine' and 'feminine'. He is, certainly, extremely careful to detach these poles from a biological sexuation (though he doesn't deny biological sexuation) when it comes to truth: 'on verra que, de l'intérieur même de l'amour, se construisent une position "homme" et une position "femme"' ['it becomes clear that a position "man" and a position "woman" are constructed within love itself'] (PE_1, p. 74; PE_2, p. 61) – just as with Badiou's truth-procedures in other domains, it is a 'truth' produced or induced by an event (of love, in this instance). In this respect, though love is fundamentally heterosexual Badiou is not necessarily homophobic as such: as he states, 'elle n'a rien à voir avec le sexe empirique des personnes engagées dans la relation amoureuse. J'admets tout à fait qu'il puisse y avoir de l'amour homosexuel [... et] le jeu de ces positions est universel' ['they have nothing to do with the empirical sex of the people engaged in the love relation. I fully recognize that there can be homosexual love [... and that] the play of these positions is, I believe, universal']. (PE_1, p. 74; PE_2, p. 61). Nevertheless, in the descriptive language Badiou uses to talk about these poles, he uses what seem to be indisputably stereotyped associations: when he describes the position 'man' as rational, imperative, mute and violent, and the position 'woman' as wandering, narrative, garrulous and demanding (see CS_2, pp. 253–73, and Tarby in PE_1, p. 73; PE_2, p. 61). Moreover, it would seem, though Badiou claims no biological basis for these positions, that 'la position masculine est assez souvent occupée par l'homme' ['the masculine position is fairly often occupied by men'] – though this is of interest to sociologists and not philosophers, claims Badiou (PE_1, p. 75; PE_2, p. 62).

There is more, however. In Badiou's difficult to parse instrumentation of Cantorian set theory *as* ontology, he replaces the standard marker for the (indiscernible) generic set (G) with the Venus symbol ♀ – a move that Burhanuddin Baki suggests may be 'in order to insinuate some Lacanian connection he leaves open to speculation'.[39] The generic set ♀ (elsewhere described as 'une vérité générique' or 'une multiplicité générique') is a 'missing subset'[40] that conditions the situation S: thus S(♀) is the set theoretical procedure through which Badiou is able to account

---

[39] Burhanuddin Baki, *Badiou's Being and Event and the Mathematics of Set Theory*, p. 171.
[40] Ibid., p. 216.

for the event (which is not contained within the situation but is its absent condition) and which, otherwise, is an ontological violation. In short, an inhabitant of S (the situation) cannot have knowledge of ♀ but can only have militant faith in it.[41] The problem with this, of course, is that Badiou enlists a distinctly feminine generic which, 'by being exterior to the situation, is essentially independent of Being and ontology'[42] and, at the same time, denies the category 'woman' any significant existence on these levels. Femininity is precisely, he claims, that which 'consists in a "logic of the Two", or "a passage-between-the-Two" that has traditionally undone the One of the masculine position'.[43] Badiou is thus charged with, as Louise Burchill describes, '"returning" to woman (pace Lacan) the universal quantifier within the sphere of the symbolic value or "the complete range of truth procedures"' and so, *encore*, a certain (absent) 'feminine exceptionality' continues to haunt Badiou's thinking.[44]

This is worth just one final word for clarification. There is no suggestion at all that only (biologically or otherwise determined) men are capable of militating faithfully for universal truth; though it is infrequent, women (as they 'appear') are occasionally accorded this success. However, as with the female protagonist, Paule (clearly a reference to the Pauline universal) in Badiou's play, *L'Incident d'Antioche*, this appears to be through a rescinding of 'womanly particularity' and thus incorporating herself to the (revolutionary) universal truth-procedure.[45] Moreover, this is explicitly framed in contrast to (a stereotyped) feminism, from which Paule distances herself when she says 'Et qui dit que la laideur, le cheveu plat, la femme éteinte au kaki de la guerre, la jupe de laine noire étaient requis, pour la promesse et l'enchantement de notre politique?' ['And who said that looking ugly, wearing your hair pulled back, hiding your femininity under military fatigues or wearing a shapeless dress were required for our politics to be one of hope and joy?'].[46] Badiou thus appears to want to have his non-/essentialist cake and eat it, so to speak, by enlisting a kind of generic feminine exceptionalism to which he can be militantly faithful, while insisting not only on the irrelevance of 'woman' as a category for politics (or indeed,

---

[41] Ibid., p. 198.
[42] Ibid., p. 227.
[43] Badiou, cited in Louise Burchill, 'Woman, the Feminine, Sexual Difference' in Steven Corcoran (ed.), *The Badiou Dictionary*, pp. 390–5 (p. 395). I would not be the first to note an unexpected complementarity between Badiou and Irigaray. See, for example, Lisa Watrous, 'Love's Universal Impetus', pp. 66–73.
[44] Burchill, 'Woman, the Feminine, Sexual Difference' in Steven Corcoran (ed.), *The Badiou Dictionary*, p. 394.
[45] Ibid., p. 392, and Act I, Scene IV of Alain Badiou, *Incident at Antioch/L'Incident d'Antioche*.
[46] See Act III, Scene IV in Badiou, *Incident at Antioch/L'Incident d'Antioche*, p. 100 [p. 101].

philosophy) but that women (as they appear in the world) continue to 'appear' sufficiently 'feminine'.

TECHNOLOGIES OF 'TRUTH' AND INSTRUMENTAL MUSIC (OR PHANTASMAGORIA AND FORMALISM)

Having laid out several key moments in Badiou's understanding of music, I would now like to probe a little more at the periodisation he offers us of music (that is philosophically identified as) participating in 'truth-procedures' by putting it into dialogue with relatively recent musicological texts by Mark Evan Bonds, Brian Kane and Emily Dolan. The earliest occurring (and frequently recurring) musical 'event', for Badiou, is the Haydn-event, and the latest appears to be the Schoenberg-event – though considerable attention is also paid to the musical 'serial' subject that emerges through fidelity to this event, with all trails drying up (or rather fully saturated without any new and generative musical event appearing) around the 1970s. The only significant exception proposed to the purely classical schema (and fairly tenuously at that, in that it isn't explicitly accorded the status of an 'event') is jazz. Badiou states that '[a]vec le jazz, on est dans une sphère de propositions formelles qui n'ont pas été toutes anticipées par la musique savante, à cause en particulier de l'introduction à grande échelle d'un élément d'improvisation' ['With jazz, we're dealing with a sphere of formal propositions that serious music hadn't wholly anticipated, particularly because of the large-scale introduction of an element of improvisation'] (PE_1, p. 96; PE_2, p. 80). For now, we will put this to one side, just noting that Badiou retains the criteria of *propositions formelles* as central to *savante* music and, though he acknowledges that a practice of (structural) improvisation exists in Eastern musics, he glosses over this without even attempting to explain why this has no relation to truth, as well as being oblivious to (or thinking unimportant) the long history of improvisation as a central feature of 'serious' European medieval (and even Renaissance and Baroque) musical practices.[47] Music which participates in truth-procedures appears to begin in the West with Haydn. Though Baroque style is sometimes mentioned, the event of which it is the incorporated trace – the Baroque subject – is never identified. Further still, the Baroque style – and certainly those early music

---

[47] Moreover, improvisation doesn't disappear after the Haydn-event, though our dominant narratives about musical practices/aesthetics may underprivilege its role; see, for example, Melina Esse's fantastic article on female improvisers in the nineteenth century, 'Encountering the *Improvvisatrice* in Italian Opera', pp. 709–70.

enthusiasts and followers of the historically informed performance movement – seem to be viewed with a certain disdain or dismissal at various points. Consequently, identifiable musical events run from Haydn through to Schoenberg, with the subjective trace of this later event being faithfully instantiated in musical works for another five decades: thus from the final years of the eighteenth century through to the last quarter of the twentieth century – a periodisation that parallels almost too perfectly the emergence and elevation of instrumental high art, rather than vocal musical forms through to its demise and the end of 'modern music' at the dawning of postmodernism. In short, music that falls fairly neatly under the particular ideological configuration of 'absolute music'.

Emily Dolan points out how 'we are used to associating "technology" with twentieth-century music'.[48] And, indeed, Badiou's own proclamations on musical technology seem to follow this narrative – while technology is never invoked in relation to the truth-procedures he identifies in 'serious' music, he does mention it – somewhat disparagingly – in relation to twentieth-century popular music (and particularly its associated socialities/social practices) as well as in relation to 'impure' art forms (that may include music within them) such as cinema. For example, to a certain extent he concurs with Lacoue-Labarthe's concern that, following certain technological advancements based in musical amplification, we live in an age of 'musicolatry' where we are presented with and immersed in music on an unprecedented scale (though the extent to which Wagner is culpable for this technologically mediated modern configuration is far less clear). Badiou seems to be scathing, for example, about portable music players, exclaiming (and referencing Mallarmé *en route*):

> Music was once 'the last and most complete human religion', but it has turned out to be a human religion in as sorry a state as the Brotherhood of the Knights in Act I of *Parsifal*. It has ended up being about having earphones in your ears – portable music players! Obviously nothing could be further removed from a ceremony than a portable music player. The ceremony is a meeting in a specific place; it is the constitution of a place, whereas the portable music player is music devoid of place. (FLW, p. 148)

The implication being, of course, that this over(t)ly technologically mediated music is in need of redemption in much the same way as was the moribund Christianity of *Parsifal*. And yet, there is no sense within any of his musical considerations that, for example, as Dolan again

[48] Dolan, *The Orchestral Revolution*, p. 22.

states, 'oboes and violins are also technologies'.[49] As mentioned in the previous chapter, the historically specific construction (and reification) of absolute music as textless, autonomous, self-referential and transcendental constellates around the work-concept; but it also (and inextricably) comes into being as – and only as – a form of *instrumental* music – it is explicitly and emphatically technological. This observation not only foregrounds the 'indivisibility between technology and aesthetics'[50] but also brings aesthetics into dialogue with explicitly material and historical concerns. For example, not only do technological developments (such as the invention of piston valves and their vast extension of brass instruments' capabilities in the early nineteenth century) shape what can be written for a particular instrument, but as with the discovery of (Brazilian) pernambuco wood – which to this day remains the most common material for professional bows – they embed aesthetics and musical practices in a history of European imperialism and colonialism (and environmental degradation – despite replanting efforts, the tree is still endangered). Dolan's work is ground-breaking in this regard, extending the now (musicologically) commonplace narrative that explains the emergence of 'absolute music' almost exclusively in relation to German philosophical idealism and the emergence of the work-concept while ignoring the materiality of musical practices. While these factors no doubt play a role, they nonetheless contribute to what is, as Dolan adroitly observes, ultimately a circular logic that continues to privilege form; her thesis is thus that 'music's perceived immateriality and absoluteness depended upon concrete, material changes in orchestral practice' and she accords Haydn (or at least his orchestral practice) a central role in this regard.[51]

Thus, while Badiou goes to great lengths to maintain his position that '[l]es événements artistiques sont de grandes mutations, qui portent presque toujours sur la question de savoir ce qui a valeur de forme et ce qui n'a pas valeur de forme' ['Artistic events are great mutations that almost always bear on the question of what counts, or doesn't count, as form'] (PE_1, p. 83; PE_2, p. 68), the relationship of formal innovation to technological and material innovations (and constraints) is necessarily obscured – or at least ignored. While Nancy attempts, albeit with some associated problems, to shore up a non-formalistic approach to listening by appealing to Venus's reposed and sensuous flesh – bodily responses firmly and necessarily in tow – Badiou is absolutely committed to perpetuating a history of listening that arises alongside the autonomous

[49] Ibid.
[50] Ibid.
[51] See ibid., pp. 5–7.

work-concept – that of structural listening. In this tradition, listeners must ideate the sonorous experience into visual or spatial concepts by validating, reifying and attending to primarily structural (often, therefore, in this repertoire, harmonic rather than, say, rhythmic, timbral, orchestral or vibrational) features: in short, you must listen to – and (re)cognise – *form* as constituting what is essentially musical. All of this ultimately hinges on the construction (both imaginary and literal) of the essentially musical experience taking 'place' at a distinct remove from its material/technological means of (re)production; paradoxically, then, this has the consequence, as we will see, of foregrounding the central role of *invisibility* in this discourse. In the imperative to pay attention to 'the formal configuration of tones alone', Brian Kane convincingly articulates how the 'separability of the sound itself from its source also grounds two positions that are closely tied to the rise of the autonomous musical work: phantasmagoria and formalism'.[52] Finally, then, a careful deconstruction of the essential disavowal of music's material bases pushes Dolan's thesis to the stunning conclusion that ideality itself 'is marked by its own particular timbre' and, moreover, that the musical transcendental is nothing more – or less – than 'simply another orchestral effect'.[53] In this respect, a strong argument could be made in support of Lacoue-Labarthe's characterisation of 'musicolatry' – the genealogy of which Badiou rejects – as emerging out of the Romantic tradition of absolute music (for Lacoue-Labarthe, writ large in the Wagnerian project), as it suggests a different understanding of where the fundamental break comes: thence not with the emergence of the mechanical reproduction of art works (i.e. the shift from acoustic to recorded and amplified music), but with the ideological, technological and material practices embedded in absolute music, that construct the art 'object' at a fundamental – and essential – *acousmatic* remove from its practice and/or performance.

(UN)VEILING BADIOU: ACOUSMATIC IDEOLOGY

> Wagner's fantasy of the invisible stage was fulfilled more literally in that immaterial stage, cinema.
> Susan Sontag[54]

As is well known, Wagner's project for a music drama which heralded back to the properly ancient Greek idea of tragedy (and thus the

---

[52] Brian Kane, *Sound Unseen*, p. 136.
[53] Dolan, *The Orchestral Revolution*, p. 264.
[54] Susan Sontag, *Under the Sign of Saturn*, p. 157.

non-separation of drama and music alongside that of theatrical and political life) was also an architectural project. It is, as John Deathridge concisely describes, a 'heroic drama art based in part on the Greek ideal and borne on the wings of German music', though, no doubt, this is a 'homogenized, idealized, unified, purified, communalized, culturally deified' version of the Greeks that is both notionally instrumentalised and yet also requires some substantial technical support itself to pull off this phantasmagorical illusion.[55] Wagner's contradictory wish for an invisible stage thus requires not only the architectural conceit of the double proscenium (which was certainly not the case for Greek theatre) to create the framing effect of depth – a transcendental elsewhere – but also the more radical – and now infamous – construction of the recessed pit that hides the orchestra from sight at the Bayreuth Festspielhaus. As Brian Kane argues, then, 'Bayreuth could be interpreted as an attempt to institutionalize the phantasmagorical power of the averted glance'.[56] Moreover, such architectural innovations played their part in a broader programme of reform, ultimately influenced by Schopenhauerian aesthetics. They sought also to unify

> concert programs, expressing the tendency toward unity and integration that had begun with Beethoven and was carried on through Wagner's *Gesamtkunstwerk*. The aim of these reforms was primarily conservative and 'spiritual,' an attempt to aesthetically shape the listening public, and in turn the social body, by creating the conditions for performances that could properly channel music's transcendent content.[57]

Ultimately, then, this move forms a central part of a story, as Kane's compelling book aptly describes, which centres on acousmatic practices – the separation of sound from its source – and which has a much longer history, whether that be in the theatre where God or the divine is often represented (so to speak) offstage; in the practice of Catholic confession; or, ultimately, in the architecture at Bayreuth.[58] At stake in acousmatic listening, then, is a practice of 'privileging hearing over seeing, of cultivating situations where sounds are detached from their causal sources, and of technologies for listening to sounds unseen' as a way of granting 'auditory access to transcendental spheres, different in kind from the purely sonic effect – a way of listening to essence, *truth*,

---

[55] John Deathridge, *Wagner Beyond Good and Evil*, pp. 106, 107.
[56] Kane, *Sound Unseen*, p. 102.
[57] Ibid., p. 103. It is worth making a clear distinction, however, between the stated aims or ideals of structural listening and actual listening practices, which inevitably and undeniably include emotional responses/associations, sensuousness, embodiment or the mundane irritation of, for example, an uncomfortable chair, and so on.
[58] Ibid., p. 6.

profundity, ineffability, or interiority'.[59]

If we return to Syberberg's film production of *Parsifal*, the question of acousmatic sound (and listening) is quite clearly foregrounded. Though Badiou reads the splitting/doubling of Parsifal into a young male *and* a young female protagonist as the representation of the possibility of a new means of sexuation in a redeemed Christianity, it is also a move that makes eerily manifest what has been happening all along: the acousmatic staging of the voice as separate from the body, of music from its instrumental source, of soundtrack from film and ultimately, following Badiou, truth from its (means of) production – the tenor voice of Rainer Goldberg is now emitted from the young Karin Krick in a move that certainly queers the portrayal of Parsifal.[60] And yet, the apparent 'queerness' of this cinematographic move seems not to be the decisive point here; in keeping with the Brechtian aesthetic throughout – the film is abundant with masks, figurines and puppets, all of which are shown as such, including the mechanics of the puppetry – the lip-synching is also made apparent. David Schwarz even describes the emergence of two Parsifals as 'an extraordinarily puppetlike gesture'.[61] There is no attempt to hide the fact that the voice supposedly emitted has not been produced by that body; quite conversely, and confirming what we have suspected throughout, this fact is made incontestably evident through this confirmational supplement, reaffirming that the voice *never was produced by the body on display* – a move that purposefully obscures or veils the auditory source. The difficulty here, then, is that 'universal truth', *contra* Badiou, is substantialised in a culturally and historically specific practice; in short, it conflates an idea with an object/practice. Just as Susan Sontag describes cinema as the 'muse' of Syberberg's *Hitler, ein Film aus Deutschland*, 'represented on the wasteland set by Black Maria, the tarpaper shack built for Thomas Edison in 1893 as the first film studio',[62] we might also see the entire Wagnerian operatic project – as heady culmination of a particular musical tradition – in all its material, mechanical, technological and architectural glory as the muse of Syberberg's *Parsifal*: an interpretation

---

[59] Ibid., p. 9, my emphasis. Again, it is worth a note to caution that this is an analysis which speaks to the dominant cultural pedagogies and the triumph of the narrative of absolute (acousmatic) music and should not be confused with a historical narrative of 'actual' listening practices. Socially informed histories of musical 'listening' practices have made this point well. See, for example, J. Q. Davies, 'Dancing the Symphonic', pp. 25–47 and Deirdre Loughridge, *Haydn's Sunrise, Beethoven's Shadow*.

[60] Queer as it may be, the feminine – as we have seen is the case in Badiou's own figuring of the feminine pole – certainly appears to be the secondary term that allows for the transformation of the first.

[61] Schwarz, *Listening Awry*, p. 154.

[62] Sontag, *Under the Sign of Saturn*, p. 142.

Figure 4.3 DVD cover. Credit: Zoetrope

that gains traction when we recall that the film's title is peculiar typographically (see Figure 4.3) layering Wagner's name above the title *Parsifal* which is then above Syberberg's name, suggesting that it is not (only) a film of *Parsifal* (as such) but also a film of or about Wagner (as character or stage – indeed, the set for the production is giant version of Wagner's death mask). Further still, it seems no coincidence that the Holy Grail is explicitly staged as the Bayreuth Festspielhaus. We might continue one step further, then, to suggest that the cultural conceit of absolute music – absolute by definition has no history, no qualification, nor can it be relative – could be seen as the all too convenient muse of Badiou's own *inesthétique* philosophical project.

Analysing the issues at stake is, of course, rather easier in this quite evidently multiply mediated format: there is no getting around the fact that cinema, as Badiou himself is aware, is a form of technology. Additionally, the 'impure' cinematic seems to legitimise commentary and analysis with strikingly little recourse to strictly musical formal features; indeed, Badiou has delineated the concerns of 'impure' arts as the formal procedures through which the different elements are combined (a Wagnerian consideration if there ever was one!). In this way, then, though non-committal about whether there was ever a Wagner-event, he certainly considers Wagner *as* art and, moreover, locates in our contemporary engagement with Wagner the fundamental question about – even the promise of – the future of 'great works of art'. However, the Wagnerian work of art – in its impure modality, an impurity which is surely augmented further in its filmic (re)enactment – seems to ask questions that at least straddle, if not outright trample on, another of the four conditions: namely politics. The question, Badiou claims, presented by *Parsifal* (including, it seems, by musical means) is the question of ceremony, and precisely the question of whether a modern ceremony is possible. This is a question which is of course structurally nested in both the dramatic narrative (the ceremony of the grail) and is also performatively enacted – strictly speaking it is not an opera, but 'Ein Bühnenweihfestspiel' (a festival play for the consecration of the stage) specifically for Bayreuth, and at which the audience is instructed not to applaud: it is not an opera for entertainment, but rather the ceremony itself. And of course, this is structurally (re)nested (for want of a better expression) in Syberberg's film, with the endless meta-, extra-, inter- and intra-textual references – above all its staging in a dilapidated landscape that turns out to be, as mentioned, Wagner's death mask (see Figure 4.3), references to the journalistic reception of Wagner at the time (see Figure 4.4) and, of course, the grail figured as Bayreuth. Though the question of *Parsifal*'s identity as a consecrational play has drawn extensive commentary, Badiou's analysis and proposition (that it asks a more complex and probably unanswered question about the possibility of modern ceremony) is a fresh and interesting perspective. At the same time, however, *Five Lessons on Wagner* seems to avoid a close engagement with how this insightful analysis stands in relation to Badiou's broader philosophical project –

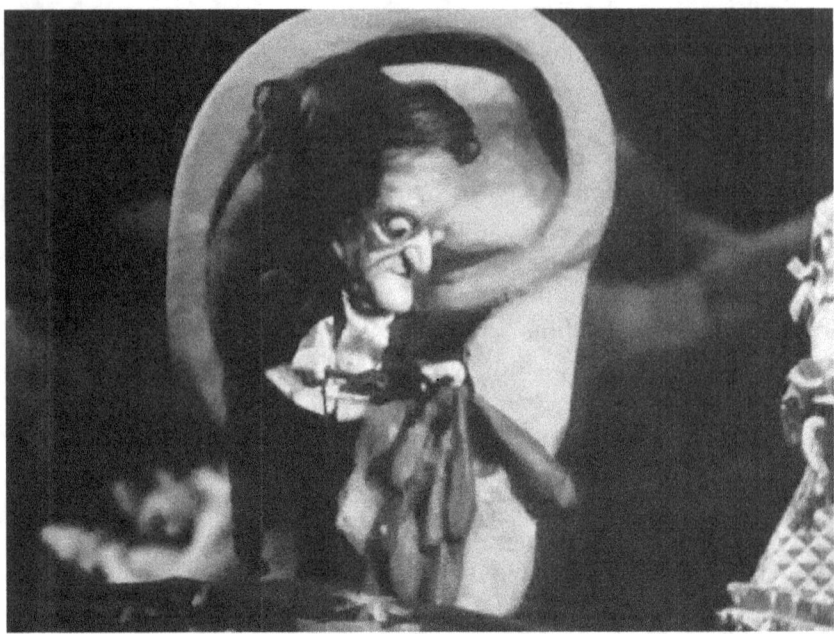

Figure 4.4   Overture. Credit: Zoetrope

especially the formalist dictates of the *Petit manuel d'inesthétique* – by skirting around the fact that, *d'après* Badiou, the questions asked by *Parsifal* are not strictly formal. By this I mean that the questions are not *merely* self-referential ways of thinking (in a domain strictly delimited to (musical) art) through formal (musical/theatrical/cinematic) procedures – the identification of points and openings and their possible responses/solutions in Badiou's terms – but rather that formal techniques are used as a means of *representing* extra-formal considerations, i.e. the question of ceremony or the representation of time and waiting. It seems pertinent to point out again the degree of hesitancy that frames this book – along with its striking lack of Badiousian philosophical jargon – and thus, perhaps, to simply suggest that this is not, in Badiou's sense, a properly philosophical book. At any rate, his admonition that philosophy's job is 'to distinguish truths from opinion' is certainly not upheld – *Five Lessons on Wagner* is replete with endless (explicit) opinions: 'my point of view' (FLW, p. 135); 'I think' (FLW, pp. 140, 147); 'we might say that' (FLW, p. 143); 'in my opinion' (FLW, pp. 144, 152); 'I personally think' (FLW, p. 145); 'as far as I am concerned' (FLW, p. 145); 'I don't think' (FLW, p. 147), and so on. Perhaps, then, Badiou is here writing without his philosopher's hat on, and is simply using the 'codes de la communication (ou des opinions que les animaux humains échangent sur "la musique")' ['codes of communication (or the opinions on "music" that human animals swap)'], safe in his faithful belief that, opinions aside, 'les grandes créations du style classique [here he is speaking about Mozart *et al.*, though the same applies to all art], subsistent éternellement' ['the great creations of the classical style, shall endure eternally'] (E_1, p. 95; E_2, p. 70).

As noted, this kind of critique is substantially easier when it comes to the 'impure' (albeit still 'high') art forms, such as opera, given that it has – as will be explored in more depth in Chapter 5 – a more complicated and contradictory relation to the emergence of absolute music as a distinct, ideologically weighty and privileged repertoire. And although I think we would do well to be suspicious of the extreme complementarity between the ideology of absolute music and that of Badiou's universal truth-procedures – they fit *too well* for domains that are allegedly distinct – if we pay close enough attention it is possible, nonetheless, to find moments where difficulties reveal themselves even in this *instrumentally* privileged repertoire. Most clearly, this can be found in the problem – already mentioned – that continues to plague any philosophy of music that starts from literate (often European high art) music and hopes to extrapolate from that an understanding of music (writ large): that of its allographic nature and the seemingly irreducible chasm between the score-copy and the performance(s) of the musical work – the ontological location/identity of music is left in limbo and is reducible to neither one nor the other. In Badiou's work, this question enters through a side door which in broad strokes can be understood as the gap between the notated formal procedures (i.e. the place where the self-referential formal procedures are worked out in strictly formal terms – the sole locus of Badiou's identification of truth-procedures in 'Scolie') and music which *sounds like* it is participating in the same exploration of the sonic universe – experientially and sonically it seems to share a musical sound world or genealogy – though in terms of formal innovations it is doing nothing of the sort. Here Badiou flounders, wanting neither to drop Debussy (and the expressionistic soundscape he shares both with, say, moments in Wagner's late tonal vocabulary or the way it pre-figures the (proto-)electronic work of a composer like Varèse) nor to accord him a proper place in the hall of truth-procedures fame.

Finally, then, this touches on what is one of the more frequent critiques of Badiou: that of the passage from being to appearance (and which *Logiques des mondes* sought, at least in part, to deal with), and how apparently 'universal truths' figure within this. Even Peter Hallward, a prominent and long-time exponent of Badiou's philosophy, shows more than a little hesitation over the specifically musical question, asking in his interview with Badiou included in the English translation of *L'éthique*, '[j]ust what is culturally specific here? How do we measure the immanent universality of an artistic truth, to limit the question only to that?' or previously '[w]hat relation is there between an artistic – let's say musical – truth, and the (culturally specific) system of tonality which ensures that the truths of Haydn and Schoenberg – to take examples from your *Ethique* – are always truths *for* certain listeners?'[63] When pushed, Badiou is notably hesitant, shifting the core question away from the cultural specificity of tonality and towards the *scale* of change induced by the Haydn- or Schoenberg-event (i.e. not every novelty is an event) and reminding the reader that his approach forms part of a necessary shift away from author/composer centred accounts of 'great art' and towards a focus, instead, on the genealogies of the bodies of work(s) produced. Nonetheless, the question of the relation between cultural specificity and universal truths continues to hang, rather ominously.

The invocation of universal truths, the seemingly non-culturally-specific essence of music (or all that Badiou will allow under the term 'music' in its properly artistic guise), the mathematical basis of Badiou's ontology and the dependence on acousmatic listening practices brings to mind the work and practices of an ancient philosopher other than Plato – that of Pythagoras.[64] Pythagoras, well known as both the first self-appointed philosopher and founder of the first philosophical school, traded well off the power of acousmatic sound by demanding that his probationary pupils, the *acousmatikoi*, were lectured to from behind a veil or screen in order that they could better concentrate on the message of his teaching. Considered the more religious branch of Pythagoreans (in relation to the other branch, the *mathematikoi*) their trust in their master depends not on empirical demonstration (nor even on abstract reasoning/logic, dialogue and understanding – they were forcedly silent) but on faith. Central to this story is of course the fact that the practice requires the use of *techne* – the veil – for its exposition and yet, as Brian Kane describes is so often the case with acousmatic

---

[63] Peter Hallward, 'Appendix' in Badiou, *Ethics: An Essay on the Understanding of Evil*, pp. 141, 138.

[64] Interestingly, mathematicians Nirenberg and Nirenberg have also suggested that Badiou's mathematical basis is considerably more Pythagorean than Platonic and, moreover, their close reading of Badiou and in-depth understanding of the mathematics at stake highlight Badiou's piecemeal adoption of set theory, posing some interesting angles of critique for the relationship between his supposedly mathematical ontology and identity. See Ricardo L. Nirenberg and David Nirenberg, 'Badiou's Number', pp. 583–614. Tarby, too, has noted that '[p]our Pythagore ce principe était constitué par les nombres [et en] un sens, Badiou reprend cette intuition' (Tarby in PE_1, p. 156) ['For Pythagoras this principle was constituted by numbers. In a sense, Badiou takes up this intuition'] (PE_2, p. 135).

sound in general, the contribution of *techne* is 'for the most part, dismissed or bracketed out of consideration. The simultaneous necessity and expulsion of *techne* aligns the tradition of acousmatic sound with a tradition of phantasmagoria, or the occultation of the means of production.'[65] Most importantly, perhaps, this brings us into direct confrontation with notions of authority, power and faith – concerns that seem particularly pertinent given both Badiou's philosophical project based around the faithful subject, and the difficulties in accounting for the passage from being to appearance in his work. Kane's discussion and analysis of Mladen Dolar's work on the acousmatic voice is worth citing at length here:

> The Pythagorean veil also grants the voice an 'authority and surplus-meaning.' The very act of hiding the voice is also a technique for giving the voice certain power – namely, omnipresence and omnipotence. These powers of the voice are irreducible to the meaning of the statement; they are the product of a surplus-meaning that has nothing to do with logos. Surplus-meaning emerges from the difference between the voice and its bearer or source, that is, between *phoné* and *topos*. Thus it is no coincidence that Pythagoras enjoyed cultic status in the ancient world. By means of the veil, he imbued his utterances with special powers. Dolar's reading of the Pythagorean veil is emblematic for philosophy in general; the power of philosophy itself does not wholly rely on the meaning or logic of its statements; rather, it resides in a hidden kernel of meaninglessness in excess of the statement. The voice becomes the voice of authority the moment it detaches from the speaker. The statement (logos) is enriched by this extra (alogical) power, a magic trick for compelling conviction.[66]

Kane continues to identify this phantasmagoria as a mode of belief, and the modality 'je sais bien mais quand même . . .' as the structure of fidelity.[67] All of this brings the structures of disavowal, faith and fetishism into a heady Marxist-Lacanian combination that taps into key questions of authority, gender and sexuality, commodity capitalism and authority, centred on the seen/unseen *techne* that allows the seamless ideological passage between being and appearance, granting apparently unmediated identification, *en route*, of universal, self-authorising, non-relativisable truth(s), without recourse to the way these supposed truths are produced or the way they are incontrovertibly enmeshed in social and cultural contexts. Just as Pythagoras's veil gave his philosophical voice the power of incontrovertible truth, so too does the 'invisible' instrumental basis of absolute music grant it a status that appears universal and transcendent. Just as Kane articulates Wagner's own

[65] Kane, *Sound Unseen*, p. 220.
[66] Ibid., pp. 209–10.
[67] Ibid., p. 222.

mode of phantasmagoric belief as 'I, Richard Wagner, know very well that the orchestra is a machine, but nevertheless [when I construct a theatre to hide the machinery of musical production] I believe that I enter a state akin to hypnotic clairvoyance',[68] we might propose that Badiou's is 'I, Alain Badiou, know very well that music arises from specific cultural contexts, but nevertheless [when I construct an elaborate philosophical system that sets the terms of the possibility of truth in relation to the art works of my own cultural context] I believe that I can identify the universal truth of these great works of art.'

FROM *INESTHÉTIQUE* TO *ANESTHÉTIQUE*: MEDIATION, TRUTH, OPINION

As demonstrated above, Badiou's cherished canon of music that he nominates as participating in universal truth-procedures runs from Haydn through to Schoenberg (and the body of work produced under that name up to the second half of the twentieth century). Not only, as mentioned, was Haydn one of the chief proponents of new orchestral techniques and forms, but it is with Haydn (and his contemporaries in the years leading up to 1800) that the process of orchestral standardisation begins (with regards to instruments, scoring and layout, and so on). As the orchestra grew in size, so different performance practices emerged – for example, pitch was increasingly standardised (let us not forget that until the nineteenth century there is little consensus as to the pitch of notes, and no 'universal' pitch until the twentieth century) and performances moved from the often rowdy chambers of court patrons to newly built concert halls (again, this is occurring throughout the nineteenth and into the twentieth centuries). A combination of inadequate architecture (hearing unamplified instruments at a distance is notoriously difficult without the best thought-out acoustics) and an ideological shift in what it meant to listen to (certain types of) music brought with it concert hall etiquette: silence, reverence and no clapping between movements as it would interrupt the organic whole of the musical work. Again, practices which have sedimented over time to seem natural or the 'proper' way to listen to music – unlike with headphones, according to Badiou – have quite clear material and ideological genealogies. Concurrently, the assumption that these practices form the 'natural' site for (appropriately reverent) musical audition – and this is certainly the narrative that Badiou implicitly valorises – privileges a (partial) story that ignores a myriad of other listening practices, even

[68] Ibid., p. 221.

within elite musical cultures, such as domestic chamber music, aristocratic salon culture and promenade concerts.

Again, Haydn and his contemporaries are highlighted as some of the names which mark the beginning of this shift, with works appearing around the turn of the nineteenth century described, as Bonds has noted, as revelatory – even oracular – with truth-disclosing properties.[69] Whereas previously dominant narratives about music emphasised an understanding of music in terms that parallel rhetoric or oratory – the listener is simply swept along – with an oracle 'listeners struggle to understand [...] an oracle requires – demands – interpretation [... and] obscurity becomes a virtue'.[70] The extent to which Badiou has assumed this legacy as a non-historicisable given is quite extraordinary; his identification of 'truth' as synonymous with formal innovation aligns him fairly straightforwardly with German idealism which reifies 'pure' art (i.e. divorced from any function and ceasing to be dependent on anything but itself) by elegantly bringing together both a metaphysical aesthetic perspective (non-functional transcendence) and the imperative of 'free-play' and self-referential form. It places Badiou on common ground with musicologists writing prior to the emergence of critical musicology, such as Carl Dahlhaus, who famously spoke of music in this tradition (particularly Beethoven, as paradigmatic exemplar of the *idea* of absolute music that emerged around 1800) as 'a revelation of the absolute [...] specifically because it "dissolves" itself from the sensual, and finally even from the affective sphere'.[71]

Attempts to inculcate acousmatic listening as a practice come to something of a head with Wagner and the building of Bayreuth (he also famously hissed at an audience member for making noise).[72] It should be noted, however, that Wagner is simultaneously committed – at least at points – to art's potential for revolution and social transformation – the complexity of the 'case of Wagner' will be explored in more detail in Chapter 5. A crucial aspect of the ideology of absolute music (and its attendant listening practices, successful or otherwise) is therefore the denial of bodily responses to music – the sacrificial tradition of musical listening to which Badiou adheres demands we attend to structure rather than sonority – by sidelining or attributing no essential or important role for somatic perception, nor for pleasure, desire and emotion

---

[69] See Bonds, *Absolute Music*, p. 112.
[70] Ibid., p. 115.
[71] Carl Dahlhaus, *The Idea of Absolute Music*, p. 17.
[72] Though Wagner is able to hide the orchestra there is, of course, little he can do about the singers. In this respect, Badiou's commitment to Syberberg's *Parsifal* (as the underlying 'truth' of Wagner's *Parsifal*) where the means of vocal production are also made in/visible is particularly revealing, as noted above.

in the musical experience.[73] And Badiou says precisely this: 'Le plaisir viendra, par-dessus le marché' ['Pleasure will come, as an additional bonus'] (Sc, p. 96; Sch, p. 86); pleasure is superfluous to what he considers to be the essential – or truthful – musical experience. Badiou is so evidently beholden to this particular tradition of musical listening as the sole locus of legitimate academic – certainly philosophical – enquiry, and yet his less properly philosophical work, *Five Lessons on Wagner* (and even moments in 'Scolie') betrays a deeply passionate and profoundly emotional relationship with music – most obviously Wagner. Moreover, his often insightful and poignant analyses of Wagner's works seem so clearly to be drawn from this deep love of and intimate – cognitive and somatic – knowledge of Wagner's music rather than from the kind of formal or structural analyses he advocates as the locus of truth-procedures (remembering that is the sole interest of philosophy *vis-à-vis* art). As mentioned, any kind of formal analysis when it comes to music in Badiou's texts – especially when compared to the sustained analysis devoted to, say, a poem by Mallarmé – is scant at best. This is not to say that his analyses are invalid because of this, but rather it is to point out that whatever their validity – infused as they are with great passion – they are not valid on the terms set by his own *inesthétique*. Ultimately, it seems hard to conceive of Badiou's project of *inesthétique* – interesting history it offers of the relationship between philosophy, art and truth aside – as distinguishable from its minimal pair, *anesthétique*, and the denial of the body as co-site of perception and understanding as found in the short history of the emergence of absolute (instrumental) music, sacrificial or structural listening, and its attendant acousmatic and concert hall practices. Perhaps this shouldn't be so surprising, given the Platonic basis Badiou claims for not only for his philosophy but for philosophy in general; nonetheless, in theory – if not in practice – Badiou upholds an ontological duality as does Plato, that aligns intellect (i.e. the intelligible world of universal forms) with truth(s) and renders embodied and bodily perception/experience (i.e. the sensible, aesthetic in its etymological sense – from the Greek αἰσθητικός, meaning sensory perception) secondary, inferior and ultimately irrelevant to a philosophy interested in truth. Needless to say, the privileging of rational, cognitive and intellectual properties over somatic, experiential and bodily ones has a long and well-trodden history of mapping pretty neatly onto the long established binaries of male/female, culture/nature, mind/body, and so on. Of course, part of what Badiou is trying to do is

---

[73] As Adrienne Janus has shown, it is precisely this sacrificial tradition of musical listening that Nancy is working against or trying to overcome. See Janus, 'Soundings'.

reclaim categories such as 'truth' and the idea of 'universality' (*contra* the full gamut of all he subsumes, rather crudely, under 'identity politics'), but this comes at the expense of an unproblematic (for Badiou) hierarchisation of perception and rehabilitation of a binary opposition borne of a singular and specific musical tradition that already privileges the same things he sets out to espouse the value of: the argument is circular. And indeed, as other commentators have argued, Badiou's universality in no way demands or even necessarily aspires to any kind of equality.[74]

Finally, then, I would simply like to draw attention to Badiou's own role as invisible (acousmatic?) mediator in setting up this frame of understanding. Not only does Badiou continuously evade formal, structural analysis in his Wagner book, but even in 'Scolie' where some formal analysis (or at least reference to intra-music(ological) distinctions and terminology) is present, all Badiou is able to do *vis-à-vis* his own philosophical system is to homologically map predetermined categories (anxiety, terror, justice and courage) onto certain musical responses to the 'Schoenberg-event', without any consideration of how these links arise or how they are mediated (nor of the value judgements they imply, despite his command that philosophy abstains from *judging* the artwork). Though self-referential formal procedures invite (inexhaustible) formal analysis, their supposed autonomy is thus at odds with the rather active, interpretative role of the analyst; just as, for Badiou, truth is itself an empty category, so too is music, in this tradition, into which you deposit . . . well, whatever you deem to have been determined from your analysis. Again, the invisible (and apparently unimportant) role of the critic/philosopher/analyst is precisely the problem that Brian Kane highlights, writing elsewhere on Badiou's *Five Lessons on Wagner*, when he asks 'what is to prevent us from simply reading into Wagner's work the accomplishments we want to find? Where is the resistance to lie?'[75] Ultimately, for Kane, this hinges on the central role of faith or fidelity in Badiou's work; authority, in Badiou, simply comes from the fidelity to the event, but this leaves us in a muddle of tautology and confusion. As Kane continues, '[h]ow are we to know where Wagner's greatness really lies? Without criteria, the answer is simply "Because I said so." If the faithful subject believes it, then, for the faithful subject it is so.'[76] In addition, it is not at all clear what there is to stop us from using the philosophical framework that Badiou has given us to nominate

---

[74] See, for example, Christopher Watkin, 'Thinking Equality Today', pp. 522–34 and Jeff Love and Todd May, 'From Universality to Inequality', pp. 51–69.
[75] Brian Kane, 'Badiou's Wagner', pp. 349–54 (p. 5).
[76] Ibid., p. 5.

non-Badiousian events as events – so long as we can (rhetorically) justify them as such. Obvious examples would be, say, the militant suffragette campaign or Rosa Park's refusal to give up her bus seat;[77] both, though told as part of the longer history of what we now term identity politics, could also be understood as events which induce universal truths and new subjective forms. Ultimately, this brings us back to the problematic role of language and rhetoric, despite Badiou's admonition against sophistry and his dependence on language as a transparent medium through which to convey philosophical ideas in a way that is not contaminated by the slippery and contingent, or by metaphorical and polysemic implications and associations. This also seems to be, at best, a question of faith rather than a demonstrable fact and, at worst, a convenient way of refusing linguistic/political responsibility for the misogyny found in his language on numerous occasions. While much of this reluctance to adhere to Badiou's project (despite his astute articulation of many of our present political realities) is the product of a difference in orientation, as mentioned, it seems evident that even on its own terms, when it comes to music and its analysis, Badiou is unable to offer what he demands – though perhaps trained musicologists would be better placed to do so.

CONTRA A MUSICAL(OGICAL) THERMIDORIANISM

Trained musicologists may be better placed to offer the kinds of formal analyses of 'strictly' musical processes that Badiou seems to view as the sole locus of truth-procedures in his maieutic system; however, this chapter will finally suggest that a return to purely formal analysis would be a regressive or reactionary move – loosely Thermidorian in Badiou's terms. This suggestion is articulated both in relation to Badiou's philosophy, and in relation to the contemporary study of music (including but not limited to musicology). Badiou describes the Thermidorian subject as a subject who is initially faithful but then

---

[77] Evidently the 'universal' aspect of the suffrage campaign is contestable for several crucial reasons which in no way would I suggest ignoring. But in terms of Badiou's philosophy, and in particular what he allows rhetorically under the remit of 'universal truth', it remains coherent; in particular, see Badiou's major text on the universal, *St Paul*, where one of the justifications offered for Paul's problematic statements on gender/women is the caveat that 'il est absurde de le faire comparaître devant le tribunal du féminisme contemporain. L'unique question qui vaille est de savoir si Paul, compte tenu de l'époque, est plutôt progressiste ou plutôt réactif en ce qui concernant le statut des femmes' (StP_1, p. 111) ['there is something absurd about bringing him to trial before the tribunal of contemporary feminism. The only question worth asking is whether Paul, given the conditions of his time, is a progressive or a reactionary so far as the status of women is concerned'] (StP_2, p. 104). Other people have also nominated Rosa Park's refusal to give up her bus seat as an event in a Badiousian sense, though as far as I am aware Badiou himself has not.

subsequently renounces their fidelity to a particular (truth) event and the new situation it entails. At the risk of instrumentalising a system whose fundamental tenets this chapter seeks to challenge, the notion of a Thermidorian reaction seems a useful explicatory schema to describe a certain type of reaction. I want to suggest that – whether we are happy to set the accompanying Badiousian baggage for the moment to one side – the emergence of what was called 'new musicology' in the 1980s and its flourishing in the 1990s and early 2000s could aptly be described as an event. The (universal) truth it announced was, in perhaps overly grand and yet rather simplified terms, that music is an irretrievably social and cultural endeavour and is thus never neutral but rather is embedded and implicated at every level in politics and ideology – and, perhaps most importantly of all, this includes the practice of apparently transcendental and absolute works of the European concert hall. The trace of this event (of which 'new musicology' is but the name) continued to be felt in the new subjective forms of musicological practice, which expanded dramatically to include cultural, sociological, anthropological and ethnographical, geographical, literary theoretical, feminist, queer and explicitly political perspectives, among others, along with the diversifying of legitimate types of music up for academic consideration. Though the task of trying to unpick and better understand these complex relations has at times been fraught, a vast and engaging body of work was produced in its name, asking quite different – and much harder – questions about the way music not only reflects particular socio-cultural configurations but also its role in creating and sustaining them, as well as pushing important but more vexed questions of its relation to social control, surveillance and terror.[78]

Though there seems to be a sense of anxiety about the identity of musicology as a discipline – given its now strikingly diverse toolkit – and difficult questions about the limited efficacy of what gets crudely characterised (in an implicitly and sometimes explicitly Badiousian vein) as the neoliberal, politically correct kowtowing to difference (or identity) *as* political category in and of itself,[79] it is difficult to see in what way Badiou's understanding and conceptualisation of music is distinguishable as *post*-postmodern rather than, simply, pre-postmodern; a return to (modernist) formalism, staged as a phantasmagoria of rehabilitated

---

[78] See, for example, Suzanne G. Cusick, 'Musicology, Torture, Repair', p. 24 pars, and 'You Are in a Place that is Out of the World', pp. 1–26, and Juliette Volcler, *Le Son Comme Arme*.

[79] James Currie, for example, claims that 'many in the academy have been tempted by the belief that difference is a kind of Trojan horse: a seemingly singular entity, which, once it has been allowed entry into the enemy's compound, will unleash a vanquishing swarm of plurality', in 'Music After All', p. 160.

beliefs in universal truths (and, apparently, musical values and tastes) constructed, rather impressively, as a militant leftist philosophy. This is neither to say that many of the premises or methodologies of 'new musicology' were unproblematic nor is it a condemnation of formal analysis; even less is it an apology for the neoliberal faux concern for minority and oppressed groups. It is simply to highlight Badiou's reliance on an ideology and understanding of music that reifies a particular musical tradition as arbiter of universal truths; not only does Badiou conflate an idea with an object[80] from behind his own Pythagorean veil, but the identification of truth solely in terms of formal, abstract, rational and structural procedures also rehabilitates the seemingly never-ending propensity to oppose mind and body or reason and emotion, often in moralising terms that validate love over desire and truth over pleasure, all the while claiming these perspectives as neutral universals. When it comes to the study of music, the same questions are still off the table as were prior to the 'new musicology' inaugurated in the 1980s – music's worldliness, situatedness, enmeshment in politics, bodies, technologies and means of production are deemed simply not *musical* questions. Moreover, the musics whose relation to such concerns seems unavoidable – rap, pop, etc. – are simply sidelined and deemed 'not art'. In short, the possibility of the deep thinking of hugely complex but extremely interesting and politically important questions about what it means to be a musicking humanimal in the twenty-first century are simply ignored. In this regard, the critical toolkit of musicology still has a lot to offer contemporary philosophy.

Badiou's narrative quite evidently serves to justify the canonical historical narrative of great art – a cause in which he is deeply invested. Despite his supposed leftist radicality, however, his novel philosophical system offers little more to music scholarship or appreciation than a robust defence of what the discipline had uncritically assumed to be valid, true and aesthetically superior for most of the discipline's history. Badiou's own position, then – whether as critic or philosopher – is all the more vexed: while one kind of universalism – neoliberal human rights discourse in particular – is contaminated by social, historical and (capitalist) political concerns, Badiou's universalism is, conveniently, absolute – like the music he reifies – and non-historical (or even historicisable). Again, all this seems to be premised on is a leap of faith and our fidelity to the master's voice – to his apparently unmediated utterances of truth from behind the veil.

---

[80] See Mark Evan Bonds and Carl Dahlhaus for more on this and its role in reification.

5. From Parnassus to Bayreuth: Staging a Music which is Not One

> Between him and the picture to be looked at there is nothing clearly discernible, instead, only a shimmering sense of distance [...] in which the remote picture takes on the mysterious quality of a dream-like apparition, while the phantasmal sounding music from the 'mystic gulf', like vapours rising from the holy womb of Gaia beneath the Pythia's seat, transport him into that inspired state of clairvoyance in which the visible stage picture becomes the authentic facsimile of life itself.
> Richard Wagner[1]

RESONANCE/DISSONANCE: SONOROUS, RHYTHMIC AND UNIVERSAL SUBJECTS

This final chapter highlights more clearly both the irresolvable differences as well as the points of contact or resonance between the works of the three philosophers previously considered: Nancy, Lacoue-Labarthe and Badiou. Despite the unequivocal dissonance between the post-metaphysical destabilisation of the possibility of universal philosophical truths in the Nancy-Lacoue-Labarthian approach and the neo-Platonism of Badiou, this chapter also aims to show, even more forcefully than in the previous chapters, the way in which all three – albeit in different ways – inherit and deploy aspects of a Romantic and idealist conception of music in their work; it also foregrounds the way in which this often relates to an essentially psychoanalytic model of the subject. Consequently, it demands that closer attention be paid to the way in which music is instrumentalised as a metaphor for progressive thinkers in a manner that has a tendency to reinforce, rather than challenge, both inherited conceptions of what music is and also certain hierarchical binaries – most especially, though by no means only, in

---

[1] Wagner, cited in Frederic Spotts, *Bayreuth: A History of the Wagner Festival*, p. 52.

regards to the continued enlisting of gender as an organisational category for philosophy.

However, this chapter also aims to emphasise what is most useful in each of these thinkers' work to the philosophy of music, namely: Nancy's insistence on sensuous and aesthetic experience as meaningful in and of itself, rather than possessing a meaning that needs to be located elsewhere; Lacoue-Labarthe's (and sometimes Nancy's) implicit but underdeveloped attention to music as *techne*, both as a technology in its normative sense, but also as a technique of the self – as a mode of training, forming, conditioning or shaping; and, finally, Badiou's conception of the *événement*, and the way in which the event *actively* impels a subject (to a kind of labour/commitment that perpetuates the 'truth' of the event). Above all, it seeks to radicalise the materialist gesture implicit in both Nancy and Lacoue-Labarthe by urging closer attention to the practices, technologies and techniques (cognitive, bodily, compositional, theoretical, and so on) that constitute a broader conception of music – a music that is neither wholly reducible to nor is entirely distinct from any one of these mediating planes – that better understands the relation of labour to the work of making music (*œuvre/opus/opera*). Most importantly of all, perhaps, this allows for a more cogent account of both the systems and mechanisms by which affect is instrumentally created and shaped in music, alongside a more rigorous account of the 'epistemic frames that organize music/noise distinctions'.[2] In short, by drawing in part on the work of Luce Irigaray, this final chapter has no less grand aims than to propose that we consider music no longer as philosophy's (or language's) Other – an Other that is all too often sacrificed as the prior condition or ground for the philosophical or linguistic gambit – but as a sensuous, theoretical, material, cognitive and bodily creative and regulatory practice that, though difficult to pin down, is nonetheless as thoroughly and demonstrably worldly as any other social or cultural endeavour. Along with the indispensible work of musicologists such as Robin James, Emily Dolan, Daniel Chua and Benjamin Piekut, the theoretical perspectives of Bernard Stiegler – most prominently his proposition of an *organologie générale* [general organology] and his work on philosophy's 'forgetting' of *techne* – have also been influential in the attempt to articulate these kinds of approaches to the understanding of music.

So far, then, this book has taken each philosopher in turn and explored how music is understood, characterised, described: in short, how it is

---

[2] Robin James, 'Affective Resonances', p. 60. I would also add distinctions between 'music as art' and 'music as entertainment'.

conceived of on the ontological level and in relation to the wider philosophical project, as well as how this resonates with the musical examples offered, used, exploited or argued to demonstrate the earlier claims. The relationship between these two distinct ways in which music is constituted in these philosophers' œuvres has been problematised, drawing largely on the poststructuralist-influenced musicology of the late twentieth and early twenty-first centuries. This final chapter aims to take things further, both in terms of the problematics identified and in terms of the musicological resources it draws on by moving beyond what is largely a context-oriented hermeneutic approach. Indeed, as Adrian Daub has described, 'while the New [or critical] Musicology of the 1980s was characterized by a sense of its own belatedness', new critical and methodological approaches such as 'ecomusicology, media studies, and new materialisms in music departments have unfolded largely parallel with their cognates in literary studies'.[3] These developments suggest that it is a particularly rich and exciting time to be considering the relationship between the kinds of thinking about music happening both inside and outside of music departments, and particularly across supposed practical/theoretical divides – in turn illuminating surprising points of contact, contamination, cross-pollination and conflict. This chapter will also return to many of the central issues raised in the first chapter in order to better understand how these philosophers' work relates to previous topics in the philosophy of music, namely: essence and effect; the relationship between music, emotion and meaning; form, performance and technology; gender and sexuality; and politics.

We will start by bringing together the work of Nancy, Lacoue-Labarthe and Badiou, by taking as a starting point one of their most obvious points of musical overlap: their contributions to the question of the relationship of music to politics through the prism of the 'case of Wagner' and his compromising and complicated relationship to National Socialism. Though it will not seek to settle the debate on Wagner (impossible!), this relentless topic is not only a nodal point shared by all three philosophers, but in the way that the question brings together (fascist) politics and (musical) aesthetics in a particularly decisive way (no matter which side of the fence one is on) it brings us back to the question of *what music is capable of* – a question that has been lurking and provoking anxiety, as we have seen, since Plato – and the unanswered question as to whether this is to be understood in relation to music's essence, its effects, or both. Both Lacoue-Labarthe and Badiou have full books devoted to the Wagner question, and Nancy

---

[3] Adrian Daub, in Azade Seyhan and others, 'Forum: Romanticism', pp. 344–60 (pp. 348–9).

makes reference to Wagner – as we have seen – and also considers the larger political question of the relationship between music and Nazism in 'March in Spirit in our Ranks' – a short essay added to the English translation of À l'écoute and which seems not to exist anywhere in an original French version. Lacoue-Labarthe also considers the question in several of the essays collected in *Pour n'en pas finir*, notably 'Une lettre sur la musique' and 'Pour n'en pas finir' itself. With all of this in mind, however, it seems necessary to signal, yet again, that this chapter is less concerned with adjudicating on the question of whether Wagner's music is fundamentally and irretrievably aesthetically compromised by anti-Semitism and (proto-)Nazism, than with probing at what these thinkers characterise as ethico-aesthetically problematic (or not) in the first place. Indeed, it would be easy to simply rehash the various arguments extant since Nietzsche's seminal and historical turn *contra* Wagner – especially given that Badiou and Lacoue-Labarthe offer fairly oppositional analyses – and so instead this chapter homes in on how the relationship between music, its ethical 'content' and politics more broadly is constructed in these texts, as well as in relation to their broader conceptions of what music 'is', as explored in the previous chapters.

MUSIC AND POLITICS

As Badiou has described, Wagner serves as a useful 'litmus test' for considering the relationship between music and philosophy and, more broadly, ideology; underlying this supposition is the sense in which music is presumed to be 'a fundamental operator in contemporary ideology' (FLW, p. 1). This conviction is nowhere proven, but is assumed – I think it is fair to say – across the work of all three of the philosophers in question.[4] Less clear, however, is any analysis or justification of the distinct ways in which different musical genres are treated in relation to ideology: in the texts we have already considered in the previous chapters, popular music genres are often assumed to be playing an ideological role (to a lesser or greater extent in line with Adorno's critique of the culture industry) while *musique savante* often seems to be given a *carte blanche* to function as music (or what is *essentially* musical) freed of ideological constraints – a lineage that as we have seen has strong links in German idealism and the emerging dominance of absolute music in the nineteenth century. In this respect, Wagner's role is often seen as pivotal: he marks both the closure of one tradition

---

[4] Badiou only seems to consider 'entertainment' music in this manner, however.

(the end of both opera and tonality as the dominant organisational system in high art music) and, according to some commentators, the beginning of the art of the masses. As Badiou describes, all that has been (negatively) attributed to Wagner had already been identified by Nietzsche; it is also Badiou who lays out with utmost clarity the raft of charges historically laid against him; charges which tend to constellate around the roles of myth, technology, unification and totalisation of the *Gesamtkunstwerk*, along with the spectacularised theatricalisation of suffering and the saturated and overly sentimental 'nature' of Wagner's 'endless melody'.[5] In short, as Badiou describes, the influential quartet of Wagner's primary detractors (Nietzsche, Heidegger, Adorno and Lacoue-Labarthe) views Wagner 'as someone who forces musical unity upon a variegated mass, upon differences whose essential character of otherness disappears or dissolves as a result' (FLW, p. 57). All differences are erased or at least sublimated to the totalising whole which, despite the inordinately delayed gratification typical of Wagner's operas, nonetheless resolves in an all the more spectacular and conclusive fashion as a result of this delay. Further still, this unifying gesture is in the service of a mythological vision that is ultimately that 'of the nation in general and of the German nation in particular' (FLW, p. 58). For Badiou, it is because of the way in which the 'musical operation is also and at the same time a political operation by virtue of its mythological resonance' (i.e. 'the unifying regime of music [. . . is] in collusion with a conception of the mythological origins of Germanness') that the Nazis were able to co-opt Wagner (FLW, p. 58). On this point, however, Badiou is rather circumspect: he both resists an analysis that identifies this as the essence of the Wagnerian project, while also conceding that the 'term "proto-fascist" was virtually invented to describe Wagner', and though Badiou doesn't 'go into detail about it', he nonetheless claims that 'the reasoning behind it does exist and there is solid support for it' (FLW, p. 58). This seems like an extraordinarily bold and central claim to make (especially in a text devoted to Wagner) and then instantly to drop – especially given that it is only refuted implicitly in the remainder of the work. With this in mind, it is perhaps unsurprising that Badiou is uncharacteristically non-committal as to whether Wagner's innovations actually constitute full-blown truth-procedures.

---

[5] See Badiou, FLW, particularly lessons one and three, and FLW, pp. 59–60 for Nietzsche's identification of these features.

I. Logos

In contrast to the negative charges levelled at Wagner, then, Badiou attempts to rehabilitate – at least in part – an alternative reading located largely in the (infra)structure underlying the appearance of endless melody and its totalising and unifying effects and (the claim of) its violent aesthetic fashioning of national identity. He directs our analysis of Wagner towards a consideration of 'greatness, as distinct from totality' by articulating five rules or directives he claims are found in the musical resources deployed by Wagner and which counter the prevailing critique of the *Gesamtkunstwerk*: the creation of possibility; the toleration of a multiplicity of hypotheses; the toleration of a split subject; a non-dialectical way of creating resolutions; and transformation without finality (FLW, pp. 130–1). All of these 'clues' quite obviously point towards ways in which it might be possible to rehabilitate a version of Wagnerian music that isn't co-optable to a totalising logic; at the same time, as already noted in Chapter 4, Badiou's defence of Wagner is made not only in terms of strictly 'musical' (i.e. formal, for Badiou) aspects, but also in relation to the broader musical-dramatic narrative, framing or staging, and/or in relation to particular performances that apparently excavate the underlying truth. Badiou also offers a number of hypotheses about what Wagner's 'great' art affords philosophical thought, including: intra-musical theses such as 'the most important thing we can learn from Wagner is [. . .] the relationship of the local to the global' (FLW, p. 132) and that Wagner invented a new relationship between continuity and discontinuity (though both have political and not only musical ramifications); and an extra-musical proposition that Wagner created a new situation with regards to the relationship between music and philosophy (see FLW, pp. 56, 69–70).

For now, we will focus on a claim that appears to be made through reference to specifically 'musical' transformations in order to try and focus on how Badiou conceives of the relationship between music and politics: the claim about dis/continuity. Badiou describes a fundamental formal innovation of the Wagnerian music drama in the way that Wagner disrupts and transforms prior operatic conventions that depended on the alternation of static arias and kinetic recitative; in short, in the past, the dramatic action was propelled forward through the speech-singing of recitatives, while arias deployed largely melodic means (i.e. melisma, ornamentation, coloratura, and so on) to express a mood or emotion while pausing the narrative element for this reflection. This strategy involved a fundamental discontinuity which meant that the relationship 'between the drama and the music was *decided* rather than being undecidable' (FLW, p. 69, Badiou's emphasis). Wagner's innovation was to make 'the interplay between drama and music [...] undecidable' and though discontinuity was not 'eliminated' it was significantly 'displaced' (FLW, p. 69). Similarly, earlier on in the text he commends the way in which Boulez's 'analytical kind of conducting' reveals the 'underlying discontinuity' to contest the charge of 'endless' melody that is so often pressed on Wagner (FLW, p. 6). All of this leads Badiou to suggest that Wagner's innovative approach to transitions has profound implications not only for musical questions but also for political and philosophical ones. Specifically, Badiou suggests it offers a fresh perspective on how we think about the relationship between 'the local and the global, between continuity and discontinuity [...] if] discontinuity is no longer expressed politically in the traditional figure of revolution, how then *is* it expressed?' (FLW, p. 69). Though it is a fascinating and thought-provoking gesture to attend to the structural innovations of a musical/dramatic text and use these changes as a tool for rethinking political or philosophical questions, it remains entirely unclear – in any precise sense – what the relation between musical procedures and politics or philosophy is. Though Badiou entrusts Wagner with having 'invented a new *model* of the relationship between continuity and discontinuity' (FLW, p. 70, my emphasis), the implication is more that this affords us a resource with which we can think of political questions that are in no essential sense connected to the music 'itself'. This observation is, in itself, by no means a fundamental objection to Badiou's instrumentalisation of formal musical procedures as a tool for philosophical reflection – far from it – but it is entirely unclear how this claim could play any role in the exculpatory project. It is an interesting, but ultimately inconsequential, remark that, though couched in relation to political concerns, does little to clarify Wagner's aesthetic relationship (or not) to National Socialism. Concisely, it simply confirms Badiou's *a priori* commitment to an understanding of music that locates its essence (or, more accurately for Badiou, its 'truth') not in its effects, but in its formal procedures. In short, Wagner is not acquitted because Badiou's musical analyses offer a counter-argument to the charges at hand, but because Badiou has *already decided* that music's essence is independent of contextual, political or ethico-aesthetic responsibility, relation or contamination. In this respect, Badiou is concerned only with music as a form of *logos* in the sense that it is a musical manifestation of rational and reasoned discourse as identifiable through structural and formal innovations that invite the philosophical identification of truth-procedures (though, as noted, Badiou is non-committal as to whether Wagner warrants being identified in this way); indeed, as we have already noted in the previous chapter, there is no relation between music's effects – especially on the level of musical pleasure – and truth. In short, though music may yield powerful effects, this is merely superficial (*vis-à-vis* truth) and is not indicative of generic universal truth and so is, therefore, of no interest to philosophy.

II. Pathos

Unsurprisingly, Nancy's and Lacoue-Labarthe's understanding of the problem is rather different. Though a superficial reading highlights similar terminology in the Wagnerian analytic – for example, both Lacoue-Labarthe and Badiou speak of 'saturation' and the need for 'une "lecture" micrologique' ['a micrological reading'] (LMus, p. 68) or 'microscopic' (FLW, p. 68) – these descriptive terms are framed, in terms of value, in entirely oppositional ways. The crucial feature for Lacoue-Labarthe is Wagner's pivotal role in bringing art and politics together through the aestheticisation of the political (see MF_1/MF_2). This critique is developed from one of the central claims in *Musica Ficta* (and elsewhere) which is that *musique savante* has been principally understood as 'musica ficta' since the end of the Renaissance. Lacoue-Labarthe draws on the etymological valence of *ficta* to describe the way that music has been subjected to an aesthetic principle and thus a mimetic logic of representation; more specifically, (early) modern music is constituted (alongside parallel cultural movements in other spheres) as a nostalgic attempt to recover the music of the ancients. In (re)discovering ancient texts on music, two things were made clear: for the ancients, music was powerfully and inextricably bound up with *pathos* – it 'agissait, avec une efficacité étonnante, sur les affects' ['would act, with astonishing affectiveness, on the affects'] (LMus, p. 63). Thus, what was discovered was 'une musique du *sujet*, au sens du sujet de la passion (de l'être-affecté)' ['a music of the *subject*, in the sense of a subject of passion (of the affected being)'] (MF_1, p. 14; MF_2, p. xvii, Lacoue-Labarthe's emphasis). Secondly, and crucially, the only available description of *how* these effects were achieved – given that we have no knowledge of what ancient music/tragedy actually sounded like – was through the description of a codified grammar of the passions; each mode 'était charg[é] d'exprimer ou d'imiter – de représenter, dira-t-on à la Renaissance – ou bien de susciter' ['was required to express or imitate – to represent, we will say in the Renaissance – or else to sustain'] a particular passion or affect (LMus, p. 64). As Nancy describes, though the pathetic or affective dimension of 'music' has been well attested to since its inception as *mousike*, the 'expressive, communicative, pulse-shaping, disseminating power had acquired an entirely new consideration in the age of subjectivity' (MSR, p. 52). The task at hand, then, was the perfecting of techniques capable of moulding or shaping the passions (and thus the subject) in modern music; or, rather, 'c'est en cela qu'ils sont précisément modernes' ['it is in precisely this way that they are modern'] (LMus, p. 62).

The early modern tendency outlined above is then radicalised – and, most crucially of all, politicised – through Romanticism's potent combination of politics, metaphysics and the invention of the singular category of 'Art'. As Lacoue-Labarthe describes, the 'tâche *moderne* par excellence' ['*modern* task *par excellence*'] is assigned jointly to '*critique*' (philosophy) and art, and is 'la collusion effective d'une politique révolutionnaire, d'une philosophie-idéologie et d'un projet religieux-artistique' ['an effective collusion of revolutionary politics, a philosophy-ideology, and a religious-artistic project'] (PNPF, p. 103). Thus, the Wagner question is not only about the relation of the *Gesamtkunstwerk* to National Socialism, but about the Romantic lineage from which it stems 'et dont le Troisième Reich [. . .] est à bien des égards l'accomplissement' ['of which the Third Reich [. . .] is in many regards the accomplishment'] (MF_1, p. 20; MF_2, p. xxi). As Nancy describes, National Socialism (and its music) 'is not purely foreign to the musical possibilities awakened long before Nazism' but rather Nazism 'benefited from an encounter, which was not a chance one, with a certain musical disposition [. . .] something had already been preparing itself for a long time – something that did not as such prefigure the Third Reich, but that offered it a choice space' (MSR, pp. 55, 50-1). Though, to a certain extent, then, Wagner can be seen as merely the culmination and Germany the repository of this heady constellation of art, philosophy and politics, for Lacoue-Labarthe, Wagner is nonetheless decisive. It is through Wagner's formidable combination of myth and technology that he continues, and, most crucially, *amplifies*, the (German) Romantic legacy – a legacy that reveals itself to be founded on a desire for a religious (and thus political) art – and so he is able to manifest, 'pour la première fois [. . .] la possibilité d'un "grand art" qui aurait la force de suppléer à la défaillance politique (ou "religieuse") de la philosophie, qui est la conséquence inéluctable d'une défaillance quant à la vérité elle-même' ['for the first time [. . .] the possibility of a "great art" that would have the force to supplement philosophy's political (or religious) loss of strength, which is the ineluctable consequence of a loss of strength as to the truth itself'] (MF_1, p. 174; MF_2, p. 91). Wagner therefore continues the quintessentially modern task of 'perfectionnements techniques' ['technical perfecting'[6]] but also brings this trajectory to a certain limit – to a point of saturation (LMus, p. 65). The technical means deployed by Wagner are far from 'purely' musical; as Lacoue-Labarthe has articulated they include, among others, many elements of scenography, 'une métaphysique de l'Art complaisamment pessimiste et rédemptrice' ['a metaphysics of Art which was smugly both pessimistic and redemptive'] and 'le dispositif de Bayreuth' ['the whole system of Bayreuth'], all of which are 'mi[s] au service d'une idée nationale et d'une *katharsis* hypnotique de masses' ['put in the service of a nationalistic idea and a hypnotic catharsis of the masses'] (PNPF, pp. 105, 106). Crucially, all of this works to render a music that is able to express the subject – its interiority and destiny – more powerfully than ever before; it is 'the propagation of subjectivity' (MSR, p. 51) as Nancy describes or similarly, as Lacoue-Labarthe states, it is subjective appropriation, or the 'retour à soi ou [. . .] la] réappropriation de l'âme exaltée par la musique' ['return to self or [. . .] the] reappropriation of the soul exalted by music'] (MF_1, p. 78; MF_2, p. 32). The definitive motif in this regard, then, is 'anamnesis' – a structure of recognition affirmed in Baudelaire's audition of Wagner (Baudelaire is one of the four vignettes through which Lacoue-Labarthe considers 'figures de Wagner') and which Lacoue-Labarthe explains as the experience of already having heard this music (even though it is your first hearing) because it feels so intimately to express what is already yours: it is a matter of 'la *destination du sujet*' ['*destination of the subject*'] (MF_1, p. 62; MF_2, p. 21, Lacoue-Labarthe's emphasis).

III. Ethos

Though music and *ethos* have been understood to have a long and privileged relationship in philosophical considerations since Plato – most notably under the auspices of a psychagogical model – whereby music (or more broadly, *mousike*) has a central role in shaping, moulding and training the psyche (in order to achieve psychical, social and even cosmic harmony) the relationship of *pathos* to *ethos* in the Wagnerian project takes a new and distinct form. Indeed, it is worth highlighting, as Nancy does, that the claim is not that the Nazis and their ideologues invent music's ability to affect or effect, to mobilise and manipulate subjects, but it is rather a question of locating, within a longer continuity, 'the turning point of a shift or of a specific perversion' (MSR, p. 55). For Nancy, this turning point is figured as a reversal: it is 'no longer a

---

[6] This could also be rendered as a 'perfecting of techniques'.

question so much of letting a fundamental affect come to expression but of shaping such an affect, of forming it and conforming it to a measure not yet registered in nature or in history' (MSR, p. 55). In a similar figure of reversal or inversion, for Lacoue-Labarthe, it is no longer that 'l'œuvre d'art (la tragédie, le drame musical) offre la vérité de la *polis* ou de l'Etat, mais que le politique lui-même s'institue et se constitue [...] dans et comme l'œuvre d'art' ['the work of art (tragedy, music, drama) offers the truth of the *polis* or the State, but that the political itself is instituted and constituted [...] in and as [a] work of art'] (FP, p. 98; HAP, p. 64) – it is in the figuring of the *Gesamtkunstwerk* at the *Festspiel* of Bayreuth as, for Germany, 'ce que les grandes Dionysies avaient été pour Athènes et la Grèce entière: le lieu où un peuple, rassemblé dans son Etat, se donne à lui-même la représentation de ce qu'il est, et de ce qui le fonde, comme tel' ['what the Greater Dionysia was for Athens and for Greece as a whole: the place where a people, gathered together in their State, provide themselves with a representation of what they are and what grounds them as such'] (FP, p. 97; HAP, p. 64). In short, music is enlisted as a way of affectively training the subject to recognise itself in the historical destiny of a particular collective or community (in this instance, the German *Volk*), and thus in terms of another resonance of *ethos* (as in 'habitat' or 'community'); crucially, however, this *'national-esthétisme'* ['national-aestheticism'] (see PNPF, p. 105, and elsewhere) is in the service of a collective destiny figured by way of mythological origins but ultimately *yet to come*. For both Lacoue-Labarthe and Nancy, then, it is not music's sensuousness (though the critiques of Wagner's work are so often framed in terms of excess, hysteria, and so on) but rather the co-optation of music's sensuousness to a signifying logic: Lacoue-Labarthe speaks of 'surcodification' ['overcodification'] (LMus, p. 68) whereas Nancy describes the way that music becomes 'indexed to a mode of signification and not to a mode of sensibility' (MSR, p. 57). It is a 'signifying imposition' that refuses any resonance or dissonance (i.e. sense rather than *meaning*) precisely because it is the 'sensuous' *representation of* a signified ideal; the form is also indistinguishably the (spiritual) content and thus '*feeling* manages to be identified all at once as signified and signifier of realities, images, or concepts like "people," "community," "destiny," "mission" and so on' (MSR, pp. 57, 58). It is thus not music's supposed ineffability – its 'beyond-signifiance [*outre-signifiance*]' – which is on trial, but the Romantic obliteration of the '*distance* between sound and sense, a distance without which sonority would cease to be what it is' and which paves the way for the *oversignifying* proto-fascism of Wagner (MSR, p. 58).

Though Badiou's critique of Lacoue-Labarthe (and by association, Nancy) is that he '*prescribes* a certain Wagner on the basis of a theory of politics as aestheticization' (FLW, p. 10), it would seem to be equally true that Badiou, too, simply finds in Wagner what he wants to find. When he argues that 'we need to make a distinction between what Wagner saw as his own greatness [. . .] and the place where his greatness really lies, namely, in the accomplishments that *we* can discern today' (FLW, p. 130), though he suggests an incontrovertibly welcome shift beyond an intentional fallacy, there is ultimately nothing, as Brian Kane has astutely described, 'to prevent us from simply reading into Wagner's work the accomplishments we want to find'.[7] Though Badiou does admit that it is 'hard to deny that Wagner created a new kind of sensuality in music' (FLW, p. 64), this appears to be of no consequence for political or philosophical analysis; by having no concern for the affective dimension of Wagner's works (or of music more generally) Badiou is simply able to sidestep the far more complex question of the relationship of sensuous musical experience to politics. Indeed, the sensuous (and potentially manipulative – this is after all the Platonic concern) dimension of music is reserved, in Badiou, for the not-really-music of entertainment – a 'music' that is shackled to the whims of capital. 'Real' music (i.e. 'Art') may be affective but its truth lies in the rational apprehension of its form. Badiou, therefore, not only 'dismiss[es] the *Gesamtkunstwerk* as mere slogan' (FLW, p. 15), but rejects all the technological, material, performative and mediating practices associated with music (and not just Wagner's) in favour of a philosophical-political assessment that simply rehabilitates the (ultimately idealist) identification of essence with form – a claim to which we will return. On the level of truth, and in keeping with his self-professed neo-Platonism, particular re-presentations (i.e. performances, recordings, and so on) of musical truth-procedures are superfluous or irrelevant to the identifiable truth 'content' (which is an ostensibly mental rather than sonorous or experiential phenomenon); its truth is independent of any of the material/technological/bodily props upon which it depends for its sounding. In summary, then, music's effects are strictly independent of its essence. For Lacoue-Labarthe and Nancy, the question is more complex: though Badiou claims that Lacoue-Labarthe locates the essence of Wagner in the effects produced – and this would certainly seem to be a defensible argument – this is not the same as claiming that music's essence is locatable (only) in its effects. As we have seen, both Lacoue-Labarthe and Nancy figure the *Gesamtkunstwerk* as a perver-

---

[7] Kane, 'Badiou's Wagner', p. 5.

sion of music's essentially sensuous dimension (though this, too, is problematic) into a logic of (over)signification – as the annihilation of sense, resonance and dissonance.

Finally, then, before moving on to suggest some of the ways in which critical thought on music might attempt to broach this seeming impasse, I want foreground in perhaps more stark terms the extent to which the Badiousian and Nancy-Lacoue-Labarthean analyses are opposed and, especially, the severity of the Nancy-Lacoue-Labarthian critique. While their work is certainly oppositional, this chapter aims to highlight the extent to which both parties recuperate a certain transcendental Romanticism. Before doing that, however, it is also important to recognise the extent to which they all simply retread variations on long-standing themes. On the one hand, music is to be understood in quasi-scientific terms as the formalistic exploration of sonic forms that are in themselves merely an ideation of music's rational, structural, *visual* aspect. Badiou betrays his indebtedness to this lineage when he says, 'Wagner's music can actually be *seen* to consist of a very complicated play of little cells [... Boulez's conducting makes] us hear the complexity of Wagner's compositional techniques behind the flow of the music in the service of mythification' (FLW, p. 6, my emphasis). To this extent, Badiou never strays far from the positivism of score-based musicological approaches that were dominant until the latter years of the twentieth century, which, even when attending to the sonorous dimension of music, does so in terms of 'literate or "structural listening"', which, as Fred Moten describes, is a way of 'imagining composition: the listener's impossible inhabitation of the imagination of the composer in order to discern those structural intentions upon which the interinanimation of individual and universal autonomy is supposed to rest'.[8] What we actually *hear* (beyond the analytic conducting of Boulez) is of no consequence or interest to Badiou. What is essential in music thus has nothing to do with its sound, but rather its ability to model/imitate/form (or rather create, for Badiou) the (eternal, universal, etc.) Idea. This kind of approach also absolves music of any relation to context – no matter how that is figured – as inessential to and independent of 'the music itself'. On the other hand, then, music is indelibly and essentially linked to the senses, the body and, in the final reading, the maternal feminine; indeed it is privileged in its ability to reveal to us some kind of deeper, more original, pre-symbolic essence. As noted in Chapters 2 and 3, Nancy and Lacoue-Labarthe make this quite explicit, although I hope to make a case, in what follows, for the critical valence of their more fluid conception of music's essence as

---

[8] Fred Moten, 'The Phonographic Mise-En-Scène', pp. 269–81 (p. 271).

found in the writings on Wagner. Nonetheless, the question remains as to whether this is sufficient so as to recuperate a non-reductive and non-essentialising account of music in general. With all this in mind, then, Badiou and Nancy/Lacoue-Labarthe's work could not be more opposed, and it seems that the depth of this disagreement has not yet been noted nor explored sufficiently in critical responses to date: the music to which Badiou remains a faithful subject (i.e. *musique savante*) is figured in Nancy's and Lacoue-Labarthe's work as not only affording fascist co-optation, but has the very possibility of fascism inherent in its structures and practices. While the critical reception of *Musica Ficta* has often focused on the already radical claim that Adorno simply didn't go far enough in his critique of Wagner – that he was still enthralled or enlisted in a certain Wagnerianism himself – it seems the underlying claim (that is certainly more severe) has been largely ignored. It is nothing short of the (enormous) claim that Western musical-aesthetic practices, in nascent form from the early seventeenth century and amplified by Romanticism at the beginning of the nineteenth century, have embedded within them if not the promise, then at least the possibility, of totalitarianism and fascism. Nancy, too, insists 'stubbornly, on the intrinsic membership of fascisms [. . .] in the history of Europe and consequently in its essence or its truth' (MSR, p. 54). This is not essence or truth in a timeless sense (as is Badiou's interest in universal/generic truths) but as the constituting essence or kernel of a particular historical construction; the implication thus being that – assuming music isn't cleanly severable from the society whence it emerges – music has no fixed essence but is co-constituted or relates in some fundamental way to the historical epoch from which it comes. In this regard, it is less that Adorno remained enthralled to a certain Romantic/Wagnerian/proto-fascist legacy, but that so too does Badiou.

TO PERFORMANCE AND BEYOND (SIGNIFICATION)

As we have seen above, the debate about Wagner's relation to or prefiguring of National Socialism through musico-theatrical means constellates primarily around music's relation to signification, affect and truth. It hinges most crucially of all, for Badiou, on the disjuncture between the location of truth in the truth-event and its transient but associated practices of performance and (re)production. Though a great performance, in Badiou's eyes, may reveal or excavate the universal truth of a particular musical subject – and thus the performance event interacts in important ways with the more essential truth-event – it in no way constitutes it, nor is performance itself an event in the Badiousian sense of the term. In sharp contrast, neither Nancy nor Lacoue-Labarthe are concerned with the location or existence of absolute truths; indeed, it is such Platonic/metaphysical fictions that their entire philosophical projects set out to debunk. Instead, for Nancy and Lacoue-Labarthe, it is the co-optation of the sensuous or sonorous dimension of music into the representational logic of signification that paves the way for Wagner's mythological music-drama, which aesthetically prefigures or anticipates National Socialism.

However, it is Lacoue-Labarthe's misappropriation of the term 'musica ficta' that points us in the most productive directions for thinking about what is at stake. Lacoue-Labarthe takes the term (nominally via Adorno[9]) to mean the way in which music – at least since the Renaissance – has been subjected to the principle of the '"esthétique", de la *mimèsis*, présentation ou représentation. Le *fingere* auquel renvoie *ficta*, dans *musica ficta*, est l'équivalent latin du *plassein/plattein* grec: façonner, modeler, sculpter – figurer, donc' ['"aesthetic" principle of *mimesis*, presentation or representation. The Latin *fingere*, to which *music ficta* refers, is the equivalent of the Greek *plassein/plattein*: to fashion, to model, to sculpt – thus to figure'] (MF_1, pp. 13–14; MF_2, p. xvii). Though Lacoue-Labarthe is clearly aware of the usual connotation of 'musica ficta',[10] this symptomatic forgetting or omission nonetheless forces our reading of Lacoue-Labarthe in productive directions. Though Lacoue-Labarthe's misappropriation is without doubt strategic, as it allows for a detailed consideration of the way in which Western musical practices also participate in the mimetic logic that both governs metaphysical thinking and to which Lacoue-Labarthe devotes so much of his philosophical musings, it also gestures towards a constituent forgetting in this very tradition. While *ficta* is taken in a flight of etymological fancy to relate to music's submission to a representative logic in the Western tradition, what the term actually refers to – in standard historical and musicological discourse – is notes outside the accepted gamut of notes in *musica recta/vera*, and so, in practice, the way in which 'some accidental inflections were conventionally implied by the musical context' and were thus not notated though they were performed.[11] As Margaret

---

[9] This is a clarification added in the English translation. See Philippe Lacoue-Labarthe, *Musica Ficta: Figures of Wagner*, p. xvi.

[10] In 'Une lettre sur la musique' Lacoue-Labarthe states '[j]e prends le terme, non au sens strict, par opposition à la *musica vera* des Anciens ou de certaines spéculations médiévales, mais au sens "détourné" que lui a conféré Adorno' ['I use the term not in the strict sense, in opposition to the *musica vera* of the Ancients or of certain medieval speculations, but in the "re-imagined" sense which Adorno gives to it']. See LMus, p. 63.

[11] Karol Berger, *Musica Ficta*, p. xi.

Bent describes, 'the application of unwritten accidentals was essentially part of the medieval [and Renaissance] performer's art. Modern performers are no longer able to perceive instinctively the problems and choices involved', meaning that in current performances of such works the manuscript editor stands in for the medieval performer, by adding suggested accidentals (sharp or flat signs above the note).[12]

As Eric Prieto argues, then, the notion of 'musica ficta' offers a useful contribution to Lacoue-Labarthe's theory of the relationship between the rhythmical subject and the mimetic paradigm of onto-typology (and thus his attendant concerns about the relation between politics and aesthetics). I would even go so far as to suggest that it allows us to flesh out much of what is implicit, but ultimately underdeveloped, in Lacoue-Labarthe's (and possibly Nancy's) reflections on music. As Prieto describes, 'musica ficta' 'presupposes the need for a subject, the musician, who is able to interpret correctly the incomplete symbols in the score'.[13] Thus, the *aide-mémoire* of the notated graphic representation as found in the score-copy has limited ability to guarantee with any exactitude the becoming sonorous or audible without the interpretive or intuitive actions of a performer. Similarly, I wish to suggest that it is highly revealing, to say the least – and, at worst, deeply problematic – that Badiou so often has to resort to performed instantiations of the works he comments on in order to even locate what he claims as the (formally derived) truth of the work. This is not to suggest, however, that we should simply switch from an immaterial gnosticism which locates the essence of the musical work in its abstract formal innovations (as with Badiou) to a drastic but ineffable performance-as-essence. Indeed, while truth (or so Badiou claims) is located only in the formal innovations of the musical subject 'itself', external to and uncontaminated by the practices of the material world, the turn to performance risks equating music's essence with (still immaterial) transience, ineffability and irrational or a-logical beyond language and/or (representational) meaning. As Robin James has explored in some detail, the philosophical recuperation of ineffability often performs its own kind of othering – it locates an excess or beyond (often strongly coded in racialised/gendered terms) – that the (white, male) philosopher can attempt to domesticate or rescue.[14] Instead, a more thoroughgoing conception of the performer-function brings into play some (though

---

[12] Margaret Bent, 'Musica Recta and Musica Ficta', pp. 73–100 (p. 73).
[13] Eric Prieto, 'Musical Imprints', pp. 17–32 (p. 31).
[14] See the text available on Robin James's website of her 'drastic' talk: Robin James, 'Eliza's "Ai"s'. I am referring in passing to the well-known work by Carolyn Abbate, 'Music – Drastic or Gnostic?', pp. 505–36 and Vladimir Jankélévitch, *La Musique et l'ineffable*.

by no means all – the list is not exhaustive) of the interrelating ways in which the musical process is constituted. As Prieto describes,

> a musician is engaged in an immersive mimetic task – the (re)presentation of a (partially) pre-inscribed intention to an audience [... However,] it is not the musician's [innate] character or sensitivity that makes possible the correct interpretation of the score, but a combination of expertise, analytic ability, training, long experience, thorough preparation, mastery of tonal syntax, and musical intelligence.[15]

Crucially, then, this also allows us to (re)think the role of instinct in performance via the notion of 'musica ficta': though it may certainly be true that '[m]odern performers are no longer able to perceive instinctively the problems and choices involved', the instinct involved here by no means equates to an innate capacity, but rather one that is learned through a specific constellation of situated practices, instruments and internalised social, cultural and artistic norms.

TECHNE/EPISTEME/DOXA

A more nuanced consideration of performance, then, leads us towards a contemplation of the musical work/process not only in terms of the drastic act of performance itself, but in terms of the accumulated and enculturated norms, knowledge and practices it utilises, deploys and exploits. More precisely, a consideration of music demands not only that we 'enter the debate between episteme (*epistēmē*) and techne (*technē*), between "knowledge" and what can be translated as either "craft" or "art"',[16] but also gestures towards the way in which practical and theoretical forms of knowledge are never entirely separable from one another, nor are they entirely distinct from the environment from which they emerge or in which they participate. As Lehmann goes on to explain, for both Plato and Aristotle – albeit in different ways – though *episteme* and *techne* are contrasted with one another, there is no fundamental or radical separation between these two aspects in the way that we separate pure theory from experiential practice in contemporary conceptualisations: '[i]n the history of philosophy this apparent division between abstract theory and experiential practice has often been only a rhetorical one, as the interest lay in discovering productive relationships between theory and practice and not in separating them into cognitive entities'.[17] Nonetheless, it has been the

---

[15] Prieto, 'Musical Imprints', p. 31.
[16] Ulrich Lehmann, 'Making as Knowing', pp. 149–64 (p. 150).
[17] Ibid., p. 150.

central commitment of Bernard Stiegler's work that underlying the practice of most Western philosophy is the premise of an (illusory) distinction between *episteme* and *techne*. 'L'héritage de ce conflit' ['the inheritance of this conflict'], as Stiegler describes, is that 'l'*épistémè* philosophique lutte contre la *tekhnè* sophistique, dévalorisant par là tout savoir technique' ['the philosophical *épistēmē* is pitched against the sophistic *tekhnē*, whereby all technical knowledge is devalued'].[18] In a specifically musical vein, Stiegler draws attention to the way in which organology (the study of musical instruments) has still not been assimilated into discourse on music in general, confirming 'une séparation absurde entre objets d'une pratique (les instruments comme condition de possibilité de la musique) et phénomènes esthétiques (tels que les œuvres, les styles et les langages musicaux, les pratiques d'écoute, etc.) ['an absurd separation between the objects of a practice (instruments as music's condition of possibility) and aesthetic phenomena (such as musical works, styles and languages, listening practices, etc.)'].[19] Similarly, Emily Dolan and John Tresch speak of the 'urgency with which both the history of science and music studies are turning to studies of instruments'.[20] Dolan and Tresch highlight the way that music and science have been intimately related since at least Pythagorus, and suggest the similar if inverted way in which music and science seem to relate to their respective instruments: 'musical instruments express the inner states of the composer or performer, moving outward from the mind to the world, while scientific instruments bring external states of the world into the consciousness of observers, moving from the world to the mind'.[21] Though the scientific and musical paradigms seem to operate in opposite directions, as it were, they clearly share an investment in the fantasy of a '"transparent" instrument' – a fantasy that for science would be capable of transmitting the natural world *as it is* to the scientific observer's mind/eye, and for music delivers us directly to a kind of transcendental communion with the harmony of the spheres – with little concern for the way in which instruments themselves 'transmute or modify', mediate or, indeed, *create* these illusions of direct and unmediated access.[22] In this regard, as Heidegger describes, '*techne* is the name not only for the activities and skills of the craftsman, but also for the arts of the mind and the fine arts. *Techne* belongs to bringing-

---

[18] Bernard Stiegler, *La Technique et Le Temps*, p. 15 [Stiegler, *Technics and Time, 1*, p. 1].
[19] Bernard Stiegler, *De la Misère Symbolique 2*, p. 29 [Stiegler, *Symbolic Misery, 2*, p. 11].
[20] Emily I. Dolan and John Tresch, 'Toward a New Organology', pp. 278–98 (p. 279).
[21] Ibid., p. 281.
[22] Ibid., pp. 290, 281.

forth, to *poiesis*; it is something *poietic*.'[23] As an undeveloped corollary, then, we are presumably every bit as able to speak of a poetics of scientific practice as we are of artistic or cultural modes. Given that the invention of new instruments extends, by prosthesis, the threshold of the human in the way that they create new possibilities through the extension and expansions (and subsequent redefinition) of intellectual and bodily capabilities (among others) there is, then, an inherent ethics of instruments to be explored. Most crucially, as Dolan and Tresch, again, describe, an ethics of instruments 'turns out to be important for epistemology: knowledge appears not merely as a set of ideas or even practices, but as a form of life, with distinct ideals, moral codes, activities, and understandings of the self'.[24]

As I have attempted to show in the previous chapters – particularly with regards to Badiou – there is a pervasive forgetting or disavowal of the constituent *techne* of *musique savante* (evidently in terms of instruments and notation, but also the extent to which composition itself is a *technique* and thus a practice) that plays into the way it is conceptualised as a wholly autonomous, self-referential, auto-poietic and absolute entity, whereas contemporary popular music (whether in performance or listening practices) appears to be so evidently and obviously mediated through technological means. This is not to suggest that different genres or epochs of music should be directly equated or conceived of as having the same relation to *techne* or technology more broadly – it may indeed by one very interesting axis of consideration to explore processes of continuity and change in music's technological aspect – but to insist on the quite indisputable facticity of absolute music's technological mediation and the consequences this brings to bear for any philosophy of music. In fact, it is not only the forgetting or disavowal of *techne* that occasions the supposedly acousmatic foundations inherent to the construction of absolute music – a fantasy that allows this repertoire to be heard as if from a '"mystic gulf", like vapours rising from the holy womb of Gaia' – but that acousmaticity is itself a practice and thus a *techne*;[25] as Brian Kane describes, *techne* 'is the supplement that allows the acousmatic effect to emerge. To ignore that is to remain faithful to phantasmagoria'.[26]

Though the framing of the argument above might most obviously seem to extend the critique of Badiou's conception of music, it also

---

[23] Martin Heidegger, *The Question Concerning Technology, and Other Essays*, p. 13.
[24] Dolan and Tresch, 'Toward a New Organology', p. 282.
[25] And is nowhere more evident than in Wagner's practical-technological endeavour to hide the orchestra from view.
[26] Kane, *Sound Unseen*, p. 222.

has important ramifications for the thinking on music as outlined in Nancy's and Lacoue-Labarthe's projects. Though Stiegler suggests that we can trace this illusory distinction between *techne* and *episteme* most clearly in music 'puisque, toujours déjà *médiate*, la musique n'advient qu'à travers un système technique (comprenant aussi bien l'instrument que l'outil d'écriture ou la technologie d'écoute)' ['since music, which is always already *mediated*, does not take place except by way of a technical system (which includes the instrument just as much as the writing tool or the listening technology)', the consequences of this line of thinking extend beyond the (technologically) mediate nature of music and into the terrain of the co-constituted realm of aesthetic experience and affect.[27] In a sense, it offers a way of de-naturalising the account of aesthetic (especially affective) experience which we sometimes find in Nancy and Lacoue-Labarthe. Stiegler suggests that 'il s'agirait de penser les techniques esthétiques depuis le point de vue d'une *organologie générale*, où les organes du vivant, les organes artificiels et les organisations sociales constituent le fait esthétique complet en nouant ce que Gilbert Simondon nomme des relations transductives (des relations qui constituent leurs termes)' ['it would then be a matter of thinking aesthetic techniques from the perspective of a *general organology*, where the organs of the living, together with artificial organs and social organizations, constitute the total aesthetic occurrence, combining in what Gilbert Simondon refers to as transductive relations (relations that constitute their elements)'].[28] In this way, there is no originary aesthetic or affective dimension to which we can return, or which we can unveil; rather, though our musical-aesthetic experiences are no doubt meaningful (in Nancy's non-foundational sense) in and of themselves and require no transcendental grounding through reference to meaning (in terms of signification), it is not because music is a sonorous residue of an effectively (affectively) pre-symbolic domain; rather, music's affective dimension is not prior to – either logically or chronologically – but coeval and co-emergent with its technical and epistemic practices. The Stieglerian approach insists on the co-individuation of organs (whether biological, prosthetic or social) such that our affective responses to music are not founded on a myth of origins but are co-created alongside or along with the specific practices in a particular context (that, crucially, is also not *prior* but co-constituted). This is a claim which no doubt highlights how easy it is to be blind to our own (intuitively 'natural') social doxa – in the sense that the force of doxa 'has nothing

---

[27] Stiegler, *De la Misère Symbolique 2*, pp. 21–2 [Stiegler, *Symbolic Misery*, 2, p. 7].
[28] Ibid., p. 29 [p. 11].

to do with Truth. Its impact derives from its being accepted, or rather its being seen as probable.'²⁹ The claim about 'musica ficta' is exemplary in this regard: the practice of adding inflections not notated in the score is no longer intuitive to contemporary performers and thus it is seen as a distinct historical practice (and one worthy of scholarly attention). At the same time, there is enough continuity in prevailing Western musical traditions to make a vast amount of the work involved in performing this repertoire seem 'natural' or intuitive – in short, 'normal'. Much is taken for granted, whether it is in the assumption that making/performing music involves the ability to read a score, the training of vocal chords or the development of instrumental technique, or the hours of repetitive rehearsal leading to a (hopefully) perfect or at least accurate rendition – none of which is a natural given but forms a specific constellation of socio-aesthetic practices. Moreover, and most centrally to the concluding arguments of this book, there is also no music (or indeed musical essence) that we can 'salvage' prior to the amalgamation of these musico-aesthetic, cognitive, affective, bodily and social practices or conventions.

To ground this potentially contentious claim a little more, it is worth thinking in greater depth about what it is we really mean when we talk about emotion or affect in music – at least as it appears in philosophy. As Robin James has so convincingly highlighted, '[m]usic, like affect, emotion, or implicit understanding, is the Other of philosophy, at least as it's conventionally defined and practiced' (and therefore sensuous, feminine, bodily, and so on).³⁰ James is in no way refuting the sometimes intensely affective dimension of music – far from it – but is rather cautioning that if we fail to (or choose not to)

> understand all the work that goes into making music – from the epistemic frames that organize music/noise distinctions, to the logic of specific compositional strategies (like tonality or ragas), to more practical matters like audio engineering or how to play the piano – it might appear to affect us in relatively *immediate* ways.³¹

We can thus better understand music's affective dimensions by attending to the specific practices, systems and mechanisms by which affect is instrumentally created and shaped, and the discursive practices that allow us to hear it precisely *as* music, rather than noise (or, indeed, as 'art' rather than mere 'entertainment'). Indeed, if music were 'extra-logical [. . .] then it would be indistinguishable from noise or

---

[29] Ruth Amossy, 'Introduction to the Study of Doxa', pp. 369–94 (p. 371).
[30] James, 'Affective Resonances', p. 59.
[31] Ibid., p. 60, my emphasis.

sound'.³² Although I am hesitant to draw such a sharp distinction between music and noise/sound (because noise/sound must also be discursively produced and multiply contingent) it is nonetheless worth emphasising that it is *music* – and explicitly not sound and/or noise – that tends to stand in as a generic synonym or placeholder for affect. For all the discussion of resonance and rhythm as the underlying (essentially musical) condition of this pre-symbolic and affective dimension, it is music (and, again, not sound in general) that is claimed – by philosophers – to have such a powerful effect (affect). It is thus even more surprising that closer attention is rarely paid to the specific practices that afford this socio-cultural affectivity. As Rita Felski describes (speaking about literature, though I think it applies equally to music), 'aesthetic pleasure is never unmediated or intrinsic [. . . because] even our most inchoate and seemingly ineffable responses are shaped by dispositions transmitted through education and culture'.³³

THE WORK OF OPERA

Given that the ethico-aesthetic in question is the operas (or *Oper und Drama*) of Wagner, it is now worth a moment to consider what the relationship between *episteme* and *techne* outlined above contributes to the debate. Returning to the birth of the genre not only elucidates certain key points, but also adds weight to Lacoue-Labarthe's firm conviction that it is no accident or mere chance that the *'paroxysme du Moderne'* [*'paroxysm of Modernity'*] was attained through music-drama (i.e. Wagner's *Gesamtkunstwerk*) (PNPF, p. 104). As he goes on to explain, much of what Wagner was trying to achieve (for the moment, irrespective of whether he met his aims) was already in place – was simply a repetition of – its Florentine/Mantuan incarnation: it is written into the story of the birth of opera itself. Though a full history of the birth of opera is far beyond the time or space available here, it is worth noting that there are few other genres that have such a clear point of origin (in this instance, Florence at the end of the sixteenth century) and about which we have such a detailed understanding of the social and cultural contexts that gave rise to the genre. Additionally, its hybrid form and socio-political context – the combination of not only musical and dramatic but literary, mythological and theoretical aspects (opera emerges in the academic culture of late Renaissance courtly life) – makes opera a focal point for the discussion and exploration of

---

³² Ibid., p. 60.
³³ Felski, *Uses of Literature*, p. 15.

the role of music and the arts more broadly. At the same time, though the intellectual climate was indispensable in formenting the birth of this new genre, it was by no means an entirely abstract or theoretical endeavour, but rather one that plays between what we might now think of abstract theory (*episteme*) and concrete practices (*techne*): indeed, though it was informed by ancient music theory, the techniques sought were an overtly musical practice. Further, the word 'opera' itself means 'work'– both in the sense of the work carried out, the labour involved – and the resulting work itself: the *œuvre*. Similarly, it is also acutely clear in the context of the emergence of opera that the genre is distinctly and indissociably bound up with the cultural context from which it emerged: its birth is inseparable from the context of the wealth and power of Florence – and particularly the Medici family; the intellectual and practical labour of the Camerata de' Bardi (the Florentine Camerata); and the Renaissance rediscovery of ancient philosophy. Opera is not, however, merely a reflection of the context whence it emerges, but it too played its own formative and influential role by displaying the cultural, intellectual and artistic wealth, sophistication and innovation – in short, their proximity to birth of Western civilisation in ancient Greece – of Renaissance Florence.

Lacoue-Labarthe draws our attention to the distinctly modern paradox upon which much of this is built: a *new* genre is founded in order to return us to the tragic dramas of ancient Greece and thus, from the off, opera is caught between the nostalgic 'perfection' of the ancients and the modern need of 'perfectionnement technique' ['technical perfecting'] aimed at surpassing the (already perfect) model that it is trying to revive (LMus, pp. 60–1). As already mentioned above, then, not only did the Camerata de' Bardi engage in a sustained attempt to resurrect ancient tragedy, but through the discovery of ancient texts (primarily Plato and Aristotle) their attention was drawn to the profound effects that music was apparently capable of in the ancient world. As Lacoue-Labarthe attests, this is not only reflected in the choice of subject matter for the earliest operas (Peri's *Euridice* (1600) and Monteverdi's *Orfeo* (1607) being cases in point) but in the attempt to (re)construct musical techniques for the excitation of the passions inspired by the ancient association of particular modes with particular affects. It is an explicit attempt to create a more expressive (but by no means *excessive*) music that is nonetheless founded on the recovery of a music that is, in its essence, (already) expressive – and particularly of the subject. Of course these developments do not take place in a vacuum – aside from anything else, early 'composers' (often court musicians alongside librettists and scenarists) of opera did not limit themselves to opera alone but also wrote madrigals, motets, intermedi, and so on – and resonances can be found more widely in relation to broader cultural process. Notions of perfection, modernity and novelty abound: 'stile moderno' (previously 'seconda pratica') was coined by Caccini in *Le nuove musiche* (1602), while Monteverdi planned to write a book called *Seconda pratica, overo perfettione della moderna musica* (though he never did). Equally, in terms of new musical practices, it is through the development of 'stile rappresentativo' – a style that is more expressive than speech but not as melodious as song – that the difficult task of balancing the demands of both the musical and linguistic/dramatic elements of opera was attained: this is one aspect of the aesthetic or mimetic principles to which music, according to Lacoue-Labarthe, is submitted (for the first time) (see, for example, LMus, p. 63). In a related vein, it is also this period which sees the first use of the word 'technology' (1612 in English, and 1607 in its Latinate root 'technologia' according to the *OED*); surprisingly (or not), in its earliest form it refers specifically to a treatise on the arts.[34]

These developments no doubt correspond to the periodisations offered by Mark Evan Bonds as laid out in Chapter 1. He marks 1550 as a threshold of a shift from ancient, medieval and early Renaissance thought which figured music's effects (fairly uncomplicatedly) as a consequence of its essence to a looser relationship between these two aspects; though essence and effect continue to be related, there is a shift towards music's capacity for expression decoupled from an entirely clear sense of its essence. This brings it into parallel with language and a quest for origins: as we reach the eighteenth century, it became increasingly unclear what language is and music, as we have noted, is posited as a possible pre-linguistic origin of language itself, linking the natural and non-semantic to the semantic and cultural.[35] In short, in the eighteenth century in particular, as Andrew H. Clark describes, music is made to *speak*.[36] What Lacoue-Labarthe brings so forcefully into frame is an insistence on how what is at stake is not an 'innate' or unconstructed musical expressivity (whatever that might be) but a rigorous and laborious theoretical and practical endeavour that sets out to find (or invent) the *techniques* that will allow for a resurgence or reanimation of ancient music's (supposed) expressive capacity.

---

[34] See 'technology, n.', *OED Online* (Oxford University Press, 2009).
[35] See Chapters 1 and 2.
[36] See Andrew H. Clark, 'Making Music Speak' in Keith Moore Chapin and Andrew Herrick Clark (eds), *Speaking of Music*, pp. 70–85. It is notable that this is figured in terms of 'common good' and the ability of music, in a Platonic vein, to 'effect and potentially control the public [. . .] and to create a sense of shared sentiment, purpose, and citizenship'; see p. 70.

At the same time, Lacoue-Labarthe skates perhaps a little too quickly over what is of course a more complicated process of transformation: though the decoupling or loosening of the relationship between music's essence and its effect can be traced back to the late sixteenth century, it only really comes into full force in the seventeenth and eighteenth centuries – and even then remains dynamic rather than static, whether in terms of ontology, epistemology or technology. Daniel Chua has described this process as a 'naturalisation' of music by which music is no longer understood as *super*natural (i.e. part of a unified totality that was at once worldly and magical, human and cosmic) but is instead aligned with nature – hence that whole raft of enlightenment binaries – and is therefore 'amenable to the interrogation and technological control of human rationality'.[37] This is, however, an ambivalent transformation: though there is an 'attempt towards the end of the sixteenth century to transfer music from the medieval quadrivium of music, geometry, astronomy and arithmetic to the rhetorical arts of the trivium; the shift split the nature of music'.[38] It is, on the one hand, an object – rational, scientifically and empirically knowable, and concerned with 'truth' – and, on the other, a subject (or at least subjective/subjectivising) – thus natural, expressive and concerned with voice, words and meaning. Philosophers, musicians and critics – depending on their own epistemological commitments – thus locate music's essence on different sides of the split: whereas Rameau clearly locates music (itself grounded in the *corps sonore*) on the side of objectivity, Rousseau is evidently committed to music's essential linguistic and expressive nature.[39] This split of course reflects the changing experience and expression of subjectivity in this period. As Gary Tomlinson carefully outlines:

> The distinction between Cartesian and pre-Cartesian subjectivity is not the difference between a mechanism and something nonmechanistic that preceded it. Rather the change is from a mechanism whose workings were thought to be fully explicable – a mechanism that seemed in the workings of its spirit to span physical and metaphysical realms – to one whose central operations had become opaque. The name this opacity assumed in the seventeenth century is *representation*, which we define simply, for now, as the presenting over again of one thing in another place.[40]

---

[37] Daniel Chua, 'Vincenzo Galilei, Modernity, and the Division of Nature' in Suzannah Clark and Alexander Rehding (eds), *Music Theory and Natural Order*, pp. 17–29 (p. 18).
[38] Ibid., p. 18.
[39] Ibid., see pp. 18–19. Chua goes so far as to place different musical genres on either side of this split (i.e. symphony vs. opera) but to my mind, while this might work on a descriptive level, it runs the risk of ignoring the ambivalent or even conflicting elements of this split that are present *within* each genre's self-construction.
[40] Tomlinson, *Metaphysical Song*, p. 35.

Importantly, then, music does not merely reflect – symptomatically – this epistemic shift from an ancient/medieval to an early modern worldview in which 'the price of progress [...] is the loss of meaning', but (modern) music is central to this narrative and is one of the very grounds on which this shift is played out or constructed, and thus bears within itself the trace of this essentially modern splitting.[41] Or again, in other words: music is not, and never was, an essence distinct or neatly separable from the theories and practices that constitute it.

BACK TO THE FUTURE: PHILOSOPHY, (GREAT) ART AND ORIGIN(ALITY)

Before we bring this chapter to a close, it is perhaps worth retreading one more time what is by now, one hopes, fairly familiar, and also to highlight a constellation of philosophical commitments that bring all three philosophers – Nancy, Lacoue-Labarthe and Badiou – at once into close proximity while also maintaining the fundamental rift between the opposing camps. Having laid out immediately above the broad sweep of operatic development from its inception in late Renaissance Italy, it is necessary to rejoin this to the second, broad epochal sweep (as laid out already in Chapter 1 and in the intervening chapters): the notion of absolute music – with which opera has a complicated relationship, for obvious reasons. It is perhaps this trajectory that is least clearly plotted out in Lacoue-Labarthe's account – an observation that leads Tomlinson to note a residual universalism (because of a generically unified and static conception of opera over time) in Lacoue-Labarthe's otherwise 'deeply thought' account in *Musica Ficta*.[42] As we have already noted, under the influence of Kant and Hegel and along with changing practices – such as the separation of musical life from courtly or religious functions; technological developments that impact the ability to make new or more complex instruments; the growth and standardisation of the orchestra; the emergence of the canon (a musical museum cf. Lydia Goehr), concert halls, institutions, and their attendant social and cultural practices – from around 1800 – and especially after about 1850 – music reaches its Romantic apex. Instrumental music is validated as the highest form of elite European art: through a

---

[41] Chua, 'Vincenzo Galilei, modernity, and the division of nature' in Clark and Rehding (eds), *Music Theory and Natural Order*, p. 18.

[42] Tomlinson, *Metaphysical Song*, p. 157 n. 3. It is not that Lacoue-Labarthe is unaware of the absolutising and Romantic trajectory – far from it, and his co-authored work with Nancy, *L'Absolu littéraire*, is a case in point – but opera's changeable metaphysical journey, from its inception in Florence through to the specifically Wagnerian project, is never considered in any detail; nor is its (Italian/German) relation to French opera addressed.

potent combination of formalist self-referentiality and (staged) separation from the (functional) mundane, this repertoire manifests an interiority that transcends the world of mere appearances and drab, prosaic, daily life. Music and its attendant theories and practices thus again correspond to the changing nature of subjectivity over time – Tomlinson outlines these shifts as follows:

> The history of Western subjectivity since the Renaissance might be written as this story of a shift from a *participating* subject, in contact with a unified cosmos extending smoothly from materiality to immateriality; to a *transcended* subject, whose knowledge depends on an unknowable harmony granted by a loving God between material and immaterial realms utterly out of touch with one another; and finally to a *transcendental* subject, encompassing within itself all the material and immaterial means necessary in order to know.[43]

The difference here being that, while we can show how music evolves over time – informing and informed by changing conceptions of subjectivity and the place of the human in the world – music 'itself' takes on a particular role in the Romantic conception because (absolute, instrumental) music becomes prized as the ideal vehicle to express the transcendental subject. The split that was noted in the early modern period – between a subjective and objective understanding of music – is thus radicalised in the modern (Romantic) period. Autonomous and absolute works of music become concrete, formally analysable, independent objects aligned with rationality, truth and transcendence (so long as we only attend to what is understandable in music as *logos*, i.e. form/structure). At the same time, music in its subjective guise (all that escapes *logos* and is thus aligned with nature, emotion, bodies, the feminine, and so on: in short, philosophy's Other) – particularly as taken up by Schopenhauer – becomes a cipher less for subjectivity at large than for *what has been lost* of subjectivity: its constitutive lack; the Will oppressed by representation; the underlying *Trieb* that manifests symbolically or symptomatically; or the Lacanian-Kristevan *sémiotique*. It refers us to a pre-linguistic or pre-symbolic dimension which, as noted in Chapter 1, is a crucial point of contact between modern philosophy and psychoanalytic approaches. Crucially, and this cannot be emphasised enough, this (subjective) conception of music is nonetheless equated with a particular repertory: largely post-1800 *musique savante* in the German tradition. At the end of this lineage (and by no means in an uncomplicated or uncontested way) stands Wagner who, depending on one's perspective, either succeeded in the totalising metaphysical gesture

---

[43] Ibid., pp. 38–9.

par excellence of submitting both language and politics to a musical adequation of the 'idea' itself, or who represents one of the last possibilities of 'great' art – who 'represents a music for the future' (FLW, p. 133).

In this regard, the Nancy-Lacoue-Labarthian and Badiousian projects are entirely incommensurable with one another: Badiou is fully committed to the idea not just of art, but of *great* art. His wager is that, no matter how compromised Wagner may be by his historical, philosophical and political associations, the Wagnerian work *itself* explores formal possibilities that gesture towards the possibility of a great art of the future. It is of central importance, then, that 'truth' only enters the Badiousian lexicon during the period of music/art history in which 'great Art' (singular, rather than *les beaux-arts*) emerges: as laid out in Chapter 4, Haydn, a 'founder of the classical style' is the earliest mention of truth-procedures in music because of his 'systematic use of the plasticity of short cells' (i.e. his formal innovations) (FLW, p. 132). Nonetheless, all three find a moment of relative consensus over a related issue, then: the crisis of contemporary 'Art'. For Badiou, this is indexed to (liberal) socio-cultural processes which have validated pluralism, diversification, the democratisation of taste, and have created a fundamental in-distinction – the inability, or perhaps just the lack of desire to distinguish – between art and non-art; between music (as Art) and music (as entertainment). These processes seem to have been amplified by the increasing capacity and availability of recording technologies and playback devices – the implication being that we live in a world in which (entertainment) music is ubiquitous – though we (the generic populace) are unable to discern that it is not 'Art' proper. In stark contrast, then, though Lacoue-Labarthe speaks, using one of his favoured privative prefixes, of 'la *désaffectation* de l'art lui-même [... parce que] l'art est désormais hors d'usage [...] "hors-service"' ['the *abandonment* of art itself [because] art is already out of use [...] "out of service"'] (PNPF, p. 98), he identifies this as a closure induced by the impossibility of the very concept of Art itself. In contradistinction to Badiou, then, he suggests that once we have finished blaming 'l'industrie culturelle, la société spectaculaire-marchande, le libéralisme postmoderne, la mondialisation, l'étatisme social-démocrate, etc. [in short, everything Badiou holds accountable] la question reste entière: pourquoi l'art s'est laissé *assimiler?* Pourquoi a-t-il fait preuve d'une telle apathie, d'un tel manque de *résistance?*' ['the cultural industry, the society of the spectacle-commodity, postmodern liberalism, globalisation, social-democratic state politics, etc., the question remains: Why does art allow itself to be *assimilated*? Why does art reveal such apathy, such a lack of *resistance*?'] (PNPF, p. 98). Lacoue-Labarthe goes on to remind us, as we have just outlined above and elsewhere, that the very concept of Art 'est un phénomène récent' ['is a recent phenomenon'], which is found in its nascent form during the *querelles* but only reaches fruition in Jena Romanticism around 1800 (he notes, for example, that 1790 is the last mention of *les beaux-arts* in Kant's *critique*) (see PNPF, pp. 98–9): thus the early modern and modern phases outlined above. The point of Lacoue-Labarthe's excursus is to highlight the inherent impossibility – the artifice – upon which the entire project of Art is built, urging us not to be misled by this notional rupture instigated by the modern: though '[o]n l'a saluée comme une naissance; elle était peut-être mortifère, ou suicidaire. Et l'Art, comme le Moderne, sont peut-être mort-nés, ou avortés' ['we welcomed it [Art] as a birth; it was perhaps fatal, or suicidal. And Art, like modernity, were perhaps stillborn, or aborted'] (PNPF, p. 99). Its own crisis is built into its (illusory) auto-conception, whereby it is charged (by philosophy) with manifesting the absolute, but all it can manifest is its capacity to manifest the absolute (and not the absolute itself): 'l'Art naît sous le signe de sa fin, c'est-à-dire sous le signe de la réflexion (philosophique) sur l'art' ['Art is born under the sign of its own end, that is to say under the sign of (philosophical) reflection on art'] (PNPF, p. 100). In moving forward, Lacoue-Labarthe draws on Adorno's concept of *Entkunstung* – which he tentatively translates as 'désartification' – a neologism that has embedded within it Art's constituent finitude and, yet, in figuring art as no longer singular (in the Romantic sense), allows the possibility of something 'artistic' to remain through its dis-articulation.

Despite their profound differences, however, what all three philosophers share is a commitment to or validation of the 'new'. Indeed, it is in this regard that the most valuable aspects of both Nancy's and Badiou's approaches to art can be discerned; for Badiou, truth is, by definition 'something new' – this stands in sharp contradistinction to knowledge, which 'only gives us repetition, it is concerned only with what already is'.[44] It is this capital newness and the potentiality for a reconfiguration not only of the subject but of the situation that seems to be most promising; indeed, the subject does not exist prior to the truth-event but it is the event itself 'which calls a subject into existence, into the creation of a truth'.[45] In asserting the productive value of figuring the event as that which founds a (faithful) subject anew I am largely following Simon Critchley, who likewise finds value in Badiou's concept of the event as a creative (rather than imitative) thrust that

---

[44] Badiou, 'On the Truth-Process', open lecture at the European Graduate School, para. 2, https://www.lacan.com/badeurope.htm (accessed 11 June 2019).
[45] Critchley, *Infinitely Demanding*, p. 45.

impels a new subjective configuration. Critchley, I think rightly, maintains suspicion over the need to describe this in terms of truth, however – not only on an ethical level, but also in terms of the circularity and tautology of the logic that figures the subject and its constituent truth as equiprimordial.[46] 'Truth' is identifiable only by way of a fidelitous commitment from the subject who is instantiated by the very same truth that it, itself, identifies.

Similarly Nancy, on the best reading, privileges the arts because of their aesthetic (in its fully etymological sense) rerouting of the senses – art is able to (re)configure the senses anew. As Christopher Watkin highlights, speaking of the Nancean body, this is precisely where *techne* figures for Nancy: *techne* is not a (Heideggerian) strategy that reveals something truer or more originary, but is instead a creative practice; in short, *techne* simply is '"art", "craft" or "creation" in the broad sense that blurs the distinction between the natural and the artificial, so the *techne* of the body is the medicinal, prosthetic and technological extensions of, modifications to and replacements for parts of the body that blur limits of the body'.[47] Indeed, as we saw in Chapter 2, Nancy is cautious in referring to raves – as Michel Gaillot does – as a 'return' to a something originary, often figured as festive and Dionysian. Instead, Nancy rearticulates this in terms not of origin but of originality – as something entirely novel 'qui n'a jamais eu lieu' ['that has never taken place'] (SM, p. 72; MM, p. 76). Similarly, the radical indistinction between subject and object in Nancy's articulation of the *corps sonore* at least affords the possibility of a philosophy of music that understands the affective dimension of music not as a 'natural' unidirectional effect of an object on a subject, but as something that is created in relation – where there are no naturally occurring subjects and objects (of music) but rather the *sens* of this distinction is in permanent and mutual flux and where music is one of the modalities through which the body and affect – as *techne* – is created (and not refound or excavated from its burial 'beneath' representation).[48] As a final point, *vis-à-vis* Nancy, one of the novelties – or so Nancy claims – that 'rock, comme le jazz' ['rock,

---

[46] Ibid.; see p. 48 in particular.
[47] Christopher Watkin, *Difficult Atheism*, p. 85.
[48] Though I am insisting on this as one of the most valuable aspects of Nancy's thinking for the philosophy of music, Nancy nonetheless often risks implying that affect/pathos is something to return to or to be refound – for example, when he characterises rock in strict opposition to art music (itself founded, he claims, on a signifying logic): 'un certain refus de tout ce qui peut faire construction du sens [. . .] parce que] le rock déclare au contraire qu'il faut au sens quel qu'il soit autre chose que la signification, qu'il lui faut l'énergie, la force' ['a certain refusal of everything which constructs meaning [. . . because], in contrast, rock declares that what is necessary for meaning is something other than signification, that it requires a certain energy, a power'], see SMR, p. 83.

like jazz'] (and subsequent genres such as techno), attests to is the centrality of the body through its co-instantiation as both music and dance (SMR, p. 79). I want to both insist on and *desist* from this narrative: though it is welcome and necessary to admit the body 'into' musical ontology, this is not because 'toutes les innovations musicales de notre histoire [musique savante] n'ont pas été accompagnées d'innovations de danse' ['all the musical innovations of our history [classical music] were not accompanied by innovations in dance'] (SMR, p. 79) (what about *Le Sacre du printemps?*) nor because *musique savante* doesn't co-instantiate a vast repertoire of bodily techniques. Indeed, '[w]ho would deny' as Benjamin Peikut describes, 'the agency of a training regimen that develops fine motor skill in the hands' or the 'corporeal protocols that discipline the performing body' – not to mention the composite bodily practices (seated stillness, silence, applause at appropriate moments) that are demanded by idealised and reverent concert hall listening.[49] Just because they are bodily practices that aim at transcending the body – at subsuming the body to the total aesthetic truth – does not mean that they are not, still, bodily practices. Moreover, and as I hope to have highlighted in the previous chapter on Badiou, this kind of approach continues to privilege an idealised narrative about musical listening and performance practices at the expense of considering the diverse ways in which people use, make and experience music (including that which is included in the repertoire of absolute music); in short, it perpetuates the idealism that denies the body as a legitimate co-site of expression in this repertoire.[50] This is, indeed, one of the fault lines in the construction of the absolute musical work, and one which warrants more attention and better understanding in philosophical attempts to think about music – especially in work, such as Nancy's, that is so concerned with bodily sensuousness.

BEYOND HYSTERIA: TOWARDS A FEMINIST ETHICS OF MUSIC (THAT IS NOT ONE)

This final section draws attention to the perhaps obvious fact that there is both a long and a more recent history that associates music with the feminine; as Lacoue-Labarthe, in the scene in *Musica Ficta* dedicated to Heidegger's (and Nietzsche's) 'figures de Wagner', states: 'Selon une très ancienne, très profonde et très solide équivalence – peut-être indestructible –, c'est [la musique] un art féminin, et destiné aux femmes

---

[49] Piekut, 'Actor-Networks in Music History', pp. 202, 191.
[50] See, for example, J. Q. Davies, *Romantic Anatomies of Performance*, which refuses this idealism and attends to the undeniably physical expression of nineteenth-century virtuosos.

ou à la part féminine des hommes. C'est un art, en tous sens, hystérique. Et c'est pour cette raison, essentiellement, que la musique est l'hystérie. Tout au moins une certaine musique' ['According to a very old, very profound, and very solid equivalence – perhaps indestructible – it [music] is a *feminine* art, destined for women or for the feminine part of men. It is a *hysterical* art, in every sense. And for this reason, essentially, music *is* hysteria. At least, a particular music'] (MF_1, p. 198; MF_2, p. 105). As stated at the beginning of this book, I want to suggest that the – not always intentional – intertwining of these related histories is worth paying closer attention to and clues us in to the reasons for Lacoue-Labarthe's concluding qualification: 'tout au moins une certaine musique'. In the way that Lacoue-Labarthe makes his claim, he asserts with absolute authority that music, fundamentally or essentially, *is* hysteria and/or feminine; and yet, at the same time, he entirely undermines this claim. By restricting the purchase of his earlier claim to that of 'une certaine musique' he identifies the constitutive aporia of this trope: though music is defined as feminine, by delimiting the scope of that supposed essence to only certain music, it no longer holds as a definition for music at large. (It is significant, I would suggest, that a similar and de-essentialising gesture is also at play *vis-à-vis* gender). Indeed, as Lacoue-Labarthe continues, this anxiety over music's (potentially feminine or feminising) essence does not lead Plato to condemn all music: again, he condemns only certain music. From the beginning, then, music has been a matter for both politics and philosophy, and thus a question of disciplining dissonance – of setting the boundaries of the *polis* and of knowledge. As Laura Odello has described, in this regard throughout

> the whole occidental tradition of metaphysics, from Plato onward, philosophy [has] tried to contain and neutralise music by reducing it to logos that resonates without harm in the political community. Yet, in the manner of a lapsus, music comes back to haunt the philosophical ear and to expose it to its own excess, that of an uncertain or lacking discourse – another discourse.[51]

It is a narrative that points us towards philosophy's problematic desire for pure knowledge – the quest for (original, unmediated) truth – uncontaminated by the messy unpredictability and contingencies of the mundane. This much is, for the most part, known – indeed the anti- or post-Platonic approaches of Nancy and Lacoue-Labarthe are indebted to this kind of observation – even if, as this book has shown, it is

---

[51] Laura Odello, 'Waiting for the Death Knell: Speaking of Music (So to Speak)' in Chapin and Clark (eds), *Speaking of Music*, pp. 39–48 (p. 39).

sometimes (constitutively) forgotten. The aspects of music (but by no means *only* music) which are not subsumable to *logos* are subsequently redefined as the *essentially musical* and, in this sense, music is figured as philosophy's conditioning 'outside' – its constituent 'other'.

As Odello, again, describes, '[s]ince the Sirens appeared in the twelfth book of the *Odyssey*, they have dwelled in the margins, on the outer borders of the Western stage of speech, which they endlessly haunt with their song, with a bewitching and seductive music'.[52] Indeed, as we have seen, this peripheral figuring of music is explicitly manifest in the texts we have considered: with the exception of *Le chant des Muses*, in all instances in the works devoted to the question either of the relation between music and theory/philosophy (Nancy's *À l'écoute* and Lacoue-Labarthe's 'L'écho du sujet') or offering a musical 'demonstration' or exemplar of philosophical system (Badiou's 'Scolie: Une variante musicale de la métaphysique du sujet'), music's marginal status is textually performed. *In fine*, for philosophy, music remains inessential, supplementary or explicatory. It is in the 'Coda' of Nancy's *À l'écoute* and 'La clôture maternelle' of Lacoue-Labarthe's 'L'écho du sujet' that the aspect of music that is irrecuperable to *logos* (and therefore philosophy) is most explicitly delineated: in both instances, this is also figured through an essential relation to the maternal (hysterical) feminine. Badiou's brief musical excursus in *Logiques des mondes* is explicitly figured as marginal: both in the sense that it is a remarkably brief segment in an otherwise hefty book, and also through its description as a 'Scolie' which, as we have already noted, usually concerns an explanatory comment given in the margins. In remarkable contrast, then, when discussion turns to 'actual' music (for want of a better way of putting it) – and not simply what music does for or demonstrates of philosophy – music appears to have a central and by no means marginal role in our political, social and cultural lives. Nowhere is this tension more obvious than in the vast difference between Badiou's texts: he is clearly a passionate Wagnerian (as is so evident from *Five Lessons on Wagner*) but pleasure, for Badiou, has no place in philosophy. As Odello has provocatively argued, in insisting that music (or what is *essentially* musical) escapes the bounds of philosophy – is located beyond its logical purview – philosophy has also violently forced music into silent submission: music (which *is not music*, but a metaphor for what philosophy is not) is figured as

> a prostitute. We exploit it, we force it, we do violence to it, we rape it, for we desire it, it arouses our desire: we push it, we urge it into prostitution or

[52] Ibid., p. 40.

substitution, putting it to good use (to our good use) by trading it, by selling it in the exchange of speech.[53]

This is not, then, a discourse about musical pleasure – philosophy has already delimited that as outside its own bounds – but about control. Similarly, Badiou's rejection of pleasure as a legitimate concern for philosophy is underpinned by (an unawareness of his own) authoritarianism: for Badiou, the philosopher must have total power as evidenced through his ability to identify (universal) truth. In the Romantic and sophistic relationship to aesthetics that he is so steadfast on critiquing, it is because art (the hysteric) reveals philosophy's (the Master's) partiality – her symptoms are resistant to a final or absolute reading – that 'il [le philosophe] rechigne à l'asservissement amoureux' ['he balks at amorous servitude'] and as a result 'n'a guère d'autre choix [. . .] que de lui donner du bâton' ['hardly has another choice than to give her a good beating'] (PMI, p. 10; HI, p. 2).[54] Rather than being the 'master' who runs the risk of being emasculated by the revelation of his non-totalising access to truth, Badiou simply opts to switch role in the drama, playing himself not as art's 'mistress' but instead as her Madame: it is the philosopher's (and the brothel keeper's) prerogative to identify, for their own benefit, the good, the beautiful and the true, and to cast out all and any who refuse to work on their terms. It is telling, I wish to suggest, that Badiou explicitly figures the relationship between art and philosophy in this way, revealing his desire for music that is silent and submissive; one which never rubs philosophy up the wrong way, so to speak. Though it is welcome that Badiou, unlike Nancy and Lacoue-Labarthe, attributes no feminine 'essence' to music as such, he nonetheless identifies generic truth (to which Art, as one of philosophy's conditions, can attest) with the feminine (♀), and which is itself figured as beyond not only experience but the world as it appears; in short, music must be (philosophically) seen and not heard.

The question of how each of the philosophers achieves their disparate aims, however, takes on a distinctly modern flavour. Though the longer history has always stood music in a compromised relationship to philosophy, in the modern period – as we have described above – musical theories and practices change alongside changing conceptions

---

[53] Ibid.
[54] This is not the only place Badiou tacitly condones gendered violence. Elsewhere, he describes love as 'une procédure sanglante qui peut entraîner des violences, des meurtres' ['a bloody procedure that can generate acts of violence and murder'] and so encodes sexual violence as a product of love rather than having to do with structural power differentials, coercion and control (otherwise known as patriarchy, racism and (neo)colonial violence, lesbophobia, transphobia, classism and ableism, among others) (see PE_1, p. 56; PE_2, p. 44).

of subjectivity. Nancy and Lacoue-Labarthe, in similar ways, arguably fall prey to the very trap they themselves identify: though their commentary on the historical emergence of a modern concept of Art (and thus music) is welcome, and thus points towards a much more fluid conception of what music 'is' than in Badiou's work, they nonetheless replicate in their own work what they identify elsewhere. Though, on the one hand, Lacoue-Labarthe so clearly identifies this quintessentially modern conception of music – music's essence is identified with the nostalgic figuring of a lost expressive immediacy – on the other, this is precisely how music is identified for Lacoue-Labarthe. Music – or again, the fundamentally *musical* – once stripped of its representational trappings is, in the final reading, nothing other than this archeoriginal emotivity; a cathartic and hysterical fantasy that allows us to play out our own imagined maternal-oceanic obliteration. At the same time, however, though this is precisely how music's essence is identified (in both 'L'écho du sujet' and *Le Chant des Muses*), it causes irresolvable problems in *Musica Ficta*, where there is an ethico-aesthetic endeavour to critique Wagner's artificial hyper-staging of music's emotional but non-signifying fundamental essence through figurative (thus signifying) means. As a result, music's ability to occasion powerful effects is: (1) its fundamental, pre-symbolic, maternal, essence, (2) a source of (feminine) danger when perverted to a significatory logic, and (3) what philosophy has repressed or rejected. Though it is logically difficult to entertain all three premises, it is this willingness – intentional or otherwise – to entertain such dissonance that makes Lacoue-Labarthe's project the most productive. There is similarly, for Nancy, an attempt to recoup for philosophy the repressed beyond (*outre*) of signification that is endemic to music: an endeavour that seems also to be modelled on a distinctly modern nostalgia that also figures 'woman' beyond signification (cf. Lacan).

Even Badiou's project takes on an unmistakeably modern flavour. Though, as a neo-Platonist, his ongoing commitment to truth and his rubbishing of hermeneutics, relativism, rhetoric and sophistry position him as distinctly anti-(post)modern in orientation, he nonetheless accepts the (entirely modern) doctrine of absolute music wholesale: by aligning the possibility of truth with formal innovation and a repertoire spanning a mere 200 years he conflates eternal and universal truths with a distinctly modern practice. He simply aligns himself with the side of the modernist split which seeks to reconcile its inherent tension by committing to an objectification of music in the name of rationality and reason. He participates in the kind of gesture that musicologist Richard Taruskin has described as 'a police function rather than a scholarly one [. . . and] an abuse of disciplinary authority'.[55] Quite clearly, a major problem in Badiou's project is the location of *his* role: while he lambasts sophists for their relativism, their concern with rhetoric and with language's inability, in the final measure, to authorise or identify truth, he can only concede truth as something philosophy can identify through a process configured on nothing more than *fidélité*. As a result, he (necessarily) refuses to accept that he, too, is a product – and not just an omniscient observer – of the 'truths' he identifies, and which ultimately depends upon 'invidious clichés of judgment that, by giving an aesthetic cloak to social discrimination, perpetuate a foolish and needless (albeit familiar) class system'.[56] In short, Badiou codifies the musical practices specific to his milieu as neutral or the norm, and thus others all others; indeed, it is extraordinarily difficult to see what is radical about re-codifying something as universal that has coded itself as universal since its inception. Moreover, this is all within a discourse which all too often seems merely to perpetuate an assumption of European exceptionalism and ethnocentric universalism and which figures modern Western culture as the pinnacle of all civilisation(s).

Finally, then, this chapter turns briefly to Irigaray's powerful critique of philosophy's (and psychoanalysis's) phallogocentrism in both *Ce Sexe qui n'en est pas un* and in *Speculum de l'autre femme* to critique the ongoing deployment of gender as an organisational category in philosophy. Through a kind of feminist archaeology, Irigaray sounds out the way in which philosophy has tended to identify the feminine through an analogy between 'woman' and 'mother' in such a way that the 'transcendent movement toward the Platonic ideal begins [. . . in] representational culture which produces an illusion of nature in the form of a maternal other'.[57] Instead, Irigaray critiques Plato's *hustera* for the way in which it locates the mother-earth-matter as the illusory ground upon which the originary scene of representation is played out and thus positions the maternal-feminine as a nostalgic projection of patriarchal Western epistemology. She is thus able to deconstructively critique the masculinist fantasy that has heretofore constructed the story of origins and the subject as self-same, teleologically determined and driven from an original 'oneness' or 'wholeness' in the pre-symbolic union with the mother. Likewise, through her infamous invocation of female *lèvres* in 'Ce sexe qui n'en est pas un', Irigaray playfully deploys a strategy that at once mimics and subsequently destabilises the conflation between

---

[55] Richard Taruskin, 'Agents and Causes and Ends, Oh My', pp. 272–93 (p. 277).
[56] Ibid., p. 277.
[57] Huffer, *Maternal Pasts, Feminist Futures*, p. 79.

penis and phallus in psychoanalysis. She identifies the way in which the feminine sex (at least in philosophy and psychoanalysis) is not one – both in the sense that it has been conceived of as a lack, a grounding fantasy to secure the stability of the masculine subject and bares little relation to the 'actual' feminine, and in the sense that it is not singular (the feminine has multiple resonances). She therefore carves out a space for woman's specificity – both in terms of sexuality and language – that is positioned not in opposition to the masculine, but as supplementary. In so doing, she reveals men, also, to be 'not all'.

Notwithstanding the potential essentialism of which Irigaray herself has been accused – the fact that she too arguably reinstates a pre-discursive feminine essence to be excavated – her broader critique of philosophy's phallogocentrism seems cogent for our purposes. Just as postcolonial scholars such as Chandra Talpade Mohanty have drawn on and then substantially critiqued and radicalised such notions to show how not just 'women' but also '"the east" are defined as others, or as peripheral, [so] that (Western) man/humanism can represent him/itself as the centre. It is not the centre that determines the periphery, but the periphery that, in its boundedness, determines the centre',[58] I want to insist on the way that (European high art) music *continues* to be deployed in similar ways – even when it claims entirely otherwise, as in Nancy's *À l'écoute*. Moreover, this often participates in the kind of logic identified above, and not only constructs music as a category prior to analysis but 'woman' too (along with assuming whiteness and heterosexual reproductivity as the norm).[59] Badiou, quite explicitly, identifies music's essence *a priori* with formal innovation – a move that derives from a specific historical understanding of music and that makes the actual happening of music (whether live, recorded, imagined, etc.) irrelevant to philosophy; it is avowedly beyond experience and so too, then, is the feminine generic truth that it births – though only with the help of the philosopher midwife. Nancy and Lacoue-Labarthe, though often keenly aware of music's historical constructedness, nonetheless attempt to recuperate music as philosophy's other and in doing so identify a lost musical essence with a timeless maternal-feminine. This seems particularly unfortunate as, at other moments, their philosophies offer exciting ways to move beyond a singular musical essence that can be neatly separated from the broader context of its happening; both Nancy's sensuous relational approach and Lacoue-Labarthe's emphasis on *formation* and *techne* (as well as his larger commitment to originary

---

[58] Chandra Talpade Mohanty, *Feminism without Borders*, pp. 41–2.
[59] Ibid., particularly p. 22 for the way in which 'woman' is often deployed as a pre-analytic category.

mimesis) point towards the way in which context does not exist apart from the music. The very best readings of Nancy and Lacoue-Labarthe go so far as to entirely destabilise the text/context opposition to the extent that neither the subject (including gendered identity) nor the (musical) text/object *nor even the context* is identifiable in advance: instead, as Piekut describes, 'context' and 'music' are

> persistently re-enacted in patterns and ruptures that strengthen or weaken existing attachments. When we speak of music reproducing as well as affecting politics, we are really attempting to come to terms with a network of associations – neither strictly musical nor political – that falls across, and mixes up, disciplinary assumptions about what counts as context.[60]

It is, thus, not a question of excavating the 'true' nature of music from a philosophy that has simply held it hostage, but instead of better recognising that though music may often have an identifiable origin (for example, opera, absolute music, rock) that doesn't mean, to rephrase Derrida, that there is an essence of music. It even means the opposite.[61] Accordingly, then, as Lawrence Kramer and others have argued, 'music is not one thing'[62] – and this applies both to Badiou's explicit attempt to identify a singular music and also to Nancy's and Lacoue-Labarthe's implicit re-essentialising of music's apparently feminine essence. One of the strategic methodologies that could be deployed to offset this tendency – especially given Nancy's and Lacoue-Labarthe's identification of the inherent impossibility of the absolute – would be to attend more closely to music's practical and technological dimensions to better hear music as, at once, utterly material, mediate and discursively, heuristically and experientially constituted through a constellation of theories and practices. It is also the case necessarily, then, that music relates to gender not at the level of 'essence', *qui n'en est pas une [which is not One]*, but across multiple mediating planes. As Georgina Born has described, this might be in the micro-sociological division of musical labour and the hierarchical striation of different musical roles – the way it informs, refracts or animates (imagined or actual) publics and hierarchical social identity formations (gender, race, class, nation, and so on) through sonorous, affective, ideational and practical means (including ideologies attached to different instruments, styles of performance or listening practices) – or in its means of (re)production (because, again, even *musique savante* does not operate in a vacuum beyond capitalist, institutional and state funding structures or indeed instruments

---

[60] Piekut, 'Actor-Networks in Music History', p. 205.
[61] Derrida says this about literature in 'A Strange Institution Called Literature'.
[62] Lawrence Kramer, 'Philosophizing Musically', pp. 387–404 (p. 400).

and technologies), among others.[63] Though music might be *irreducibly* composite – and indeed, irreducible also in the sense that its ontology cannot be pinned down to one plane alone (whether epistemological, technological, political, experiential, cognitive, affective, and so on) – what escapes in any attempt to pin it down is emphatically not the *musical*, but is rather a constitutive openness (and one that is by no means limited to music) that leaves it available to multiple – though not necessarily infinite or arbitrary – interpretations. To figure music, essentially, as that which always escapes is to place it forever *en abyme*, and to render lived musical practices (and theories), ironically, as *not musical*. Indeed, not only does such a move figure music's essence as the (non-existent) ground, periphery or elsewhere upon or against which philosophy can stage its own (illusion of a) bounded centre, but it does so in incontrovertibly gendered terms, with the philosophical Idea of music (or its 'truth') figured as irretrievably feminine, and so sends both music and women, *encore*, to the beyond of either pre-, inter- or post-signification.

---

[63] See Georgina Born, 'For a Relational Musicology', pp. 205–43 (p. 231) and 'Music and the Materialization of Identities', pp. 376–88 (p. 378).

Encore: *After Music*

> What is important now is to recover our senses. We must learn to see more, to hear more, to feel more [. . .] The function of criticism should be to show how it is what it is, even that it is what it is, rather than to show what it means.
>
> Susan Sontag[1]

In conclusion, then, this book has sought to analyse and identify the way certain ideas about what music 'is' inhabit recent and contemporary philosophy – focusing especially on writers whose aims are guided by their own deeply critical agendas to challenge certain key assumptions of their own philosophical forebears. For Nancy and Lacoue-Labarthe, music tends to be figured as the Other of language (and therefore representation/signification); for Badiou, music is accorded no special status *vis-à-vis* language but is one domain within the condition 'Art' in which (eternal, universal, generic and feminine) truths can be created. It has been important to note, also, that these considerations often come hand in hand with the invocation of gender as an organising category for philosophy. In both instances, then, the (metaphorical) musical-feminine is aligned, *encore*, with the beyond of the symbolic, signification, or the world as it appears (and in which we live); at the same time, 'music' is something to which these philosophers aspire – or which offers, *in its essence*, some liberatory potential beyond the constraints of the mundane.

In so doing, I am offering little – if anything – to the academic study of music but have instead highlighted some of the genealogies of the conceptions of music that animate the philosophies of Nancy, Lacoue-Labarthe and Badiou. To do this, it has been necessary to emphasise

---

[1] Susan Sontag, 'Against Interpretation' in Neil Jumonville (ed.), *The New York Intellectuals Reader*, pp. 243–54 (p. 252).

the (geographically specific) historicity of the concept of singular Art (of which instrumental, absolute music was the pinnacle); its reduction to (functionless) form *as* content (thus a way of conceiving music in terms of visualised ideation); its (illusory) abstraction from the mundane; and, finally, the philosophical (largely Schopenhauerian and Nietzschean) cross-pollination with a psychoanalytic conception of the subject that figures music's sonorous, rather than ideated, dimension (along with the feminine) in terms of the semiotic, pre-linguistic or pre-symbolic. None of these aspects, of course, necessarily has anything *essential* to do with 'music' in its multiple, variable, changeable determinations, but rather describes a specific configuration that inhabits the assumptions of the philosophers at hand. Indeed, a major criticism of this work might be that in my attempt to identify this singular story of music I, too, have simply replicated a singular story of music: and that is precisely my point.

Throughout, and especially in the previous two chapters, I have insisted on the way in which inherited narratives (derived largely from German idealism) demand that we divert our attention from music's material and technological means of production in order to make their accounts coherent – an imperative that also obscures some of the ways in which music's affective and emotional dimension is also discursively and instrumentally mediated, preferring instead to draw on a mysterious maternal pre-symbolic reservoir of *immediate* emotion. In these final pages, then, I wish to go further, and to heed the calls made by various scholars, including Benjamin Piekut and Deborah Wong, that we should, in fact, not only move beyond music as a singular category but should jettison the category of 'music' altogether. As Piekut describes, once you start to consider 'music' as an 'unpredictable conglomeration of things and processes [. . . the] distinctions between social, technological, or musical domains are difficult to make'[2] – indeed, a major critique of the poststructuralist-influenced musicology of the late twentieth and early twenty-first centuries was that it took context as a fixed given that could be mapped onto the music (or that the music could be identified to be constructed by) rather than something co-created with and by music. In this respect, it would be particularly interesting to better understand how 'musical' theories, practices and discourses also coproduce ideas about and experiences of gendered identity.

In a different vein, Wong writes as an ethnomusicologist and convincingly highlights ethnomusicology's perennially marginal status within music departments because 'its radical relativism challenges

---

[2] Benjamin Piekut, 'Actor-Networks in Music History', p. 212.

logocentric thinking about music'.[3] Wong turns our curiosity about the lack of a word connoting (what we assume to be) 'music' in the majority of global cultures on its head, and suggests that the more pressing issue is to better understand the extent to which we have reified music *as* an ontological construct;[4] indeed, this chimes with some of Gary Tomlinson's work as mentioned in Chapter 3, whereby 'music' is deconstructed as a geo-historically specific (and very recent) sub-species of a much broader human capacity for organising sound phenomena, often including various forms of vocalisations.[5] Music as an ontological category is, then, already inter-constituted through its relation to (the historically specific emergence of) aesthetics, such that in considering 'music' – even in remote geographical areas and specifically as a practice – there remains the tendency to recapitulate to the underlying assumptions and preconceptions of a romantic Eurocentric concept. As Wong states, 'if we [ethnomusicologists] hope to say what we really want to say, we will need to reject music'.[6] Moreover, and beyond the specifically ethnomusicological context, Wong argues that music as a construct 'contains the very terms for our unimportance and irrelevance' – 'it *cannot* matter (and those who focus on it cannot matter, either) due to an extended post-Enlightenment ideological process casting Music as the feminine corner of the humanities'.[7]

Though in Chapter 5 I tentatively advocated for Stiegler's project of an *organologie générale* as a productive way to consider 'music' – given that it insists on a non-essentialist co-individuation of biological, technological and social organs – this now comes with the caveat that it should be so *without* the category 'music'. The risk, otherwise, is already present in Stiegler, when he identifies 'music' as a privileged site of analysis in a theory that is, nonetheless, a philosophical one: yet again (as so often), music is instrumentalised as the thing that best exemplifies the theory because it is easy – too easy – to make music say whatever the theory demands of it. If none of the organs (somatic, sensory, prosthetic, technological, social ...) precede – in any essential *sens* – their co-individuation, then it follows, too, that neither does music. For future philosophy, then, this means far more caution about the assumptions brought into play, presumed and carried by 'music' as a site for the com-position of minds, bodies and practices – including, even especially, with regards to gender.

---

[3] Deborah Wong, 'Sound, Silence, Music: Power', pp. 347–53 (p. 348).
[4] Ibid., see p. 350.
[5] See Gary Tomlinson, 'Vico's Songs', and also Chapter 3.
[6] Wong, 'Sound, Silence, Music: Power', p. 349.
[7] Ibid., p. 350.

Bibliography

Abbate, Carolyn, 'Music—Drastic or Gnostic?', *Critical Inquiry*, 30 (2004), 505–36, https://doi.org/10.1086/421160

Agon, Carlos, Gérard Assayag and Jean Bresson (eds), *Penser La Musique Avec Les Mathématiques? Actes Du Séminaire Mathématiques/Musique/ Philosophie*, Musique-Sciences (Paris: [Sampzon]: IRCAM, 2006).

Ahmed, Leila, *Women and Gender in Islam* (New Haven: Yale University Press, 1992).

Ahmed, Sara, 'Melancolic Universalism', *Feministkilljoys*, 2015, https://feministkilljoys.com/2015/12/15/melancholic-universalism/ (accessed 14 December 2016).

Albright, Daniel, *Modernism and Music: An Anthology of Sources* (Chicago: University of Chicago Press, 2004).

—, *Panaesthetics: On the Unity and Diversity of the Arts*, The Anthony Hecht Lectures in the Humanities (New Haven: Yale University Press, 2014).

Amossy, Ruth, 'Introduction to the Study of Doxa', *Poetics Today*, 23 (2002), 369–94, https://doi.org/10.1215/03335372-23-3-369

Aristotle, and Peter L. Phillips Simpson, *The Politics of Aristotle*, trans. Peter L. Phillips Simpson (Chapel Hill: University of North Carolina Press, 1997).

Assoun, Paul-Laurent, *Freud et Nietzsche*, Quadrige, Grands textes, 4e éd. (Paris: Presses universitaires de France, 2008).

Attridge, Derek, *The Singularity of Literature* (London; New York: Routledge, 2004).

Austern, Linda Phyllis (ed.), *Music, Sensation, and Sensuality* (New York; London: Routledge, 2002).

Austern, Linda Phyllis and Inna Naroditskaya (eds), *Music of the Sirens* (Bloomington: Indiana University Press, 2006).

Aviram, Amittai F., *Telling Rhythm: Body and Meaning in Poetry* (Ann Arbor: University of Michigan Press, 1994).

Babich, Babette E., *Words in Blood, like Flowers: Philosophy and Poetry, Music and Eros in Hölderlin, Nietzsche, and Heidegger*, SUNY Series in Contemporary Continental Philosophy (Albany: State University of New York Press, 2006).

Badiou, Alain, *Court traité d'ontologie transitoire* (Paris: Seuil, 1998).
—, *Ethics: An Essay on the Understanding of Evil*, trans. Peter Hallward (London: Verso, 2001).
—, 'Who Is Nietzsche?' in *Pli: The Warwick Journal of Philosophy*, 11 (2001), pp. 1–11.
—, *Briefings on Existence: A Short Treatise on Transitory Ontology*, ed. and trans. Norman Madarasz (Albany: State University of New York Press, 2006).
—, *Second manifeste pour la philosophie* (Paris: Fayard, 2009).
—, *Five Lessons on Wagner* (London: Verso, 2010).
—, *Petit manuel d'inesthétique*, L'Ordre philosophique (Paris: Éditions du Seuil, 2011).
—, *Second Manifesto for Philosophy* (Cambridge: Polity, 2011).
—, *Incident at Antioch/L'Incident d'Antioche* (New York: Columbia University Press, 2013), http://ezproxy.lib.cam.ac.uk:2048/login?url=http://www.degruyter.com/doi/book/10.7312/badi15774
Badiou, Alain and Fabien Tarby, *Philosophy and the Event*, trans. Louise Burchill (Cambridge: Polity, 2013).
Baki, Burhanuddin, *Badiou's Being and Event and the Mathematics of Set Theory* (London: Bloomsbury Academic, 2016).
Bartlett, Adam John, Justin Clemens and Alain Badiou (eds), *Alain Badiou: Key Concepts*, Key Concepts (London: Routledge, 2010).
Begbie, Jeremy, *Resounding Truth: Christian Wisdom in the World of Music*, Engaging Culture (Grand Rapids: Baker Academic, 2007).
Belhaj Kacem, Mehdi, Alexandre Costanzo and Alain Badiou, *Esthétique et philsophie: Actes du colloque, Musée d'Art Moderne de Saint-Étienne Métropole, 22 octobre 2008*, Pensées contemporaines (Saint-Étienne Métropole: Éd. du Musée d'Art Moderne, 2008).
Bent, Margaret, 'Musica Recta and Musica Ficta', *Musica Disciplina*, 26 (1972), 73–100.
Berger, Karol, *Musica Ficta: Theories of Accidental Inflections in Vocal Polyphony from Marchetto Da Padova to Gioseffo Zarlino* (Cambridge: Cambridge University Press, 1987).
—, 'Concepts and Developments in Music Theory' in *European Music 1520–1640*, ed. James Haar (Woodbridge: Boydell Press, 2006).
Berio, Luciano, Rossana Dalmonte and Bálint András Varga, *Two Interviews*, trans. David Osmond-Smith (New York: M. Boyars, 1985).
Bloch, Georges, 'Lettre à Philippe Lacoue-Labarthe' in *Penser la musique avec les mathématiques? Actes du séminaire mathématiques/musique/philosophie*, ed. Carlos Agon, Gérard Assayag and Jean Bresson, Musique-Sciences (Paris: IRCAM, 2006), pp. 173–202.
Bloechl, Olivia with Melanie Lowe, 'Introduction: Rethinking Difference' in *Rethinking Difference in Music Scholarship*, ed. Olivia Ashley Bloechl, Melanie Diane Lowe and Jeffrey Kallberg (New York: Cambridge University Press, 2015), pp. 1–52.

Bloechl, Olivia Ashley, Melanie Diane Lowe and Jeffrey Kallberg (eds), *Rethinking Difference in Music Scholarship* (New York: Cambridge University Press, 2015).

Bogue, Ronald (ed.), *Mimesis in Contemporary Theory: An Interdisciplinary Approach, Volume 2: Mimesis, Semiosis and Power*, Cultura Ludens (Philadelphia: John Benjamins Publishing Company, 1991).

—, *Deleuze on Music, Painting, and the Arts* (New York: Routledge, 2003).

Bonds, Mark Evan, *Absolute Music: The History of an Idea* (New York: Oxford University Press, 2014).

Born, Georgina, 'V. Techniques of the Musical Imaginary' in *Western Music and Its Others: Difference, Representation, and Appropriation in Music*, ed. David Hesmondhalgh and Georgina Born (Berkeley: University of California Press, 2000), pp. 37–58.

—, 'For a Relational Musicology: Music and Interdisciplinarity, Beyond the Practice Turn', *Journal of the Royal Musical Association*, 135 (2010), 205–43, https://doi.org/10.1080/02690403.2010.506265

—, 'Music and the Materialization of Identities', *Journal of Material Culture*, 16 (2011), 376–88, https://doi.org/10.1177/1359183511424196

Born, Georgina and David Hesmondhalgh (eds), *Western Music and Its Others: Difference, Representation, and Appropriation in Music* (Berkeley: University of California Press, 2000), http://search.ebscohost.com/login.aspx?direct=true&db=nlebk&AN=66372&site=ehost-live

—, 'I. Postcolonial Analysis and Music Studies' in *Western Music and Its Others: Difference, Representation, and Appropriation in Music*, ed. David Hesmondhalgh and Georgina Born (Berkeley: University of California Press, 2000), pp. 1–3.

Bowie, Andrew, *Music, Philosophy, and Modernity*, Modern European Philosophy Series (Cambridge: Cambridge University Press, 2007), http://site.ebrary.com/lib/bodleian/docDetail.action?docID=10209502

Brennan, Teresa (ed.), *Between Feminism and Psychoanalysis* (London: Routledge, 1989).

Brett, Philip, Elizabeth Wood and Gary C. Thomas (eds), *Queering the Pitch: The New Gay and Lesbian Musicology*, 2nd edn (New York: Routledge, 2006).

Buchanan, Ian, *Deleuze and Music* (Edinburgh: Edinburgh University Press, 2004).

Buchanan, Ian and Marcel Swiboda (eds), *Deleuze and Music*, reprinted (Edinburgh: Edinburgh University Press, 2006).

Bull, Anna, 'The Musical Body: How Gender and Class Are Reproduced Among Young People Playing Classical Music in England' (unpublished PhD, Goldsmiths, University of London, 2014).

Butler, Judith, 'The Body Politics of Julia Kristeva', *Hypatia*, 3 (1988), 104–18, https://doi.org/10.1111/j.1527-2001.1988.tb00191.x

Campbell, Edward, *Music after Deleuze*, Deleuze Encounters (New York: Bloomsbury Academic, 2013).

Carby, Hazel V., 'White Woman Listen! Black Feminism and the Boundaries of Sisterhood' in *Empire Strikes Back: Race and Racism in 70s Britain*, Centre for Contemporary Cultural Studies (London: Hutchinson, 1982).

Carroll, Mark, '"It Is": Reflections on the Role of Music in Sartre's "La Nausée"', *Music and Letters*, 87 (2006), 398–407, https://doi.org/10.1093/ml/gcl047

Cassin, Barbara, *L'effet Sophistique*, NRF Essais (Paris: Gallimard, 1995).

Castanet, Didier, 'Éditorial. "L'impossible, c'est le réel, tout simplement"', *L'en-je lacanien*, 7 (2006), 5–7, https://doi.org/10.3917/enje.007.0005

Cavarero, Adriana, *For More Than One Voice: Toward a Philosophy of Vocal Expression* (Stanford: Stanford University Press, 2005).

Chapin, Keith Moore and Andrew Herrick Clark (eds), *Speaking of Music: Addressing the Sonorous* (New York: Fordham University Press, 2013).

Chion, Michel, *La Voix Au Cinéma*, Cahiers Du Cinéma (Paris: Editions de l'Etoile, 1982).

Christensen, Thomas, 'Eighteenth-Century Science and the "Corps Sonore:" The Scientific Background to Rameau's "Principle of Harmony"', *Journal of Music Theory*, 31 (1987), 23–50, https://doi.org/10.2307/843545

—, *Rameau and Musical Thought in the Enlightenment*, Cambridge Studies in Music Theory and Analysis, 4 (Cambridge: Cambridge University Press, 1993).

Chua, Daniel K. L., *Absolute Music and the Construction of Meaning*, New Perspectives in Music History and Criticism (Cambridge: Cambridge University Press, 1999).

Clark, Suzannah and Alexander Rehding (eds), *Music Theory and Natural Order from the Renaissance to the Early Twentieth Century* (Cambridge: Cambridge University Press, 2001).

Clément, Catherine, *L'Opéra, Ou, La Défaite Des Femmes* (Paris: B. Grasset, 1979).

Clifton, Thomas, *Music as Heard: A Study in Applied Phenomenology* (New Haven: Yale University Press, 1983).

Cohen-Levinas, Danielle, 'Deleuze Musicien', *Rue Descartes*, (1998), 137–47.

— (ed.), *Musique et Philosophie*, Orfeo, Recueil d'esthétique et de Philosophie de l'art, op. 2 (Paris: Harmattan, 2005).

Colebrook, Claire and David Bennett, 'The Sonorous, the Haptic and the Intensive', *New Formations*, 66 (2009), 68–80, https://doi.org/10.3898/newf.66.05.2009

Connor, Steven, *Beyond Words: Sobs, Hums, Stutterers and Other Vocalizations*, Popular Science/Linguistics (London: Reaktion Books, 2014).

Corcoran, Steven (ed.), *The Badiou Dictionary* (Edinburgh: Edinburgh University Press, 2015).

Crenshaw, Kimberle, 'Demarginalizing the Intersection of Race and Sex: A Black Feminist Critique of Antidiscrimination Doctrine, Feminist Theory and Antiracist Politics', *The University of Chicago Legal Forum*, 140 (1989), 139–67.

Critchley, Simon, *Infinitely Demanding: Ethics of Commitment, Politics of Resistance* (London: Verso, 2012).
—, *The Ethics of Deconstruction: Derrida and Levinas*, 3rd edn (Edinburgh: Edinburgh University Press, 2014).
Criton, Pascale and Jean-Marc Chouvel (eds), *Gilles Deleuze: la pensée musique* (Paris: Centre de documentation de la musique contemporaine, 2015).
Crowley, Martin, 'Being Beyond Politics, with Jean-Luc Nancy', *Qui Parle*, 22.2 (2014), 123–45.
—, 'Review: Philippe Lacoue-Labarthe: (Un)Timely Meditations. By John McKeane. Oxford: Legenda, 2015', *French Studies*, 70 (2016), 130, https://doi.org/10.1093/fs/knv249
Currie, James, 'Music After All', *Journal of the American Musicological Society*, 62.1 (2009), 145–203.
Cusick, Suzanne G., 'Musicology, Torture, Repair', *Radical Musicology*, 3 (2008), 24 pars.
—, '"You Are in a Place That Is out of the World . . .": Music in the Detention Camps of the "Global War on Terror"', *Journal of the Society for American Music*, 2 (2008), https://doi.org/10.1017/S1752196308080012
Dahlhaus, Carl, *The Idea of Absolute Music*, trans. Roger Lustig (Chicago: University of Chicago Press, 1989).
Davies, J. Q., 'Dancing the Symphonic: Beethoven-Bochsa's *Symphonie Pastorale*, 1829', *19th Century Music*, 27 (2003), 25–47, https://doi.org/10.1525/ncm.2003.27.1.25
—, *Romantic Anatomies of Performance* (Berkeley: University of California Press, 2014).
Dayan, Peter, *Music Writing Literature, from Sand via Debussy to Derrida* (Aldershot: Ashgate, 2006).
Dean, Jodi, *Solidarity of Strangers: Feminism after Identity Politics* (Berkeley: University of California Press, 1996).
Deathridge, John, *Wagner Beyond Good and Evil* (Berkeley: University of California Press, 2008).
Deleuze, Gilles and Félix Guattari, '1837 – De la ritournelle' in *Mille plateaux: capitalisme et schizophrénie 2* (Paris: Minuit, 1980), pp. 381–433.
Derrida, Jacques, *De La Grammatologie*, Collection 'Critique' (Paris: Minuit, 1967).
—, 'Tympan' in *Marges de la philosophie* (Paris: Minuit, 1972).
—, *Psyché: Inventions de l'autre*, Collection La Philosophie En Effet (Paris: Galilée, 1987).
—, *The Ear of the Other*, ed. Christie McDonald (Lincoln: University of Nebraska Press, 1988).
—, 'Introduction: Desistance' in Philippe Lacoue-Labarthe, *Typography: Mimesis, Philosophy, Politics*, ed. Christopher Fynsk (Stanford: Stanford University Press, 1989).
—, 'A Strange Institution Called Literature' in *Acts of Literature*, ed. Derek Attridge (London: Routledge, 1992).

—, *Of Grammatology*, trans. Gayatri Chakravorty Spivak (Baltimore: Johns Hopkins University Press, 2016).

Derrida, Jacques, Claude Lévesque and Christie McDonald, *L'Oreille de l'autre: Otobiographies, Transferts, Traductions: Textes et Débats Avec Jacques Derrida* (Montréal: VLB, 1982).

Dolan, Emily I., *The Orchestral Revolution: Haydn and the Technologies of Timbre* (Cambridge: Cambridge University Press, 2013).

Dolan, Emily I. and John Tresch, 'Toward a New Organology: Instruments of Music and Science', *Osiris*, 28 (2013), 278–98.

Dolar, Mladen, *A Voice and Nothing More*, Short Circuits (Cambridge, MA: The MIT Press, 2006).

Duncan, Michelle, 'The Operatic Scandal of the Singing Body: Voice, Presence, Performativity', *Cambridge Opera Journal*, 16 (2004), 283–306.

Esse, Melina, 'Encountering the *Improvvisatrice* in Italian Opera', *Journal of the American Musicological Society*, 66 (2013), 709–70, https://doi.org/10.1525/jams.2013.66.3.709.

Felski, Rita, *Uses of Literature*, Blackwell Manifestos (Malden, MA: Blackwell, 2008).

Fuld, James J., *The Book of World-Famous Music: Classical, Popular, and Folk*, 5th edn (New York: Dover Publications, 2000).

Gallope, Michael, 'Review: Jean-Luc Nancy. 2007. Listening Translated by Charlotte Mandell', *Current Musicology*, 86 (2008), 157–66.

—, 'The Universal Form of Badiou's Wagner', *The Opera Quarterly*, 29 (2013), 342–48, https://doi.org/10.1093/oq/kbt029

Goehr, Lydia, *The Imaginary Museum of Musical Works: An Essay in the Philosophy of Music* (Oxford: Clarendon Press; Oxford University Press, 1992).

Gracyk, Theodore and Andrew Kania (eds), *The Routledge Companion to Philosophy and Music*, Routledge Philosophy Companions (Abingdon: Routledge, 2011).

Graham, Gordon, *Philosophy of the Arts: An Introduction to Aesthetics*, 3rd edn (London: Routledge, 2005).

Grant, Roger Mathew, 'Review: Jean-Luc Nancy's "Listening"', *Journal of the American Musicological Society*, 62 (2009), 748–52, https://doi.org/10.1525/jams.2009.62.3.748

Grimshaw, Jean, 'Philosophy, Feminism and Universalism', *Radical Philosophy*, 76 (1996), 19–28.

Groddeck, Georg, 'Musique et Inconscient', *Musique et Jeu*, 9 (1972), 3–6.

Gutting, Gary, *French Philosophy in the Twentieth Century* (Cambridge: Cambridge University Press, 2001).

Guyer, Paul, *Values of Beauty: Historical Essays in Aesthetics* (Cambridge: Cambridge University Press, 2005), https://ezproxy-prd.bodleian.ox.ac.uk:6038/core/books/values-of-beauty/0FC264C2A70D9A1169DC1468B9846755

Haar, James (ed.), *European Music 1520–1640*, Studies in Medieval and Renaissance Music, 5 (Woodbridge: Boydell Press, 2006).

Hanslick, Eduard, *On the Musically Beautiful: A Contribution Towards the Revision of the Aesthetics of Music*, trans. Geoffrey Payzant (Indianapolis: Hackett Pub. Co., 1986).

Hasty, Christopher, 'The Image of Thought and Ideas of Music' in *Sounding the Virtual: Gilles Deleuze and the Theory and Philosophy of Music*, ed. Brian Hulse and Nick Nesbitt (Aldershot: Ashgate, 2010), pp. 1–22.

Havelock, Eric A., *The Muse Learns to Write: Reflections on Orality and Literacy from Antiquity to the Present* (New Haven: Yale University Press, 1986).

—, *Preface to Plato* (Cambridge, MA: Belknap Press of Harvard University Press, 2004).

Hegel, Georg Wilhelm Friedrich, *Aesthetics: Lectures on Fine Art, Vol. 1*, trans. T. M. Knox (Oxford: Clarendon Press, 2010).

Heidegger, Martin, *The Question Concerning Technology, and Other Essays*, Harper Colophon Books, CN 419, 1st edn (New York: Harper & Row, 1977).

Hesiod, and Norman O. Brown, *Hesiod's Theogony*, trans. Norman O. Brown (Indianapolis: The Liberal Arts Press, 1953).

Hickmott, Sarah, *'(En) Corps Sonore*: Jean-Luc Nancy's "Sonotropism"', *French Studies*, 69 (2015), 479–93, https://doi.org/10.1093/fs/knv152

—, 'Beyond Lacoue-Labarthe's *Alma Mater*: Mus(e)ic, Myth and Modernity', *L'Esprit créateur*, 57.4 (2017), 174–88.

Hobson, Marian, 'Kant, Rousseau, et la musique' in *Reappraisals of Rousseau: Studies in Honour of R. A. Leigh*, ed. Marian Hobson et al. (Manchester: Manchester University Press, 1980), pp. 290–307.

Hobson, Marian, Simon Harvey, David Kelley and Samuel S. B. Taylor (eds), *Reappraisals of Rousseau: Studies in Honour of R. A. Leigh* (Manchester: Manchester University Press, 1980).

hooks, bell, *Feminist Theory: From Margin to Center* (London: Pluto Press, 2000).

Horkheimer, Max and Theodor W. Adorno, *Dialectic of Enlightenment: Philosophical Fragments*, ed. Gunzelin Schmid Noerr, trans. Edmund Jephcott, *Cultural Memory in the Present* (Stanford: Stanford University Press, 2002).

Howells, Christina, *Sartre: The Necessity of Freedom* (Cambridge: Cambridge University Press, 1988).

Huffer, Lynne, *Maternal Pasts, Feminist Futures: Nostalgia, Ethics, and the Question of Difference* (Stanford: Stanford University Press, 1998).

—, 'Blanchot's Mother', *Yale French Studies*, (1998), 175–95, https://doi.org/10.2307/3040736

Hulse, Brian Clarence and Nick Nesbitt (eds), *Sounding the Virtual: Gilles Deleuze and the Theory and Philosophy of Music* (Farnham: Ashgate, 2010).

Hutchens, B. C., *Jean-Luc Nancy and the Future of Philosophy* (Montreal: McGill-Queens University Press, 2005), http://site.ebrary.com/id/10455559 (accessed 23 April 2013).

Ihde, Don, *Listening and Voice: Phenomenologies of Sound*, 2nd edn (Albany: State University of New York Press, 2007).
Irigaray, Luce, *Speculum de l'autre Femme*, Collection Critique (Paris: Minuit, 1974).
—, *Ce Sexe Qui n'en Est Pas Un* (Paris: Minuit, 1977).
James, Ian, 'Art – Technics', *Oxford Literary Review*, 27 (2005), 83–102, https://doi.org/10.3366/olr.2005.007
—, *The Fragmentary Demand: An Introduction to the Philosophy of Jean-Luc Nancy* (Stanford: Stanford University Press, 2006).
James, Robin, 'Affective Resonances: On the Uses and Abuses of Music In and For Philosophy', *PhaenEx*, 7 (2012), 59–95.
—, 'Eliza's "Ai"s: Musical Ineffability, Implicit Understanding, & Racialized Virgin/Whore Dichotomies', presented at the American Philosophies Forum, Emory University, 2013, http://www.its-her-factory.com/2013/04/my-talk-paper-on-musical-ineffability/ (accessed 24 January 2017).
Jankélévitch, Vladimir, *La Musique et l'ineffable* (Paris: Éditions Points, 2015).
Janus, Adrienne, 'Listening: Jean-Luc Nancy and the "Anti-Ocular" Turn in Continental Philosophy and Critical Theory', *Comparative Literature*, 63 (2011), 182–202, https://doi.org/10.1215/00104124-1265474
—, 'Soundings: The Secret of Water and the Resonance of the Image', *The Senses and Society*, 8 (2013), 72–84, https://doi.org/10.2752/174589313X13500466751001
Jay, Martin, *Downcast Eyes: The Denigration of Vision in Twentieth-Century French Thought* (Berkeley: University of California Press, 1993).
Jumonville, Neil (ed.), *The New York Intellectuals Reader* (New York: Routledge, 2007).
Kane, Brian, 'Jean-Luc Nancy and the Listening Subject', *Contemporary Music Review*, 31 (2012), 439–47, https://doi.org/10.1080/07494467.2012.759413
—, 'Badiou's Wagner: Variations on the Generic', *The Opera Quarterly*, 29 (2013), 349–54, https://doi.org/10.1093/oq/kbt030
—, *Sound Unseen: Acousmatic Sound in Theory and Practice* (New York: Oxford University Press, 2014).
—, 'Badiou's Wagner: Variations on the Generic', *The Opera Quarterly*, (2014), https://doi.org/10.1093/oq/kbt030
Kanngieser, Anja, 'A Sonic Geography of Voice: Towards an Affective Politics', *Progress in Human Geography*, 36 (2011), 336–53, https://doi.org/10.1177/0309132511423969
Kant, Immanuel, *Critique of the Power of Judgment*, ed. Paul Guyer, trans. Paul Guyer and Eric Matthews, The Cambridge Edition of the Works of Immanuel Kant (Cambridge: Cambridge University Press, 2000), http://search.ebscohost.com/login.aspx?direct=true&db=nlebk&AN=206893&site=ehost-live
Keeling, Kara and Josh Kun (eds), *Sound Clash: Listening to American Studies*,

A Special Issue of American Quarterly (Baltimore: Johns Hopkins University Press, 2012).

Kramer, Lawrence, 'Philosophizing Musically: Reconsidering Music and Ideas', *Journal of the Royal Musical Association*, 139 (2014), 387–404, https://doi.org/10.1080/02690403.2014.944824

Kristeva, Julia, *La Révolution Du Langage Poétique: L'avant-Garde à La Fin Du XIXe Siècle, Lautréamont et Mallarmé* (Paris: Seuil, 1974).

—, *Pouvoirs de l'horreur: Essai sur l'abjection*, Points Essais, 152 (Paris: Seuil, 1980).

—, *La Révolution du langage poétique: l'avant-garde à la fin du XIXe siècle: Lautréamont et Mallarmé*, Points Essais, 174, Neudr. (Paris: Éditions du Seuil, 1985).

Kristeva, Julia, *Powers of Horror: An Essay on Abjection* (New York: Columbia University Press, 2014).

Kristeva, Julia and Leon S. Roudiez, *Revolution in Poetic Language*, trans. Margaret Waller (New York: Columbia University Press, 1984).

LaBelle, Brandon, *Lexicon of the Mouth: Poetics and Politics of Voice and the Oral Imaginary* (New York: Bloomsbury, 2014).

Lacan, Jacques, 'Le Stade du miroir comme formateur de la fonction du Je telle qu'elle nous est révélée dans l'expérience psychanalytique', *Revue française de psychanalyse*, 13 (1949), 449–55.

—, *On Feminine Sexuality The Limits of Love and Knowledge, 1972–1973 (Encore: The Seminar of Jacques Lacan, Book XX)*, ed. Jacques-Alain Miller, trans. Bruce Fink (New York: W. W. Norton & Company, 1999).

Lacan, Jacques and Jacques-Alain Miller, *Encore: Le Séminaire , Livre XX (1972–3)*, Le séminaire de Jacques Lacan, Livre 20 (Paris: Éditions du Seuil, 2005).

Lacan, Jacques and Alan Sheridan, *The Four Fundamental Concepts of Psycho-Analysis*, ed. Jacques Alain Miller (London: Vintage, 1998).

Lacoue-Labarthe, Philippe, *Le Sujet de la philosophie: Typographies I* (Paris: Flammarion, 1979).

—, 'The Fable' (Literature and Philosophy), trans. Hugh Silverman in *Research in Phenomenology*, vol. 15 (1985), pp. 43–60.

—, *Musica Ficta: Figures of Wagner* (Stanford: Stanford University Press, 1994).

—, *Musica Ficta: Figures de Wagner* (Paris: C. Bourgois, 2007).

—, *Pour n'en pas finir: écrits sur la musique*, ed. Aristide Bianchi and Leonid Kharlamov (Paris: Christian Bourgois éditeur, 2015).

Lacoue-Labarthe, Philippe and Jean-Luc Nancy, *L'Absolu littéraire: théorie de la littérature du romantisme allemand*, Collection Poétique (Paris: Seuil, 1978).

—, 'Le "retrait" du politique', in *Le retrait du politique: Travaux du Centre de recherches philosophiques sur le politique*, ed. Jacob Rogozinski (Paris: Galilée, 1983).

Leaman, Oliver (ed.), *The Future of Philosophy: Towards the Twenty-First Century* (London: Routledge, 1998).

Lefebvre, Henri, *Eléments de rythmanalyse: introduction à la connaissance des rythmes* (Paris: Syllepse, 1992).
Lehmann, Ulrich, 'Making as Knowing: Epistemology and Technique in Craft', *The Journal of Modern Craft*, 5 (2012), 149–64, https://doi.org/10.2752/17 4967812X13346796877950
Leppert, Richard D, *The Sight of Sound: Music, Representation, and the History of the Body* (Berkeley: University of California Press, 1993).
Lester, Joel, 'Rameau and Eighteenth-Century Harmonic Theory', in *The Cambridge History of Western Music Theory*, ed. Thomas Christensen (Cambridge: Cambridge University Press), pp. 753–77, http://university publishingonline.org/ref/id/histories/CBO9781139053471A031 (accessed 8 May 2013).
Levinson, Jerrold, *Musical Concerns: Essays in Philosophy of Music* (Oxford: Oxford University Press, 2015).
Leyshon, Andrew, David Matless and George Revill, *The Place of Music* (New York: Guilford Press, 1998).
Loughridge, Deirdre, *Haydn's Sunrise, Beethoven's Shadow: Audiovisual Culture and the Emergence of Musical Romanticism* (Chicago: University of Chicago Press, 2016).
Love, Jeff and Todd May, 'From Universality to Inequality: Badiou's Critique of Rancière', *Symposium: Canadian Journal of Continental Philosophy*, 12 (2008), 51–69.
McClary, Susan, *Conventional Wisdom: The Content of Musical Form*, The Bloch Lectures (Berkeley: University of California Press, 2001).
—, *Feminine Endings: Music, Gender, and Sexuality* (Minneapolis: University of Minnesota Press, 2002).
—, 'Why Gender Still (As Always) Matters in Music Studies' in *Dichotonies: Gender and Music*, ed. Beate Neumeier (Heidelberg: Universitätsverlag Winter, 2009), pp. 49–60.
McKeane, John, *Philippe Lacoue-Labarthe: (Un)Timely Meditations* (London: Legenda, 2015).
Maclachlan, Ian, 'Contingencies: Reading between Nancy and Derrida', *Oxford Literary Review*, 27 (2005), 139–58, https://doi.org/10.3366/olr.2005.010
Mallet, Marie-Louise, *La Musique En Respect*, Collection La Philosophie En Effet (Paris: Galilée, 2002).
Marchart, Oliver, *Post-Foundational Political Thought: Political Difference in Nancy, Lefort, Badiou and Laclau*, Taking on the Political, transferred to digital print (Edinburgh: Edinburgh University Press, 2008).
Martis, John, *Philippe Lacoue-Labarthe: Representation and the Loss of the Subject*, 1st edn (New York: Fordham University Press, 2005).
Marty, Nicolas, 'Deleuze, Cinema and Acousmatic Music (or What If Music Weren't an Art of Time?)', *Organised Sound*, 21 (2016), 166–75, https://doi.org/10.1017/S1355771816000091
Meschonnic, Henri, *Critique Du Rythme: Anthropologie Historique Du Langage* (Lagrasse: Verdier, 1982).

Milbank, John, Catherine Pickstock and Graham Ward (eds), *Radical Orthodoxy: A New Theology* (London: Routledge, 1999).

Mohanty, Chandra Talpade, 'Under Western Eyes: Feminist Scholarship and Colonial Discourses', *Boundary 2* 12.3/13.1 (1984), 333–58.

—, *Feminism without Borders: Decolonizing Theory, Practicing Solidarity* (Durham, NC: Duke University Press, 2003).

Molino, Jean, 'Fait Musical et Sémiologie de La Musique', *Musique et Jeu*, 1975, 37–62.

Molino, Jean and Craig Ayrey, 'Musical Fact and the Semiology of Music', trans. J. A. Underwood, *Music Analysis*, 9 (1990), 105–56, https://doi.org/10.2307/854225

Moten, Fred, 'The Phonographic Mise-En-Scène', *Cambridge Opera Journal*, 16, 269–81, https://doi.org/10.1017/S0954586704001867

Murray, Penelope and Peter Wilson (eds), *Music and the Muses: The Culture of 'Mousikē' in the Classical Athenian City* (Oxford: Oxford University Press, 2004).

Nadrigny, Pauline, *Musique et Philosophie Au XXe Siècle: Entendre et Faire Entendre*, Philosophies Contemporaines, 1 (Paris: Classiques Garnier, 2014).

Nancy, Jean-Luc, *Les Muses*, Collection La Philosophie En Effet (Paris: Galilée, 1994).

—, *The Sense of the World*, trans. Jeffrey S. Librett (Minneapolis: University of Minnesota Press, 1997).

—, *Le Sens Du Monde*, Collection La Philosophie En Effet (Paris: Galilée, 2001).

—, *À l'écoute* (Paris: Galilée, 2002).

—, *La Communauté désoeuvrée* (Paris: Christian Bourgois, 2004).

—, 'La Scène mondiale du rock', *Rue Descartes*, 60 (2008), 74–85, https://doi.org/10.3917/rdes.060.0074

—, *The Inoperative Community*, ed. Peter Connor (Minneapolis: University of Minnesota Press, 2012).

Neumeier, Beate (ed.), *Dichotonies: Gender and Music*, American Studies, vol. 181 (Heidelberg: Universitätsverlag Winter, 2009).

Nietzsche, Friedrich, *The Birth of Tragedy out of the Spirit of Music* (London: Penguin, 1993).

—, *Twilight of the Idols, or, How to Philosophize with a Hammer*, trans. Duncan Large, Oxford World's Classics (Oxford: Oxford University Press, 1998).

—, *The Gay Science: With a Prelude in German Rhymes and an Appendix of Songs*, ed. Bernard Williams, trans. Josefine Nauckhoff and Adrian Del Caro, Cambridge Texts in the History of Philosophy (Cambridge: Cambridge University Press, 2001).

—, *Thus Spoke Zarathustra: A Book for All and None*, ed. Adrian Del Caro and Robert B. Pippin, trans. Adrian Del Caro (Cambridge: Cambridge University Press, 2006), http://dx.doi.org/10.1017/CBO9780511812095 (accessed 27 October 2016).

—, *Ecce Homo: How One Becomes What One Is*, trans. Duncan Large (Oxford: Oxford University Press, 2009).

Nikolopoulou, Kalliopi, '"L'Art et Les Gens": Jean-Luc Nancy's Genealogical Aesthetics', *College Literature*, 30 (2003), 174–93, https://doi.org/10.2307/25112725

Nirenberg, Ricardo L. and David Nirenberg, 'Badiou's Number: A Critique of Mathematics as Ontology', *Critical Inquiry*, 37 (2011), 583–614.

Pelosi, Francesco and Sophie Henderson, *Plato on Music, Soul and Body* (Cambridge: Cambridge University Press, 2010), http://dx.doi.org/10.1017/CBO9780511778391 (accessed 27 October 2016).

Peraino, Judith Ann, *Listening to the Sirens: Musical Technologies of Queer Identity from Homer to Hedwig* (Berkeley: University of California Press, 2006).

Perpich, Diane, 'Corpus Meum: Disintegrating Bodies and the Ideal of Integrity', *Hypatia*, 20 (2005), 75–91, https://doi.org/10.2307/3811115

Pickstock, Catherine, 'Music: Soul, City and Cosmos after Augustine' in *Radical Orthodoxy: A New Theology*, ed. John Milbank, Catherine Pickstock and Graham Ward (London: Routledge, 1999), pp. 243–77.

Piekut, Benjamin, 'Actor-Networks in Music History: Clarifications and Critiques', *Twentieth-Century Music*, 11 (2014), 191–215, https://doi.org/10.1017/S147857221400005X

Pinhas, Richard, *Les Larmes de Nietzsche: Deleuze et La Musique* (Paris: Flammarion, 2001).

Plato, *Phaedo*, trans. Benjamin Jowett (Blacksburg: Virginia Tech, 2001).

—, *Republic*, trans. Robin Waterfield, Oxford World's Classics (Oxford: Oxford University Press, 2008).

Potolsky, Matthew, *Mimesis* (Abingdon: Routledge, 2006).

Prieto, Eric, 'Musical Imprints and Mimetic Echoes in Philippe Lacoue-Labarthe', *L'Esprit Créateur*, 47 (2007), 17–32.

Rameau, Jean-Philippe, *Traité de l'harmonie réduite à ses principes naturels* (Paris: Jean-Baptiste-Christophe Ballard, 1722).

—, *Treatise on Harmony*, trans. Philip Gossett (New York: Dover, 1997).

Redner, Gregg, *Deleuze and Film Music: Building a Methodological Bridge between Film Theory and Music* (Bristol: Intellect, 2011).

Reich, Willi, *Schoenberg: A Critical Biography* (London: Longman, 1971).

Ross, Alison, *The Aesthetic Paths of Philosophy: Presentation in Kant, Heidegger, Lacoue-Labarthe, and Nancy*, Cultural Memory in the Present (Stanford: Stanford University Press, 2007).

Rousseau, Jean-Jacques, *Essai Sur l'origine Des Langues; Où Il Est Parlé de La Mélodie et de Limitation Musicale*, ed. Charles Porset (Bordeaux: Ducros, 1970).

—, *Essay on the Origin of Languages* in *On the Origin of Language: Two Essays*, trans. John H. Moran and Alexander Gode (Chicago: Chicago University Press, 1986).

Ruti, Mari, *Between Levinas and Lacan: Self, Other, Ethics* (New York: Bloomsbury Academic, 2015).

Sallis, John, *Chorology: On Beginning in Plato's Timaeus* (Bloomington: Indiana University Press, 1999).

Sartre, Jean-Paul, *La Nausée*, Collection Folio, 805 (Paris: Gallimard, 2008).

—, *Nausea* (London: Penguin, 2014).

Sartre, Jean-Paul and Arlette Elkaïm-Sartre, *L'Imaginaire: psychologie phénoménologique de l'imagination*, Collection Folio Essais, 47 (Paris: Gallimard, 2007).

Scherzinger, Martin, 'On Sonotropism', *Contemporary Music Review*, 31 (2012), 345–51, https://doi.org/10.1080/07494467.2012.758933

Schopenhauer, Arthur, *The World as Will and Representation (Vol. 1)*, ed. Judith Norman, Alistair Welchman and Christopher Janaway, trans. Judith Norman and Alistair Welchman (Cambridge: Cambridge University Press, 2010), https://ezproxy-prd.bodleian.ox.ac.uk:6038/core/books/schopenhauer-the-world-as-will-and-representation/6AA41648D7C79FD5C01EDFBA37B9FBD2

Schwarz, David, *Listening Awry: Music and Alterity in German Culture* (Minneapolis: University of Minnesota Press, 2006).

Scruton, Roger, *Death-Devoted Heart: Sex and the Sacred in Wagner's Tristan and Isolde* (Oxford: Oxford University Press, 2004).

Sève, Bernard, *L'Altération Musicale, Ou, Ce Que La Musique Apprend Au Philosophe*, Poétique (Paris: Seuil, 2002).

—, *L'Instrument de Musique: Une Étude Philosophique*, L'Ordre Philosophique (Paris: Seuil, 2013).

Seyhan, Azade, *Representation and Its Discontents: The Critical Legacy of German Romanticism* (Berkeley: University of California Press, 1992).

Seyhan, Azade, Adrian Daub, Jocelyn Holland, Leif Weatherby, Joseph D. O'Neil and Nina Amstutz, 'Forum: Romanticism', *The German Quarterly*, 89 (2016), 344–60, https://doi.org/10.1111/gequ.12005

Sheridan, Alan, 'Translator's Note' in Jacques Lacan and Alan Sheridan, *The Four Fundamental Concepts of Psycho-Analysis*, ed. Jacques Alain Miller (London: Vintage, 1998), pp. 277–82.

Silverman, Kaja, *The Acoustic Mirror: The Female Voice in Psychoanalysis and Cinema* (Bloomington: Indiana University Press, 1988).

Small, Christopher, *Musicking: The Meanings of Performing and Listening* (Hanover: University Press of New England, 1998).

Sontag, Susan, *Under the Sign of Saturn* (New York: Farrar, Straus & Giroux, 1980).

Spotts, Frederic, *Bayreuth: A History of the Wagner Festival* (New Haven: Yale University Press, 1994).

Steans, Jill, 'Debating Women's Human Rights as a Universal Feminist Project: Defending Women's Human Rights as a Political Tool', *Review of International Studies*, 33 (2007), 11–27.

Sterne, Jonathan, *The Audible Past: Cultural Origins of Sound Reproduction* (Durham, NC: Duke University Press, 2003).
Stiegler, Bernard, *La Technique et Le Temps*, La Philosophie En Effet (Paris: Galilée, 1994).
—, *Technics and Time, 1: The Fault of Epimetheus*, trans. Richard Beardsworth and George Collins (Stanford: Stanford University Press, 1998).
—, *De La Misère Symbolique 2: La* Catastrophè *Du Sensible* (Paris: Galilée, 2005).
—, *Symbolic Misery, 2: The Catastrophe of the Sensible* (Cambridge: Polity, 2015).
Taruskin, Richard, 'Agents and Causes and Ends, Oh My', *The Journal of Musicology*, 31 (2014), 272–93, https://doi.org/10.1525/jm.2014.31.2.272
Tho, Tzuchien and Giuseppe Bianco (eds), *Badiou and the Philosophers: Interrogating 1960s French Philosophy*, trans. Tzuchien Tho and Giuseppe Bianco (London: Bloomsbury Academic, 2013).
Thomas, Downing A., *Music and the Origins of Language: Theories from the French Enlightenment* (Cambridge: Cambridge University Press, 1995).
Thomson, Iain D., *Heidegger on Ontotheology: Technology and the Politics of Education* (Cambridge: Cambridge University Press, 2005).
Tomlinson, Gary, 'Vico's Songs: Detours at the Origins of (Ethno) Musicology', *The Musical Quarterly*, 83 (1999), 344–77, https://doi.org/10.2307/742419
—, *Metaphysical Song: An Essay on Opera* (Princeton: Princeton University Press, 2014).
Tucker, Sophie, *Some of These Days: An Autobiography* (London: Hammond, 1948).
Vasse, Denis, *L'Ombilic et la voix: deux enfants en analyse* (Paris: Seuil, 1999).
Volcler, Juliette, *Le Son Comme Arme: Les Usages Policiers et Militaires Du Son* (Paris: La Découverte, 2011).
Watkin, Christopher, *Difficult Atheism: Post-Theological Thinking in Alain Badiou, Jean-Luc Nancy and Quentin Meillassoux* (Edinburgh: Edinburgh University Press, 2011).
—, 'Thinking Equality Today: Badiou, Ranciere, Nancy', *French Studies*, 67 (2013), 522–34, https://doi.org/10.1093/fs/knt148
Watrous, Lisa, 'Love's Universal Impetus: Luce Irigaray and Alain Badiou', *L'Esprit Créateur*, 52 (2012), 66–73, https://doi.org/10.1353/esp.2012.0030
Wong, Deborah, 'Sound, Silence, Music: Power', *Ethnomusicology*, 58 (2014), 347–53.

Index

1968 protests, 9

À *l'écoute* (Ec, Nancy)
  corps sonore, 51–2, 53–4, 62, 63–5, 77–8, 79, 80–1, 83–5, 86
  diction, 66
  Venus with an Organist and Cupid (Titian), 50–2
absolute music, 26, 30, 31, 32, 35, 201, 208–9, 208–10
  Badiou, 130, 171, 175, 177–8, 217–18
  Dolan, 166
  Lacoue-Labarthe, 103–8
  see also instrumental music
acousmatic ideology, 167–76
acousmatic listening, 168, 174–5, 177
Adorno, Theodor W., 46, 196, 211
advertisement, 62
aesthetic genesis, 73–7
aesthetics, 23–4, 26, 68, 69, 70, 106–7, 166; *see also anesthétique*; *inesthétique*
affect, 77, 190–1, 193, 203–4
Albright, David, 27, 28, 39, 49, 99
allography, 19–21, 105, 173
allothanatography, 98
analytical philosophy, 103–4
anamnesis, 123–4, 192
anesthétique, 178
angoisse, 141, 142–3
anti-essentialism, 5
anti-ocular turn, 6–7, 62, 63; *see also* ocularcentrism
anti-philosophy, 132
antiquity, 28, 29, 39
anti-Semitism, 153, 154–5, 186
Apollonian, 25–6, 30
appropriation, 26–7, 192

art
  Badiou, 144, 149–52, 210, 216
  Hegel, 24, 41
  Lacoue-Labarthe, 210–11
  Nancy, 56–9, 212
  Plato, 44, 92
  v. science, 35–8
Austern, Linda Phyllis, 48
authority, 44
autobiography, 95–7, 98
autography, 19, 21
Aviram, Amittai F., 95, 110

Babich, Babette E., 40, 42
Badiou, Alain, 126–30
  acousmatic ideology, 167–76
  anesthétique, 178
  anti-essentialism, 5
  art, 149–52, 210, 211
  being, 133, 134–5
  conditions of philosophy, 143–4
  event, 133, 135–8, 184
  feminism, 159–64
  history, 144–5
  inesthétique, 149–52, 176–80
  music, 215–16, 217–18, 219, 222
  musical exceptionalism, 4
  musical subject, 138–43
  particularism and universality of truth, 145–9
  performance, 196–7, 198
  philosophy, 59, 130–3
  poststructuralism, 9–10
  technology, 165–7, 171
  thermidorianism, 180–2
  truth-procedures, 164–5, 173
  on Wagner, 152–9, 186–90, 194, 195–6
Baki, Burhanuddin, 162

239

Baroque style, 164–5
Bayreuth Festspielhaus, 168
Bayreuther Festspiele, 193
Beethoven, Ludwig van, 139
Begbie, Jeremy, 22–3
Being, 60, 92–3, 134–5
Bennett, David, 10
Bent, Margaret, 197–8
Berg, Alban, 139, 140, 142
Berger, Karol, 36
Berio, Luciano, 18
Birth of Tragedy, The (Nietzsche), 25–6
'blackness', 102
Bloch, Georges, 19, 20
Bloechl, Olivia, 32
blues, 102
Bogue, Ronald, 44–5
Bonds, Mark Evan, 28, 31, 206
Born, Georgina, 26, 220
Boulez, Pierre, 142, 189
bourgeois identity, 106–7
Bowie, Andrew, 29
Bull, Anna, 106–7
Burchill, Louise, 163
Butler, Judith, 80

Caccini, Giulio, 206
Camerata de' Bardi, 205
Cantorian set theory, 135, 162–3
capitalism, 137, 146, 147
catacoustic subject, 108–12
  and education, 112–15
catacoustics, 95
chora, 34, 79–80, 110
Christianity, 154–7, 158–9
Chua, Daniel, 37, 207
Clark, Andrew H., 206
classical music, 104, 105–7, 129;
  see also European high art music
classical style, 139, 140
Clemens, Justin, 143, 144
Clifton, Thomas, 26
Cohen-Lévinas, Danielle, 39, 40
Colebrook, Claire, 10
community, 67–9
composer-function, 20–1, 37, 57
concert hall etiquette, 176
concert halls, 86
contemporary music, 150
context, 220
continuity *see* dis/continuity
'Copernican revolution', 23

corps sonore
  Nancy, 51–2, 64–5, 77–83, 84, 85–6, 212
  Rameau, 65–6
courage, 141–2
courage, 143
Crenshaw, Kimberlé, 11
Critchley, Simon, 56, 144, 211–12
critical / new musicology, 32–3, 42, 53, 181, 182, 185
Critique of Pure Reason (Kant), 23
Crowley, Martin, 60
cultural values, 112–13
culture, 26–7, 38–9, 72–3

Dahlhaus, Carl, 177
Daub, Adrian, 185
Dayan, Peter, 7
Deathridge, John, 168
déconstruction, 90–1
Deleuze, Gilles, 10
democratic materialism, 144, 145, 147
Derrida, Jacques, 88, 113–14, 114–15, 121
Derridean *déconstruction*, 90–1
désistement/désister, 93
differences, 147, 159–60, 161
Dionysian, 25–6, 30, 33
dis/continuity, 188–9
Dolan, Emily, 126, 165–6, 200, 201
Duncan, Michelle, 11
During, Elie, 149
Dutilleux, Henri, 143

Ecce Homo (Nietzsche), 121
education, 39–40, 41, 45, 92, 112–15
effect, 31–2
emotions, 61, 107, 116
Enlightenment, 36, 74
Entkunstung, 211
episteme, 199–200, 202, 205
Essai sur l'origine des langues (Rousseau), 66–7
essence, 31–2
ethical ideology, 159
ethics
  of difference, 159–60
  feminist, 213–21
  of instruments, 201
ethnomusicology, 223–4
ethos, 22, 29, 40, 98, 111, 112, 192–6
European high art music, 4–5, 42, 82, 101, 120, 208–9, 219; *see also* classical music; *musique savante*

European musical world, 143
event, 135–8, 184, 211–12; *see also* 'Haydn-event'; 'Schoenberg-event'

Felski, Rita, 204
Feltham, Oliver, 131
femininity, 5–6, 11
   Badiou, 163, 164
   classical music, 106
   Irigaray, 218–19
   Lacoue-Labarthe, 123, 124–5, 213–14
   Nancy, 73–7, 78, 80, 81
   see also muses; sirens
feminism, 159–64
feminist ethics, 213–21
feminist philosophers, 75
Five Lessons on Wagner (FLW, Badiou), 152–9, 171–2, 178, 179, 186–90, 194, 195, 210
Florence, 204–5
form, 31, 130, 167
formal analysis, 180–2
French music, 37, 142
Freud, Sigmund, 33

Gaillot, Michel, 57, 69–70
Gay Science (Nietzsche), 38
gender, 5–6, 11, 155–7; *see also* femininity; feminism; masculinity; muses; sirens
gendered identity, 158
Génération harmonique (Rameau), 65
Gesamtkunstwerk, 31, 43, 187, 188, 191, 193, 194–5
Goehr, Lydia, 19–20, 21, 103–4, 105, 108
Goodman, Nelson, 21
Götterdämmerung (Wagner), 154, 155
Grant, Roger, 52
Groddeck, Georg, 119–20
Guattari, Félix, 10

Hallward, Peter, 173–4
Hanslick, Eduard, 18, 31
harmonic theory, 65–6
harmony, 36, 40, 68–9, 106, 107–8
Hasty, Christopher, 21
Haunting Melody, The (Reik), 95–8, 109
Havelock, Eric A., 43–4
Haydn, Joseph, 176
'Haydn-event', 129, 139, 164, 173
hearing, 63, 81

Hegel, G. W. F., 24, 41–2
Heidegger, Martin, 91, 135, 200–1
Hesiod, 42–3
Hesmondhalgh, David, 26
heterothanatography, 98
high art music, 4–5, 42, 82, 101, 120, 208–9, 219; *see also* classical music; *musique savante*
hip hop, 103
history, 144–5
Hobson, Marian, 23
Horkheimer, Max, 46
Howie, Gill, 75
Hutchens, B. C., 55, 60

identarian liberation movements, 146–8
identity politics, 148
idols, 2
Imaginary Museum of Musical Works, The (Goehr), 103–4, 105, 108
imitation *see* mimesis
inesthétique, 149–52, 178
instrumental music, 24, 29, 30, 31, 39, 208–9
   and technologies of truth, 164–7
   see also absolute music
instruments, 200–1
intersecting identities, 11–12
Irigaray, Luce, 11, 48, 78, 161, 218–19
Italian music, 37

Jaeger, Werner, 113
James, Ian, 56, 57, 68, 91
James, Robin, 77, 198, 203
Janus, Adrienne, 62, 64, 78, 82, 83–4, 86–7
Jay, Martin, 6, 11
jazz music, 86, 102, 150, 164
justice, 142

Kane, Brian, 7–8, 167, 168, 174–5, 179, 201
Kant, Immanuel, 23–4, 27, 108
katakouein, 113
Keeling, Kara, 6, 7
knowledge, 23, 62, 75, 136, 199, 201, 211
Kramer, Lawrence, 220
Kristeva, Julia, 34, 48, 79–80, 110
Kun, Josh, 6, 7

La communauté désœuvrée (Nancy), 67, 68

La Nausée (Sartre), 15–17, 48
'La Scène mondiale du rock' (SMR, Nancy), 53, 71
Lacan, Jacques, 33–4, 137
Lacoue-Labarthe, Philippe, 88–9
  absolute music, 103–8
  art, 210–11
  femininity, 123, 124–5, 213–14
  maternality, 5–6, 117–21, 122–5
  music, 1, 2, 184, 217, 219–20: and language, 96–7, 99–103, 122, 222
  musica ficta, 197–8; see also *Musica Ficta* (Lacoue-Labarthe)
  musical subject, 94–8, 108–12: and education, 112–15
  opera, 204–5, 206–7
  philosophical inheritance, 89–94
  poststructuralism, 9
  on Reik, 95–8, 115–17
  on Wagner, 185, 186, 190–2, 194–6
language, 22, 27, 28, 29–30, 206
  Badiou, 131–2, 180
  Enlightenment, 74
  Lacoue-Labarthe, 96–7, 99–103, 122, 222
  Rousseau, 66–7
Laruelle, François, 127
Le Chant des Muses (CM, Lacoue-Labarthe), 88–9, 104, 105, 114, 117–18, 121, 123
'Le 'retrait' du politique' (Lacoue-Labarthe and Nancy), 5–6
'L'Écho du suject' (ES, Lacoue-Labarthe), 88, 89, 94–8, 104, 114, 115–17, 118, 119, 123
Lehmann, Ulrich, 199
Leibniz, Gottfried, 35
Leppert, Richard, 86
Les Muses (M$_1$, Nancy), 56–7, 58–9, 59–60, 76–7
L'Être et l'événement (EE, Badiou), 133, 134, 135
Levinson, Jerrold, 24
liberation movements, 146–8
Librett, Jeffrey S., 60
L'incident d'Antioche (Badiou), 163
listening
  acousmatic, 168, 174–5, 177
  Badiou, 166–7, 174–5, 178
  Nancy, 63, 64, 83–4, 86
  sirens, 46
  structural, 167, 195
Liszt, Franz von, 31
literacy, 43–4

literary writing, 131
literature, 39
Logiques des mondes (LM, Badiou), 138, 145
logos, 188–90
love, 144, 162
Lowe, Melanie, 32

McClary, Susan, 32, 106
McKeane, John, 90, 93, 122
Maclachlan, Ian, 55–6
Mahler, Gustav, 96, 97, 107, 109, 112
Marchart, Oliver, 133
Martis, John, 93, 124
masculinity, 45, 77, 81, 106
maternal metaphorisation, 77–80
maternality, 5–6, 117–21, 122–5
mathematics, 35, 36
matter, 133
meaning, 27–35, 77, 90, 93; see also *sens*/sense
Meistersinger, Die (Wagner), 154, 155
melody, 36
melos, 29
metaphysics, 91, 92, 144, 145
mimesis, 21–7, 44–5, 91–3, 197
Mnemosyne, 39, 99
Mohanty, Chandra Talpade, 219
Molino, Jean, 18
Monteverdi, Claudio, 206
moral values, 112–13
Moten, Fred, 167
mousike, 28, 29, 38–42, 43, 45, 99, 112, 113
Mozart, Wolfgang Amadeus, 82, 139
Murray, Penelope, 38, 40, 43
muses, 38, 39, 42–5, 111
  Lacoue-Labarthe, 88–9, 99–103
  Nancy, 56–7, 58–9, 59–60, 76–7
music
  definitions and conceptions, 17–18, 31, 35, 37, 223–4
  as metaphor, 77
  naturalisation, 207
  non-musical factors, 2–4
  and philosophy, 203
  philosophy of, 17
music ficta, 203
Musica Ficta (MF, Lacoue-Labarthe), 123, 124, 197–8, 217
  femininity, 213–14
  Wagner question, 190, 191, 192, 196
musical exceptionalism, 4–5
musical form see form

musical instruments, 200–1
musical meaning, 27–35
musical ontology, 19–21, 123; see also sonorous ontology
musical representation see representation
musical subject, 103–4, 106, 108–12, 138–43
  and education, 112–15
musical 'work', 104–5
musicking, 3–4
musicolatry, 165, 167
musicology, 26, 53
  critical / new, 32–3, 42, 53, 181, 182, 185
'Musique et inconscient' (Groddeck), 119–20
Musique et philosophie au XXe siècle (Nadrigny), 72
musique savante, 54, 186, 190, 196, 201, 209; see also high art music

Nadrigny, Pauline, 72
Nancy, Jean-Luc, 50–4
  art, 56–9, 212
  Being, 60
  collaboration with Lacoue-Labarthe, 90
  community, 67–8, 69
  femininity, 73–7
  feminist ethics, 217, 219
  maternality, 5–6
  muses, 56–7, 58–9, 59–60, 76–7
  music, 222
  poststructuralism, 9
  rock music, 71–3, 212–13
  sens/sense, 51, 55–6, 58–9, 60–1, 63–4, 69, 212
  sonorous ontology, 62–5, 77–87
  techno music, 54, 68, 69, 70
  on Wagner, 185–6, 192–3, 194–6
Naroditskaya, Inna, 48
National Socialism, 91, 189, 191
naturalisation of music, 207
Nazis, 91
Nazism, 191
needs, 67
neoliberal capitalism, 146
neoliberal economic system, 148
new / critical musicology, 32–3, 42, 53, 181, 182, 185
Nietzsche, Friedrich, 33
  Birth of Tragedy, The, 25–6
  Ecce Homo, 121
  Gay Science, 38
  Thus Spoke Zarathustra, 30
  Twilight of the Idols, 1–2
Nikolopoulou, Kalliopi, 76
noise, 203–4
non-musical factors, 2–4
nostalgia, 67–8, 69, 70
noumena, 23
noumenal reality, 24

ocularcentrism, 11; see also anti-ocular turn
Odello, Laura, 214, 215–16
Odysseus, 46–7
opera, 30, 37, 153–4, 204–8
orality, 43, 44
orchestral standardisation, 176
organologie générale (Stiegler), 11
organology, 200, 202, 224
Orpheus, 29
Othering, 26–7, 103, 198
Otobiographies (Derrida), 113–14, 114–15, 121

Parsifal (Wagner), 129, 152, 154–5, 155–9, 169–72
particularism, 145–9
passions, 67, 190–1
Pater, Walter, 37
pathos, 190–2
Peikut, Benjamin, 213
Peraino, Judith, 47
performance, 196–7, 198–9
Perpich, Diane, 81
Phaedo (Plato), 40–1
phallogocentrism, 218–19
phenomena, 23
philosophical discourse, 91
philosophical writing, 131–2
philosophy
  analytical, 103–4
  Badiou, 59, 130–3
  conditions of, 129, 143–4
  and gender, 75–6
  and *mousike*, 40–1
  and music, 203
  and musicology, 53
  phallogocentrism, 218–19
  see also anti-philosophy
philosophy of music, 17
Pickstock, Catherine, 108
Piekhut, Benjaimin, 141, 220, 223

Plato
  episteme and *techne*, 199
  hustera, 218
  mimesis, 44–6, 91–2
  music, 61, 68, 214
  ontological duality, 178
  Republic, 22, 40, 41, 111, 127
  Timaeus, 34
Platonic view of art, 150
poetry, 38–9, 43, 45, 99–100
poets, 44
politics, 144, 185–96
  Badiou, 188–90
  Lacoue-Labarthe, 190–2
  Nancy, 192–6
popular art, 149, 152
poststructuralism, 9–10, 32
Potolsky, Matthew, 45, 92
presentation, 134
Prieto, Eric, 198, 199
'programme music', 31
Pythagoras, 29, 35, 174, 175

quadrivium, 35

Rameau, Jean-Philippe, 36, 37, 65–6, 68–9, 207
rap music, 103
reading, 90–1
Reik, Theodore
  The Haunting Melody, 95–8, 109
  The Ritual, 115–16
repertoire, 35, 37, 41, 209
representation, 21–7, 31, 77, 85–6; *see also* mimesis
Republic (Plato), 22, 40, 41, 111, 127
rhetoric, 43
rhythm, 7, 82, 94, 109–12, 115–16
Ritual, The (Reik), 115–16
rock music, 53, 54, 62, 71–3, 86, 212–13
Romanticism, 2, 4, 57, 107, 144, 150, 209
Ross, Alison, 23, 93
Rousseau, Jean-Jacques, 36, 37, 66–8, 69, 207
Ruti, Mari, 161

Saint Paul (StP$_1$, Badiou), 145–6, 147, 160
Sallis, John, 34
Sartre, Jean-Paul, 38, 48
  La Naussée, 15–17
Schaeffer, Pierre, 7

Scherzinger, Martin, 4, 53, 61
Schoenberg, Arnold, 27, 138
'Schoenberg-event', 129, 139, 140, 142, 164, 173, 179
Schopenhauer, Arthur, 24–5, 28, 30, 33, 37–8, 61
Schwartz, David, 156, 169
science, 118, 144, 200
  v. art, 35–8
scientific discourse, 122–3
'Scolie' (Sc, Badiou), 138–40, 141–3, 179
score-copies, 21
Second Viennese School, 140
self, 94
sémiotique, 34, 48, 79
sens/sense, 51, 55–6, 58–9, 60–1, 63–4, 69, 212; *see also* meaning
serial music, 140, 143
sexuality, 155–7
sexuation, 158
Seyhan, Azade, 23, 111
shofar, 115–16
sirens, 46–9, 215
'situated universality', 144
social values, 40, 41, 112–13
Socrates, 40–1, 45
sonata form, 106
sonorous ontology, 61–5, 77–83; *see also corps sonore*
sonotropism, 4, 61–2
Sontag, Susan, 222
sophistry, 132–3
sound, 46, 51, 58, 63, 66, 81–2, 86, 203–4
Sound Unseen (Kane), 7–8
Spariosu, Mahai, 44, 45
spatiality, 65
state educational institutions, 114–15
Sterne, Jonathan, 81
Stiegler, Bernard, 11, 184, 200, 202, 224
Stravinsky, Igor, 142
structural listening, 167, 195
structuralism, 9–10
student protests 1968, 9
style, 96, 98, 113, 124
subject *see* musical subject
subjectivity, 64, 124, 207, 209
Syberberg, Hans-Jürgen, 129, 155, 156, 158, 159, 169–70, 171

Tarby, Fabien, 131, 133
Taruskin, Richard, 217–18

techne, 38, 199–202
  Badiou, 174–5
  Lacoue-Labarthe, 99, 100, 117, 184, 219
  Nancy, 57, 212
  opera, 205
techno music, 54, 68, 69–70, 86
technological innovations, 3
technology, 165–7, 171
terreur, 141
Theogony (Hesiod), 42–3
theory, 9
theory of art, 24
thermidorianism, 180–2
thing-in-itself, 23, 24
Thomas, Downing A., 66, 68
Thus Spoke Zarathustra (Nietzsche), 30
Timaeus (Plato), 34
Titian, 50–1, 81, 83, 129
Tolbert, Elizabeth, 74
Tomlinson, Gary, 105, 207, 209, 224
tonality, 85, 106, 107, 143
Traité de l'harmonie (Rameau), 36
Tresch, John, 200, 201
Tristan and Isolde (Wagner), 153–4
'Tristan chord', 85
truth, 132–3, 136–7, 143–4, 169, 179, 211–12, 217
  and art, 151, 210
  and gender, 162, 163
  and history, 144–5
  new musicology, 181, 182
  universality of, 145–9
truth-procedures, 164–5

Twilight of the Idols (Nietzsche), 1–2

values, 40, 41, 112–13
Varèse, Adgard, 18
Venus with an Organist and Cupid (Titian), 50–1, 81, 83–5, 129–30
vision, 62, 77, 81
voice, 12, 28, 66, 67, 74, 96–7, 175

Wagner, Richard
  absolute music, 31
  acousmatic listening, 177
  Badiou on, 129, 152–9, 171–2, 178, 179, 194, 195, 209–10
  Lacoue-Labarthe on, 123–4, 204
  music drama, 167–8
  Nancy on, 85
  Nietzsche on, 26
Wagner question, 185–96
  Badiou, 186–90, 194, 195–6
  Lacoue-Labarthe, 190–2, 194–6
  Nancy, 192–3, 194–6
Watkin, Christopher, 212
Webern, Anton, 140, 143
Western Music and Its Others (Born and Hesmondhalgh), 26
Will, 24–5, 33, 61
Wilson, Peter, 38
woman, 161–2, 163
women composers, 141
Wong, Deborah, 223–4
writing, 131–2

Zeus, 39, 99

EU representative:
Easy Access System Europe
Mustamäe tee 50, 10621 Tallinn, Estonia
Gpsr.requests@easproject.com

www.ingramcontent.com/pod-product-compliance
Lightning Source LLC
Chambersburg PA
CBHW071203240426
43668CB00032B/2049